Worlds of E–Commerce: Economic, Geographical and Social Dimensions

Worlds of E–Commerce: Economic, Geographical and Social Dimensions

Edited by

THOMAS R. LEINBACH
University of Kentucky

and

STANLEY D. BRUNN
University of Kentucky

Graphic Design and Production by

Donna Gilbreath & Richard Gilbreath
Gyula Pauer Cartographic Information Laboratory
University of Kentucky

JOHN WILEY & SONS, LTD
Chichester • New York • Weinheim • Brisbane • Singapore • Toronto

Other Wiley Editorial Offices

John Wiley & Sons, Inc., 605 Third Avenue,
New York, NY 10158-0012, USA

WILEY-VCH Verlag GmbH, Pappelallee 3,
D-69469 Weinheim, Germany

John Wiley & Sons Australia, Ltd, 33 Park Road, Milton,
Queensland 4064, Australia

John Wiley & Sons (Asia) Pte Ltd, 2 Clementi Loop #02-01,
Jin Xing Distripark, Singapore 129809

John Wiley & Sons (Canada) Ltd, 22 Worcester Road,
Rexdale, Ontario M9W 1L1, Canada

Library of Congress Cataloging-in-Publication Data

British Library Cataloguing in Publication Data

A catalogue record for this book is available from the British Library

ISBN 0-471-494550

Typeset in 10/12pt Times from the authors' disks by Vision Typesetting, Manchester
Printed and bound in Great Britain by Biddles Ltd, Guildford and King's Lynn
This book is printed on acid-free paper responsibly manufactured from sustainable forestry,
in which at least two trees are planted for each one used for paper production.

Contents

List of Contributors

Yuko Aoyama, School of Geography, Clark University, 950 Main Street, Worcester, MA 01610-1477, USA   email: yaoyama@clarku.edu

Stanley D. Brunn, Department of Geography, University of Kentucky, Lexington, KY 40506-0027, USA   email: brunn@pop.uky.edu

Kenneth Button, The Institute of Public Policy, George Mason University, Fairfax, VA 22030, USA   email: kbutton@gmu.edu

Sharon Cobb, Department of Economics and Geography, University of North Florida, South Jacksonville, FL 32224, USA   email: scobb@unf.edu

Neil M. Coe, School of Geography, University of Manchester, Manchester M13 9PL, UK   email: neil.m.coe@man.ac.uk

James Curry, El Colegio de la Frontera Norte, Tijuana, Mexico. US Mail: POB L, Chula Vista, CA 91912, USA   email: jcurry@colef.mx

Martin Dodge, Center for Advanced Spatial Analysis, University College London, 1–19 Torrington Place, London, WC1E 6BT, UK   email: m.dodge@ucl.ac.uk

Thomas M. Edwards, Microsoft Corporation, Building 3/1064, One Microsoft Way, Redmond, WA 98052-6399, USA   email: tomedw@microsoft.com

Marina van Geenhuizen, School of Systems Engineering, Policy Analysis and Management, Technical University of Delft, PO Box 5015, 2600 GA Delft, The Netherlands   email: mariag@sepa.tudelft.nl

Michael F. Goodchild, Department of Geography, University of California, Santa Barbara, CA 93106-4060, USA   email: good@geog.ucsb.edu

Sean P. Gorman, Department of Geography, University of Florida, Gainesville, FL 32611, USA   email: spg1x@aol.com

Martin Kenney, Department of Human and Community Development, University of California, Davis, CA 95616, USA   email: mfkenney@ucdavis.edu

John Langdale, Department of Human Geography, Macquarie University, North Ryde, 2109 Australia   email: jlangdal@ocs1.ocs.mq.edu.au

Thomas R. Leinbach, Department of Geography, University of Kentucky, Lexington, KY 40506-0027, USA   email: leinbach@pop.uky.edu

Edward J. Malecki, Department of Geography, University of Florida, Gainesville, FL 32611, USA   email: malecki@geog.ufl.edu

Peter Nijkamp, Department of Spatial Economics, Free University of Amsterdam, de Boelelaan 1105, 1081 HV Amsterdam, The Netherlands
email: pnijkamp@econ.vu.nl

Dominic Power, Kulturgeografiska Institutionen, Uppsala University, Box 513, 751 20 Uppsala, Sweden   email: Dominic.Power@Kultgeog.uu.se

Darren Purcell, Department of Geography, Florida State University, Tallahassee, FL 32306-2190, USA   email: dpurcell@garnet.acns.fsu.edu

Priscilla M. Regan, Department of Public and International Affairs, George Mason University, Fairfax, VA 22030, USA   email: pregan@gmu.edu

Samantha Taylor, PPK Environment and Infrastructure, South Melbourne 3205, Australia   email: STaylor@ppk.com.au

Barney Warf, Department of Geography, Florida State University, Tallahassee, FL 32306-2190, USA   email: bwarf@coss.fsu.edu

Mark I. Wilson, Department of Geography/Urban and Regional Policy, Michigan State University, IPPSR – 321 Berkey Hall, East Lansing, MI 48824-1111, USA email: wilsonmm@pilot.msu.edu

Henry Wai-chung Yeung, Department of Geography, National University of Singapore, 10 Kent Ridge Crescent, Singapore 119260   email: geoywc@nus.edu.sg

Preface and Acknowledgements

In 1991 we collaborated on the editing of a book entitled *Collapsing Space and Time: Geographic Aspects of Communications and Information* which attempted to capture the enormous international impact of the expansion of information and communication in a variety of dimensions. That volume is now out of print. Since the mid-1990s our interests have been captured by continued developments in this area and particularly the way in which technology has exploded and allowed even greater information and communications accessibility. But the triggering mechanism for this book of original essays has been the explosive growth of electronic commerce (e-commerce), broadly defined, over the past five years. This phenomenon and its implications and impacts are still in the very early stages of maturation. Nonetheless, urged on by a variety of colleagues, we felt that it was important to produce a volume which examines e-commerce especially from the perspective of the social scientist. The diversity of themes within the broad topic immediately suggested an edited volume which would capture as much as possible the rich applications and theory which attend this theme. After a number of conversations about the structure of such a book we began to contact authors and were pleasantly surprised by the existence of ongoing research and the willingness of authors to produce an original paper specifically for this volume. The set of 16 essays covers a wide span of applications and we trust that the reader will be stimulated by still other research topics.

Our appetites for information, communications, and technology driven matters have grown largely through our own curiosity. We have, of course, appreciated the scholarship and have been influenced more generally by several individuals over the course of our careers. One of the editors (TRL) is particularly indebted to Peter Gould, former Emeritus Evan Pugh Professor at the Pennsylvania State University, who passed away in January, 2000. Peter wrote, at our request, the initial essay for *Collapsing Space and Time*. We know that an essay on this new theme would have been eagerly produced had he had the opportunity. We hope this book captures some of the flavor, insights, and scholarship exemplified in his writings. The other editor (SDB) acknowledges the many discussions spanning several decades with Don Janelle and Don Ziegler on time–space issues, cartographic innovations, and human geography futures.

Our interests in this theme have been spirited by contacts and communications with a variety of other individuals, many of whom are contributors to this volume. We are especially grateful to have had the opportunity to interact with colleagues at a variety of regular professional meetings and also several special ones. Noteworthy are the recent annual conferences of E-Space, organized by Mark Wilson and Kenneth Corey of Michigan State University, as well as several workshops organized under the National Science Foundation sponsored Varenius Project at the Department of Geography, University of California, Santa Barbara. We also wish to acknowledge the National Science Foundation for support under NSF/INT 99-07474 for our ongoing work on Nokia and its internationalization process. Last, but not least, we are tremendously appreciative of the contributions of Donna and Richard Gilbreath for both editing and cartographic skills delivered through the University of Kentucky"s Cartographic Laboratory. This effort could not have been completed without their wonderful assistance.

Finally, we truly hope that this work will be read, critiqued, and used widely. As editors we can think of no better reward than for individuals in various disciplines to use the book in courses or seminars and have it stimulate new inquiry. We welcome hearing from readers as we continue to explore the new paths which seem to develop daily in *The Worlds of E-Commerce*.

Thomas R. Leinbach and Stanley D. Brunn
Lexington, Kentucky
June 2000

Introduction

E-Commerce: Definitions, Dimensions and Constraints

THOMAS R. LEINBACH and STANLEY D. BRUNN

University of Kentucky, Lexington, KY, USA

Speed, accessibility, globalization and information are four key attributes of e-commerce. These distinguishing features and their impacts in the main explain the explosive growth of the phenomenon which is being broadly labeled e-commerce. They distinguish the ways individuals, businesses, organizations, and governments conduct their operations from those in pre-e-commerce periods. While speed was important then, it was not measured or valued in the same commercial context and environment as today. Accessibility or connectivity has always been important to those producing agricultural or industrial raw materials and finished products, but the associated movements relied most heavily on traditional transport networks rather than electronic connections. World trade and transfer of products have long been the driving force of many companies and states, but globalization implies a broader geographic set of linkages and interdependent components, whether the objects are corporations, cities, or states. Information as the final distinguishing feature is the hallmark of post-industrial economies. This quaternary and quinary sector includes those producing, consuming, transferring, and regulating information for all other sectors. Banking, health, education, leisure, computing, and telecommunication represent a few of the evolving 'new economies' which are heavy users and promoters of e-commerce.

These four attributes need to be considered alongside other concepts that scholars from different disciplines and perspectives use to describe and theorize economies and economic change. The geographer will seek to comprehend the whys and wherefores of e-commerce not only with regard to the meanings of distance and space, but also notions of scale, hierarchies, surfaces, networks, and regions. For the economist e-commerce presents challenges in theorizing cost, production, and consumption. And for the policy analyst e-commerce presents new challenges when discussing old issues of taxation, regulation, protection, ownership, and policing. Finally for the regional scientist and international development specialist there are issues about the importance of culture in e-commerce innovations, the innovation and adoption rates of new technologies, and fostering e-commerce initiatives at local and grassroots levels in developing countries as well as connecting creative regions worldwide. In short, e-commerce is a phenomenon or development that benefits from scholars and practitioners coming from different backgrounds, experiences, and perspectives.

We consider e-commerce as the collective of numerous individual, not always commercial, electronic strands of information that move at local, regional, and global scales between and among individuals, universities, corporations, non governmental organizations (NGOs), and states for a variety of purposes. It can include the sheepherder in the Gobi Desert using a cellular phone to contact her/his family about children's health and it can include an investment banker on the fiftieth floor of New York's World Trade Center who in the middle of the night uses the World Wide Web (WWW), e-mail, and fax to exchange information with potential clients in Singapore and Tokyo. E-mail, fax, the WWW, chatrooms, and listservs are used to communicate with others, share and obtain information from others. Sometimes these exchanges are in our own language, but often simultaneously in multiple languages. Information is conveyed by words, but also by symbols, numbers, and codes. While e-commerce is the term most widely used to refer to the exchange of information using the electronic medium, not all traffic on the Internet is of an economic nature. Individuals use the various media, especially e-mail and the WWW, for personal reasons, groups to promote social agendas, and organizations to empower marginalized groups.

E-commerce literally burst onto the scene during the last three years of the 20th century. Its origin is associated especially with electronic data interchange (EDI), the growth of personal computing, and in particular, the rapid diffusion of the Internet and WWW as a medium to display and promote one's goods and services. As noted above these might be real estate opportunities, information on health care, travel, and investment, employment possibilities, and sites to obtain information from libraries, states, and NGOs for use by individuals, scholars, farmers, activists, and politicians. The Internet, another new word added to the electronic lexicon of the 1990s, has become a household word, at least in many rich countries, and one understood by preschool children, working adults, and retirees. The associated features of the Internet, and in particular that associated with e-commerce, permit one to order or bid on books, music, household items, and almost any consumer service through WWW sites and eBay (the major online auction), to be connected with literally thousands of other individuals, libraries, companies, and organizations, and converse electronically with those we know and do not know on a wide variety of topics. The 'worlds' of e-commerce are of a different size, shape, and configuration than before the 'wired' worlds. The vocabulary used by specialists, scholars, and lay people includes terms such as digital economy, DVD, viruses, spamming, surfing, hacking, portals, windows, browsers, and bookmarks, as well as multiple words (with cyber, virtual, and web as adjectives). Young children and technology specialists use the same terms. Moreover, English has become the international language used in e-commerce speech and print.

The inspiration to develop this book came from authors and users of our earlier volume, *Collapsing Space and Time* who urged us to prepare a volume on the spatial, temporal, economic, social, and political dimensions of e-commerce. But mostly it is the explosive and conspicuous growth, as well as the potential impact of this topic and theme, which explains how and why this book came together. We consider it important that social and policy scientists be cognizant of the meanings and importance of e-commerce in the early 21st century. As geographers, we recognized the importance of space, distance, diffusion, networks, interactions, and accessibility in addressing the topic of e-commerce, and we deliberately sought out senior and junior scholars who either were engaged in research on e-commerce or would be intrigued by the opportunity to delve into this theme. But we also deliberately ferreted out scholars in other fields who also have interests or emerging interests in e-commerce. We were most anxious to include both younger and senior scholars in economics, regional economics, public, community, and international policy. Furthermore, we wanted to include authors who come from regions other than North America and Europe where e-commerce has already a firm hold or is likely to very shortly. We were eager to include materials that discussed e-commerce in non Western countries and societies and are pleased that contributing authors have experiences in working with these themes in the Netherlands, Japan, Singapore, and Australia as well as the UK and the USA.

To our knowledge, this book represents a first in the English language which addresses, from a largely social science perspective, the emerging field of study called e-commerce, including theoretical underpinnings, individual case studies, and pertinent policy and development issues. All 16 chapters are original, that is, they have not appeared previously in journals, as chapters, or as books. Most were written within the first five months of 2000. Their bibliographies reflect the recency of materials used in their analyses. An examination of the literature cited reveals the use of newspaper and magazine articles from business, financial, and popular sources, unpublished and recently published documents, and WWW sources from companies, organizations, and countries. References appear in languages other than English.

We feel it important also to call attention to some existing works in e-commerce and related themes which have already been extremely illuminating in their path-breaking efforts. Among these are:

Cronin, M.J. (1996) *Global Advantage on the Internet.* New York: Van Nostrand Reinhold.

Geographical Review (1997) **97**, (2) (special issue on cyberspace and geographical space).

Graham, S. and Marvin, S. (1996) *Telecommunications and the City: Electronic Spaces, Urban Places.* London: Routledge.

Schiller, D. (1999) *Digital Capitalism.* Cambridge: MIT Press.

The Information Society (1997), **13**(1) (March) (special issue on e-commerce).

Westland, J.C. and Clark, T.H.K. (1999) *Global Electronic Commerce.* Cambridge: MIT Press.

Wheeler, J., Yuko A. and Barney W. (eds) (2000) *Cities in the Telecommunications Age.* New York and London: Routledge.

Whinston, A.B., Stahl, D., and Choi, S-Y. (1997) *The Economics of Electronic Commerce.* Indianapolis: Macmillan Technical Publishing.

Wilson, M. and Corey, K. (eds) (2000) *Information Tectonics: Spatial Organization in the Electronic Age.* Chichester: John Wiley.

The current book is organized in three main parts. Part I entitled, 'E-Commerce: Meaning, Theory and Impacts' has five chapters which focus on e-commerce and the Internet. Chapter 1 by Leinbach examines the reasons and bases for the rapid growth in the digital economy as well as two of its facets: e-commerce *per se* and the information technology (IT) industries that drive e-commerce. The former addresses definitions of e-commerce and especially e-commerce between businesses, the digital delivery of goods and services, and the electronic retail sale of tangible goods. The latter includes specific attributes and characteristics, both spatial and aspatial, of the IT industries and their employment–wage implications in the 'new economy'. The chapter concludes with a discussion of the likelihood of continued growth as well as the constraints and challenges which lie ahead.

Chapter 2 by Button and Taylor focuses on the importance of economics in understanding the way in which the spatial use of the Internet and the growth of electronic commerce can affect the location of economic activities. It looks at the theoretical issues and the implications of public policy interventions in markets. Chapter 3 by Kenney and Curry views the Internet as a newly developed space with the power to give rise to novel forms of human social interaction in almost any area of human endeavor, commercial or otherwise. By enabling certain types of activities, the Internet will impact consumer behavior, firm behavior, and industrial organization. The final configuration caused by the Internet is difficult to predict because the features of the Internet interact in problematic and contradictory ways. Perhaps the most problematic question relates to the economic impacts of the Internet in regards to market niche and firm formation. Chapter 4 by Goodchild focuses on e-commerce and the Internet through the concept of distributed computing, namely, if one can compute anywhere, but must compute somewhere, how does one decide where to compute? This chapter addresses a complete range of computing activities (storage, processing, archiving, user interfaced) and includes wireless computing. The basic argument is embedded in classical location theory, and examines appropriate models of individual behavior and impediments to distance. Related concepts of accessibility and potential are examined as well. The final chapter in this first section, by Malecki and Gorman, examines the Internet as a connected structure. This topic has not been analyzed to date in the scholarly literature. The authors examine the Internet as a system of nodes and links, with metropolitan areas as the nodes and fiber-optic lines as links. Traditional network analysis of connectivity and measures of network structure are applied to the network within the USA in order to analyze the connectedness of major US metropolitan areas.

Part II 'Electronic Commerce in Firm, Regional, and International Context' contains six chapters, all of which describe specific e-commerce applications in a variety of commercial and global contexts and at different scales. Yuko Aoyama examines the partnership between convenience stores and e-commerce in Japan; it provides an alternative model of IT use. The Japanese example suggests that e-commerce can develop without requiring all elements of support structures necessary to promote home-based e-commerce use, which is now common in many developed states. For

Japanese consumers, using e-commerce means adopting new business practices and a consumer behavior that comes with the technology, and having to develop and implement a necessary infrastructure and regulations that facilitate this mode of exchange. The convenience store model of e-commerce in Japan has numerous implications and suggests alternatives to that used in the USA. This chapter is followed by that of Sharon Cobb which picks up the debate regarding the nature of the economics of the Internet in a specific context. Essentially, do basic economic principles remain the same even when played out through a new and innovative medium? Internet economics, including issues of capitalization, and consideration of the relationship between electronic space and real space, are analyzed using case-study evidence from the electronic online recruiting industry, seen by many observers as the result of the rapid growth of the IT sector over the past decade.

Coe and Yeung, at a different scale, use Castell's concept of 'nodes in global flows' to explore the potential for particular localities to emerge as hubs within the rapidly emerging world of e-commerce. Singapore provides an excellent case study, due to the wide-ranging efforts of the government to establish the city-state as a premier e-commerce hub in the Asia–Pacific region. In exploring these policy initiatives, the potential impacts of hub development in terms of attracting employment, technology and infrastructure to Singapore are considered. Second, they evaluate the potential impacts on national competitiveness and consider some implications of their analysis for geographical theories of spatially bounded competition in a rapidly changing world economy. Following this chapter, Dodge examines Amazon.com, billed as the 'world's largest bookstore'. Among the themes discussed are the origins, operations, products sold, the process of brand establishment on the Internet, the guiding vision of the founder, customer profile, and the attempt to develop a sense of community. Finally Dodge examines the challenges which the entity faces. Van Geenhuizen and Nijkamp discuss electronic banking in the Netherlands. Since the introduction of electronic banking, the restructuring of banking networks shows remarkable spatial impacts, ranging from the financial abandonment of specific local areas to an increased importance of particular medium-sized towns as a marketplaces for financial services. Electronic banking has brought about the decline of local branch offices, because automated teller machines (ATMs) and home computers now perform routine transactions such as cash withdrawals and other operations. At the same time, the regional offices increase in importance in order to supply specialized services based on a face-to-face contact with customers in the retail and business segment. The final chapter in this section by Langdale investigates the impact of 24-hour trading in Singapore, a critical Asia–Pacific foreign exchange hub. He examines the question of how foreign exchange firms operate in a global environment and also considers the interrelationships between the Asian economic and currency crisis and the global electronic environment in foreign exchange markets.

Part III 'E-Commerce: Financial, Legal and State Issues', like the first, contains five chapters. The focus is on electronic funds, regulatory and governance issues regarding e-commerce and related developments. The section opens with Warf and Purcell's chapter 'Currency of Currency'. They note that the emergence of floating exchange rates, electronic funds transfer systems, and digital money in the late 20th century progressively undermined the capacity of national governments and central banks to control their own currencies. The chapter provides a theoretical and historical survey of money and its complex, often contradictory, impacts on time and space, emphasizing the extreme volatility of contemporary electronic currency trading systems under global post-Fordist capital. It then offers three case studies using the European Union, Russia, and East Asia to illustrate differential ways in which the loss of national monetary controls during the 1990s have played out in various regional contexts, ranging from the relatively harmonious to the utterly chaotic.

Power, in the second chapter of this section, addresses the policy debate which suggests that the creation of electronic realms for dealing with transactions in global money and finance has little rational need to be tied to high cost locations in financial centers such as London. He argues against such logic by showing how information and communication technologies have in many ways reinforced the role of major financial centers. Furthermore, the chapter highlights the importance of innovation, and the agglomeration economies of information and knowledge, to the continued role of urban financial centers in European financial markets. It provides an empirical analysis of derivatives exchange integration and innovations in order to complement theoretical claims made about the continued importance of face-to-face interaction to financial centers and the interaction and collaboration between financial centers.

The third chapter, by Regan, also looks at regulation issues, but in a different arena. She tackles the issues of taxation and e-commerce, specifically, how does a government tax goods and services that are obtained electronically? Liquor and gaming are the case studies. Here the difficulties of enforcing legal and regulatory regimes in cyberspace, as well as the interdependence of legal and regulatory infrastructures, which are technology based, are discussed. The enforcement difficulties appear to reveal something of a paradox: the enforcement of laws and regulations in cyberspace may necessitate more authentications of personal identities. An activity such as e-shopping in the virtual world may require a more complete check of one's identity than would result from the same activity in the physical world.

Wilson's chapter is concerned with the international dimensions of e-commerce, and specifically the pluses and minuses of diffusing 'dot com' technologies. The role of IT in economic development, and the viability of advanced electronic infrastructure for developing countries are explored. It is maintained that while IT may well be important or essential for economic development, its implementation and use raises questions about the 'best use' and 'opportunity costs' associated with a country's scarce resources. Issues addressed include the political and social processes surrounding the adoption of IT; the contribution of IT to developing country trade; and the spatial patterns of IT development between and within countries. While there are promises to these technologies entering a country, there are also pitfalls of which governments and organizations need to be aware.

Owing to rapid social, political, and technological changes in the past decades, transnational corporations (TNCs) have become geopolitical entities that not only conduct business across international boundaries, but also act as carriers of technological advance, political viewpoints, cultural values, and a 'global' information context. The TNC thus becomes a form of 'corporate nation', a hegemonic form of sovereignty working above and beyond international boundaries. The final chapter by Tom Edwards, addresses this theme and focuses on the concept of 'information geopolitics' – the movement of geopolitical from the purely corporeal realm into the virtual world of information, where disputes are fought over the control of the perception of sovereignty. Microsoft Corporation is used as an example. He posits that a new political and economic entity is appearing, the corporate nation, which has many of the features of an electronically wired state.

The volume, as a foundation text and state-of-the-art effort (July, 2000), illustrates examples of original scholarly work by specialists in a number of disciplines and from different national and international perspectives. It is our hope that the readings will be useful in introductory and advanced classes on e-commerce in a variety of disciplinary, interdisciplinary, and transdisciplinary settings. We envision new courses and additional courses offered in the future with such titles, for example, as 'E-commerce and Local Entrepreneurship', 'E-commerce in Industrializing Economies', 'Liberalization and E-commerce', 'E-commerce and the State', and 'E-commerce and International Development'. Chapters and sections could also become the foundation for workshops, corporate seminars, and short-term courses in cities, regions, and countries that are already 'wired', as well as those that aspire to be connected. Small businesses, large city business organizations, multistate economic development initiatives, and transnational corporations interested in ITC (information and telecommunications) might wish to expand on one or another theme. Of one development we are sure, and that is the introduction, implications, uses, and regulation of e-commerce, in a broad context, will be a major topic for attention by governments, corporations, and scholars in the coming decade.

There remain many topics that are ripe for disciplinary and interdisciplinary research in e-commerce. We suggest five of promise. One is the use of electronically accessed information in education or 'E-education', and in particular, distance learning and the various library, laboratory, translation, and databases services used by students, faculty, and other professionals. Second, is the uses of e-commerce in health fields; the burgeoning developments in 'E-health' during the past two years have multiple and unknown, individual and international, ramifications not only for those having direct access to medical attention nearby, but those in remote and poor areas. A third topic deals with the conventional travel industry, which must adapt to the direct access competition now provided through Internet sites. Increasingly, individuals and corporations are planning their own itineraries and arranging directly for accommodations in both leisure and business travel. A fourth is the uses of e-commerce in retailing and professional services. The popularity of eBay suggests that many other businesses will utilize the Internet and thus may change the mall landscapes of large cities and the use patterns for personal individual services, such as attorneys, physicians, and care-givers. The final topic that merits the attention of scholars and policymakers is the 'digital divide'. The social and spatial dimensions of this 'divide', whether gender, age, race, class, disability, rural or urban based, and at local and international scales, are ones that best not be avoided. Ethical and moral issues of technological innovations also need to be part of these discussions. Contributions to these and other topics can and should come from those with interests in different cultures and world regions, within different economies and stages of e-commerce development, with different disciplinary backgrounds and training, and with varying commitments to local and international scales of innovations. Our understanding of the 'whys and wherefores' of the worlds of electronic commerce will be enhanced by developing new or refining existing theories but also by case studies, comparative research, and policy applications. We chose our title, *Worlds of E-Commerce*, to illustrate the multifaceted, transdisciplinary, and international contributions scholars can offer to this rapidly developing and vital field of inquiry.

PART I

E-COMMERCE: MEANING, THEORY, AND IMPACTS

1

Emergence of the Digital Economy and E-Commerce

THOMAS R. LEINBACH

University of Kentucky, Lexington, KY, USA

INTRODUCTION

While there has been much speculation about the impacts of the information explosion in an increasingly digital society, surprisingly little is known about how particular applications of technology have and will affect the future paths of firms, cities, regions, and other places people live and work and with whom they interact (Lohr 1996). It is only within the last half decade that we are beginning to see through various innovations how IT can influence the ways in which people react and respond to opportunities. A current example of this is the spread of the cellular telephone and the behavioral changes which it has produced in communications and other facets of life. Similarly, in order to maintain competitive advantage, firms are racing to apply IT in a variety of ways. The focus on efficiency through the implementation of e-business has now become a standard by which firms measure their profitability and success. In order to accommodate the shift to a new focus these firms are undergoing numerous spatial and structural adjustments. While the bulk of this innovative behavior is taking place in the USA, Canada, Europe, Australia, and parts of Asia gradually applications are seeping into more economically peripheral states on the globe. Both electronic mail (e-mail) and electronic data interchange (EDI) are powerful instruments which have begun to stimulate and promote development in the Third World. The gradual adaptation to these new modes of operation will almost certainly affect profoundly behaviors and geographical influences in non-Western economies and cultures more rapidly over the ensuing decades (Stuck 1996).

The application of IT is perhaps most conspicuous and best seen in examining the changing nature and global reach of electronic commerce (e-commerce), and this constitutes the subject of this volume. In order to capture e-commerce in detail it is necessary first to examine its economic base and genesis especially within the USA. It is the economic environment and the changing nature and structure of that environment which has supported the tremendous explosion of e-commerce in its many forms (Schiller 1999).

The first objective of this chapter is to define and examine the 'theory' surrounding the 'new or digital economy'. In addition, it is important to capsule how it has developed and also provide the context of the several debates surrounding its nature and origins. The essence of the digital economy lies in the developments commonly referred to as high (information) technology industries. An assessment of the growth and importance of such technological developments in both a spatial and structural manner is essential to a full appreciation and understanding of e-commerce.

Following this, and because this is the initial chapter, we lay out the definitions, partial theory, and basic applications of e-commerce. An important aspect of all recent developments is the impact of the Internet and e-commerce on individuals, firms, cities, and regions including the changing nature of employment (Cronin 1996; Graham and Marvin 1996; Lohr 1996; Sternberg 1996). While it is far too early to delineate these impacts with great precision, it is clear that important developments have already been felt and these are the topics and themes of subsequent chapters. Thus in order to lay the groundwork for later chapters, it is important to present and review the essential tools or instruments of e-commerce. Even though the rapid pace of developments make predicting the future of e-commerce difficult to forecast, certain constraining issues, as well as promising developments, loom large on the horizon. These are also discussed.

THE DIGITAL ECONOMY

It is acceptable in scholarly and corporate communities to refer to the 'digital or new' economy as ways in which IT industries and electronic communication and distribution methods have produced an unexpectedly strong performance in the American economic fabric since 1996. The measurement of the digital economy may be documented through incomes, growth, the stock market, interest rates, employment, and productivity. In many circles, however, the notion and definition of the 'new economy' is a contentious topic. Essentially the crux of the debate is whether important relationships that underlie our economy and bind it together have really fundamentally changed. Have the 1990s marked the beginning of a unique era or are we simply at a virtuous point in the business cycle whereby a dynamic system is increasingly conspicuous? Some observers claim that globalization and technology have combined to create new rules for the US economy, while others argue that recent events can be explained satisfactorily by existing economics (Stiroh 1999).

The new economy paradigm comprises a variety of ideas, and assembling these views into a simplified framework of explanation is useful. One can argue that there are really three broad versions of the new economy: a long-run growth version, a business cycle version, and a sources of growth version. The defining characteristic for a new economy viewpoint is a focus on increasing globalization and expanding information and communication technologies. These two basic forces are the driving prongs of the new economy in all three versions.

The 'long-run' version argues that the US economy will continue, as a result of the above influences, to enjoy a period of permanently faster output growth that will not lead to increased inflation. New economy proponents point to spreading capitalism and widespread deregulation, both of which place pressure on the market and allow resources to be used more efficiently while accelerating output growth. Simultaneously, IT industries are transforming the economy as they account for an increasing share of growth, falling prices, and wage acceleration. Implicit here is that IT is a 'transcendent technology' which is analogous to the railroads in the 19th century and automobiles in the 20th century, and may be only the initial edge of a stronger era of technological, business and financial creativity (Mandell 1998; Shepard 1997). Embedded in this view is the notion that IT boosts productivity, which is in turn enhanced by globalization, deregulation, and innovation. One of the important questions in the new economy debate focuses precisely on the degree to which productivity is present, where it is most conspicuous, and how it is growing.

A second view is a business cycle version; the focus here is on the behavior of inflation and unemployment, both of which are key characteristics of the new economy. The argument is that short-run supply shocks are a plausible explanation for the recent decline in both inflation and unemployment. Specifically in the past few years the US economy has benefited from the sharp decline in oil (despite the mid-2000 situation of high oil prices) and commodity prices, a strong dollar, a balanced budget, and reduced military expenditures. These are all transitory factors that could have led to conditions of low unemployment and inflation. The dilemma here is distinguishing between temporary factors and structural changes in short-run data series.

Finally, the sources of growth version posits a wholly different explanation of how economies grow. This view takes the idea of total factor productivity as its main thrust and argues that important sectors benefit from increasing returns, externalities, standards, and network economies (Solow 1956). The latter assumes that growth is accumulating and geometrical, for example that the values of IT products such as an Internet connection, a fax machine, or a piece of software increase as other individuals and firms invest in similar equipment and facilities. This production spillover, it is maintained, allows for ongoing growth that can rapidly overwhelm and outpace a more traditional explanation of growth. Included here are mutually reinforcing feedback effects in industrial situations of varying scale and complexity. These range from the isolated industrial district to the assembled firms within the Silicon Valley. In addition, the increase in quality via technology and scale economies is an important element of the same spillover effect. Coupled with this, since 1994, is the entrepreneurship which has been triggered by the Internet. The proponents of this view point to the myriad innovations of IT such as hardware and software development and their applications, combined with the impact of globalization, on critical sector growth, and achievement of scale effects. As part of this debate there is the question of performance and productivity in the current economy to which we now turn.

The Productivity Debate

A major question in the controversy surrounding the new economy is whether high-tech industries and the IT that propel them are making the economy more productive. Proponents agree that the new economy means more than 'numbers of high-tech workers and firms'. Thus a key ingredient in the new economy debate is the matter of productivity: how deep it is, where it is found, and how long lasting it will be. As recently as a few years ago prominent economists argued that although high technology applications had affected people and firms in obvious and visible ways, the slowdown in productivity growth since the 1970s remained unaffected. Since 1996 the US nonfarm productivity has improved on average by 2.2 percent a year (in contrast to the 25-year average of barely 1.1 percent per year). But since 1998 nonfarm productivity grew by an annual average of 3.4 percent. These figures do not resolve the matter as such increases have occurred previously and may be a function of the way in which inflation is measured. But more discouraging for the new economy proponents is that the measured productivity since the mid-1990s is extraordinarily concentrated in one small sector of the high-tech economy: computer manufacturing. Although computer manufacturing is just 1.2 percent of the US output, the improvement (42 percent a year from 1995 until 1999) was substantial enough to increase non-farm productivity growth. Overall the manufacturing performance of the US economy decelerated in 1995–99 compared with the period, 1972–95. A plausible conclusion is that the IT revolution may mean that computer technology has been very effective at reproducing itself, but has not had a perceptible overall positive impact (Gordon 1999).

Against this negative finding about productivity are several arguments. First these data exclude the certain impact of IT in services where productivity is notoriously difficult to measure. Another is that firms may be compelled to embrace and invest in technology in order to preserve or extend their share of the market but are not producing much additional product for these additional expenditures. Also it is quite certain that industry's investment in capital which embodies high technology must be resulting in productivity improvements. Especially important is that the easy accessibility of information has allowed numerous improvements in corporate efficiency. Among these are production planning, inventory reductions, and altered distribution systems. In sum, capital goods are made more flexible and as a result capital investment is more attractive and productive. In this process firms are encouraged to substitute capital for scarce labor. The resultant employment shifts with the application of IT will continue to be of interest. The regional and structural implications of employment losses and gains as jobs are created and eliminated will be important barometers of the new economy's impacts.

Clearly the debates on the new economy will only be resolved as long-run growth prospects and labor market dynamics, for example, are integrated into existing data. In many ways it is far too early to determine whether the new economy is in fact unique or can be explained by conventional economics. We next turn to a more detailed examination of high technology industries within the new economy.

Information Technology Producing Industries

A conspicuous aspect of the digital economy in recent years has been the rapid increase in the IT industries' share of investment activity and the gross domestic product. From 1985, with 4.9 percent of the economy, it grew to 6.1 percent in 1990 and 8.2 percent in 1998 (Figure 1.1). The initial spurt in the last half of the 1980s was triggered by the dramatic rise in personal computer ownership in both residences and offices. From 1993 onward the growth may reasonably be attributed in large part to the commercial

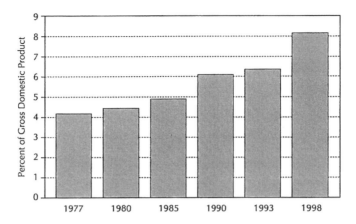

Figure 1.1   *Information technology's share of the US economy. Source: US Department of Commerce 1999 [http://www.ecommerce.gov/fig2.htm]*

activity which has been driven by the growth of the Internet. This growing share of the economy is remarkable in and of itself, but also because IT product prices, adjusted for quality and performance improvements, have been falling while the prices in the other sectors of the economy have been rising. For example, as a result of microprocessor research and development, transistor prices have fallen from $230 to $3.42 per MIPS between 1991 and 1997 (US Department of Commerce 1998). Another gauge of the IT industries' contribution to production in the economy is in real terms. During the late 1990s IT industries were responsible for more than 25 percent of real economic growth. Another obvious and major aspect of this growth is the ways in which these industries have contributed to employment, a theme discussed below.

The forecasts of future economic growth are exuberant and what is most interesting is not only the growth in the IT sector itself, but also the spillovers created across all sectors as the Internet expands and its commercial impact multiplies. Although it is likely that new facets and applications will appear which will generate growth, there are now principally four types of economic activities which are driving the expansion.

First, 'building out' the Internet, that is the growing numbers of people who use the Internet will generate increased investment in computers, software, services, and communications. One simple example is the expected continued growth in not only personal computers in desk and mobile formats, but especially in hand held and run devices (mobile device demand) with wireless connections to the Internet. By 2002 perhaps 400 million additional devices beyond the current 600 million stationary devices will be purchased. The competition for this market by manufacturers of devices, software, and associated add-ons will be considerable. Second, electronic commerce among businesses is already expanding in dramatic fashion as firms realize that in order to compete effectively they must interact and carry out business using a variety of electronic means. Despite the debates on productivity impacts of the digital economy, there is considerable confidence and growing evidence that electronic networks are allowing this expansion to occur through the creation, purchasing, selling, distribution, and servicing of goods and services. Third, the digital delivery of goods and services is an increasingly important aspect of e-commerce. Airline tickets and securities have been the leading edge of an expansion that now includes software programs, music, and newspapers–journals. The presence of the digital economy and the power of the Internet are altering the ways in which most industries are doing business. Education, health care, consulting, and financial services are among those industries in which considerable changes in the modes of operation are already apparent. Fourth, the retail sale of tangible goods that are stored, produced, and delivered physically is an additional growing aspect of the contemporary economy. Although Internet sales are now minute as a portion of total retail sales, this statistic will change dramatically over the next decade as Internet connections, especially via cheaper hand held devices and web television, takes place.

As we survey the IT producing sector as driver of the digital economy an important question is: what are the included industries? The US Department of Commerce includes 29 separate industries and services under four major categories: hardware, communications equipment, software/services, and communications services (Table 1.1). On the other hand, an additional important definition is that constructed by the American Electronics Association (AEA) which eschews the inclusion of numerous related industries such as biotechnology, engineering, testing, and related services. The AEA uses 45 Standard Industrial Classification (SIC) categories to define 'high-technology' industry. The basic categories include the largest which is high-tech manufacturing; it includes computers and office equipment, consumer electronics, communications equipment, electronic components and accessories, semiconductors, industrial electronics, photonics, defense electronics, and electromedical equipment. Other major groups are communications services, and software and computer-related services (software services, data processing and information services, and rental and maintenance services). Additional industry groups not covered in AEA's definition

Table 1.1   *Information technology producing industries*

Hardware industries	Software/services industries
Computers and equipment	Computer programming services and
Wholesale trade of computers	equipment
Retail trade of computers and equipment	Prepackaged software
Calculating and office machines	Wholesale trade of software
Magnetic and optical reading media	Retail trade of software
Electron tubes	Computer integrated systems design
Printed circuit boards	Computer and data processing
Semiconductors	Information retrieval services
Passive electronic components	Computer services management
Industrial instruments	Computer rental and leasing
Electricity measuring instruments	Computer maintenance and repair
Laboratory analytical instruments	Computer related services
Communications Equipment Industries	**Communications Services Industries**
Household audio and video equipment	Telephone and telegraph communications
Telephone and telegraph equipment	Radio and TV broadcasting
Radio, TV, and Communications Equipment	Cable and other pay TV services

Source: US Department of Commerce. The Emerging Digital Economy: II, June 1999, p. 15.

include wholesale and retail trade of high-tech goods. The biotechnology industry is not included because US government statistics do not distinguish and clearly identify which portion is 'bio' and which is 'tech'. There is no clear consensus on the definition of the biotechnology industry. Thus the AEA definition is more conservative and limiting.

We noted above the growing share of the US economy accounted for by IT producing industries and their contributions to real growth. In addition, IT producing industries and services accounted for an increasing share of US international trade from 1993 to 1998. During these years the IT producing sectors averaged annual growth of 11.9 percent against 7.6 percent for all other goods. Increases in both exports and imports raised the negative balance in goods trade by IT industries from $33 billion in 1993 to $55 billion in 1998. In the same period exports and imports of services from this sector grew at 13.2 percent per year, reaching $20.7 billion in 1997. The rate of growth in exports (17.2 percent) over that in imports (9.5 percent) signals good prospects for a surplus balance in the sector (US Department of Commerce June, 1999).

Labor in the Digital Economy

Another critical aspect of the IT industries is the employment dimension. The expansion of these industries and the concomitant growth in e-commerce have produced an energizing influence on the economy. The application of technology has allowed, and sometimes forced, firms to become more efficient in order to be competitive and survive in a broader global context (Singh 1994; Porter 1990, 1996). At the same time the heightened competition, global access and need for flexibility have affected the respective labor markets by influencing employment demand, wages, skill requirements and, consequently, education delivery at a variety of institutions (Aaronson and Housinger 1999). In general the IT industries are characterized currently by increasing employment demand, rising wages and skill requirements (American Electronics Association (AEA) 1999b). By the middle of the current decade nearly 50 percent of the private workforce will be employed by IT related industries and this has grown from 44 percent in 1989. Perhaps most conspicuous is the increased demand for 'core' IT workers (computer scientists, engineers, programmers and system analysts).

In addition the digital economy is generating new IT occupations and changing both skill requirements for non-IT jobs as well as raising the minimum skill requirements for many non-IT jobs (US Department of Commerce 1999). High-tech firms have been hiring employees vigorously over the past decade. Successful examples are Cisco Systems, Compaq, and Dell Computers, among others (Figure 1.2). This hiring trend is true of both startups and well-established firms. In June 2000 there was some evidence, however, that a number of the startup firms were downsizing in order to become profitable. Recent analysis has discovered evidence of a 'churning' effect of employment gains and losses among IT industries and occupations. Basically the innovations which have been applied as a result of computing and telecommunications technologies have had the effect of expanding employment in some industries while decreasing it in others. Flexible, multiskilled workers who must accept continuing education and retraining are essential for rapidly changing labor markets. An import-

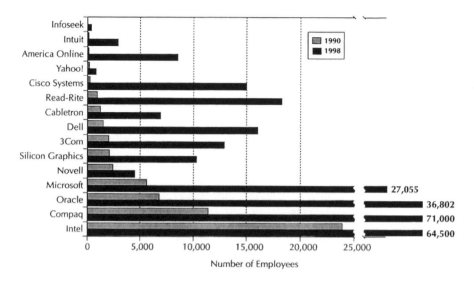

Figure 1.2   *Employment growth in select high-tech industries. Source: AEA 1999d*

ant part of this employment theme is the explosion of the 'online' employment recruitment industry, a topic discussed by Cobb in Chapter 7 of this volume. Increasingly for high-tech as well as more traditional employment, Internet web sites such as hotjobs.com, govworks.com, and kforce.com provide information on job opportunities to a growing number of increasingly sophisticated employment seekers.

Employment growth in IT-producing industries is outpacing average employment growth. Over the period from 1989 to 1997 employment grew 2.4 percent annually compared with the 1.7 percent growth in all private industry. Since 1996 the US Department of Commerce reports that IT-producing industries have added 350 000 jobs (a total of 4.8 million jobs) compared with average total employment growth of only 3 percent. Software and services is the fastest growing group. It is now the largest (1.43 million workers) and has surpassed communications employment (1.42 million). By contrast hardware industries have experienced only slight gains, despite some high growth sub-industries.

Spatial Expressions of US Information Technology Producing Industries

While the locational results are not completely surprising, it is useful to examine briefly the digital economy in spatial perspective. Using 1997 high-tech employment (AEA definition above) as a measure of the importance of individual states' contribution to and representation in the digital economy, the top 10 cyberstates are: California, Texas, New York, Illinois, Massachusetts, Florida, New Jersey, Pennsylvania, Virginia, and Georgia. The figures reveal that California's employment is more than twice that of its nearest rival, Texas, and almost six times that of Georgia. These leading states are depicted along with all others in a pattern derived from the total number of high-tech jobs (Figure 1.3). Excluding the 10 leaders, conspicuous states are Washing-

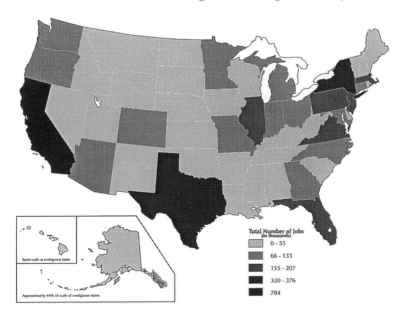

Figure 1.3   *Total jobs in high-tech industry, 1997. Source: Cyberstates v3.0, AEA 1999*

ton (software services), Oregon (semiconductors and software), Minnesota (electromedical equipment), New Mexico (semiconductors), North Carolina (communication services), Missouri (communication services), Indiana (communication services, electrical components, consumer electronics), Colorado (communication and software services), and Connecticut (communication services). More interesting is the distribution revealing the number of high-tech workers per 1000 private sector workers. (Figure 1.4). It is clear that certain states are seeking to attract and focus on information and communication technology production and services as the transformation to a digital economy continues and deepens. Conspicuous among the smaller states are Vermont (semiconductors), New Hampshire (electronic components and accessories, computers), Maryland (software and communication services) as well as Colorado and Virginia (software and communications services). These employment ratios reflect well-seeded centers of specialized industry and/or locations proximate to larger centers of high-tech development (e.g. Vermont (Essex Junction) and New Hampshire (Manchester) namely Rte 128 in the Boston area). Similarly, Maryland (Bethesda) and Virginia (Fairfax) on the doorstep of the nation's science and technology policy hearth fit this explanation. Finally, and in the same vein, the fastest growing cyberstates as measured by high-tech employment growth over the period from 1990 to 1997 are South Dakota, North Dakota, Delaware, Idaho, and Washington. In the case of the Dakotas the deagrarianization process as the family farm disappears has been countered by a growing trend toward high-tech industry.

A final theme in spatial context emphasizes high-tech exports as a percentage of

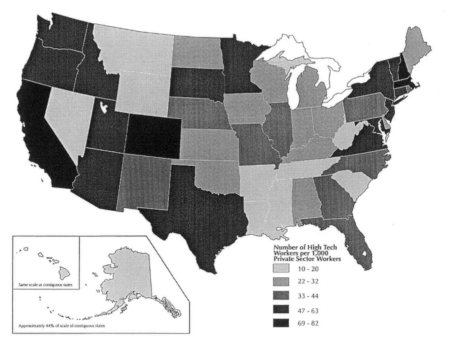

Figure 1.4 *Employment in high-tech industry, 1997. Source: Cyberstates v.3.0, AEA 1999*

total exports (Figure 1.5). Roughly two-thirds of the high-tech products produced in Arizona, California, Colorado, Massachusetts, New Hampshire, New Mexico, and Vermont are exported. This static pattern, however, does not reveal the leading growth states in such exports over the period of 1990–97, which are New Mexico, Oregon, Maine, Tennessee and Nevada. The spatial expression of information and communications technology and services reflects our intuitive knowledge of the US economy. Heavily populated states where industry is strong are also doing well in the production of new economy goods and services. Yet it is also clear that the expansion of the digital economy is filtering down into many nontraditional industrial states as they seek to gain a competitive foothold in the strengthening economy and seek to replace jobs lost through agriculture and basic industry.

E-Commerce: Definitions and Structure

We noted above the major influences which will drive the IT sector over the coming decades. A major aspect of the propelling force behind the growth of the IT sector is of course e-commerce, a topic we now turn to. There are a growing number of both basic and specialized treatments of e-commerce (e.g. US Department of Commerce 1998; Wigand 1997; Westland and Clark 1999; Whinston *et al.* 1997) and the reader is referred to these for more detail and further readings. The intent here is simply to provide a definitional, conceptual and structural road map for readers as they launch themselves into our volume on e-commerce.

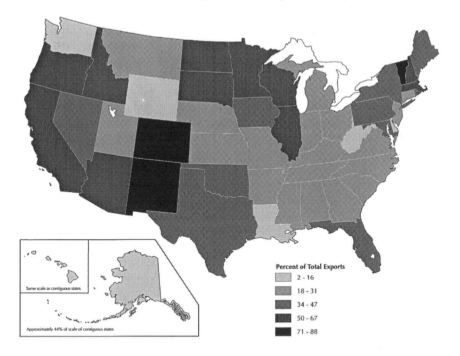

Figure 1.5 *High-tech exports, 1998. Source: Cyberstates v.3.0, AEA 1999*

The term 'electronic commerce' has been in existence since the 1970s. But the growth of e-commerce in the past few years has generated considerable diversity and complexity in its structure and applications. The 'old e-commerce' is in fact putting on new clothes as we write and it remains a shifting target in the attempt to define and understand its nuances. Related terms often used synonymously with e-commerce are e-business and e-markets. Among the various definitions of e-commerce one states that it:

> includes any form of economic activity conducted via electronic connections and denotes the seamless application of information and communication technologies from their points of origin to the endpoints along the entire value chain of business processes in pursuit of a business goal. The bandwidth of electronic commerce spans from electronic markets to electronic hierarchies and also incorporates electronically supported entrepreneurial networks and cooperative arrangements (electronic networks) (Wigand 1997, pp. 2, 5).

Another definition is:

> the use of information and communication technologies to network economic activities and processes, in order to reduce information related transaction costs to gain a strategic, information advantage (Garcia 1997, p. 18).

This definition emphasizes networks and economic processes and outcomes rather than marketing and consumers or firms. Still another view states that electronic commerce includes commercial activities conducted through an exchange of information generated, stored, or communicated by electronic, optical, or analogous means, including electronic data interchange (EDI), electronic mail (e-mail) and so forth (Hill 1997, p. 33).

Finally, e-commerce may be

the use of electronic means to pursue business objectives. This can include the use of information technologies such as electronic data interchange, electronic funds transfer, electronic auctions, and other telecommunication technologies as well as the interactive technologies of television and the Internet (Palmer 1997, p. 75).

While there are many different technologies that enable electronic commerce it is, of course, more than the mere use of technology (Wigand 1997, p. 5).

While all of the above definitions are useful, it is the one which stresses the use of information and communication technologies to network economic activities and processes in order to reduce information related transaction costs and/or gain a strategic, information advantage that is the most rewarding. This working definition also captures, in our view, the strongest theoretical view of e-commerce as it focuses upon networks, economic processes, and outcomes rather than specific activities, actors or organizational forms. Such a definition thus provides a basis for analyzing how e-commerce networks alter business procedures and transcend organizational and geographical boundaries. In this context, wealth is generated and transaction costs are reduced. It is also suggested that by viewing electronic commerce in this way one can begin to forecast the long-term impacts of e-commerce on infrastructure deployment, labor and employment, and the evolution of networking industries. The merging of electronically oriented industries are also part of this calculus. One example is the linkages between computing and legal firms, in particular those that produce software and deal with intellectual property, especially copyright issues. These linkages are among the reasons the packaged software industry is so vibrant in the USA.

Theoretical Approaches to E-Commerce

There are clearly a variety of ways to examine this concept in a theoretical sense. Notions such as marketing, information retrieval, strategic networking, and diffusion, each of which has some legitimacy and is particularly suited to the context of use and application, are capable of supporting and developing theory (Wigand 1997). For social scientists, however, the concept of transaction costs embedded within the larger framework of institutional economics (which generally emphasizes the significance of information and communications for the coordination of economic activity) has perhaps the strongest appeal and is potentially a fruitful way of looking at e-commerce and the relationship to competitive advantage. Transaction costs may be viewed as analogous to the friction or impediments in a movement system and are incurred as a product is channeled along the value chain in the production and distribution process. The objective of transaction cost theory is the explanation and reduction of these transaction costs within an adequate theoretical framework and organizational design. Clearly the tools and mechanisms of e-commerce have considerable potential to reduce costs for contracting, monitoring, and adaptation.

Information Technology Effects and E-Commerce

The products of the IT-producing industries as noted above are varied. But in terms of the effects on e-commerce, it is principally those products and processes (effects) that influence the firm's ability to coordinate business transactions within itself and with other firms, as well as between the firm and its customers, that are critical. These effects lead to the reduction of transaction and coordination costs and may be enumerated as four separate but overlapping forces (Malone *et al.* 1987, 1989; Wigand 1997). They are, first, the communication effect, whereby advances in information technology allow for more information to be transmitted in the same amount of time, thus reducing transaction costs. Second, the electronic integration effect which means that through information technology a tighter connection or linkage is effected within a business, among businesses and between a firm and its customers. Third, the electronic brokerage effect whereby the electronic marketplace brings together buyers and sellers to compare offers. A most conspicuous and growing example of this effect is the electronic auction phenomenon, e.g. eBay. Finally the electronic strategic networking effect enables the design and deliberate strategic deployment of linkages and networks to gain competitive advantage among cooperating firms intended to achieve joint, strategic goals (Wigand 1997, 3).

Tools of E-Commerce

Electronic commerce has expanded quickly as a result of the application of two primary tools: e-mail and electronic data interchange (EDI). Both tools may be viewed as value added network services and allow the user to substitute electronic forms for their paper-based counterparts (e-tickets for example) (Wigand 1997). Electronic mail is now, of course, quite common and is gradually replacing traditional mail flows. EDI is defined as the computer-to-computer exchange of business documents between or among organizations in a standard format. Moreover, EDI requires a contractual agreement to trade.

But it is the development of the Internet and the WWW medium that have allowed these tools of e-mail and EDI to rapidly stimulate electronic commerce (Andresssen 1997) (Figures 1.6 and 1.7). The Internet phenomenon represents a paradigm shift governing business and IT systems, and is an immense resource aiding business to be conducted electronically among millions of small, medium, and large firms.

The bulk of the development, innovation and advantages of the application of these tools has focused upon the private sector. What is not really clear is how the public sector–the state–and nonprofit groups will utilize the advantages of IT effects and associated tools to foster development and produce competitive advantage. There is a continuing effort on the part of a variety of public agencies to attract and further stimulate high-tech industry in regions peripheral to the dominant clusters in the major cyberstates. An important aspect of such efforts is the role of capital and financing. Venture capital funding has been extremely important to the development of high technology industry (Leinbach and Amrhein 1987) and especially influential in moving the Internet developments from universities, government and large corpora-tions to consumer media services. Netscape, one of two major 'browsers' is largely a result of venture capital investment. Typically such entrepreneurial efforts demand ownership

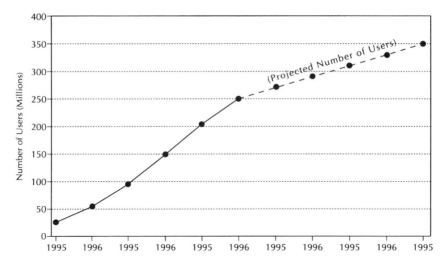

Figure 1.6   *Number of online users worldwide. Source: Datamonitor 1998; Nua Internet Surveys [http://www.nue.ie/surveys/graphs_charts/comparisons/how_many_online.html]*

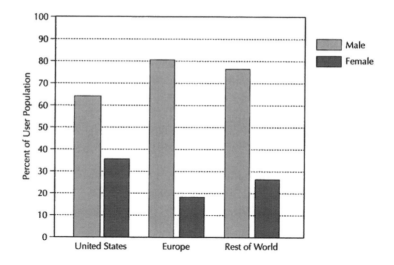

Figure 1.7   *Internet users by gender, 1998. Source: Datamonitor 1998; GVU User Survey [http://www.nue.ie/surveys/graphs_charts/1998graphs/gender.html]*

of four-fifths of a company's equity before they will sell stock shares through an initial public offering (IPO). Venture capitalists pumped $1.8 billion into US information technology firms in 1992 and this expanded to $7.1 billion by 1997 (Schiller 1999). The new twists are the roles of venture capital in the development of business accelerators and incubators, where the focus is not only on traditional information technology but more critically the stimulation of smaller firms which seek to be innovators in either the development or application of Internet business. Against these positive developments are the ways in which regulatory bodies may restrict the use of the Internet and the

WWW and perhaps limit and constrain and/or direct development. This issue is especially critical in the developing world. Within our own economic system, e-commerce must be seen in the context of markets and the market consists of all goal-seeking firms, government agencies or individuals producing some commodity.

E-Commerce Between Businesses

The leading edge of the e-commerce revolution has been, and in many ways continues to be, transactions and applications between businesses. E-commerce is used in a variety of ways including coordination of purchasing operations with suppliers, planning logistics with distribution firms that move products, linking the sales organizations and wholesalers/retailers who sell its products, and producing efficient customer service and maintenance operations. The first real application of e-commerce occurred during the 1970s, as firms were able to send and receive purchase orders, invoices and shipping notifications electronically through EDI. EDI became a standard mechanism for compiling and transmitting information between computers, over private communications networks called value added networks (VANS) (US Department of Commerce 1998). Initially these relatively costly private networks restricted Internet usage to all but the largest firms. Over time these costs as well as those associated with more public means of access have been reduced. The result is that companies of all sizes can, and increasingly will, use electronic transactions in order to remain competitive. Lower purchasing costs, reduced inventory, lower cycle times (the time required to produce a product), lower sales and marketing costs, and new sales opportunities are all benefits derived from carrying out business on the Internet. The estimates of the value of e-commerce between businesses continue to be revised upward. The dramatic growth of e-commerce, with contrasts between business-to-business and business to consumer traffic is readily apparent from the graphic below (Figure 1.8).

Digital Delivery of Goods and Services

One of the earliest and most important applications of e-commerce was, and continues to be, the digital delivery of goods that do not rely on a physical form. The production of and demand for intangible goods has strengthened as the acquisition of personal computers and other access means such as television, cellular telephones, and personal digital assistants have expanded the power of the Internet. Sales of mobile telephones was 283 million units in 1999, a 65 percent increase over 1998, and is expected to surpass 410 million units in 2000 (Table 1.2). Software for a variety of purposes, journals, news, stocks, airline tickets and insurance policies are among the most examples of such goods which continue to drive Internet traffic. The utility and advantage of online delivery of information includes easier access to limited circulation items, acquisition of supplementary information such as maps, video and audio clips and above all more complete and recent information.

Recent surveys show that the acquisition of personal information remains, as in previous surveys, among the most important primary uses of the Internet. Other critical categories such as education, shopping, entertainment, and work in part at least make use of intangible goods (Figure 1.9). As technology advances and content sites become easier to use, the popularity of intangible goods will develop further.

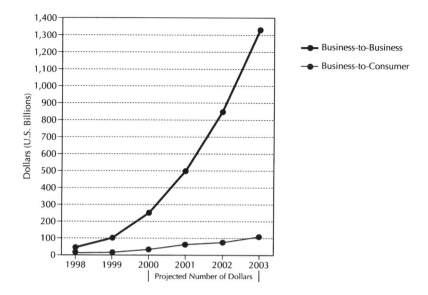

Figure 1.8   *US E-Commerce, 1998–2003. Source: US Department of Commerce 1999; Forrester Research [http://www.nua.ie/surveys/graphs_charts/comparisons/ecommerce_us.html]. See also Figure 6.1*

Table 1.2   *Worldwide mobile telephone terminal sales estimates, 1999 (millions)*

Company	1999 Unit sales	1998 Unit sales	Percentage growth
Nokia	76 335	38 622	97.6
Motorola	47 817	33 379	43.3
Ericsson	29 785	25 906	14.8
Samsung	17 686	4687	277.4
Panasonic	15 580	14 463	7.7
Others	96 376	54 536	76.7
Total market	283 581	171 594	65.3

Source: Dataquest, February, 2000.

While the usage patterns and economics of hard copy versus electronic versions of newspapers and journals continues to be debated, it is clear that ease of access and delivery are critical determinants of which form will prevail. The trend seems to be that content sites are eschewing a fee for use access in favor of building an audience and attracting advertising and direct marketing revenues. These revenues will continue to grow and perhaps grow dramatically. The current trends in classified and local advertising reveal a shift that is toward niche publications, direct mail and especially online services. All projections seem to indicate that significant growth will occur in revenues for online content businesses, which include those from transactions, advertising and fees (Figure 1.10).

Another major topic of current interest, especially for individual businesses seeking to expand their presence through the Internet, is the way in which the access to the Internet will evolve.

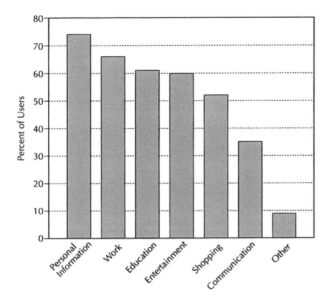

Figure 1.9 *Primary uses of the web, 1998. Source: Datamonitor 1998; GVU User Surveys [http://www.nua.te/surveys/graphs_charts/1998graphs/primaryuses.html]*

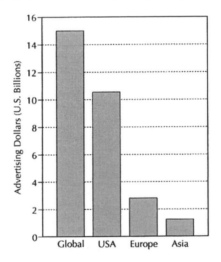

Figure 1.10 *Online advertising revenue in 2003 by region. Source: Datamonitor 1998; Forrester Research [http://www.nua.ie/surveys/graphs_charts/comparisons/advertising_by_ region_2003.html]*

The most conspicuous pattern currently is the 'funnel' model whereby a limited number of sites guide a viewer through the vast content. In this model, businesses seeking a larger audience may increasingly be required to pay large fees to secure 'shelf space' on these sites. The contrasting model is one where such funneling sites disappear because advertising and marketing costs become prohibitively expensive. Easier personal navigation, which is clearly a trend, would produce the latter scenario (US Department of Commerce 1998).

In the quest for information it is in the area of travel where individuals have most benefited from the power of the Internet (Figure 1.11). For example, all airlines now have Internet sites, which allow consumers to search out and construct itineraries, choose from fare options and obtain paperless e-tickets (see e.g. United Airlines at www.ual.com). Increasingly, there are incentives, such as additional frequent flier miles, to book tickets via the Internet. Another common strategy for airlines is to advertise via e-mail subscription specially priced E-fares for those travelers who either travel regularly and/or can schedule travel without long lead times. Passengers benefit from bargain fares where yield management reveals city pairs where excess capacity is evident or the attempt to bolster revenues by encouraging travel in particular corridors, as well as in off-peak periods. The individual web sites also allow fliers to monitor their frequent flier mileage accounts and request mileage award tickets using this accumulated mileage. Online surveys are frequently being used as a way for carriers to monitor the satisfaction and changing needs and complaints of passengers. In addition to air travel, it is also increasingly common to schedule rail travel and purchase tickets via the Internet. One of the most impressive sites is Rail Europe (www.raileurope.com) which allows individuals to obtain schedules, rail tickets (e.g. Eurailpass), auto rentals and lodging for both internal and transborder rail travel. In addition there are now at least a half dozen major sites which function as virtual travel agents (e.g. Expedia, Travelocity, etc.) and allow consumers to search for inexpensive airfares, book lodging and auto rentals. In addition it is common to be able to track fares for a particular itinerary with e-mail notification of these.

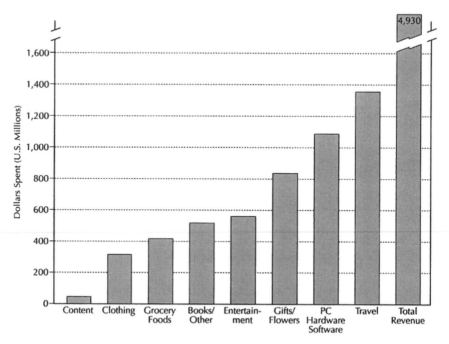

Figure 1.11   *US consumer spending online, 1998. Source: Datamonitor 1998; Yankee Group [http://www.nua.ie/surveys/graphs_charts/1998graphs/consumer_spending_us.html]*

Perhaps the most important development is the surge in access to and availability of information on particular places in global context. Online travel agencies, web driven travel guides, and a variety of other publications aimed at 'off the beaten path', ecologically sensitive and budget travelers have all developed within the last few years. It is now common to be able to purchase and download from commercial web sites to personal digital assistants, city (e.g. In Sync) and country travel guides complete with maps. Such guides exist for cities such as London, Paris, Tokyo, New York and other major tourist destinations. Place 'boosterism' via the Web has also become conspicuous as urban and regional agencies seek to disseminate information on tourism and industry in their respective locales (Brunn and Cottle 1997).

In addition to travel, there is great potential for Internet banking which seems to still be in its infancy. While many banks have their own web sites only a couple of dozen are classified as true Internet banks that permit consumers to review balances, transfer funds and pay their bills electronically. Online retail banking is being driven by lower operating costs, the ability to offer new services, and the ability to do one-on-one marketing (US Department of Commerce 1998). It is conservatively estimated that the cost of an Internet banking transaction is one hundredth of the cost of a teller physically carrying out the transaction. This costing, of course, does not consider the additional energy and other costs associated with physical travel to a bank. It is already apparent that despite the dramatic growth of ATM machines over the last decade (Figure 1.12) and the ability to make payments by phone, or personal visits, electronic payment of bills is the payment mode of the future. It is quite likely that web-based bill payment will become dominant. Vendors will send electronic images and customers will electronically authorize the bank to pay the bill, the bank in turn will debit an account and the vendor will receive payment electronically. Printing and mailing costs are eliminated and the processing cost is greatly reduced. Approximately 4.5 million households were

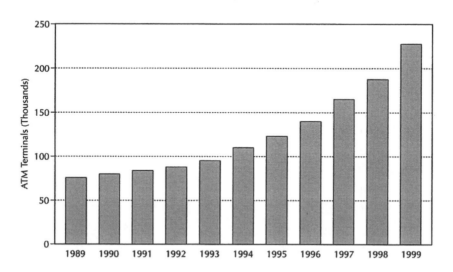

Figure 1.12   *Number of ATM terminals. Source: Bank Network News, EFT network data book 2000 edition, vol 18, no. 6, 1 August 1999*

banking online in 1997. By the end of 2000, as many as 16 million households will be carrying out banking transactions via this mode (Weiner 1999).

Retail Sale of Tangible Goods

The sale of physical goods via the Internet has become incredibly important for all retailers (see Figure 1.11). The contrast between US consumer spending online and that of Europe is readily apparent where Germany and the UK stand out (Figure 1.13). In the US initially it was the catalog sellers and telephone orders which began the surge toward online shopping, but many other large and small establishments doing business on the Web have followed this. By 1997 more than 10 million Internet users (roughly 16 percent of all Internet users in North America) had purchased goods via the Web. Apparel, books, music, toys, food, and flowers are among the most popular goods sold. Most virtual stores have aggressive and clever marketing strategies to accompany the offering of a wide range of goods often at discounted prices. Among these are the suggestion lists provided to consumers for future purchases based on initial interests or previous purchases, the notion of a virtual 'shopping cart' or 'suitcase' which allows the Internet shopper to accumulate a variety of pieces of different merchandise before purchase, and the ability to compile annotated 'wish lists' for goods desired on particular occasions. Amazon.com is perhaps one of the most distinctive firms in its use of these devices to attract shoppers.

An important related development associated with the growth of purchases via the Internet is the sharp expansion of distribution services and the improved efficiency of logistics. As a result of the growth of catalog shopping in the 1980s these services began to grow in order to handle telephone and mail traffic orders. The real key has been the growing popularity of 'time definite services' (overnight and second day) as the world's

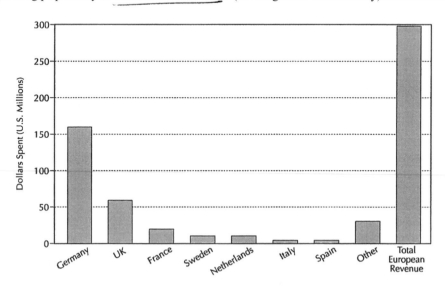

Figure 1.13 *Consumer spending online at European sites by country, 1998. Source: Data-monitor 1998 [http://www.nua.ie/surveys/graphs_charts/1998graphs/consumer_spending_europe.html]*

leading integrators (firms that integrate both air transport and ground delivery functions) have invested in aircraft, vehicles and distribution facilities. The two most important air cargo hubs in the US currently are Memphis and Louisville, which are the home bases of Federal Express and United Parcel Services respectively. The purchase and development of Subic Bay, the former US naval base, by Federal Express for its Asian air cargo hub is well known and a harbinger of developments being considered by other integrators.

A related topic is the growing popularity of electronic auctions (see e.g. Westland and Clark 1999, 343–5). Many occasions arise in both commercial and personal situations in which the buyer or seller of a commodity or service does not know its value. Antiques or used goods, especially, fit this description. Under these circumstances it is a distinct advantage to buy or sell at an auction rather than posting a fixed price. Reserve prices may be established below which the seller is unwilling to sell the article. A positive feature is that the seller is able to take advantage of a substantially larger market. Similarly the seller is able to find both routine and specialized or rare items. The growth of the Internet auction market has been dramatic. Forrester Research in Cambridge, Massachusetts, and Prudential Securities in New York estimate that the consumer to consumer and small business to consumer online auction market will reach $4.8 billion in gross merchandise sales in 2000 and $41.6 billion by 2003. The largest portion of this auction market is accounted for by the enterprise, eBay. The idea for eBay, based in San Jose, California, came from a French national, Pierre Omidyar, living in the mid-1990s in the Silicon Valley. The 'world's largest flea market' has spawned thousands of imitators and has literally changed the way people think about shopping online. eBay was launched on Labor Day, 1995 and in 1998 had revenues of $47.4 million representing a 724 percent change over the previous year. The eBay.com community includes 7.7. million registered users who buy and sell items in more than 2900 categories. Each day eBay.com is host to more than 2.5 million auctions with more than 350 000 items going on sale every 24 hours. Since its initial launch the site has listed more than 126 million auctions. A relatively recent development has been the creation of a new division called eBay Great Collectibles. This up-market move followed the eBay purchase in 1999 of a 134-year-old auction house, Butterfield and Butterfield. The new site focuses solely on trading in antiques and works of art.

The discussions throughout this volume will highlight the ways in which the Internet collapses the traditional divisions of social class and geography. In this vein just as interesting as the commercial success story of eBay is the impact that the electronic online auction, and more generally the Internet, has had on people and places. The auction has served to create or expand livelihoods by providing distributing products to a broad audience otherwise inaccessible to isolated and perhaps minimally funded enterprises. The story of an entrepreneur in Baker, Montana, 225 miles from the largest city of Billings, is one of perhaps thousands of illustrations, which reveal the impact of the Internet and particularly eBay. With the decline of the oil and cattle economy, a family-owned motel business evaporated and as a result the proprietor turned to a former hobby in crafts for income. From the growth in contacts and sales, the hobby became a livelihood.

One of the more interesting international applications of the electronic auction is that of the Dutch flower industry. The Netherlands is the leading producer of cut flowers and dominated the world market in the late 1990s with approximately a 60 percent share. Since the end of the 19th century flowers have been marketed by cooperatives through an auction mechanism. Two major auctions at Aalsmeer and Naaldwijk/Bleiswijk dominate the industry and every day on average 30 million flowers from the Netherlands as well as Israel, Kenya, and Zimbabwe are traded in over 100 000 transactions. The current debates in the industry center around the decoupling of price discovery and logistical processes in the Dutch flower auction,[1] the increasing imports of foreign flower products and the use of new information technology in the industry. Flower Auction Aalsmeer and Flower Auction Holland each had an annual turnover in 1996 of $1 billion. The application of IT to the flower industry is complex for it involves a complex set of markets (diverse situational circumstances involving buyers and sellers) which comprise the whole industry. An initial problem is to specify a general model of exchange and a process–stakeholder framework to evaluate market designs. At least three experiments with electronic auctions are currently being carried out with sample-based flowers using (1) EDI, (2) a teleflower auction, and (3) a 'buying at a distance' auction. A major consideration currently is how to deal with the weakness of the Dutch auction concept, which is supply oriented, and to develop an electronic system which recognizes the increasing demand orientation of these markets through brokerage trading (van Heck and Ribbers in Westland and Clark 1999, 360–4).

Guyanan Weavers Go Dot.Com

Finally there is the experience of the village of Lethem, Guyana, a community of 2000 people, which had no telephone service until two years ago, and the concept of paying with money is still awkward for many of its residents. Recently an organization was formed by indigenous women of two tribes which have revived the ancient art of hand weaving large hammocks from locally grown cotton. As the weavers tried to sell their hammocks to museums and other collectors by unreliable postal services, Guyana Telephone and Telegraph installed telephone lines using an innovative satellite system. A few months later the company through its chief executive offered the weavers' society two telephone lines, free Internet access and $12 000 worth of equipment, including a desktop computer and scanner.

The group hired a young member to create a web site to take their wares online and last year they sold 17 hammocks to people around the world for as much as $1000 per piece.

Unfortunately the weavers were too successful bringing attention and income to a place where powerlessness and poverty are common. Threatened by the women's success regional leaders intervened and took control of the weavers' organization. The woman who created the web site has left and the group has been struggling since that time. This represents the 'classic tale of old power reacting to new power' and suggests even though the Internet may empower people, that does not bring the status quo so the status quo quite rationally reacts to defend its interests (Romero 2000).

FUTURE PATHS: TRENDS AND CHALLENGES

The emergence of the digital economy and especially the further development of e-commerce have already challenged the traditional ways in which the production and consumption process has been viewed. Major changes must and will occur in a variety of realms if the brief success we are witnessing is to continue. A major aspect of these changes focus on labor. The rapid growth of IT industries has already created a large demand for a technically trained workforce. Witness the employment calls for programmers, computer scientists, and engineers with varying specialties. As e-commerce becomes more widespread it too will drive changes in the labor force, essentially employment will shift from traditional occupations to those requiring IT skills. In addition a growing trend, which is increasingly conspicuous, is the need for and accommodation to a more flexible workforce. Basically firms will need to produce products and services with less rigid organizational structures. Work organizations are replacing well-delineated, task-rigid job descriptions with flexible cells and team approaches that are intended to improve quality by reducing return rates, lowering cycle times, and reducing costs. Moreover, it is increasingly common for research and development teams to produce new ideas and products via a communications network that links team members from Singapore and France with those in California and Kentucky. IT is critical in both driving the need for a new workforce and enabling the greater flexibility. Teleworkers, now only a small fraction of the total workforce, will more than double over the next decade (Figure 1.14). The users of cellular phones and personal digital assistants capable of receiving and sending faxes, e-mail and accessing the Internet has jumped from 77 million in 1998 to well over 300 million in 2000. The training demands on the firm will increase and educational institutions will continue to restructure their offerings to respond to these new demands.

As the creative process is enhanced by IT, more individual entrepreneurs will emerge with ideas to be implemented. The emergence and viability of especially smaller firms has great potential to enhance development in nonhigh-tech cities and regions around the globe, whether well connected or remote. In addition to the requirements of specific human capital skills is the need for financial capital. Both the fluidity of external venture capital and the stimulation of local capital are matters of great importance in this changing scene (Westland and Clark 1999; Schiller 1999).

As has been noted previously, the digital revolution is changing the roles of both government and the private sector. The major cost burden of developing communications infrastructure, in contrast to the historical development of transport and other infrastructures, has shifted from the federal (and local) governments to the private

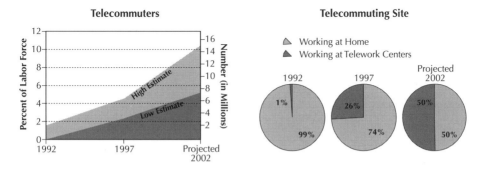

Figure 1.14 *Projected future of US telecommuting. Source: US Dept of Transportation, Bureau of Transport Statistics 1999*

sector. In many ways the pace of technological development and the borderless environment will set a new framework for governments and private sector. Emphasis will be on creating an environment of optimal conditions which will not constrain growth, but foster it. Governments will be forced to allow e-commerce to rely on markets unburdened by extensive regulation, taxation, and censorship. An important role for government will be to address, with the cooperation of industry, issues of privacy, security, and human resource policies (Drummond 1996; Garcia 1997).

END NOTE

1. The Dutch flower auction concept uses a clock for price discovery, whereby a computerized auction clock provides information on producer, product, quality, and minimum purchase. The flowers are transported through the auction room and shown to buyers. The price is set high and drops to some point at which the buyer will stop the clock and relay how much he/she wishes to purchase.

2

Towards an Economics of the Internet and E-Commerce

KENNETH BUTTON

George Mason University, Fairfax, VA, USA

and

SAMANTHA TAYLOR

PPK Environment and Infrastructure, Melbourne, Australia

INTRODUCTION

This chapter is concerned with some features of the Internet and e-commerce, broadly defined, that raise particular economic questions. Strictly there is no such thing as 'The economics of the Internet and e-commerce' but it is useful shorthand. What there is, is a set of features associated with the Internet and e-commerce that differentiate them from many other activities and, therefore, require a particular portfolio of economic techniques and theories to understand the nature of their supply and appreciate why they are demanded. They also have characteristics that make it interesting to see how they influence the markets for other goods and services such as transportation and land.

A primary focus is on the importance of economics in understanding the way in which the spatial use of the Internet and the growth of e-commerce can affect the location of economic activities, either directly or through changes in travel behavior. It looks at the theoretical issues and the implications of public policy interventions in markets. In particular, conventional economic analysis assumes that markets offer optimal solutions, but many of the underlying assumptions of simplistic Marshallian neoclassical economics are not relevant to the Internet.

In practice, for example, the realities of the e-commerce sector could potentially lead to under-supply in certain parts of the market. This is particularly so when, to adopt economic jargon, the core is empty. What this means is that incentives in the market are such that in the long term insufficient companies will enter, or those in it under-supply, despite the fact that from an overall economic perspective this is economically

i.e. public good problem

inefficient. There are many good reasons to suppose that the particular structural features of network industries, such as shipping and air transport, make them potentially prone to severe core problems and that many of these conditions are common to the supply of e-commerce services. From a geographical perspective, an empty core in one network would seem to imply distortions in linked, competitive and complementary networks, and with this a suboptimal spatial distribution of land use may result. Issues then arise as to how public policy should be developed to deal with this issue and how to define the appropriate conditions that ensure workable competition evolves.

The overall topic of the economics of the Internet and e-commerce is a large one and here attention is largely on only two elements. The first is concerned with the implications of the Internet for sales activities and what this in turn may mean for supply, distribution, and deliveries. The second is on the links between teleworking and travel demand. The notion that teleworking can help alleviate some of the congestion found in many cities is an attractive one, especially for policymakers unwilling to tackle the problem at its source. It does, however, raise a number of economic issues. Tied to this, although not fully explored here, are the changes in the labor market that a wider adoption of teleworking could induce.

THE CURRENT SITUATION REGARDING ELECTRONIC COMMUNICATIONS

Advanced communications technologies are growing and evolving at a very rapid rate. Penetration rates of mobile phones are expanding globally while household Internet access in the US is at 30 percent of all homes. Globally the number of people with access to the Internet is growing and, if the stock market is a reflection of future expectations, is seen as the world's most dynamic sector. While still in its infancy, some 17 percent of US homes have used the Internet for purchasing goods and services in 1999 (although over half spent more than $500), and online and business-to-consumer (B2C) transactions were worth about $20 billion. This compares with 10 percent in the UK, 9 percent in Canada, and 2 percent in Italy. Some 2 percent of the US travel transactions were carried out over the Internet. In terms of physical movements a study by Forrester Research shows that 20 percent of package traffic in the US is by electronic retailers (cited in Gardiner 2000).

Although Internet commerce is still relatively limited, it is growing rapidly and Internet commerce is expected to have a significant impact on the supply chain. A recent forecast by one US organization suggests growth in consumer purchases over the Internet of 2500 percent, between 1997 and 2001, albeit from a very low base (Konezny and Beskow 1999). The most popular purchases over the Internet are items such as books, CDs, electrical components, and those goods perceived as having a known quality. The phenomenon is also certainly not purely American. As early as 1994 1.2 million French were buying over the Web compared with 0.8 billion in the US at the same time. Now retails over the Web in Europe amount to about $3.6 billion (Peet 1999).

The largest growth though is in business-to-business (B2B) transactions which now amount to about \$114 billion annually in the US or about 80 percent of total Internet transactions (Cohn and Brady 2000). For example, Ford, DaimlerChrysler, and General Motors are transferring all their purchases to the Web over the next few years via a single e-hub exchange for auto parts and General Electric has been rapidly moving in that direction. Internationally, Sear, Roebuck and Carrefour have moved to an Internet retail exchange to handle the \$80 billion they spend annually with suppliers. Some explanations for these developments are the fact that B2B transactions are purely commercial in their orientation, there is no utility involved in the act of shopping per se, and because of their frequency of purchase, they generally involve a known quality. They effectively cut transactions and search costs. In contrast, consumers often enjoy the act of shopping and require nonquantitative information about products. That is largely why, although as many as 40 percent of car buyers consulted the Internet at some point, only 2.7 percent of new car sales in the US in 1999 took place online.

Simultaneously, as Internet use has risen traffic volumes are also constantly growing; congestion and environmental issues are causing major political and social concerns in the US and Europe (UK Royal Commission on Environmental Pollution 1994). Road traffic levels have grown in all countries. With the widespread growth of urban sprawl, however, public transit is seldom a viable alternative for the car and with limited scope for additional road building in most cities, alternative transportation solutions are being sought. Further, while much of the local pollution associated with the automobile has been considerably reduced through the adoption of new technologies, it has not been eliminated and the problem of greenhouse gas emissions remains.

In response to these concerns, some public authorities in Britain have launched travel awareness initiatives, predominantly aimed at increasing individuals' and firms' 'susceptibility to change'. Alternatives may take the form of teleworking, transit, nonmotorized transport or car-pooling. The European Union (EU) has wider initiatives aimed at fostering a system of what it considers 'sustainable transport' (Commission of the European Communities 1992). This seeks to establish policy packages of 'sticks and carrots' that would stimulate the use of alternatives to the automobile. A large part of the focus is the correction of transportation prices and taxes to reflect externality costs.

In the US there is a greater overt and popular interest in the ability for advanced technology to contribute to alleviating traffic congestion. This includes intelligent transportation systems but also the use of technological alternatives to travel. Inherently, the American culture is proudly car dependent and the US urban form is also different from most European cities. There are fewer desirable alternatives available so a slightly different emphasis to that in Europe is required. This is not to say that the results from Europe and the UK are not relevant, but rather, they are not always entirely transportable across the Atlantic.

Some Features of the Market for E-Commerce

Increased per capita income, changes in the composition of the workforce, intelligent electronic technologies, and the footloose nature of employment, to name a few, have had a major effect on increasing the demand for flexibility in lifestyles and in employment. It is often claimed that the late 20th century marked the beginning of the Information Age; an age in which knowledge management is a real issue and many organizations' biggest assets are their employees (Hewson 1999). Partly, this is reflected in the growth of industries in the service sector such as marketing and information technology (IT) that are strongly people dependent, and are essentially concerned with communicating and persuading. These ethereal concepts of human capital and tacit knowledge are purported, in a generic sense, to be driving factors in an organization's success, and essentially they depend on interaction or communication.

It is in this context that communication can be usefully discussed along with its subsystems, telecommunications and transportation. Many enthusiasts, particularly in the US context, have had high hopes for the favorable impact of communication technology, and specifically the opportunity to telecommute, on traffic congestion (Salomon and Mokhtarian 1997). These have included popular predictions about the potential for large-scale vehicle commuting to be replaced by virtual offices in the home, at 'village' sites or on-board vehicles connected by dial-up communication. Linked to this, the growth of e-commerce and the reduced need to physically visit retail outlets is seen as a mechanism for reducing nonwork travel, and of simplifying what are currently complex journey-to-work patterns.

These expectations, however, often neglect some of the innate features of the Internet. The market for the Internet has complexities on both the supply and demand sides. On the demand side there is the oft-cited argument that since the Internet is essentially a network activity, it can be associated with network externalities and very strong increasing returns. In the past, Metcalfe's law, whereby the utility of a network is proportional to the square of the number of people it connects, has been used to support this type of argument. This has dynamic implications. In general, it is hardly worth joining a small network, but once a certain threshold size has been reached the benefits are explosive. Simple arithmetic supports this. If two cities, each of 100 people, are joined electronically, this provides 10 000 possible two-way communications. Adding a third city increases this by 990 000 and a fourth city by a further 99 000 000.

The extent of network externalities, however, is likely to be seriously tempered once one introduces variations in the size of markets and their nature. Cities vary considerably in their population sizes and the compositions of both their populations and industrial bases. Assuming commercial rationality on the part of network suppliers, the law of diminishing returns implies that the most valuable connections will be made first with centers of lesser value being added subsequently. This pattern was historically appreciated when postal services were regulated or state provided to ensure ubiquitous supply and why there has been a tendency to encourage cross-subsidization. Without these measures, many links deemed politically or socially necessary, would not have been provided.

Looking at the current US situation, in many sectors there is mounting evidence of market concentration, for example 75 percent of B2C e-commerce is done through five sites (Amazon, eBay, AOL, Yahoo! and Buy.com). The reason is that the market is far from perfect on the supply-side. Indeed perfection may not be desirable if the market is to remain viable. Varian (1999) points to the decreasing cost nature of providing information goods. Information goods have high fixed costs, but then extremely low marginal costs. This poses problems of what is often termed an empty core.

A noncore situation can be illustrated by taking the situation of two identical carriers supplying service on a link, with standard U-shaped average cost curves. There is, thus, an assumption of fixed costs. Marginal cost is a discontinuous function of total carrier output and is equal to the minimum average cost of the carriers at two points in Figure 2.1, namely Q_1 and Q_2. The demand for service is represented by D. In this situation if one carrier provides a service then excess profits will be earned. Expansion to two carriers, as the second carrier is attracted to the market, will result in both making a loss, since competition will lead them to operate at a price equal to marginal cost. Only if by chance the demand curve intersects the average cost curve at a point coincidental with the marginal cost curve will a stable outcome emerge. Increasing the number of firms does not affect the outcome until the number becomes very large, at which point the Pareto-optimal number of undertakings is reached.

This type of situation is not uncommon in network industries (Button and Nijkamp 1998). Regulation of the market and/or direct supply through a monopoly state supplier is one possibility. This was the de facto approach in the past of many countries in terms of postal networks, telephone systems, railroads, and air services. The alternative, less likely to stifle longer-term technological developments, is to allow concentration of supply. This situation is already happening and is largely a function of how network services are provided. There is not a homogeneous product, but rather there is market segmentation. In air transport and shipping this has taken the form of yield management, in the Internet it is rather through 'versioning'. Shapiro and Varian (1998) offer a range of types of versioning that include such practices as 'features and function variations' (the high version has more features and functions); 'image resolution' (low-resolution images sell for a low price, high-resolution images sell for a high price) and 'user interface' (the professional version has an elaborate user interface; the popular version has a simple interface).

Versioning is important because it involves price discrimination and, thereby, a mechanism for potentially recovering outlays when there are decreasing costs. Price

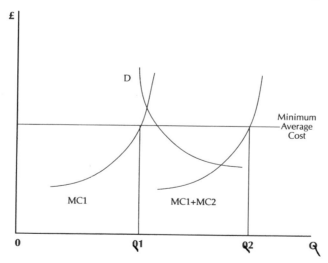

Figure 2.1 *Decreasing costs and the empty core problem. Source: Button*

discrimination, however, is only possible if a supplier has a degree of monopoly power in the market. Again drawing on the airline parallel, this has been attained through loyalty schemes such as frequent flyer benefits and through mergers of carriers. Loyalty schemes are somewhat different in Internet markets where transactions are potentially more frequent than flights. As with frequent flyer schemes they should also be nonlinear, involving plateaus above which the bonuses are greater. The discrimination can also be through 'shopbots' whereby the e-commerce company separates out those users who search out lowest cost generic products systematically and those who do not. By holding periodic sales, the careful searcher can get the lowest price, but at the expense of both search costs and foregone loyalty payments. Such segmentation also allows consumer surplus to be translated into producer revenues for the Internet provider.

Market concentration through mergers is only likely if there is adequate incentive for suppliers to combine. Take the simple case discussed in Varian (1999). If it is assumed that the benefit of a network is proportional to the number of users on that network (n) and for simplicity the constant of proportionality is taken as unity, then following Metcalfe's law the value of the network is n^2. A simple calculation shows that combining two networks of size n_1 and n_2 yields:

$$\Delta v_1 = n_1(n_1 + n_2) - n_1^2 = n_1 n_2$$
$$\Delta v_2 = n_2(n_1 + n_2) - n_2^2 = n_1 n_2$$

Each network has equal value (v) from the interconnection. Those on the small network (2) each has considerable value from linking with the large number on the other network. The large number of people on the other network (1) each has smaller additional utility, but there are a lot of them. This offers scope for reciprocation with the networks having settlement free access to the other network. The problem is that the large supplier may need to keep its market power to allow adequate price discrimination to recover costs and make an acceptable long-term return. In this case the larger concern may merge with the smaller and attain twice the value of interconnecting:

$$\Delta v_1 = n_1(n_1 + n_2)2 - n_1^2 - n_2^2 = 2n_1 n_2$$

This market pressure for concentration in providing Internet services ripples through the economy. It has potential implications for those supplying inputs into the process (e.g. transportation as discussed below) and for users of the services (e.g. in terms of the costs they bear and the services that they can receive that can in turn have implications for, among other things, the growth of teleworking).

THE IMPACT OF TECHNOLOGY ON PHYSICAL DISTRIBUTION

The development of telecommunications has already impacted significantly on the freight transportation sector. It is now an integral part of modern supply chain management, of which transport is a central component, and is especially relevant for just-in-time activities. As each producer and manufacturer strives to gain market power, the elasticity of the supply chain is critical in ensuring quality (e.g. the cold chain requires goods to be maintained at or below a certain temperature and delays can affect quality and the production life cycle), convenience, and time compression. Customers are increasingly able to shop around at a minimal cost for a product and service that satisfies their individual needs. From a producer perspective, this equates to the threat of competition and the opportunity for greater market share.

The growth in the e-commerce market in its various forms is already having implications for the demand for transportation and on land use. While it is possible to deliver some goods online (e.g. airline tickets and music), most goods ultimately have to be produced, shipped, and consumed. The rise in B2B interactions is stimulating greater sophistication in supply chain management and furthering the development of just-in-time production. The development of such features as auto-exchange web sites, such as Ford's ConsumerConnect (Kerwin and Stepanek 2000) are aimed at reducing inventory holdings, lowering transactions costs, permitting tailored vehicles, and fostering faster delivery. The savings in doing business can be considerable, with estimated savings up to 39 percent for electronic components, 20 percent for computing, 25 percent for forestry products and 22 percent for machining. These savings have inevitable implications for delivery patterns involving smaller consignments and more frequent deliveries. Added to this, e-commerce also helps improve the efficiency of the freight transportation industry by as much as 15–20 percent according to recent Goldman Sachs data (cited in Cohn and Brady 2000). This saving will itself keep the commercial costs of transportation down, although the social and environmental implications may be somewhat different.

The B2C e-commerce market is likely to become even more oligopolized for the reasons set out above. Delivery patterns will then depend very much on how the major suppliers develop their logistics. At present much of the traffic is handled by UPS (which had 55 percent of the 1998 Christmas e-commerce delivery market), the US Post Office (32 percent), and FedEx (10 percent). Some short-term changes in market share are inevitable as FedEx restructures its operations to meet the emerging market conditions, but there are longer-term, structural issues.

It is within this context that there have been noticeable changes in the way freight transportation services are supplied and used. Although different regions may have different propensities toward readily adopting new communication technologies, the capability of the Internet as a medium for consumer shopping is real and its success will require changes to the logistics process. It is interesting to observe, for example, that the freight transportation sector, an industry that in the recent past has been notoriously slow in adopting new technology and cultures, has shifted its focus to developing so-called strategic alliances with shippers. In the case of maritime transportation, for example, the first alliance emerged in 1994 when APL, OOCL, MOL, and Nedlloyd formed the Grand Alliance and by the end of 1999 only MSC and Evergreen were the only major carriers outside of alliances. Relations involving alliances are more than ever concerned with interpersonal communications and trust. In some cases carriers have physically located personnel in shippers' offices to facilitate this process, linking individuals technologically and personally to communicate effectively with customers and clients in a timely manner (Taylor 1999).

Potentially, significant volumes of goods will be delivered directly from the manufacturer or major distributor to the customer, who could be located anywhere on the globe. While the trend in recent years has been to increase the productivity of long haul carriers through larger vehicles, [distribution resulting from Internet shopping is expected to increase the population of delivery vans. In the 1980s, coincident with a trend toward reducing inventories, and a greater focus on customer service, a trend toward smaller quantities of product and more frequent deliveries was observed] (Brugge 1991). In Japan, the average weight of goods carried on each trip dropped by 36 percent, from 3.8 tons in 1980 to 2.4 tons in 1990 (Harutoshi 1994). For a constant aggregate amount of production, more vehicle movements were, and are, required to transport these smaller quantities. This change often entails larger vehicles operating through transshipment and consolidation facilities with collections and deliveries by smaller trucks. The high growth in Internet commerce is leading to an increase in demand for delivery vehicles. Growth of 15.3 percent and 25 percent for small/medium and larger vans respectively, have been reported. Fedex also stated in 1999 that it saw delivery of business generated by Internet transactions as a key to its future growth. If a proliferation of commercial deliveries to residential areas does result, there will likely be concerns about the environmental and aesthetic impact of delivery trucks in residential areas.

To date the distribution of web-based purchases has often been problematic. In the US there were many disruptions to deliveries over the Christmas period in 1999 and the problem extended to many other countries. In Australia, for example, major online retailers such as d-store and ToySpot admitted their fulfillment systems were inadequate over that period (Gardiner 2000). Indeed, shipping costs are seen as one of the main deterrents to shopping for physical goods online. In particular, consumers often did not appreciate their own time costs of collection at stores, but now delivery charges make these transactions costs transparent. The legacy businesses that expanded from traditional retailing into Internet activities have generally found their warehouse and distribution centers ill suited to e-commerce. Companies such as Land's End and J. Crew with a tradition in mail order business have had less difficulty, but the transition has still been far from smooth. The new suppliers of e-commerce services have generally been inexperienced in logistics and have found problems in containing costs. Many e-commerce companies are now constructing large automated warehouses to handle the picking-and-packing of their sales to ensure an acceptable level of customer service. These developments take time and this has meant that distribution costs have often been higher than they need be.

Outsourcing has grown in importance with UPS playing a prominent role for long-distance distribution. This change implies the potential for considerable consolidation with limited additional vehicle movements if distribution remains oligopolized. The Internet has helped foster confidence in outsourcing solutions. Logistics management is evolving to what can metaphorically be referred to as the 'glass pipe', that is emphasizing the need for transparency to the client. Delays are visible which places greater emphasis on the connectivity of the supply chain, namely integrated transportation networks, seamless information exchange, good communication and coordination (Taylor 1999). Communications technology allows businesses to reduce the quantity of paper transactions, which in freight movement, especially regarding import/export activities, can be extremely high, and to provide customers with information on where their goods are in the chain. Having paid for the goods, customers are understandably anxious to keep track of the physical movement of their investments, that is where are the delays, where is the commodity in the chain, what is the estimated arrival time?

The extent to which B2C e-commerce will affect transportation and land use also crucially depends on the types of markets where it will achieve its greatest penetration. Market research into e-shopping has generally found that the physical shopping experience is attractive to some people, particularly women. For example, in apparel retail, displays are manipulated to attract female shoppers interested in finding something that looks and feels right. Studies distinguish the female shopper from the male, arguing that female shoppers browse, are interested in what is new, and touch garments. Men, on the other hand, go shopping to satisfy a need; they have a purpose and are often reluctant to try new trends. In addition, with the increasingly popular outlet malls and discount centers offering designer labels at discount prices, leisure shopping becomes a quasi-sport, namely hunting for bargains.

Online shopping clearly eliminates the experiential aspect of shopping, but what it can do is widen the possible choice set. Statistics of the type cited earlier regarding car purchasing show a great deal more online window shoppers than purchasers. Consumers frequently use the Internet to gather information about products, and depending on the perceived reliability of product quality and suitability, many are still purchasing offline. However, there is some evidence of consumers viewing goods at a mall and then buying online at lower prices. Again, this shopping pattern depends on the type of product and the attitudinal predisposition of the consumer.

Internet transactions involving more local deliveries, such as groceries, have grown slowly with the leader in comprehensive service, Peapod, only covering about 8 percent of the US population (Peet 1999). While some companies such as Streamline in Boston provide free refrigerators to allow them a flexible delivery schedule, a major problem is providing a guaranteed delivery time. In the short term, it seems unlikely that e-commerce will make a significant impact in this area and hence unlikely to reduce traffic at supermarkets.

THE IMPACT OF TELEWORKING ON TRAVEL DEMAND

When discussing telecommunications and transportation, there is increasingly a move to investigate teleworking (or telecommuting) and the like as alternatives to transportation. There are difficulties in estimating the current levels of telecommuting (US Department of Transportation 1992), but the widespread adoption of activities such as teleworking that the Internet and e-commerce allows could be envisaged in some circumstances as a method of reducing the need for interpersonal interactions at work and hence travel. This development is attractive politically since it circumvents the generally unpopular idea that traffic should be restrained by measures such as road pricing or traffic controls. In addition, the IT sector is promoting the introduction of its technologies and services as solutions to a range of business, societal and domestic problems. The idea is also raising expectations in the public at large, namely that information systems may be a panacea to their transportation problems.

Teleworking is defined here as any proportion of work done at home, which would normally be done at the workplace. This would include parts of days or weeks working at home. Two basic hypotheses have been proposed to describe the relationship between transportation and telecommunication. These are related to notions that information systems may be a substitution or a complement to travel (Salomon 1985).

Complementarity is commonly discussed in terms of enhancement and efficiency, although in practice complementarity is essentially a hybrid of the two (Salomon 1986). In the case of enhancement, communication stimulates the need for travel by precipitating the transfer of additional information, specifically information about available opportunities. A brief e-mail may spark one to identify relevant information (that may or may not involve transportation) on a completely different project. This type of cross-fertilization, synergy, or enhancement is more likely to occur now, purely as a result of the permeability, magnitude, and timeliness of information flows made possible by technology. An example commonly used to illustrate enhanced efficiency is in freight transportation, where communications technology makes the supply chain more 'transparent' and, therefore, assists efficiency of scheduling and customer service. In personal transportation, an individual may choose to telework in the morning, avoid the morning peak period, and drive to work later in the day attending business meetings en route. It is argued that the person's efficiency is improved.

Until recently, substitution has been the more popular of the hypotheses, i.e., where a physical trip is replaced by communication technology. Overall though, attempts to identify a wide spectrum of substitution effects have generally been inconclusive (Salomon 2000). A complicating factor of the substitution hypothesis is an assumption that the total volume of interactions, whether by travel or communication (e.g. interactions between people or between workplace and employee) is constant (Plaut 1997). This assumption may not the case. The Institute pour Frantide shows a gradual increase in passenger transport miles and the number of remote communications in France between the early 18th century and the late 20th century. In practice, the policies adopted regarding the way the transportation system is used and the way teleworking is treated by companies and government, for example regarding tax incentives, will be influential on the level of teleworking adopted (US Department of Transportation).

Supporting this hypothesis, Nijkamp and Salomon (1989) argue that over time the total of all forms of communication has increased. Incomes have risen, car ownership has risen and socioeconomic life of Western economies has evolved to encourage greater levels of interpersonal contact. High growth in the service sector and information industries, for example, has resulted in a greater inherent emphasis on face-to-face communication and the development of interpersonal relationships during work hours. Increasingly, business and pleasure are merging, and networking is a valued skill in contemporary working life. Rycroft and Kash (1999) maintain that the complexity of social, economic and technological forces are such that a firm's success frequently depends heavily on continuously adaptive organizational interactions or networks. This can be particularly so in the case of political and social complexity where a meeting face to face may be more desirable than a telephone or e-mail interaction. Individuals may be more comfortable discussing the complexities and or sensitivities of a project or process in person.

Improved and novel transportation technologies, together with additional transportation infrastructure and hardware, have allowed personal interactions to grow considerably over time. These developments have permitted both more frequent interactions between the same individuals (a deepening effect) and for a larger number of interactions between different individuals (a widening effect).

In practice, however, at any point in time there are physical and logistical constraints on the capacity of individuals to meet face to face, the constrained interaction curve is shown graphically in Figure 2.2. Public concerns about the environmental implications of further infrastructure expansion and the high financial costs of such investments, combined with changes in life styles, suggest that this interaction curve is now beginning to flatten. Questions can also be raised concerning the marginal social utility of additional transportation infrastructure provision, especially if it simply leads to additional travel (Nijkamp and Baaijens 1999).

Through telecommunications technology a greater number of interactions are possible because of the empowerment provided through timely (in some cases 'real-time') information transfer (the unconstrained interaction curve in Figure 2.2). This development means that telecommunications has the scope not only to fill the potential interactions but also to push up the unconstrained curve. What types of interactions are most efficiently replaced by telecommunications in this process is by no means certain.

The speed with which interactions can be initiated and completed has increased with advances in information technologies. This acceleration may well affect the types of situations where electronic information systems can fill the 'telecommunications gap' (Figure 2.3). For example, reduced response time is observed when using facsimile as a medium, rather than courier. This means that an individual can either achieve better quality interactions and/or a greater number of interactions in the same period of time. The advent of e-mail speeds up this type of interaction further.

Another factor is the complexity of information that has to be transferred. In

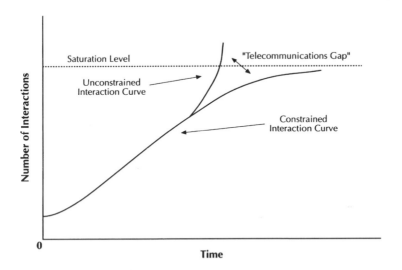

Figure 2.2 *Liberalization of the constrained interaction curve by telecommunications. Source: Button 1991*

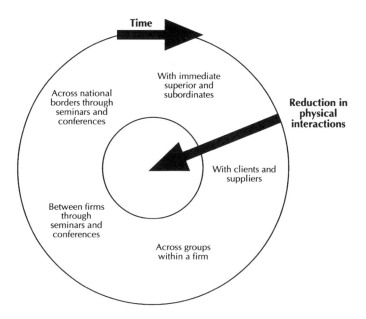

Figure 2.3   *Work-induced interactions. Source: Button 1991*

general, the more complex the information, the more important the need for face-to-face contact. There is also the uncertain issue about the additional amount of interactions that are generated by the very existence of new forms of interaction. What is evident at the current time is that people are engaged in a wider range of interactions than before and that the net effect is a greater number of interactions in total.

It is useful in looking at the link between telecommunications and transportation to review the sociological context within which personal transport exists. Much of the early modeling of travel was essentially engineering driven. While more recent work has been more closely allied to behavioral types of models, often based in micro-economic theory, they are still in many ways very simplistic. In particular it is assumed that people travel to work just to earn an income. Other motivations for making these types of trip are now seen as important and can impact on travel patterns (Fukuyama 1996).

The success of modern workplaces largely relies on its people, information and knowledge, all of which are dependent on interactions and relationships. Maslow (1954) proposed a triangle of needs which ranks the motivation of human needs from the essentials of sustenance and security, through belongingness, recognition and finally, to self-actualization. This theory fits Fukuyama's argument; that many human needs are, ceteris paribus, met by the workplace, that is, belonging, security, recognition, and, for some people, self-actualization. It is also worth bearing in mind the historically significant impact that car ownership had on improving a person's social status; in fact status was a major contributor to their popularity (Boltanski 1975). Materialism is manifest in visual evidence of status and identity thus satisfying, in a sense, the need for recognition. The workplace, and the commute to work in some respects, provides the opportunity for recognition and also satisfies the social need for interaction and security.

The journey-to-work, and associated traffic congestion, has been at the center of debates on urban transportation policy. Because road space is not provided in a market setting, and users are not fully aware of the full costs of their actions on others at the time trips are made, there tends to develop excessive levels of commuter congestion. Excessive congestion is seen as inefficient in a purely transportation sense and, because of the pollution generated, is an environmental issue. Considerable research and policy based analysis have been expended seeking a socially acceptable way of limiting the congestion problem. Recent analysis has suggests, however, that the issue may be more complex than is traditionally thought.

In much of the transportation and communications discussions, there has been an implicit assumption that individuals wish to reduce their travel time, and in particular that involved in the journey-to-work. This has stemmed, in part, from the notion that transport is largely a derived demand existing for the sake of other ends (e.g. to earn an income, shop, transport children or socialize), rather than being an end in itself. Recent research in California challenges this assumption drawing on the findings of a survey of over 1300 workers which found that only 3 percent of people desired a zero-to-two minute commute (Mokhtarian and Salomon 1999). It showed that almost 50 percent of respondents preferred a commute of 20 minutes or more. This type of finding would not be inconsistent with the notion of Zahavi's constant travel budget hypothesis. Such a time may be seen as a reasonable price to pay for a suburban lifestyle.

Policymakers and researchers focus on the negative impacts of the commute in terms of environmental impacts, congestion, stress and so on, while the positive attributes are not recognized. Mokhtarian and Salomon (1994) argue that individuals often value the transition between home and work and the ability to use the time productively. They may also value the opportunity to drive a status-oriented automobile or the chance to experience the environment by traveling. They may value a nonhome destination for work because of social/professional interaction opportunities, the scenic location, or the shopping and other locational amenities. There are also the opportunity benefits involved in not spending time in a commute such as doing household chores.

Dupuy (1999) models the positive effects of automobile travel in terms of its 'club effect'. What a person gains by joining the club are the network externalities, and from car ownership and driving there are parallels with Internet club membership. Obtaining a driver's license provides an identity card that is a sign of independence and adulthood. Acquiring a vehicle allows a driver to realize freedom and independence, travel at speed and increase accessibility, relative to those who do not have a car. Benefits increase as the number of cars in the fleet increase, for example, driving a popular car results in accessibility to spare parts, roadside service, and after-sales services, that are more difficult to acquire with a unique vehicle. Experience shows that the more people using the road network the better the quality of road and the denser the traffic network and the more accessible facilities are relative to those not using the network. The outcome is that while congestion may be a cost of being a member, the overall situation is one of benefit to the car commuter.

Given that increased teleworking could produce environmental benefits, Mokhtarian and Salomon (1994) sought to study what contributes to an individual's ability or choice to telecommute. Various pressures and constraints appear important for individuals to change their prevailing work routine. In the majority of cases, a threshold level of dissatisfaction with one or more aspects of life was necessary to cause an individual to consider an alternative to conventional work patterns. This dissatisfaction may be manifest in a desire to accomplish certain goals in work, family, leisure, or travel. Constraints could be manifest in the amount of telecommuting permitted by the nature of the job or by the employer, the availability of suitable remote technology, whether supervisors support telecommuting, and the propensity toward distractions at home. Individual are likely to be more productive if they are easily able to switch off from, and separate, home duties.

Interest has grown in the travel patterns of each gender, particularly the idiosyncrasies of travel by women (Root et al. 2000; Morris et al. 1996). More part-time work, increases in nonhome based travel, partly through a greater proportion of women in the workforce and flexible employment, have contributed to increased demand for off-peak travel (Richardson et al. 1996). Women are still largely responsible for the majority of household duties and care of children, and this leads to more complex travel patterns involving linked trips and greater car dependency. In this context, flexibility becomes a valid attribute. The flexibility, and complementarity, provided by teleworking is likely to be valued by women, particularly those with dependents.

Employers may find benefits in stimulating or facilitating teleworking. The current strong economy favors employees. Employers, particularly in the IT sectors, experience difficulties retaining staff, resulting in valuable expertise and tacit knowledge walking out the door. Employers are often creative in terms of the remuneration packages that they offer, but they also need to provide and manage the work environment. More subtly, telecommunications provides the advantage of impersonalizing communication. It may be more advantageous to employers to use telecommunications to emphasize content and minimize social influences; reduced socioemotional communication and increased task orientation can enhance group work and efficiency (Walther 1996). The success of this effort depends on the context and environment in which the telecommunications media are used.

According to Chiolcoat and DeWine (1985) the interpersonal attraction dimension of social influence is a multidimensional construct, comprising task attraction, physical attraction and social attraction. The more people are attracted to one another, the more they will communicate with one another, and the more they are attracted to another person the more influence that person has in interpersonal communication. Interpersonal attractiveness can thus enhance communication and detract from it. Strategically employers could use either telecommunications or face-to-face methods depending on the individuals involved and the company's objectives.

From a financial perspective, employers have identified benefits from savings in office space, lighting and utilities by outsourcing to one-person businesses. In some cases, new office buildings are being designed on the premise that workers will 'rent' rather than 'own' space, that is, they will have no dedicated desk, but book one when they need to visit the office. Exact estimations of savings are scant. Savings stemming from lower maintenance costs from having fewer parking spaces, however, have been estimated at £110 ($176) per parking space per year in England (York City Council 1999).

In summary, the benefits to employers are largely idiosyncratic, depending on the circumstances and environment of each firm. Transition costs may be large and they are also likely to vary according to the current working practices and fixed investments of firms. Changing working practices is not cost-less and can be disruptive in terms of meeting customer demands. Table 2.1 provides a listing of some of the considerations.

Table 2.1 *Potential advantages and disadvantages of teleworking* (Taylor *et al.* 2000)

Employer		Employee	
Potential advantage	Potential disadvantage	Potential advantage	Potential disadvantage
Reduced car parking requirements, therefore lower overheads	Requires employee self-discipline	Greater flexibility in work hours	
Reduced in-office space requirements (lighting, space, furniture)	Lower productivity due to home-based distractions, lack of supervision, reduced stimulation from face-to-face interactions	Greater flexibility in lifestyle	Requires self-discipline
Higher staff productivity through fewer interruptions	Ineffective communication between personnel may result due to lack of proximity and/or interaction	Higher productivity through fewer interruptions	Lower productivity due to home-based distractions, lack of supervision
Higher efficiency (e.g. less 'paid' time traveling)	Less opportunity for cross-fertilization resulting from both social and professional face-to-face interactions	Lower car use and less fuel consumption, therefore money saved	Reduced social/professional contact and lack of stimulation from face-to-face interactions
Less dependent on climate conditions (e.g. snow days) Greater flexibility in work hours	Provision and maintenance of equipment Not all jobs lend themselves to telecommuting, which may cause some resentment among staff	Achieve more life goals in a day Ability to avoid traveling at congested times	Requires dedicated space in the home Internal household conflicts
Facilitates outsourcing	Increased security risk		

THE NEW ECONOMICS OF LOCATION

The New Age Society is largely immersed in the dynamic world of communication. One could argue the increasing proportion of complex goods production and services provided in the economy has led to a greater proclivity toward human and company interaction. Advanced telecommunications are evolving to fill niche markets, enhancing efficiency of business and personal life through flexibility and timely information flow. Penetration of Internet connections into workplaces and households, as observed in Western economies, have allowed consumers to browse and search for services and products, communicate between 'desktops', and on average access information in a more timely manner than ever before. This may be thought of as a mechanism favoring neoclassical mechanisms for spatial convergence of economic performance.

Counter to this have been the 'New Growth Theory' arguments of Lucas (1998), Romer (1990) and others that the 'New Information Age' leads to the cumulative-and-circular divergence of economies. The regions or cities that have an initial advantage in information systems will enjoy a variety of internal and external benefits that will allow them to develop their advantages further. Their position has been supported by a body of empirical evidence, largely stemming from the new approaches of Barro and Sala-i-Martin (1992), showing that regions are not converging significantly in their economic performance and certainly not in a way consistent with neoclassical analysis.

The economic argument for the decline in spatial variation, and indeed the potential end of cities, ties in closely with the degree to which electronic communications are substitutes for face-to-face contact (Gaspar and Glaeser 1996). As we have seen the evidence on this is far from clear. Empirical analysis is constrained by data limitations and the difficulties of testing for causality over a short time period. There has been a tendency historically for urbanization to be unevenly spread, but often to broadly follow a consistent hierarchical pattern (Krugman 1996). Whether this pattern is sustainable in the context of the widespread use of the Internet is uncertain. The empirical work presented by Moss and Townsend (1998) is very much in line with the larger ideas of Romer and Lucas and the more localized analysis of Krugman. There is a high correlation in the US between those urban areas that have a high concentration of information-intensive functions or technology industries and the concentration of deployment of Internet technologies. They find a limited network of highly interconnected metropolitan areas that dominate the national network with economically distressed areas being left behind. Zook (2000b) by exploring the geographical origins of domain names also provides support for spatial concentration. Attempts to explore this situation using more sophisticated econometric analysis by Pelletiere and Rodrigo (1999), however, produced much less conclusive evidence.

This lack of any confirmation with the neoclassical convergence theory for Internet supply is also tending to be replicated in terms of physical distribution. The developments in information systems and e-commerce more generally have led, as outlined above, to a tendency to concentrate interchange and consolidation at a limited number of nodes. The focus of FedEx, the major carrier of e-commerce generated goods movements, in Memphis has been complemented by the city becoming a major trucking center and an important node in all the main railroad networks in the US.

Geography has played a part in this, but the information revolution has consolidated the hub-and-spoke nature of freight transportation.

These findings that largely refute neoclassical economics may not be that surprising, however, in light of the standard Vernon (1966) theory of product cycles. When new products emerge they tend to be located in regions with high-quality labor and access to specialized information. Time erodes these needs as the product becomes more standardized. The Internet is too new to be able to ascertain whether or not it will follow this pattern. The situation at present is that economic theories abound linking the Internet and e-commerce to land-use developments, but the empirical support for any of them is still extremely tenuous.

CONCLUSIONS

In a way this chapter highlights how little quantitative evidence and real understanding that there is of the economic implications of the Internet and e-commerce. Of course, it could be that the New Information Age is simply a modified replication of the telegraph era, or the telephone age, and that there is really little more economics to be understood. The new technology has features common to many other network activities, albeit with a few idiosyncrasies of its own, and by and large its role in society can be explained in traditional economic theories, or at least by rather minor variations to that theory. The Internet simply offers an advanced form of communication that will have implications for the way we work and travel, but fundamentally these will be similar in their implications to early trends in communications technology, namely the railways, telegraph, postal service, etc. caused important one-time shifts in the aggregate production function and were then assimilated. The empirical evidence to date does not refute this idea.

The alternative is that the Internet/e-commerce economy requires a new way of thinking and not simply a minor reformulation of traditional theory. The speed of change, the new social values and the complexity of the 'new age' makes traditional theories redundant and potentially very misleading. The evidence on this has not really materialized to date. Certainly, there are differences in the way the US economy has been performing in recent years, with low inflation and low unemployment thwarting traditional ideas such as the Phillips curve. In itself, however, this may simply be a reflection of a stepped change in the structure of the economy rather than creating a fundamental change that should reshape economic thinking. Only time will tell which school of thought is correct.

a) Network econs promote conc. of or mkt concentra.

b) Complexities of IT flow + dispta

c) ? Spot correspond equation of growth rates + spat
   des perim under IT ... Product cycle ?

3

Beyond Transaction Costs: E-Commerce and the Power of the Internet Dataspace

MARTIN KENNEY

University of California, Davis, CA, USA and Berkeley Roundtable on the International Economy

and

JAMES CURRY

Colegio de la Frontera Norte, Tijuana, Mexico

The commercial Internet is now approximately six years old. But what is most remarkable is not the speed of its adoption, the remarkable expansion in the amount of data flowing through it, or even the number of new web sites coming online. Rather it has been the remarkable redirecting of talent and capital to finding ways to commercialize what had been an entirely noncommercial system. It is this wave of talent experimenting with new ways of generating and/or conserving value that is powering an enormous burst of creativity. Our modest aims are to examine a few of the current developments in what the venture capitalists term 'the Internet space' and reflect upon what these mean to the development of the current economy. As with anything written regarding such a fast-moving economic phenomenon, any predictions or observations are based upon conditions and developments that might be rapidly outdated (Kenney and Curry 1999b).

Our central orienting theoretics are Schumpeter's (1969) metaphor of new technologies opening new spaces, and De Landa's (1991) work, derived from Deleuze and Guattari, about the self-organizing impulses which arise out of complex, chaotic phenomena. Schumpeter's perspective is particularly appropriate for the Internet insofar as it is a vast new region being colonized by a variety of activities, many of which are highly novel in their approach. As an intelligent communication technology the Internet enables the creation of virtual places, which, in prosaic terms, are only places in computers. Collectively, these new places constitute a vast virtual space which is the profound creative product of a process of machine mediated social interaction. Moreover, as Batty (1997) so brilliantly points out, these new cyber places are now beginning to reorient the world of physical places.

De Landa emphasizes the points (singularities) at which order begins to arise out of chaos, rendering previously random individual elements into a higher order, and more powerful, whole (mechanic phylum). This sort of thing is witnessed in the natural world when random air molecules and temperature variations exhibit self-organized coherence, for example to produce a storm. Taken at the individual level, the Internet can be viewed as a collection of individual processes interacting randomly.[1] At this level of analysis one might regard the Internet mainly as a sophisticated communications medium that radically reduces transaction costs between individual nodes (like the telephone). However, if one considers the virtual space of the Internet as a process resulting from the complex interaction of millions of intelligent nodes, it is entirely possible, indeed highly likely, that new processes will emerge from the medium itself. However, for us this emergence, rather than a 'natural' process, is one sparked by an entrepreneur. This is concretized in 'new ways of using the Internet' or when new e-commerce business models are 'invented' or 'discovered' and implemented in code (a new software program).

The power of the Internet belies its simplicity. At first glance the Internet is merely a medium for connections able to transmit anything digitized and a medium which allows for infinite interconnections. Unlike prior communication systems, such as telephony, which established a dedicated connection between two (or sometimes more) nodes, the Internet allows the simultaneous exchange of information in digital form among an unlimited number of nodes, each with its own computing power. The protocols used to transmit data across the Internet are standardized and readable by a multiplicity of platforms. Added to this is the innovation of hypertext, that is, the ability to almost effortlessly move from node to node at a whim – a feature that is only possible because the information has been separated from its physical carrier medium such as paper, celluloid, or plastic. The information content of the Internet is almost completely dephysicalized or dematerialized. It is reduced in its physical essence to the most abstract possible formulation: 1s and 0s carried by laser light or electromagnetic waves and stored by electrons or magnetic charges. Multi-platform accessible standards, hypertext, and dematerialization are forcing and combining with a remarkable increase in the capacity of global telecommunications systems to rapidly reduce the costs of communicating digital data – notice the reduction-in-cost dynamic itself constantly creates new opportunities. The extreme flexibility of digital representations permit their representing an almost infinite number of activities as diverse as booking airline flights, purchasing items, playing games, viewing pictures, listening to music, or accessing public information. Moreover, once objects, either physical or mental are reduced to digital (i.e. mathematical) representations, they become uniquely malleable and observable, in ways that are not possible with physical or mental objects.

As powerful as all this is, a finer power is derived from the fact that the Internet space is a collection of interconnected intelligent machines. Unlike a simple communications device like a telephone, which is merely a conduit for data, the nodes connected to the Internet are all capable of storing, retrieving, and manipulating data at constantly increasing levels of sophistication. While it is possible to use a telephone to interact with a computer – with touch tone-based menuing systems for example – it functions essentially as a dumb machine, merely transmitting pulses entered directly by the user which trigger intelligent functions in the computer located at the other end of the line. While at one level the Internet is just a communications system, at a more important level it is a communications system mediated at all its nodes by powerful computers. Each personal computer connected to the Internet is far more than a dumb terminal connected to a mainframe. Thus while it is clearly the case that much of the usage of the Internet is predicated on a broadcast model (i.e. information downloaded for user consumption), there will be a cascade of applications which will either utilize the individual user's computer or storage power in some novel and innovative way, or in some way utilize the collective computing power of the Internet as a whole. In other words, there will be applications that will emerge that are not the proverbial economist's network externalities, but rather network internalities.

Taken together, the intelligent nodes of the Internet (each with their own data and processing power) and their connective links constitute a vast, continuously growing and evolving dataspace.[2] Separated from its material basis, the Internet consists of nothing more than data of two types: code, that is, the data that instruct the machines how to perform (computer programs), and the data on which the code-instructed machines work (see, for example, Lessig 1999). These data are constantly in motion, directed and utilized by intelligent machines that are directly or indirectly in the service of their biological masters. Far from being an inert mass of digitized information stored on metal or silicon, or a virtual simulation of something else, the Internet dataspace is its own reality, sui generis, governed by its own social and technological logics. Thus, the real power of commerce, or anything else, on the Internet derives not merely from the efficiencies of a new communications medium, but from the creative singularities that emerge out of the complex chaos of the Internet dataspace. Put another way, with the interlinked intelligent nodes of the Internet, the sum is greater than the whole of the parts and even the network externalities.

There can be no doubt that the Internet is transforming the very substance of economic activity. This chapter aims to explore some aspects of this transformation by speculating upon the meaning of some of the tendencies that are appearing in the economy due to the influence of the Internet. It begins with a brief discussion of the difficulties contemporary social sciences have in explaining the Internet and its effects. The next three sections consist of a general examination of the development and capabilities of the Internet as they relate to commerce, a more focused discussion of the capabilities of the web for enhancing customer service, and a general examination of the economic and organizational impacts of web-based commerce. This is followed by three sections which examine exemplary areas in which the commercial application of the Internet is leading to new approaches to doing business, or otherwise having a major impact on the way business is already conducted. These factors underlie the current push for the development of web 'portal' sites, the direct marketing model of personal computer assembly and sales, and the use of the Internet to streamline interfirm transactions. The penultimate section addresses the advantages of being first to exploit a particular niche or opportunity. Finally, in the conclusion, we raise the question as to whether the Internet will lead to the proliferation of numerous niche businesses, or whether certain technological and economic exigencies will lead to domination by a small number of very large content aggregators or product marketers.

THE ROLE OF THE INTERNET IN THE FORMATION OF A NEW ECONOMIC SPACE

The Internet is a key aspect of the ongoing transformation of the economy to a form in which materiality becomes subordinate to information and knowledge creation. One way of thinking about this is that in the USA during the 1960s through 1980s there was one computer per 10 persons, in the PC era this had changed to 10 computers per person. In the late 1990s there were 100 computers per person, and some predict that it will soon be 1000 computers per person (Khosla 2000). This seems unbelievable, until one considers that increasingly not only automobiles, but nearly every consumer appliance now contains a computer of some type. Moreover, telecommunications networks have enormous numbers of computers, which are called routers and switches. Already, many of these computers are connected to the Internet, in the next decade all will be.

The Internet is a computer network that connects computers to computers through computers. It is an interactive communications medium through which the user accesses information that would have previously taken much time and physical effort to find.[3] The web is remarkable because the user has the sensation of traveling, though in reality the user is only electronically reaching out and retrieving data to be visualized on a computer monitor. Because of the nature of computer networks, even the path and information search are logged and therefore converted into information that may be of potential value. Moreover, this entire situation must be seen dynamically in that technical components of the system are dropping exponentially in cost; that is, what costs x today will cost half as much in 18 months. The cost of bandwidth is asymptotically approaching zero. So what appears expensive (or nearly impossible to deliver), for example a 3-megabyte data file, will have its cost of delivery halved in 18 months.

With the cost of processing power, bandwidth, and connection continuously declining, it is reasonable to assume that anything that can be digitized will be. In the commercial realm this means that all standardized activities, which have a separable information component will likely have that separated and handled electronically. Even though there is no certainty about the ultimate configuration of Internet-related commerce at maturity, businesses with standardized products such as securities, insurance, music, video, stamps, and tickets will have much of their business conducted online. Of course, sales activities can also be moved online at tremendous savings, because of the removal of paper and individuals handling paper from the value chain. Cyberspace allows the emergence of online communications and trading platforms, where economic actors can conduct businesses.

Prior to the Internet (electronic data interchange (EDI) was so costly and limited in its capabilities that the interactions were quite limited), the cost and time necessary to evaluate information were so great that physical and EDI interaction between the various parties had to be limited. In other words one normally interacted with only a small number of potential transaction partners. The Internet rapidly decreased the costs and other entry barriers dramatically increasing the potential market size. For example, in the consumer-to-consumer (C-to-C) area eBay has created the world's largest garage sale, and made it continuous (24/7), convenient, and inexpensive.

Similarly, in the business-to-business (B-to-B) area, markets are being built (i.e. the code is being written), which can become platforms on which entire industries can trade. Forrester Research estimates that over half of all B-to-B e-commerce will be marketplace based instead of direct trade between partners (Industry Standard 2000a). Finally, virtual stores (B-to-C) have been created with inventories, i.e., entries in gigantic databases, which are dramatically larger than any physical store, and also are easier to access from any computer. Smart data collection and marketing technologies enable e-store customization all the way down to the individual level, and have precipitated a major debate about the privacy rights of consumers in cyberspace. Ease of access is becoming even greater as the Internet is extended to wireless, enabling a new wave of e-commerce potential.

The increasing dematerialization of communication, i.e. its separation from paper or sound waves, would seem to argue that space no longer matters. But, in fact, it does except in new ways. It is in the transport and warehousing functions where the physical world is manifested. Some dot-coms have embarked on major building campaigns. For example, in 1999 the Internet grocer Webvan embarked on a $1 billion project to build 26 warehouses to serve the major US cities. With these warehouses, Webvan hopes to completely reorganize the way groceries and other products are delivered. In other words, it is their intention to move purchasing out of supermarkets and shopping malls by offering convenient delivery. Another major development is the shifting of product delivery from bulk long-haul trucks, which are used to deliver products to traditional stores to the less-than-load delivery industry exemplified by UPS, the USA Postal Service, and Federal Express. Since the customer base is now global, these delivery services must also become global. Finally, the Internet has made it possible for these delivery services to offer the customers the ability to track their packages online.

The stampede to invest in Internet-related businesses, in the USA nearly $20 billion in 1999 (an increase of nearly 500 percent over the previous year), has created a situation in which company valuations seem to have departed from all reasonable standards (Industry Standard 2000b). The curious economics of the Internet are exemplified by Yahoo! which is valued at over $40 billion, even though it generates a limited amount of income. And yet, it offers a plethora of services including e-mail, Internet access to a massive web database, a search engine, stock tracking, file storage, a appointment calendar, chat, a messaging service, travel booking services, news and weather, all for free. Like America On Line (AOL) and other web user aggregators, Yahoo!'s high market valuation is predicated on the vast future potential represented by its online users.

The existence of free content provided by for-profit enterprises goes far beyond simple notions of a loss leader. For example, with the drop in cost of bandwidth, if the current movement towards voice-over-IP continues, the charge for telephone calls globally might just become a monthly fee. There will be no reason to bill for the minutes themselves. From the perspective of traditional economics, giving products away for free or for a single monthly rate appears foolhardy and even perverse. The economics of a product whose cost is asymptotically approaching zero can only be expected to be unusual. Moreover, once landline and wireless telephony follow a more Internet-like pricing model, new value-added services can be marketed over the network. This has caused some economists and business theorists to begin rethinking traditional economic concepts to better account for the value-added from knowledge creation and the 'winner-take-all' aspects of capturing or becoming standards in information- and communication-intensive industries (Arthur 1994; David 1986; Shapiro and Varian 1999). The efficiencies and synergies being generated in the electronics and telecommunications realms are driving the discussion of the New Economy.

Economic puzzles like these are only the tip of the iceberg; there are other phenomena pressing beyond the boundaries of traditional social sciences. This is the case where value creation through machine-augmented interaction gives rise to new forms of value creation in both an economic and social sense. Web site user communities actually are an integral component of the value of many commercial and noncommercial sites. The user community creates value in a profoundly social sense. For example, reader's reviews are posted at Internet bookseller Amazon.com (Hagel and Armstrong 1997). In this way Amazon becomes more than a mere bookseller leveraging the disintermediative capabilities of the Internet. Users can, and often do, utilize Amazon's site as a research tool, without buying anything; a sort of hyperlinked, constantly evolving *Books in Print* and *Kirkus Reviews* all rolled into one. The social (community) interaction process, and its concomitant communication of information and opinion, and the comprehensive nature of the Amazon site creates its value (Kotha 1998). The significant lesson from both Yahoo! and Amazon is how they provide multiple reasons for the users' continued patronage. Put differently, they enmesh the user.

THE INTERNET AND COMMERCE

By the early 1990s the Internet hosted a collection of useful information and downloadable software. However, the tools for accessing this information were complicated and required a certain amount of expertise and system knowledge on the part of the user. IT was by no means plug-and-play. Most of the innovations were designed to make the Internet more useful to academics and computer scientists. The breakthrough came with the World Wide Web (WWW) and Hypertext Mark-up Language (HTML) protocols, which were developed by researchers at the European Laboratory for Particle Physics (CERN) in Switzerland in order to facilitate information exchange among physicists. The next step was the development of special software, the browser, which made these and other protocols invisible to the user. A number of different browsers were developed, some more functional than others, and were distributed freely over the net. One of the early browsers, Mosaic, developed at the National Center for Supercomputing Applications (NCSA) at the University of Illinois Urbana-Champaign became wildly popular with millions of copies downloaded in a few short months after its release. This was perhaps the first instance in which the unique characteristics of the Internet dataspace were leveraged on their own terms, in this case for the purpose of extremely rapid market penetration. Soon, the venture capitalists would develop the term 'viral' to describe products or ideas whose adoption curve could be measured in days and weeks. This confronts business with a treacherous situation in which competition can literally derail a well-planned marketing strategy overnight.

The Internet confronts businesses with four unique characteristics: ubiquity, interactivity, speed, and intelligence. The first three relate to what might be considered the extensive development phase of the Internet. The fourth, intelligence, relates to the capacity for intensive development of the Internet based on its distributed independent processing power. Those firms who wish to succeed in Internet commerce have had to confront and manage these four characteristics.

The first is ubiquity. By this we mean that all 'places' on the Internet are accessible to the user on what is essentially an unlimited and equal basis. The user can go anywhere on the net with a minimum of effort; there is no inherent technological reason for the user to start at a particular point. Only five years ago, most users had only one entry point to the WWW, either their corporate network or the proprietary network services predating the rise of the WWW in the mid-1990s, such as AOL, Prodigy, and CompuServe. Beginning in the late 1980s, most, if not all of the services provided by these network services was available at either free or subscription stand-alone web sites. Now access and availability of content and other services is increasingly available to all over a variety of media including telephone lines, television cable, and, soon, wireless. Emblematic of this ubiquity is the near universal recognition of the meaning of 'www.xxxx.com.'

The second important characteristic of the Internet is interactivity. The Internet itself was developed through a remarkable process of interaction by researchers located around the world. Commercial publishers who wish to succeed on the Internet must offer more to customers than that which is ordinarily available in print or from some other media. One of the more successful web publishers has been the *Wall Street Journal*, which has seen steady growth in its paid subscription base since it began collecting fees about two years ago. The *Journal*'s site offers not only standard print content but also a wide range of content and services not found in the print edition. These include articles from other Dow Jones publications, past article search and retrieval, customized stock quotes, job finding information, a database of company background information, interactive discussion of various current news topics, a news audio feed, the ability to customize the Web page to the user's interest, and numerous other features. The *Journal* site serves both as a substitute for those with limited access to the print version, such as overseas readers, and as a complement to print subscribers who wish to access additional services such as company and stock tracking from a brand name they know and trust.

The interactive nature of the Internet also gives rise to new forms of collaborative activity. Some software firms place nearly completed software (beta releases) at a web site and encourage computer aficionados and IT professionals to install the software and test it for bugs, functionality, and features. Consumers actually participate in the knowledge-creation process by using a new product and communicating the results back to the company. Numerous software producers leverage the communitarian power of the Internet by prereleasing unfinished 'beta' versions of new software products over the Internet, where a large number of interested users can locate problems and offer suggestions for product refinements. This diminishes some of the costly burdens of in-house testing and decreases the distance between software creators and customers by creating an information feedback loop. Moreover, integrating a subset of customers directly into the product development process also accelerates the creation of demand for the finished product. The open source 'movement', best exemplified by the Linux operating system and Apache web-server software programs, takes this logic to an even higher level. These, and other programs, are downloadable for free, and have relied on the Internet for both their dissemination and their continuing technological evolution. Open source has emerged as an important software development strategy and has been embraced by numerous startups, and in the case of Linux, even by IBM (DiBona *et al.* 1999).

The third important characteristic of the commercial Internet is speed (Davis and Meyer 1998; Kenney and Curry 1999b). Because the Internet is an ubiquitous, interactive system based on a multipurpose digital computing platform, changes such as system software upgrades, new standards and protocols, and new publications (content) can be developed and disseminated very rapidly. The availability of out-of-the-box network and network server hardware and easily adaptable software applications such as credit card billing systems and searchable relational databases enables the rapid development of commercial systems at very low cost. Moreover, many Internet-based businesses have been developed as overlays on existing infrastructure, which further reduces startup costs and time of deployment. The rapidity at which businesses can be established on the Internet places a great deal of emphasis on being the first in a particular market category. An interesting case in point is Amazon.com, an Internet bookseller based in Seattle. By relying on existing systems of distribution as a sort of retailing adjunct to them, Amazon was able to start operations quickly and efficiently (Bianco 1997). By purchasing advertising link space for itself on the Internet from frequently visited sites such as Netscape's, Amazon developed a high volume business in a very short time (Southwick 1996). Founded in 1995, Amazon had over $116 million in net sales during the second quarter of 1998, an increase of 316 percent over net sales of $27.9 million for the second quarter of 1997 (Amazon.com 1998). Barnes & Noble, an important innovator of large, high variety bookstores, has only recently recognized and introduced bookselling on the Internet as a logical extension of its own large-scale distribution and inventory-tracking system (Marcial 1997). But, being a late entrant in the Internet book sales arena, Barnes & Noble is having great difficulty catching Amazon.

The final important characteristic of the Internet is ultimately the most powerful of all. The previous three characteristics represent an extensive historical evolution of telecommunications technology, i.e. bigger, faster, and better. The fourth, intelligence, i.e. the ability, distributed throughout the Internet, to retrieve, store, and process information, renders each node something far more than a passive information conduit, and the Internet itself something far more profound than a mere communications system. The machine intelligence (i.e. processor power and code) embedded in each node (both client and server) enables a more intensive mode of development based on the potential of the Internet as a complex, technology-mediated, social relation. Business models and strategies rooted in old notions of marketing developed in the era of one-way broadcast media have met with only limited success at best. Those strategies which in some way attempt to utilize the Internet on its own terms, as a synergistic whole, understanding in McLuhan's famous words that 'the medium is the message' have been more successful.

The individual machine-based intelligence of the Internet has two aspects: node-based and net-based. Node-based intelligence refers to the systems, which, while they are net-oriented, reside primarily in servers and/or clients. This is hardware and code which make the Internet much more than a mere communications medium-extending interaction between individuals to interaction between individuals augmented by intelligent machines and, ultimately, machine-to-machine interaction. In this classification are all the functions which power the Internet beyond basic communications (like e-mail): streaming media, user-searchable databases, targeted marketing/advertising, the various tools provided by portals and other service sites, e-retail functions/sites, and all the other machine-augmented Internet interactivity. Net-based refers to the synergistic development that arises out of the Internet as a whole as a consequence of interactive machine intelligence.

Businesses (and consumers as well) are increasingly able to use their node-based intelligence to both create and utilize the collective information creation and storage capabilities of the Internet. For example, MicroStrategy builds 'data mining' and 'decision support' software, which is meant to enable the nascent B-to-B revolution. The term 'data mining' is somewhat of a misnomer conveying the impression of something along the lines of database management software for 'data warehouses', i.e. very large databases. MicroStrategy goes far beyond this, as it develops software enabling companies to make use of the Internet to make business decisions about marketing, production, and logistics, based on data 'mined' from the Internet. MicroStrategy's applications are not mere stand-alone database applications, which utilize the Internet, but rather applications that allow users to effectively and interactively utilize the vast and constantly growing Internet dataspace. In the same way that the Internet becomes a ubiquitously accessible hypermall, the Internet dataspace becomes a hyperdatabase requiring users to create metadata, i.e. distilled data such as those generated by search engines or shopping aggregators like C-Net, to effectively utilize it.

There are already numerous examples of all this, and undoubtedly there will be many more in the near future. Whispernumbers.com uses automated search technology to sweep the Internet for rumors, opinions, individual estimates, hard data, etc. on company earnings. These data are analyzed to produce earnings estimates that have been observed to be more accurate than those produced by professional analysts (Gimein 2000). Whispernumbers.com thus uses its node-based machine intelligence to access the 'group mind' of the Internet, leveraging, and going beyond, ubiquity, interactivity, and speed.

Other examples use the distributed computer power of the Internet to develop unique approaches to content distribution and work sharing, in effect, using the Internet itself as an exploitable resource. Napster is a software program that is downloaded to the hard drive where it creates a file folder in which MP3 files are inserted to make them available to Napster users anywhere in the world.[5] Unlike one of its counterparts in the MP3 space, MP3.com, which serves MP3 files to its clients out on the web, Napster.com does not store any music; it merely matches up the downloader and the provider. Napster transcends the standard client/server logic in which web surfing 'clients' access the data collected, created, or repackaged by web 'content providers', instead making every Napster user a content provider (Figure 3.1).[6] Another interesting example is the Seti at Home project based at the University of California, Berkeley. Seti at Home is a screen saver program that downloads and

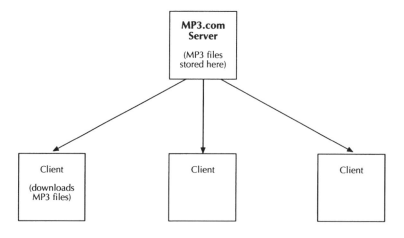

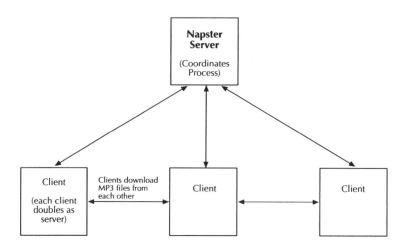

Figure 3.1   *The MP3.com (client-server) model versus Napster (dataspace) model. Source: Kenney and Curry*

analyzes radio telescope data, searching for signs of extraterrestrial intelligence. The Seti at Home project radically reduces research costs by utilizing the collective computer power of over a million users to perform analysis which would normally require enormous amounts of expensive supercomputer time. How unusual is the current conjuncture? Napster was created by a 19-year-old college freshman at Northeastern University majoring in computer science (Brown 2000; Rosenberg 2000). There are already improved versions emerging, even while Napster.com is working with universities to improve its current bandwidth-hogging characteristics. We believe Napster is only the beginning of this lashing together of computers.

BUSINESS-TO-CONSUMER E-COMMERCE

Customer service functions have always been a time-consuming person-to-person activity; however, most of the interactions are highly routinized. An important recent step in automating customer service was telephone call processing, but this was a slow system with very low bandwidth. In other words, an excessively long menu of choices leads to consumer disconnection and difficulties in creating user-friendly branching systems. More sophisticated nonhuman intermediated customer service would have to wait until the consumer had a device able to handle greater amounts of information, i.e. the PC and the computer modem. When the installed base grew and the technology was sufficiently mature it became possible to place information on a server open to customers. This redefined customer service by increasing the level of provision while decreasing the cost. This was possible because most interactions are entirely standard. For example, many customer questions are for routine information such as store hours and directions. Answers to such questions can be codified, indexed, and stored on a server to be accessed online and downloaded. For simple questions such as directions, the Internet can download a map, whereas on the telephone error-prone verbal instructions were necessary. Essentially, customers can access the information they need to find and create value for themselves from the provider's web site at practically no cost except the initial startup costs.

In addition to seeking routine information, customers are also attracted to sites that provide detailed information about products or services. A potential customer can browse several competitors' sites, as well as third party sites, which discuss the product in question, compare prices and features, gather general information about a particular product or type of product, taking as much time as desired before making a purchase. A recent study by the Fuqua School of Business at Duke University found that consumers were more likely to buy products from sites that provided comprehensive information than from sites that had slightly lower prices but little in the way of useful information (Bransten 1998). The point is that the user can select the desired amount of information, removing the need for the information provider to make decisions based on an 'average' consumer.

The types of customer service provided online depend upon the firm's product or service. For example, software companies make available various software patches, add-ons to current products, and/or demos. Increasingly, software programs such as Norton Antivirus or Netscape Communicator have the ability, upon a prompt from the user, to automatically check for updates and then download and install them. Delivery through the Internet is essentially without cost and has the added benefit of developing a connection with the customer. In other cases, service bulletins or product-related information are placed on company web sites for informational purposes. These relatively straightforward applications replace or augment previous product upgrading or information dissemination techniques.

Global logistics firms, such as DHL, UPS, and Federal Express, have taken the potential for customer service much further. Federal Express, one of the aggressive first-movers, has opened the tracking portion of its computer system to Internet users. The initial effort of Federal Express on the Internet was a one-way information provision service that customers could use to receive information about the location of the shipment and its arrival time (Lappin 1996; Grant 1997). The success of this initial effort spurred Federal Express to use the Internet in other ways. Based on its experience with the tracking service, a web site was developed to permit customers to use the Internet for all their shipping functions. The features now available include scheduling pick-ups, detailed maps of all drop-off locations, rate charts, and other information regarding international customs regulations. Moreover, the site offers free downloadable software that speeds the processing of shipments, allows the user to store addresses in an address book, maintains a shipping history in a log, and creates and prints labels (Fedex.com 1998). Many shipping office functions have been transferred onto software and into data communications networks. Human intermediaries and physical documents were replaced by software. Not only is it less expensive than previous methods, but it also provides the mechanism for creating new ways for firms and their customers to interact. Most critical, the information provided through the server gives the customer the resources to create value from the site.

The potential for e-commerce is illustrated in the highly simplified Figure 3.2. In Panel 1 we illustrate the conventional system in which products moved from supplier to the customer through the various intermediaries, and information moved the other direction physicalized in the form of paper. The important thing to understand here is that almost invariably product was pushed through the supply chain before the customer purchased the product. The information in paper form took a long time to move back to the supplier. Within the system there was the constant threat of waste in the form of production that the customer did not want. For example, in the auto industry there was on average 60 days of inventory in the channel from the producer to the customer, this is product that is simply tying up capital and losing value. Similarly, the relationship between an assembler and suppliers was driven by information on paper and, unless operated on a just-in-time basis had the same problem of push versus pull. In Panels 2a and 2b we schematically show how EDI or electronic service industries operated. In Panel 2a it is plain that paper has now been eliminated from the intermediary through to the supplier. However, we should note that the EDI systems were proprietary and quite costly to implement. Moreover, they were usually very inflexible and not open to outsiders due to their high cost and proprietary protocols. In services such as brokerages that could be reduced to electronic impulses the brokerage houses had already implemented telephone touch pad systems. In other cases, such as travel agents, the customer phoned the travel agent and made requests that the travel agent typed into the computer system. In this case the travel agent had access to the computer, but really was, for simple transactions, merely a data entry operator.

The power of the Internet is exemplified in Panels 3a and 3b. Not only is there now the ability to connect every node in the value chain, but also there is the possibility of new intermediaries joining. The point is that in a value chain that is completely networked by the Internet all the paper can be removed from the system. Moreover, if it becomes a true pull system, then risk and inventory can be driven out of the system making the entire system more efficient. The ideal example of this is Dell's management of the personal computer value chain (Curry and Kenney 1999).

The Internet provides the potential for entirely new intermediaries. These new possibilities are illustrated in the differences between Panel 1 and Panel 3a in Figure 3.2. Notice that there is the potential for entirely new intermediaries to enter the value

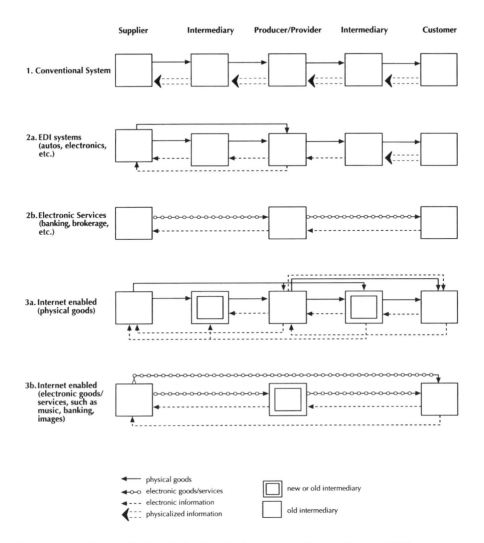

Figure 3.2 *Evolution of value chains into the Internet era: Source: Kenney 1999*

chain. This is now actively underway as venture capitalists fund startups intent upon displacing incumbents, creating new marketplaces (or platforms), and reorganizing value chains.[7] The use of Internet retailing will transfer an increment from traditional channels to online. No previous communications technology has allowed the customer to personally search databases of, for example, books, autos, software, airline schedules, and then complete the purchase without face-to-face interaction. Traditional commercial locations deployed a service worker (or intermediary) that communicated with a customer while interfacing with a computer and performing search and booking procedures. With Internet browser technology it is possible to remove the service worker as a translator between the analog customer and the digital database or to 'disintermediate' the relationship (of course, software is now the intermediary). This makes it possible to reconceptualize activities that formerly required human service workers and directly connect customers to firms' computers. With credit card payment the entire process is electronic with the exception of delivery for some goods, such as insurance, stock certificates, and financial instruments, there is nothing but an accounting notation in a computer.

There are remarkable benefits for a retailer who can transfer sales activities to the Internet, though they vary by product or service. For many services in which there is no physical component at all it may be quite easy to move the entire process online. A general benefit is that an Internet retailer can hold far lower inventory levels than a conventional retailer who must have the items in stock, thereby tying up capital. The difference can be striking. For example, Amazon.com, the online bookseller, turned its inventory over 42 times in 1997, whereas its largest competitor, retail store-based Barnes & Noble turned over inventory only 2.1 times (Willis 1998). Moreover, a significant portion of Amazon's inventory is held by distributors who ship the items directly to the customer, although this is changing as Amazon attempts to develop a system of buying directly from publishers (Bianco 1997). Though Amazon began in books, it soon expanded to various other items including CDs, videocassettes, and consumer electronics, while investing in an online pharmacy and various other Internet retailers. Simultaneously, it began constructing centrally located warehouses to serve its online customers.

Internet-based retailing eliminates the costs of retail branches, thereby lowering initial entry costs and the fixed costs associated with retail stores. Moreover, the use of the Internet for sales combined with less-than-load delivery firms such as Federal Express and UPS extends the customer base from the relatively local reach of individual stores to anyone anywhere in the world having access to a PC with a modem and a credit card. So, not only can the large Amazons enter the retail market. It is also possible for small local stores anywhere in the world to join the global market by selling their product. Thus the Internet can disintermediate retailers, but it can also connect them with a much larger customer base.

The ability to build very simple graphical representations of a potential purchase allows consumers the ability to make their purchases online. Complicated sets of purchasing decisions such as booking travel and hotels can be undertaken online without the intervention of intermediaries. For example, air travel, car rental, and accommodations can be booked at an online travel site. The online travel agent can go far beyond a telephonic travel agent by providing much broader and more detailed information including textual descriptions, images, and even reviews of the various destinations. In effect, huge databases of information can be made available to the customer in such a way as to allow users to 'customize' their travel agenda. In essence, the customer produces a uniquely customized product from an entirely standardized set of choices.

Compare the economics of an online travel agency with that of a conventional agency. At the conventional agency a person deals directly with the customer in a situation in which the time spent with a customer on a booking is a direct cost. In essence, each interaction with the customer is a cost (Department of Commerce 1988, p. 28).[8] In addition, travel agents can make mistakes; however, on the Internet the customer bears full responsibility for the reservation. In the case of the conventional travel agency, return business is dependent upon building an interpersonal relationship with the customer. The online travel agency uses the online customer community to develop relationships between the customers and with its site in the hopes of encouraging repeat business (Hagel and Armstrong 1997).

The travel agent's experience combined with a personal relationship with the traveler can be seen as a knowledge base that enabled them to make recommendations to improve the traveling experience. The travel agent was a form of expert knowledge. Customers not utilizing the travel agent's knowledge base in effect subsidized those using the knowledge. In an Internet-based system information on travel habits, previous travel, and other characteristics (i.e. a profile) allows the computer to search its database and match it with similar profiles to be used to offer 'personalized' services to a customer.

The success of online travel agencies is apparent (Needle 1998). For example, Microsoft's Expedia site launched in 1996 had more than $12 million in monthly sales in January 1998 and was growing quickly (Lipton 1998). As important, the US travel industry is being reorganized, not only with new entrants such as Microsoft, but also as the airlines are reducing the fees they pay to travel agents and encouraging customers to buy tickets directly through their web sites. In the process these web sites are being built into virtual places. For those desiring human contact, the offline travel agent will remain available, but increasingly they will be paid for directly by the user; witness the increasing use of service charges by the offline travel agencies (a tactic that will accelerate the movement of customers to the online agencies).

To recapitulate, the technical capacity for online retailing can be understood by seeing the two tendencies that were integrated by the Internet. First, the decreasing cost of long-distance telephony meant many customer transactions had already been centralized into call-processing centers especially for the purchase of products such as tickets, software, computers, etc. Second, the development of sophisticated database management software and the use of corporate intranets serviced by large-scale computer servers meant that the purchasing process had been largely computerized. The service worker using a networked computer to take an order was merely an intermediary between the customer and the corporate database. On the demand side, the increased usage of e-mail, the development of inexpensive, user-friendly browsers, personal computers with faster modems, and more persons attached to high-speed local area networks created a large installed base of potential consumers. The final step was to habituate customers to purchase items through cyberspace. As more and more consumers are online, old retail methods will be eclipsed since consumers have vastly more information at their disposal, not only about the products available, but about their prices as well. Premium list pricing will be more difficult to maintain as consumers can nearly effortlessly find the lowest-priced vendor, or go to a site that aggregates the price information of several vendors.

E-MALLS AND PORTALS

When entrepreneurs began exploring the use of the Internet for e-commerce, the question was how to attract customers. This was a thorny question because the chaotic unplanned topology of the Internet made it difficult for customers to find the vendors (Watson *et al.* 1998). One experiment was to aggregate commercial web sites at an e-mall, which was the analog of the physical world's shopping mall (*Economist* 1997). Here, the idea was that a web site developer would build a web site at which a number of vendors would create virtual stores. The aim was for the vendors to pay rent in terms of a fee or a percentage of sales for their site. The developer would be responsible for advertising the site and bringing in the web surfers. The more creative of these actually generated small buildings that the customer could click on to enter. This business model built on the suburban shopping mall seemed entirely plausible. However, the difficulties became obvious rather quickly. The shopping mall provides a centralized place for consumers, who had moved away from traditional downtown shopping districts to the suburbs. Prior to the automobile, the downtown had been served by public transit such as streetcars and subways, so commerce clustered at its nodes. The fatal flaw with e-malls was that there were no reasons such as convenience, less traffic, or crime that would impel 'shoppers' to visit the mall rather than go 'downtown'. Moreover, the cost barriers to starting an e-store were never high enough for merchants to 'locate' in an e-mall rather than building their own site.

Another problem related to the relatively slow acceptance of the e-mall idea is advertising. Many commercially oriented sites rely on advertising as either a full or partial source of revenue. The proprietary online services such as Prodigy, MSN, or AOL serve as excellent advertising vehicles since their users are forced to start with their proprietary interfaces. The rise of the ubiquitous web, however, has challenged the proprietary online service models since users with 'direct' Internet connections can essentially start wherever they want. This presents a problem for those companies who seek revenue from advertising and/or linking partnerships with online vendors. Like any other medium, the more viewers you attract, the more you can charge for advertising. Thus, with the viewer free to roam, the focus shifts from getting people online, to getting people who are online to go to your site. AOL has been particularly successful with users who can, if they wish, access the Internet directly, but who feel more comfortable using AOL's proprietary interface as their 'home base' on the Internet. Part of the reason for this is that AOL has been very successful in creating a sense of community for its members, something which it emphasizes in its advertising and has worked very hard to build through its early integration and promotion of technologies such as Internet Relay Chat (IRC) and instant messaging.

In addition to individual specialized sites such as Amazon.com for books, CDNow for CDs, and Auto-by-tel for automobiles, it was the portals that were able to capture the general traffic. The portals began by attracting web users by offering search and classification services to their users. As mentioned previously, they evolved by adding numerous other utilities and resources accessible for free by Internet users. However, because of the number of individuals that utilize these services they have an enormous audience, which means that space on the portal was very valuable. Advertising on the portals had an additional benefit of offering immediate click through to the vendor. This immediate connection meant that the customers delivered were actually searching for a product.

The portals have become the one-stop shop for all the Internet needs of consumers (Rindova and Kotha 2000). Their strategy has been to integrate the consumer into their site, thereby giving the portal an ability to deliver a habituated base of consumers to retailers and advertisers. This has led them to constantly evolve by offering more services and options: from free e-mail to free Internet access and beyond. The more a user utilizes these services, the less likely he will move to another site due to the costs involved in becoming familiar with a new interface and reentering data. It also adds ubiquity to the client side by enabling users to access their customized services, such as e-mail or appointment calendar, from any computer. It is not entirely unlikely that with the decreasing cost of bandwidth and storage capacity, most consumer computing including word processing, spreadsheets, etc. will be done through a portal. Already several startups such as Desktop.com, MyInternetDesktop.com, Launchpad.com, and iDrive, have begun to offer services such as file storage and backup and virtual desktops with everything from schedulers to purchase requisitions. The moves in this direction actualize the Sun Microsystems phrase 'the network is the computer' in new and powerful ways and will likely spark yet another new wave of innovations.

The e-mall failed because it was not a destination for anything but retailing, so it could not create synergies and, in effect, capture the web surfers' time. Portals have evolved away from the limitations of the client/server concept and toward finding ways to leverage the potential singularities of the Internet dataspace. The portals started out as web catalogs and search engines, then sought to gain audience mindshare as content aggregators and distributors, eventually reaching the current period where they are becoming useful adjuncts to users' daily life in cyberspace through their role as providers of proactive functionality. For many users, portals are net-centric PC applications as indispensable as word processors and spreadsheets. From a commercial perspective therefore, portals are in a unique position because they are central nodes in the Internet world.

BUSINESS-TO-BUSINESS E-COMMERCE

The discussions of the impacts of the Internet have focused upon disintermediation/ reintermediation which, while correct, does not fully capture the significance of the Internet as a medium for the relationship between firms (Kenney and Curry 1999a). One consulting firm, the Yankee Group (1999), in one of the more conservative estimates predicts that B-to-B e-commerce in the USA will increase at a compound annual growth rate of 41 percent over the next five years from $138 billion in 1999 to more than $541 billion in 2003. There are two levels of B-to-B that we examine. The first level is the creation of sites upon which purchasing can occur. This can be as simple as the site Cisco developed for its customers that already has over $10 billion a year in sales. However, this is not so interesting because it simply automates the mechanical aspects of the sales function. More interesting on this level are the various auction and exchange sites, which are creating new platforms upon which business can be conducted. The second level to be discussed is the building of software machinery for automating the entire purchasing function, i.e. the relationship between a buyer and a seller.

The world of B-to-B commerce has traditionally been complex and paper intensive.

It was a highly routinized process with no economies of scale. Notice that this entire process creates no value, it is simply a method of keeping track of things. Max Weber celebrated the rationality of a bureaucracy that kept track of everything on paper, and certainly large-scale enterprise would have been impossible without such bureaucracies, but entire layers of workers did nothing but in a relatively mechanical fashion collect and process this information. Their jobs were not to give meaning to the information, merely to prepare it.[9] The strength of this system is it provided information necessary to make decisions; the weakness is that it demanded lengthy decision cycles.

The entire process of procurement created inefficiencies for both the buyer and seller. The ability to move all of this online already existed before the Internet, but the establishment of one simple easy-to-use protocol meant that it became much simpler to move all procurement online. The initial efficiencies are obvious and massive including moving more and more of the human beings out of the mechanical segments of the information interchange pipeline, thereby increasing reliability and speed. But this is only the initial advantage, every step in the procurement process can be monitored and optimized. There is now an ability to collect data about the data stream to offer still more opportunities for optimization.

The recreation of any marketplace often has a power dimension; it is not simply a technical question. In the B-to-B arena this is particularly true as the owner of the transaction platform has the potential to control the transaction conducted, both in terms of rules but also in terms of rents (Bar and Murase 1998). The simplest B-to-B arrangement is for a firm such as Intel to establish a site to which its customers go to order parts according to some established price list. This is no different from the B-to-C businesses. Intel's power and the highly oligopolized market make this a viable strategy, but few other industries have such a dominant vendor with such a standardized product. For most industries a platform, which creates a market, is highly desirable from an efficiency perspective, because information can be exchanged in real time with no time-consuming, costly paper flows. In disaggregated markets it can bring more buyers and sellers together, ensuring greater efficiency. Often commercial firms have excess stock of various commodities, currently because the market is so disaggregated the firm sells the commodity at a near-total loss to an odd lot handler, who then searches for a customer. If a market platform for such odd lots can be created, then customers and purchasers can be matched without resort to such intermediaries.

The governance of a B-to-B market is very important, and there are pitfalls that discourage entry. There is a path dependency issue, because once an exchange becomes dominant, all of the users incur large switching costs that block participants from exiting. This makes all of the participants vulnerable to hold-up, despite the fact that their participation in the exchange is what gives it value. Thus the decision to join such a market is fraught with risk. For the promoter of the platform, the issue is to attract desirable or lead customers and/or suppliers depending upon where the power lies. If they announce that they will only conduct purchases on a particular platform, then a market tipping might occur making the site the platform for exchanges.

In the last three years there has been a proliferation of web sites seeking to aggregate B-to-B commerce. There are many examples. One venture-capital funded startup

VerticalNet.com has established approximately 75 vertical markets in nine major groups such as food and packaging. To illustrate, under the 'food and packaging' heading the markets are bakeries, beverages, dairy, food, food ingredients, meat and poultry, and packaging. Each market has not only a transaction platform, but also an online trade magazine. The executive responsible for the market is an 'editor'. Another startup GoCargo.com allows real-time pricing for cargo container space. Prior to the advent of the Internet, the market for cargo space was extremely disaggregated and worked primarily on the friendship ties between purchasers and suppliers. The system was human-interaction intensive, but inefficient because of the high search costs. Much of the human interaction was simple information transfer; this the computers can do. The real value humans added was in nonstandard transactions or unexpected events, i.e. times in which the system went 'nonlinear'. The creation of transparency and more perfect information flow creates the enormous efficiencies. The system removes the costs of producing and transferring paper – an important gain in itself. But, most important, when economic activities become apparent, they can be manipulated or tweaked to improve them.

The politics and power dimensions of these exchanges are becoming apparent as big buyers and sellers begin to create their own exchanges. Recently, General Motors, Ford and Daimler/Chrysler announced their intention to create a unified exchange where they plan to process about $240 billion in annual purchasing. It is predicted that the purchase-order processing fees will be reduced from $100 to $10. Initially, all three companies had planned to build separate sites, which would have created duplication and made the situation difficult for suppliers who would have to operate three separate billing systems. The Big Three automakers want their suppliers to use this site for purchasing from their own second-tier suppliers. The suppliers will be expected to pay a transaction fee for the use of the site. The launching of this site will dramatically reduce the potential for independent sites to be established. However, their control of the site and access to the information about supplier behavior and even the costs of suppliers' inputs will increase the power of the Big Three. Quite possibly, the exchange will create efficiencies for the value chain as a whole even while it increases the power of the assemblers (Dalton 2000).

The move by the Big Three is not rare. Big firms across a number of competitive, but oligopolized, sectors are considering whether they should allow the VerticalNet-type startups and capture the benefits of such exchanges. Increasingly, they are concluding, as did the Big Three, that it might be better to establish their own independent exchanges in which they hold an equity interest. In this way, rather than permit interlopers to capture the benefits from becoming electronic intermediaries, the market leaders can capture the benefits through their sponsored startup. The number of large firm driven B-to-B startups is rapidly increasing, and they may be able to outmaneuver the startups. The outcome is still uncertain.

DISCUSSION

The Internet is more than just another communications device. It is a newly developed space with the power to give rise to novel forms of human social interaction in almost any area of human endeavor, commercial or otherwise. By enabling certain types of activities, the Internet will impact consumer behavior, firm behavior, and industrial organization. The final configuration caused by the Internet is difficult to predict. This is because the features of the Internet interact in problematic and contradictory ways. Perhaps the most problematic question related to the economic impacts of the Internet regards market niche and firm formation. Will the Internet encourage the development of a vast collection of business types, marketing strategies, and market niches? Or will it lead to a small collection of mega marketers (such as portals), each dominating a particular product or service, and making the Internet seem like the proprietary online services it replaces? There are arguments to be made in favor of both possibilities.

At one level, the Internet can be conceptualized as a giant machine for reducing transaction costs. As we have seen, the Internet is being used in a myriad of ways to speed and enhance relations between consumers and firms. The Internet reduces physical and bureaucratic drag by drastically reducing the importance of location and the number of procedural steps requiring the direct intervention of firm operatives. For example, on the retail side the external costs associated with opening, maintaining, and staffing actual physical stores is reduced, and on the production/distribution side the time-related costs of generating and circulating paper is reduced. Startup costs are also greatly reduced in that all anyone really needs to begin selling things over the Internet is a connected server, or space on someone else's server. This has led to a proliferation of individuals and firms attempting to use the web for commercial purposes.

The power of the Internet, however, cannot be comprehended merely in terms of efficiency. As long as the Internet remains an essentially open platform, its ability to develop novel opportunities and novel approaches will likely remain high. It is possible that the simple dichotomy between big and small is as problematic as physical space in cyberspace. Indeed, perhaps the biggest error made by those companies who 'don't get' the Internet is the assumption that it is nothing more than a giant transaction cost reducer, or in Bill Gates's terms, a tool for friction-free capitalism. The most successful enterprises of the future will be based on the Internet's own paradigm, rather than paradigms borrowed from the past. Large-scale web enterprises which seem such inevitable successes today, could, in a few years' time, be hopelessly mired in their assumptions, rendered meaningless by the collective imagination and creativity of cyber explorers who are only beginning to learn the true contours of the new world they have created.

END NOTES

1. Care must be taken with our metaphorical extension of these characteristics of physical systems.
2. It was recently estimated that the Internet dataspace is growing at a rate of nearly 2 million web pages per day. A web page is 'a collection of information or web resources, intended to be rendered simultaneously, and identified by a single uniform resource identifier, or URI'.
3. It is interesting to note that the Internet is having another effect, namely the erasure of all history prior to the Internet. For example, university students no longer feel a need to go to the library. If it is not on the Internet, it does not exist!
4. Shapiro and Varian (1999) argue this can be integrated into traditional microeconomics.

However, their proof is dubious.

5. MP3 is a data compression standard that reduces the bandwidth necessary for the transmission of high-quality sound files.

6. MP3.com itself demonstrates communitarian power of the Internet through its creation of a large community of local and regional, and amateur and professional musicians, providing them with a very inexpensive way to access a potentially large audience, bypassing the formidable barriers to entry of the current corporate-dominated music industry.

7. There are some interesting geographical components to this as many of the new entrants are headquartered in Silicon Valley. The implications of this are a massive shift of economic power from other regions to the Silicon Valley.

8. Traditionally the travel agent retained 10 percent of the ticket cost. In late 1997 the airlines cut this to 8 percent or $50, whichever was smaller.

9. We do not underestimate the sometimes complicated task of preparing information. There clearly were nonmechanical components inherent in the activity.

(1) Network of intelligent machines:
Something really new (Deleuze & Guattari)

4

Towards a Location Theory of Distributed Computing and E-Commerce

MICHAEL F. GOODCHILD

University of California, Santa Barbara, CA, USA

INTRODUCTION

Humanity has always struggled with the impediments created by distance, through its ability to reduce or truncate communication, add cost and delays to the movement of goods, and limit the spaces of direct experience; and such impediments play an essential role in our ability to understand the uneven distribution of phenomena on the Earth's surface, and the various strategies that humans adopt to decide where to locate, whether it be for commerce, residence, employment, or recreation.

Each new innovation in transportation technology has helped to reduce the impediments associated with distance, and many such innovations have been hailed as having profound effects, whether they be in helping to reduce human misunderstandings through more frequent contact, or in enhancing trade and the assumed benefits of an integrated global economy. Terms such as 'time–space convergence' (Brunn and Leinbach 1991; Forer 1974; Janelle 1968) and 'the global village' date from transportation and communication innovations that occurred several decades ago. But of all of these stages the most recent is surely one of the most significant – the phenomenon of networked digital communication that has made it possible to communicate at close to the speed of light and at very low cost across a network that increasingly reaches every part of the planet, based on the Transmission Control Protocol/Internet Protocol (TCP/IP). Many prior innovations in transportation technology pale in comparison to the impact of the Internet. Today more than ever 'there is no more *there*, everywhere is *here*', to cite a recent advertising campaign of a major telecommunications company.

An obvious reaction to such notions is to believe that location is now irrelevant, at least as far as communication of information is concerned. Virtual and immersive technologies already allow environments to be represented in astonishing detail at remote sites, in effect transporting the individual across space without any of the impediments associated with moving matter. Yet we know that these environments are merely representations, and that there is no prospect of perfect representation – we can never build immersive environments that completely replace the human experience of being there, because representations can never fully replace the senses. Moreover, even digital information must exist somewhere, at some well-defined location on the network of hardware, software, and communication links. Pronouncements to the contrary, then, location in the digital world will be of great significance, and the impacts of digital technology on human society will be of profound importance.

Location theorists have long worked to understand and predict the locations of human activities. Many such efforts have been firmly grounded in economics, and have given primacy to transport cost as an explanatory factor. If the economic costs of transporting information have been reduced to near zero, it follows that predicting the locations of information-based activities will be increasingly difficult, since theories of location will have to give greater importance to factors that are less tangible, and more difficult to formalize and operationalize.

This chapter attempts to lay the groundwork for a theory of the location of computing, and more generally of activities that are associated with the information economy and e-commerce, and depend heavily on computing. The term *computing* is used throughout as shorthand for the acquisition, manipulation, storage, and analysis of information in digital form. The chapter is structured as follows. The next section briefly reviews classical location theory, which derives expectations about the locations adopted by the components of a system on the Earth's surface from statements about the behavior of actors controlling the components, and assumptions about relevant prior conditions. The subsequent section examines computing, and the degree to which it is influenced by location. This is followed by a discussion of the factors likely to influence the location of computing, given that the costs of overcoming distance are likely to be very small or nonexistent. The last major section of the chapter examines research libraries, as an instance of a system of physical facilities and associated services whose spatial structure will be profoundly influenced by the transition to a digital world, and as a case study for other types of facilities and services that are being similarly affected.

Any discussion of the location of computing must address the distinction between information that is and is not geographically referenced. We define geographically referenced information as having a defined geographic footprint, enclosing the area on the Earth's surface that is described by the information. Maps and Earth images clearly fit this definition, but so do certain books, reports, works of art, and other items that are associated in one way or another with some geographic area, and for which geographic location might form a basis of search. For example, footprints are essential to answer queries of the form 'what information is available about restaurants in Paris?' or 'who else wrote about the Bath of Jane Austen's time?'

CLASSICAL LOCATION THEORY

In classical location theory the locations of activities on the Earth's surface are established by decision-makers, who are assumed to behave according to certain rational principles. The central place theory of Christaller (1966) and Lösch (1954), for example, deals with the behaviors of consumers who occupy residential locations that are scattered over the surface, and entrepreneurs, who sell goods to consumers. Because entrepreneurs must invest in the high fixed costs of building stores, it is not possible to place stores at the locations of every consumer; instead, stores are established at a few central locations. In recent decades central place theory has been generalized to theories about the locations of all kinds of central services, in both the public and private sectors (Love *et al.* 1988; Mirchandani and Francis 1990). For example, location theory is now routinely used to locate such services as schools or fire stations, as well as retail stores. The classical location theory of Weber (1929) deals with the location of industrial activities, based on the costs of transporting inputs and outputs. A steel mill, for example, would locate at the least-cost point between its sources of supply (coal, iron ore, and limestone) and the markets for its products.

In classical central place theory the behavior of consumers and entrepreneurs is reduced to two simple premises: first, that consumers will travel to the central facility only if it is within some distance termed the range, and will otherwise opt not to purchase the service offered; and second, that entrepreneurs require some minimum number of consumers, known as the threshold, to continue offering the service. Much more complex models of both types of behavior have been proposed (see, for example, Berry and Parr 1988).

Clearly the predictions of the theory will be impacted if the range changes, which it can be expected to do following major innovations in transportation that reduce travel cost or increase travel speed. A consumer who had to walk to the nearest village might well be tempted to travel many times further to a larger town if able to do so at low cost by bus, and in time this change in behavior could drive stores in the village out of business. Similarly, local stores could be driven out of business if a sufficient number of consumers chose to make their requests via the Internet, and to receive goods via express delivery services. The costs of sending requests via the Internet, and shipping goods via express delivery services are both largely independent of distance, so there are no longer any incentives for entrepreneurs to locate close to consumers. Predictions will also change if the threshold changes, as a result of changed expenditure per consumer, or changes in the economies of scale of store operation or the costs of store establishment. A *category killer*, a large store operating at low margin in a market such as sporting goods, might be able to drive a number of smaller stores out of business because of its stronger scale economies, and even stronger scale economies may be associated with e-commerce operations like Amazon.com. Similarly, the predictions of Weber's industrial location theory will change if innovations in transportation result in different transport costs, or if technological innovations change the economies of scale of plant operation.

In addition to the effects of scale economies and transportation costs, locations will be influenced by prior conditions, for example concerning the availability and costs of land, or constraints on development imposed by planning agencies. Decisions will also be determined by variations in the spatial density of consumers, the presence of existing central facilities, competition between entrepreneurs, and a host of other factors. Historically, each new spatial organization has inherited the legacy of past spatial organizations, and many businesses have made their first forays into e-commerce from their existing locations, whether or not these are now optimal. The classical theorists made simplifying assumptions about many of these additional factors, and were able to derive simple predictions about the patterns of activities that would be found under such ideal circumstances. After much research in the 1960s had failed to find even vestiges of such simple patterns (Berry and Parr 1988), and after demonstrations that simple patterns would fail to emerge if the assumptions were even slightly untrue (e.g. Goodchild 1972), the emphasis in location research moved sharply away from prediction to the more normative framework of site selection.

LOCATION AND COMPUTING

Computers as Central Facilities

Computing is defined here as the set of processes associated with digital technology: the input, storage, transformation, communication, and output of digital information – in short, the core processes of e-commerce. In the earliest days of computing, in the 1950s, there were virtually no capabilities for long-distance communication of digital information at high speed, and all computing activities were therefore necessarily co-located. Input was created on paper tape or punched cards, fed into the computing system, stored there on magnetic tape until processed, and the results were output using mechanical printers. Large volumes of digital information had to be sent by mail on magnetic tape. The fixed costs of establishing a computing facility were extremely high, and as a result computing services could be offered only from a few locations where high levels of demand existed within short distances. Thus early computing resembled the classical model of a central facility providing a service to a dispersed population. The earliest computers were installed in universities, government laboratories, and large corporations where sufficient demand could be found to meet the facility's threshold, within the service's range. A major university computing center of this period might have served several thousand users with a single system. Users traveled to the facility to obtain its services, though in some instances input and output were sent by mail or express delivery. The solution of making the facility mobile, which is sometimes used in order to bring a larger number of consumers within range (as in mobile libraries or periodic markets, Bromley 1980) was not available because of the extreme weight and power requirements.

By the late 1960s the computing industry had adopted the communication technology of the telegraph industry, which allowed coded information to be transmitted over standard telephone wires at speeds of several hundred characters per second, using input and output devices similar to typewriters. Users could now process data that had been previously stored on a remote computer, and obtain simple results immediately, and more detailed results when paper output arrived by mail or express delivery. But long distance telephone charges were still a significant impediment to computing from truly remote sites, and users remained closely clustered around the computer that served them.

By the early 1980s the fixed costs of computers had begun to fall rapidly, first with the introduction of the 'superminicomputer', typified by the Digital VAX 11/750, and later with the personal computer, typified by the IBM PC and the Macintosh. The threshold demand for a computer's services fell by orders of magnitude, until it became possible to think of a *personal* computer, a system with a threshold of one user. Computing had now reached the equivalent of a retail system that provides a store for every consumer, instead of a few central stores, obviating any need for consumers to travel to obtain service. Today, approximately 40 percent of US households have at least one computer. The remaining 60 percent have decided either that the benefits of owning a computer are less than the costs, or that the costs of traveling to and using a central service, in a library or cybercafé or school, are less than the costs of owning.

Computers as Communication Media

The previous analysis was appropriate for the paradigm of computing that prevailed until the early 1990s. In this view, computing is a service that meets certain human needs: for example, the need to write letters and reports or to perform tax calculations. To a scientist, this view implies the ability to analyze, using statistical methods, or to model and predict. In all such cases the computer is performing much as a servant, responding to the user's commands and inputs with various forms of output, and exploiting its ability to perform arithmetic and logical operations much faster than a human. The computer is controlled by its users, whether these be a large group of researchers at a university, or a single user of a home PC, and everything stored in the computer has been placed there by its users.

In the late 1960s a small group of researchers began to explore the notion of connecting computers electronically, so that a user of one machine could access the services of another machine. If this could be done, it would allow software, data, and the results of analysis to be shared across machines. The ARPANet project, funded by the military Advanced Research Projects Agency, devised the necessary protocols for high-speed communication, which by the 1980s had been implemented over an extensive and rapidly growing network. The designers made the decision to adopt protocols that were largely independent of the specific communication technology, making it easy to take advantage of advances such as fiber-optic links that vastly increased the amount of information that could be communicated in a given period of time. By the early 1990s the network had evolved into the Internet, and communication speeds were reaching above a million bits per second.

By linking computers, it became possible to develop *client–server* computing, in which functions are shared between two computers. The user interacts directly with the client computer, entering commands and observing displayed output, while the much more powerful server computer might contain the database and the software used to access and process its contents. The network allows a client to switch quickly from one server to another, and supports the sending of information between any pair of computers. Client–server computing exploits the strong scale economies of computing technology, which make it cheaper to serve many users from a single machine, but to reserve certain operations associated with user interaction for local processing at the client machine because of the network's bandwidth limitations.

In this new environment the resources available to the user are those of the entire network, not merely the user's own client. The network has become in effect one massive computing resource, co-located with the user because of its high degree of connectivity and minimal transport costs. Moreover, the network has promoted entirely new applications that have little to do with data processing and much more to do with communication between users. Services such as electronic mail, chatrooms, push technologies, and electronic commerce had no equivalent in the prior paradigm, which provided only for communication between user and machine.

The measures of success of the old paradigm focused on quantity and quality of service: how much data could be processed, at what cost, and in what period of time? The new computing paradigm implies quite different measures, however. At the technical level it is important to know:

- the costs of communicating information;
- the delays or *latency* associated with communication;
- the reliability of the communication channel, in terms of the proportion of information lost, or the proportion of down time;
- the speed of the channel, or the amount of information communicated in a given time, in bits per second (bps).

But other more conceptual aspects may be equally or more important:

- whether the channel acts as a filter, bypassing only certain types of information;
- whether sender and receiver share the same systems of understanding (definitions of terms, language, coding systems);
- whether software systems are interoperable—capable of accepting and processing information from each other.

Computers as Augmentations of the Senses

Concepts of virtual reality and immersive environments are based on the notion that communication is an alternative to direct sensory perception, and the basis on which we learn about parts of the world that are beyond our immediate surroundings, either in space or in time. Thus the Virtual Field Course project (Dykes *et al.* 1999; Raper *et al.* 1999) sees technology as a substitute for the field experience that is capable not only of avoiding the high costs of travel, but also of representing information about distant environments in ways that help students to learn.

The concept of *augmented* reality is similarly based in the relationship between computer-based communication and sensory perception, but differs in that its purpose is to add to sensory perception. For example, a traveler equipped with a laptop might query a database to find information about his or her environment that is not directly available through sight, hearing, touch, or smell, such as the telephone numbers of businesses on the street that the traveler is driving along, or the availability of rooms in an adjacent hotel. This concept of augmenting the senses through technology has great commercial potential, as it allows the proximity of enterprises to be brought to the customer's attention even though they are not visible. In a commercial world in which all of the corner locations are already taken, such sensory augmentation can make other locations more attractive and competitive. Spohrer (1999) describes the World-Board project as exploring the use of devices that know where they are, and can present information accordingly. Reality can be augmented by devices that appear in the corner of the visual field—technology that is now commonly used on factory floors to allow workers to see the blueprints of structures they are assembling. Geographers might one day use such devices to display maps in the field, or data collected in prior visits. Reality can also be augmented by sound (Loomis *et al.* 1998).

The Four Locations of Computing

The previous sections allow us to identify four important types of locations in any computing task, contrasting with the two (consumer and entrepreneur) that are important in classical location theory:

- the location of the user, and of the device with which the user is interacting (the *user* location);
- the locations of the servers with which the device is interacting through a communication network (the *server* locations);
- the location of the recipient of communication from the user (the *receiver* location);
- the location that is described by the information which the user is processing (the *subject* location).

The third type of location will be relevant only for information communicated between people, and the fourth only for geographically referenced information, by definition.

In addition to these four, we should perhaps add various forms of intermediate stores, or caches. The academic's bookshelf contains books that are both more likely to be of interest than the average book in the research library, and also accessible in a shorter time. A researcher working on a given area might choose to retrieve a comprehensive collection of imagery for the area into a personal store, knowing that it could be retrieved from the personal store when needed much more rapidly than from the Internet as a whole, because of the time required to search the Internet, and the slow retrieval speed from remote stores compared with local ones, and could perhaps be retrieved using more specialized search mechanisms.

The user location will affect computing in many ways. First, it determines the nature of communication with the Internet. While the Internet is now accessible globally, the 'last mile' to the user's location can often reduce connectivity substantially. While two-way connections as fast as hundreds of megabytes per second may be available at certain campus and corporate locations, the average household one mile away and connected via the telephone network and acoustic modem may be restricted to 28.8 Kbps, and certain household communication technologies such as a digital subscriber line (DSL) provide much higher bandwidth to the user than from the user. A wireless modem operating via the cellular telephone network can provide access anywhere within cellular coverage, but at even lower communication rates. Finally, various forms of satellite-based communication extend coverage to virtually anywhere on the planet, but at much higher cost. Connectivity has become a complex function of location that is very different from the simple relationships between location and access to facilities that are assumed by classical location theories. If $C(x)$ denotes the connectivity available at location x, then the surface C has a very rugged appearance, with sharp gradients, contrasting sharply with the smooth isodapanes of Weberian theory. Moreover, if r denotes the amount a user is willing to pay for connectivity, per unit of time, then C is clearly also a function of r. Thus we write the bandwidth available at a location x at cost r as $C(x, r)$.

Suppose a user is located at distance d from a point of large bandwidth. In classical location theory the costs of overcoming this distance would be assumed to increase with d. But this seems not to be true of Internet connectivity, at least over certain important ranges of distance. The cost of a cellular connection is independent of distance within certain ranges, as is the cost of a connection through the conventional telephone network. On the other hand, very remote locations are likely to offer connections only at very high cost, so a slight negative correlation between connection cost and distance may be found at very large distances.

Second, user location affects computing through its impact on modes of interaction. At the desk the user expects to interact mostly through the keyboard, the screen, and the mouse pointing device. Laptops extend these modes to airline seats and other even less comfortable locations. But outdoors the standard laptop screen is too dim, battery power too limiting, and keyboards too prone to failure. Instead, interaction with devices outdoors is likely to be through pens and small hand-held devices, both of which restrict the flow of information between human and device. Again, ease of interaction varies over space in very complex ways, differing sharply between locations inside and outside the same building.

We assume that servers are connected to the network with large bandwidth. Murnion and Healey (1998) have shown that the bandwidth available between two locations on the network is only weakly dependent on the distance between them, and similarly that latency is only weakly correlated with distance. Because some countries exert control over Internet access, and access is generally less available in some countries, the bandwidth available between two servers tends to be unique to the countries in which they are located, that is, $B(s_1, s_2) = E[i(s_1), i(s_2)]$, where $i(s)$ is the country containing server s, E is the bandwidth available between servers in two countries, and s_1 and s_2 are the two servers. This structure induces a slight negative correlation between distance and bandwidth, because two servers further apart are more likely to be in different countries. There may also be similar effects if the two servers are located on different subnets that are relatively poorly connected to each other (see Wheeler and O'Kelly, 1999, for an analysis of the effects of network topology).

Now consider communication between a user and a receiver. The bandwidth available between them will be determined by their connectivity with the network, and also by whether they are located in different countries. The apparent connectivity between locations x_1 and x_2, using servers s_1 and s_2, and between individuals willing to pay r_1 and r_2 on connectivity will be determined by

$$\min[C(x_1, r_1), C(x_2, r_2), B(s_1, s_2)].$$

Distance between x_1 and x_2 will be a very poor predictor of this function.

Finally, any location theory of computing must consider the locational influences of the information that is being processed, if that information is geographically referenced. Goodchild (1997) has used the term *information of geographically determined interest* (IGDI) to refer to the property of geographically referenced information that interest in it is likely to vary, being highest within the footprint of the information. For example, a street map of New York City is clearly of greatest interest to a user in that city. The same effect may be reflected in variation in the spatial resolution of information: a user in New York might require a detailed street map, whereas users in Paris might be satisfied only with generalized information about New York. The concept of computers as augmentations of reality is clearly relevant here, with its emphasis on devices that access information about their immediate geographic environments.

Towards a Locationally Enabled Internet

Although the Internet is embedded in geographic space, its original conception had much to do with overcoming the impediments of geographic separation, at least within the USA. Domain names and IP addresses are assigned largely without reference to geographic location, although national domains predominate outside the USA, and state and local governments often adopt names that code geographic location (e.g. state.nc.us). Thus there is no obvious mapping between IP address and geographic location, no way to send e-mail to all users within a geographic region, and no way to readily identify the closest IP addresses. Search engines make it much easier to find World Wide Web (WWW) sites that have similar content than sites with similar locations. In short, the Internet's organizational mechanisms are predominantly functional rather than spatial.

A locationally enabled Internet would have significant benefits. A mandate from the US Congress will require cell phones to be locationally enabled by the end of 2001, so that the locations of emergencies reported using 911 from cell phones can be identified easily. As communications technologies become more and more integrated, the same capability in palmtops, laptops, and other devices connected via the Internet will be particularly useful. The concept of computers as augmentations of reality also implies an ability on the part of the device to determine its location, in order to present appropriate information. An Internet startup company, Go2 (http://www.go2on-line.com), is promoting a system of coding geographic locations as hierarchically ordered pairs of numerical digits, similar in appearance to IP addresses, to support the spatial organization of Internet information and services. Finally, there are obvious marketing benefits to enabling the sending of e-mail to addresses within a given geographic area.

FACTORS AFFECTING THE SPATIAL ORGANIZATION OF COMPUTING

As noted at the outset, although many of the impediments to interaction at a distance have been reduced or removed by the high connectivity of the Internet, nevertheless every bit of digital information must be located somewhere, and rational decisions must be made about where to compute. We will argue in this section that while economic factors have a relatively weak impact on the spatial organization of computing, other factors have risen in importance. Thus a location theory of computing and e-commerce is more likely to be driven by noneconomic factors than was classical location theory. This section examines those factors in detail.

Accessibility

Accessibility is a familiar concept in geographic research (Pirie 1979). Generally, a service is considered more accessible the closer it is, and a large grouping of services is considered more accessible than a small grouping. Thus the accessibility to a collection of services each of size z_i and distance d_i is often characterized by a summation:

$$V = \sum_i z_i/d_i$$

a measure termed *potential* (Warntz 1967).

As we have seen, however, distance is a poor indicator of accessibility to Internet services, and the comparative irrelevance of distance in ordering opportunities suggests that other approaches are needed. Consider a set of servers, S, and suppose that the needed service is known to be available from one of them, but that the user must search among them for the correct one. One interpretation of accessibility in this context is that it is measured by the inverse of the set size, $1/|S|$. If servers vary in magnitude, such that large servers are more likely to contain the service, then an appropriate measure is

$$V = \sum_i z_i$$

where z_i is the size of the ith server. In other words, the effect of making distance irrelevant to accessibility is captured by making all distances equal, and by redefining measures of accessibility based on set size rather than distance.

Geographic Footprints

Consider information related to a specific footprint. It has already been argued that interest in such information is highest within the footprint. In addition:

- an agency is more likely to be mandated to collect and disseminate such information the more closely its jurisdiction approximates the footprint;
- access to ground truth, for checking and maintaining information, is highest within the footprint.

Thus Goodchild (1997) concluded that geographically referenced information is most likely to be found on a server located in or near the footprint. Although these arguments are not as strong in the case of other types of information, it seems reasonable to assume that information of specialized interest will be more likely found on a server located where that specialized interest is densest, whether or not the information is geographically referenced. For example, special collections in research libraries tend to co-locate with research interests.

The collection-level metadata (CLM) of a server is defined as the description of its information contents. For servers containing geographically referenced information, CLM includes a description of geographic coverage. For example, Figure 4.1 shows the CLM of the geographically referenced information cataloged by the Alexandria Digital Library (http://alexandria.ucsb.edu). There is a clear concentration of information around the location of the library in Santa Barbara, but also much information about many other areas of the Earth's surface.

Ubiquity

In classical location theory the solutions to problems of location are almost always fixed: an entrepreneur seeks a permanent central location to serve a fixed residential population. The mobile service discussed earlier is an exception in that the entrepreneur adopts a roving location, and similar solutions are often suggested in locating ambulances, rescue vehicles, and other services.

Wireless services offer the potential for high mobility in computing, because they allow a user to remain connected while his or her location changes. The term *ubiquitous computing* is used to describe an environment in which it is possible to compute anywhere, and in which geographic location therefore imposes no constraints. Battery-powered devices, such as palmtops, laptops, and in-vehicle computing systems, offer enormous potential for such ubiquity. In the area of intelligent transportation systems (ITS), the ability to compute in a moving vehicle is essential for services that allow drivers to modify their travel plans based on real-time information on congestion. Similarly, there are many e-commerce applications such as search for hotels and restaurants where the ability to compute while moving is of substantial benefit.

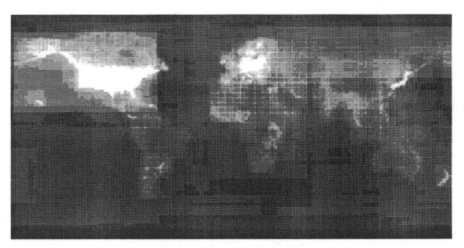

Figure 4.1 *An example of Collection-Level Metadata (CLM): the geographic distribution of data sets cataloged by the Alexandria Digital Library [http://alexandria.ucsb.edu]. Light shading indicates the highest density of data set footprints, and dark shading the lowest*

Links to Other Activities

Many applications of IT involve direct interaction between computing and other mechanical or physical operations. For example, precision agriculture (Wilson 1999) requires the presence of IT on the farm, and even on moving farm equipment. Similarly, many resource industries, such as forestry, require co-location of IT and the resource itself. In such cases the user location is determined by external factors, rather than by issues of computing per se.

In e-commerce, IT is often intimately associated with the handling of physical goods, including express delivery operations and warehouses, and the economics of transportation may therefore have an important effect on the location of computing. Image of place is also an important factor, as reflected in the way the catalog company Lands' End markets its location in rural Wisconsin.

Computing is well known as an instance of an activity that is largely *footloose*, meaning that its functions can be carried out virtually anywhere. Telecommuting, the practice of working at home by making use of high connectivity, is in many ways a product of advances in information technology, though many 'cottage industries' have a long history of allowing their workers to produce at home. Telecommuting allows workers to select locations based on amenity or other factors that have nothing necessarily to do with information technology, by making use of near-universal connectivity.

Face-to-face Communication

We have already noted that digital representations can never fully replicate the experience of the senses. Although user and receiver can often make use of very high connectivity, sufficient to support video for example, it seems that the Internet has done little to dampen the need for face-to-face meeting. Cities like New York, London, and Tokyo, which were built on the need for face-to-face business contact, continue to flourish, and tourism moves larger and larger numbers of people around the planet.

One of the major successes of the Internet has derived from its ability to transmit information independent of content, as universal packets that may contain anything from highly encrypted military signals, to e-mail text, to music. Thus it is possible to think of the Internet as a network whose ability to communicate information between people is limited only by bandwidth. But this raises an important question: are there fundamental limits to communication by electronic means that increased bandwidth will never solve? In a geographic context, it is common to note that certain sophisticated concepts such as 'sense of place' are much more difficult to express through digital channels than simple concepts such as distance, or location (Egenhofer *et al.* 1999). The issue appears intimately related to the more basic scientific issue of shared meaning: 'sense of place' is difficult to communicate, whether face-to-face or by digital means, because the sender and receiver do not enjoy shared understanding of the relevant terms.

Distance and Relevance

The need to communicate is driven by many factors, including the mutual acquaintance of sender and receiver, the likelihood of shared interests, and the existence of a common language. The probability that any two people are acquainted clearly declines with the distance between them, despite the Internet's ability to create widely scattered communities. Similarly, the probability that any two people share interest is negatively correlated with distance because many interests and information media have geographic footprints. Finally, the strongly positive spatial autocorrelation of language induces a negative correlation between distance and the probability of shared language. Thus while the impediments to communication may now be only weakly correlated with distance, the propensity to communicate is likely to continue to exhibit strong negative correlation. Wheeler and O'Kelly (1998) demonstrate this effect clearly with their analysis of Internet traffic to and from Ohio State University.

Attention

Media such as television acquire their value to commercial interests through their ability to capture attention remotely, augmenting the direct attention that is captured by outdoor advertising or direct mail. Similarly, the business case for Internet search engines, map services, and other popular applications is often based on the attention that such services can direct to advertising.

People are inevitably interested in their surroundings, and in issues of local importance. Moreover, people are more likely to avail themselves of services that require physical presence if these are close by. It follows that geographically enabled Internet services, such as directories to local businesses, are good ways to advertise other local services. The ability to target information based on the geographic location of the user and of the subject has substantial value in e-commerce, so much so that the term g-commerce is increasingly used to refer to Internet services that are geographically enabled.

Summary

This section has identified various ways in which geographic location impinges on computing. Despite the weak correlations between distance and economic cost associated with Internet communication, then, there are solid grounds for believing that location will continue to be a factor in computing, driving complex decision-making processes.

This discussion has led to the following conclusions regarding the four locations introduced earlier:

- Subject locations are likely to be strongly correlated with server locations, since georeferenced information is most likely to be found on a server within its footprint.
- Interactions between user and receiver locations are likely to be strongly negatively correlated with distance, despite the lack of impediments to communication, because of factors driving the need for two people to communicate.
- The costs associated with communicating currently show strong geographic patterns, due to the current lack of ubiquitous access, and affecting both user and receiver locations. Cost surfaces show very strong local gradients, and also strong variation between countries.

THE CASE OF THE RESEARCH LIBRARY

In this section we focus on a specific case – the location theory of the services provided by the research library. The arguments are based in large part on those presented by Goodchild (1997). The library is an immensely complex institution, and any discussion must inevitably simplify and even caricature it. This section focuses on the functions associated with the research library, as exemplified by the institutions that exist at all major research universities, as well as in some major cities and in national capitals. In addition it focuses on the functions such research libraries perform to provide information to their users, by acquiring and building collections, providing the mechanisms that allow users to search these collections for items of interest, allowing users to broaden their searches through browsing, and finally allowing users to retrieve information for use. Thus it ignores the functions of archiving, through which research libraries attempt to preserve knowledge that might otherwise be lost; as well as the provision of workspace, and direct involvement in the instructional programs of their host institutions.

Currently the number of such institutions is of order 10^4. Although the collections of the largest research libraries might include order 10^7 bound volumes, let us assume that the average collection is of order 10^6. If the average volume contains order 10^5 words of text, then a rough estimate of the number of words of text in the average research library might be 10^{11}, or order 10^{12} bytes if we allow 10 bytes per word. Thus the text content of an average research library could be captured in 1 Tb of digital storage. Today, 1 Tb file stores are readily available, and occupy a space comparable to a small room. Of course we have ignored in this calculation all of the nontext content of bound volumes, including photographs and maps, and all of the annotation that can be so valuable to historical research.

Suppose order 10^3 readers wish to access such a storage device using the Internet. If the average reader moves through text at 10 words per second, the rate at which the contents must be served is of order 10^5 bytes per second, a rate well within the capacity of large contemporary servers. In summary, it is well within the capacity of current technology to provide the information dissemination services of a research library online. To do so it would be necessary to digitize the entire collection, but this again is well within the capacity of current technology, and almost all new text arriving in the research library is already in digital form. Of course major issues of intellectual property are involved in this scenario, and much debate about them is occurring at this time (see, for example, National Research Council 1999a), but such issues are beyond the scope of this chapter.

Since its widespread inception in approximately 1993, the WWW has rapidly become a major source of information, in many ways competing with the research library. Students searching for information for papers will often use the WWW exclusively, despite the relative lack of mechanisms for ensuring quality or completeness in information discovered in this way. Much of this section derives from a comparison between the WWW and the system of research libraries, so it would be helpful at the outset to establish a consistent terminology.

The WWW currently accesses some order 10^7 servers or sites, distributed in most countries of the world. The geographic distribution of servers will be compared throughout the section to the geographic distribution of research libraries. The term 'collection' is used to describe both the set of volumes stored and cataloged by the research library, and the set of information objects accessible through a server. But while virtually all information in a research library is accessed in the form of bound volumes, there is no comparable control over the granularity of information accessible through a server.

Recent estimates put the total volume of information accessible through the WWW at order 1 Pb (10^{15} bytes), though this figure may be unreliable by at least one order of magnitude. Each information object is accessed through a universal resource locator (URL), which is roughly equivalent in function to the call number assigned to a volume by the research library. But while call numbers carry useful information about subject, a URL carries almost no reliable information to guide the user of the WWW in searching for specific content. Instead, searching on the WWW is facilitated by a number of search engines, sites that use a combination of manual and automated means to build catalogs of WWW content, or relations linking words that are indicative of content to URLs in which those words figure prominently. Nevertheless, current estimates place only 10 percent of WWW content within the reach of search engines, leaving 90 percent essentially uncataloged.

Although the position of a volume on the shelves of a research library is established by subject, it is the catalog that provides the primary search mechanism. All materials acquired by the library are identified by catalog staff using author, title, and a controlled vocabulary of subjects. In the pre-digital era, these three keys were used to build card catalogs, physical systems that arrayed volumes in alphabetical order using card records. Thus the library user could easily find volumes knowing either author, title, or subject. Without the catalog it would be very difficult to make effective use of a collection of a million volumes or more.

These three sort keys are unidimensional (each key provides a basis for a simple sort, usually in alphabetical order), finite (the number of possible key values is limited), and discrete (the key values are countable), all requirements for a system based on the physical sorting of cards. In an early stage of library automation, now almost complete, the contents of the cards were transferred to digital databases, allowing much faster searching and easier update, as well as remote access. Users were now able to determine whether a given volume was in the library without having to visit. More importantly, however, the digital catalog enabled new methods of search. Full titles could be searched for key words, a much more powerful mechanism than relying on a title card catalog that sorted only by each title's first word. But most importantly, a digital database can be searched on many keys at once, and on dimensions that are continuous and infinite rather than discrete and finite.

Location and time are two obvious candidates for such expanded search capabilities. Location is multidimensional (two-dimensional for most geographic applications), and there are an infinite number of possible locations on the Earth's surface. Thus physical catalogs could support search by location only if that property could be captured by a limited number of place names in the controlled subject vocabulary. A digital catalog can easily support search by latitude and longitude (for example, find all information relevant to the area between 120 and 121 degrees West, 34 and 35 degrees North). The term *geolibrary* has been coined to describe a library whose primary search key is geographic location (National Research Council 1999b).

Several instances of geolibraries have appeared in recent years to exploit the power of geographic location as a means of organizing information. The Alexandria Digital Library (ADL; http://alexandria.ucsb.edu) began as an effort to make the services of a major map and imagery collection available via the Internet, taking advantage of the new medium's ability to vastly increase their effective range. It rapidly became clear, however, that the ability to search by location could be applied to many other types of information that were not normally collected by map libraries, including books, photographs, and even pieces of music. ADL now contains over a million items, amounting to over 1 Tb of data, and includes a gazetteer with over 4 million entries to support users who must identify geographic locations by place name rather than by coordinates. Other instances of geolibraries include the US National Geospatial Data Clearinghouse (http://www.fgdc.gov) and Terraserver (http://www.terraserver.com).

Libraries as Central Services

In central facilities location theory each facility provides a similar service. Competition between facilities leads to a hierarchical pattern in which facilities at the same level in the hierarchy offer the same goods. Similarly, major research libraries attempt to provide similar services to their users, modified to some extent by the special or unique collections that many libraries possess, and by the varying disciplinary strengths of their supporting institutions. We can represent this in a simple model in which every library strives to acquire the largest possible proportion of all significant published works – the largest and most successful research libraries, such as the Library of Congress, succeed in acquiring the largest proportion, while all other research libraries fall below this proportion to varying degrees.

The system of scholarly publication of which libraries are a very important part relies on the economies of scale that exist in the processes of printing and publication. The unit cost of printing a book falls dramatically with the number printed, and the marginal cost of printing one copy of a popular book is far less than its retail value. These economies of scale make it inevitable that the publishing industry will favor popular books over less popular ones – and because libraries are designed as physical repositories of books, it follows that the information found in libraries will be information that is of interest to the largest number of people, and the product of the largest possible print runs. By contrast, material that is of limited interest tends to be expensive to acquire, and is only found in libraries that have specialized in that respective subject area.

Impacts of the Digital Transition

This system of research libraries has evolved within a particular technological environment, dominated by the printing press, metal shelves, card catalogs, etc. Arguably very little changed in this technological environment (a library built in the 17th century is still recognizable as such) until the advent of digital technology in the late 20th century. But over the past 20 years computerization has wrought very profound changes on this environment. Almost all information is now expressed in digital form at some point in its life, during the various stages of composition, editing, printing, dissemination, and distribution from the library. The transition to digital communication has brought enormous benefits, deriving from the economies of scale of a technology that is able to handle all kinds of information without respect to content, copy and transmit information almost instantaneously, and transform information through analysis at very low effort.

First, the digital transition has dramatically changed the parameters of the library as central facility. It has driven the effective range of the service much higher, since distance from the library is largely irrelevant if the institution is accessed and used via the Internet. Similarly the low costs of establishing and maintaining Internet servers have driven down the effective threshold, allowing services similar to those of a library to be provided at small scales by almost anyone.

Second, the digital transition has changed the economics of publishing, and made it feasible to publish information that is of comparatively low interest. An individual can create and publish a map or a paper using the digital technology of the WWW, even though it is clear that only a very small number of users are potentially interested. While the earlier environment favored publication of material of widespread interest, the much lower fixed costs of digital publication mean that publishing information of very limited interest can be economically viable.

Third, the digital transition has made new search mechanisms feasible. As noted earlier, it is now possible to think of searching library collections by location, by time, or by many new dimensions that were previously impossible. If a library is now able to support search by geographic location, it becomes a much more attractive repository for the kinds of information that are amenable to that particular search mechanism – specifically, information about places. Thus the development of new search mechanisms is likely to have a strong influence over the kinds of information we choose to store in libraries.

Towards a New Library Geography

The combined influence of these factors is likely to be profound, affecting the spatial organization of libraries, their contents, their base of users, and the services they provide. Thus the new geography of libraries and of geographic information is likely to be fundamentally different from the old. The arguments presented in the previous sections lead to the following conclusions regarding the future spatial organization of research library services, as illustrated in Figure 4.2:

1. Increased range will remove the need for a large number of research libraries with similar content. In principle a single large facility, such as the Library of Congress, could satisfy the entire need, though issues of reliability and institutional legacy will likely maintain some redundancy.
2. Decreased thresholds and lower fixed publication costs will make it economically possible to organize library services for small and highly specialized collections.
3. New search mechanisms, and the ability of digital systems to handle information independently of content, will permit the serving of information not normally found in traditional research libraries, including geographically referenced information.

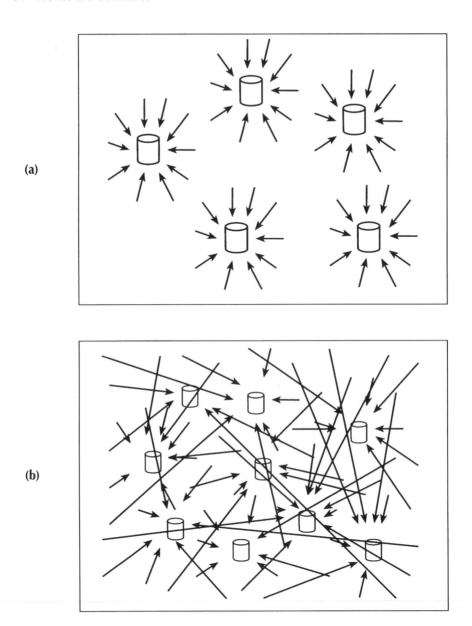

Figure 4.2   *Schematic rendering of the impacts of the digital transition on the distribution of research libraries. (a) The prior system, characterized by high threshold, short range, and uniform services, with substantial areas left unserved. (b) The emergent system of much lower thresholds, much larger ranges, universal access, and service diversification*

4. Specialized collections are most likely to be found on servers located close to the greatest number of interested users.

In summary, the current network of general-purpose research libraries that strive toward uniformity of services will be replaced by a much denser network of small collections, each representing some specialized field of interest, including geographically specialized interest, and thus striving to provide unique services. These changes are consistent with a system of central places that experience massive increases in range and massive decreases in threshold, and responds by diversifying its services. The potential for a geographic basis to that diversification suggests that the library of the future will place much more emphasis on geographically referenced information.

The transition to a new geography is likely to be slow. The existing system has many stakeholders, with economic as well as other interests in maintaining it. Changes will be incremental, as the existing system attempts to support new services by grafting them onto the old. In the long term, however, it will be impossible to sustain a system that reflects earlier realities, and is already badly out of agreement with underlying fundamentals.

CONCLUSIONS

In the early days of computing, the high fixed costs of hardware ensured a spatial organization that resembled many other instances of central facilities location, where a few facilities are located to serve a large and dispersed population. Institutions responded by creating computing centers with responsibility to install and run computing services. Through time, declines in fixed costs led to decentralization, and eventually to the personal computer, though central computing services were able to sustain themselves by emphasizing residual services of high fixed costs, such as consulting and standards setting.

The advent of high-bandwidth connectivity through the Internet has allowed users to obtain computing services from virtually anywhere on the planet, driving the effective range of computing to infinity. The impediments to computing no longer increase with distance from the nearest computer, since computers are virtually everywhere and connectivity is largely independent of distance. But the map of connectivity remains highly irregular, with massive variations in the bandwidth that can be obtained at a given location, and at a given cost.

The notion of computers as central facilities is consistent with the paradigm of computing that prevailed until the early 1990s. Since then, however, the integration of computers into a massive network has changed the paradigm, and given increasing weight to the communication function. Today, we tend to see the Internet as a means of communicating information between people, with processing as a way of adding value to what is communicated. This perspective gives much greater importance to the efficiencies of the communication channel, and to the value of digital communication vis-à-vis direct face-to-face communication.

From a geographic perspective, it is also important that computing be seen as a means of augmenting the experience of the senses, by providing access to stored representations of the user's surroundings. Such means are of great interest in geographic field work, since they allow direct connection from the field to previous work, representations of prior states, and computed predictions of future states. They require that devices be able to sense location, and respond accordingly. Other g-commerce services become possible when these capabilities are integrated with others, such as the ability to identify the geographic locations of IP addresses.

Because distance fails to impede Internet interaction as directly as it does travel, the spatial organization of computing and e-commerce will likely be influenced by a number of less tangible factors. These include the tendency of geographically referenced information to be served from locations in or near its footprint; linkages between information processing and other activities that are not so footloose; the perceived commercial value that is conferred through association with places; and the persistent tendency for human communication to be negatively correlated with distance.

The chapter used the case of the research library to examine the impacts that digital technology is likely to have on spatial organization. These impacts are likely to be profound, and to force a transition from a system of central facilities, providing essentially similar services to a much denser system of facilities providing highly specialized services, with locations determined largely by concentration of specialized user interest. However, they address only certain functions of research libraries, and examination of other functions may lead to somewhat different conclusions.

According to recent reports, fully 30 percent of recent expansion of the US economy is directly attributable to IT. This alone would be sufficient to justify detailed examination of the technology's impact on spatial organization. But IT also impacts other activities, through its effects on the costs of communication. Arguably, then, the impacts of IT on spatial organization will be comparable to those of major transportation innovations of the past, including canals and railroads, and may even exceed them in significance. As geographers, we should be in an excellent position to anticipate these impacts, and to explore their ramifications for communities, economies, and institutions.

ACKNOWLEDGEMENT

The National Center for Geographic Information and Analysis, the Alexandria Digital Library, and the Center for Spatially Integrated Social Science are supported by the National Science Foundation under cooperative agreements with, and grants to, the University of California, Santa Barbara.

a) loc~ ∫ computing: 2 types: len due to econ consideration
: other factors suggest loc~ still is imp. to computer use (79)

b) applic~ to research libys

5

Maybe the Death of Distance, but not the End of Geography: the Internet as a Network

EDWARD J. MALECKI and SEAN P. GORMAN

University of Florida, Gainsville, FL, USA

INTRODUCTION

The Internet is one of the most influential technologies of the 20th century. Its utilization of the convergence of computers and telecommunications technology has transformed industries, spurred a tremendous surge in investment, and sparked new business creation (Mandel 1999; Henry *et al.* 1999). The size and growth of the 'emerging digital economy' continue to surprise even experts (Henry *et al.* 1999). Rather than cite inevitably out-of-date figures, a number of web sites track the Internet, including www.nua.ie, www.openmarket.com, www.internet.org, and www.nw.com (Paltridge 1998b). An estimate of the Internet's size in January 2000 put it at 1 billion web pages (Inktomi Corporation 2000), an increase from 800 million pages in February 1999 (Lawrence and Giles 1999) and from 320 million pages only 15 months earlier (Lawrence and Giles 1998). The next generation of Internet Protocol (IPv6) has been designed to connect up to 1 trillion (1 000 000 000) networks (Huitema 1997). Its growth alone makes it easy to see why the Internet has received so much media attention and hype. In the process, the Internet has become one of the most pervasive technologies to impact society. It is one of the few recent 'general purpose technologies' included with such innovations as electricity, railroads, the automobile, and the wheel (Harris 1998).

The Internet is an interconnected network of hundreds of individual 'backbones', networks linking cities with fiber-optic cables operated by private companies and in some countries by government monopolies. These links are the routes by which the global Internet interconnects individual and business users with web content providers and e-commerce merchants. Residential and small business users generally connect via the local phone network or by cable modem, whereas large businesses, universities and other institutions often have 'direct connections' that bypass the telephone network and link directly to a metropolitan area network or to the fiber backbones. These technologies are the infrastructure level, together with Internet Protocol (IP) and World Wide Web (WWW) standards, necessary to enable the services, products and structures of e-commerce (Barua *et al.* 2000; Zwass 1999).

This chapter focuses on the backbone portion of the Internet's infrastructure in the USA. By examining the aggregation of individual networks, it is apparent that the Internet does not mean the 'end of geography' or the irrelevance of location. The remainder of this chapter reviews some of the emerging and still evolving features of the Internet's infrastructure, and presents empirical evidence of the uneven geographical structure of the Internet, focusing mainly on the USA. There are indications that the highest level of technological capability is increasingly concentrated at the upper echelon of the urban hierarchy. The emerging hierarchy of Internet connectivity is concentrated on a small set of urban nodes in the largest markets.

Internationally, geography has not been neutralized by the Internet. Seen globally, the Internet remains US-centric. Internet backbone capacity to the USA from Europe and Asia is far greater than that within Europe or Asia, with the result that up to 75 percent of traffic goes first through the USA, a portion of which is routed back to the region. ISDNet, a French ISP, exchanges traffic with France Telecom in the USA. Cukier (1999) believes the situation is not going to change any time soon, because the greatest increases in capacity continue to be on US-bound routes.

TELECOMMUNICATIONS AND THE FUTURE OF GEOGRAPHY

It is helpful to look at what the Internet is and from where it was conceived. First, the Internet is a new infrastructure – parallel but not identical to the public switched telephone network (PSTN). Inequalities, such as urban–rural contrasts, are not disappearing in the Internet age. The evolving telecommunications infrastructure suggests that inequalities will persist rather than vanish (Arnum and Conti 1998; Salomon 1996). Distance will not 'die' but will become less important as other forms of proximity become more significant (Duranton 1999). Second, the combination of spatial change and of temporal change, the collapsing of space and time, forces us to rethink and to accommodate – if not fully to accept – such concepts as 'Internet time' (Cusumano and Yoffie 1998), the 'space of flows' (Castells 1989, 1996), and a switch 'from places to spaces' (Kelly 1998). Third, the effects of the Internet are not unidirectional – homogenizing space, lowering agglomeration economies, facilitating mobility of services and of skilled labor, and reducing productivity differentials between large and small countries (Harris 1998). However, more discerning writers see the shades of gray: the Internet is both centralizing and decentralizing (Kitchin 1998b; Moss 1998; Peitchinis 1992). IT convergence has led to centralization of activities involving codified information; at the same time, facilitation of communication between sites has enabled decentralization of knowledge-creation activity – quite the reverse of what appeared to be the effect of information systems a decade ago (Hepworth 1989).

The new interconnectedness and interdependence of the world, linked in new ways by telecommunications and information technologies (IT), have changed perceptions of space, place, and time. There are divergent views about the effects of the new technologies. Pronouncements of the 'death of distance' (Cairncross 1997) and 'end of geography' (O'Brien 1992) have led to wide speculation across many disciplines that the IT and telecommunications revolution would be an end to the 'tyranny of geography' (Gillespie and Robins 1989). Wireless and satellite communications no longer require travel, or (in many cases) even cables or wires, making any place seem as near as any other. The technological optimists see the elimination of the 'scale disadvantage of small regions' (Harris 1998), the 'death of cities', and economic functions made 'more footloose' – all because electronic communications can replace face-to-face activities that formerly occurred in central locations (Harris 1998; OTA 1995). In sum, the argument goes, communication technologies have allowed population and economic activity not to be tied to geography and specific locations, but free to decentralize from the core to the periphery and still be connected by telecommunications networks (Abler 1970; Toffler 1980). The end of the 'tyranny of geography' is based on the assumption that telecommunications and IT technology are available equally or ubiquitously.

Geographers and other spatial analysts, on the other hand, tend to be aware that all technologies are 'inherently spatial' (Falk and Abler 1980; Gillespie and Robins 1989). Communication systems collapse, compress and shrink time and space and reduce, even if they do not fully eliminate (or annihilate), the effects of distance (Atkinson 1998; Brunn and Leinbach 1991; Castells 1989; Harvey 1989; Negroponte 1995). Space and time remain significant for two reasons: (1) cyberspace depends on some degree of real world spatial fixity, and (2) connections and their quality are unequally distributed. Location or conventional space will not become irrelevant because of cyberspace, and we will have to learn to deal with both traditional and cyber-geographies (Kitchin 1998a).

For example, large cities will not be replaced completely by cyberspace and 'tele-mediated' services, but will continue to be essential (Goddard and Richardson 1996; Graham 1997). Face-to-face contact is central to nonroutine and creative activities, while routine activities are made ever more locationally flexible (Coyle 1998; Gaspar and Glaeser 1998; Moss 1991). Telecommunications is both centralizing and decentralizing – not only decentralizing, as early accounts predicted – because of the importance of face-to-face contact (Hanson 1998; Kellerman 1993; Moss 1998). The result is that some cities have become 'the nodes or switching centers of this network-based economy' (Goddard 1991, p. 193). These cities are the nodes in the network of world cities (Graham 1999; Knox and Taylor 1995; Sassen 1994).

A second effect is that travel is increasing, rather than declining, among the 'islands' of competence within corporate networks, because telecommunications and travel are not substitutes (Lorentzon 1995). Claims that telecommunications substitute for transportation 'ignore the synergetic effects of improved communications on the need for face-to-face contacts that . . . cannot be handled on-line . . . [B]etter telecommunications services are likely to both encourage substitution away from transportation and induce new transportation demands' (Nicol 1985, p. 195). The complementarity between telecommunications and face-to-face communication has been a repeated research finding (De Meyer 1993; Gaspar and Glaeser 1998). Moreover, although telecommunications may reduce some travel for shopping trips, it necessitates greater use of transport for delivery of goods. While some observers continue to predict the 'death of distance' and the 'end of geography', overall there is little sign that this is actually taking place.

The telecommunications revolution is not only technological; it is also a result of widespread deregulation of the telecommunications industry, which has changed the landscape of telecommunications providers from one of state-subsidized monopolies into one of numerous private market competitors. Corporate needs have shaped telecommunications infrastructure – and its geography – and continue to influence the Internet (Langdale 1989; Schiller 1999). Privately operated networks in a competitive environment respond almost exclusively to market demand: where demand is greatest, telecommunications will be supplied. The result is a geographic bias that agglomerations of population and economic activity will be disproportionately supplied with telecommunications services and infrastructure (Gasper and Glaeser 1998; Moss 1998; Salomon 1996). If communication innovations bifurcate geography into a core and a periphery, the agglomeration of demand and of skilled labor reinforce the argument that communication technologies will not cause the 'end of geography' and decentralization of economic activity.

The Influence of Bandwidth

An important aspect of 'concentrating information-intensive activities' is the need for access to high-capacity bandwidth (Moss 1998, p. 113). Bandwidth is the term commonly used to designate transmission speed, measured in bits per second. A simple 'rule of thumb is that good video requires about a thousand times as much bandwidth as speech. A picture is truly worth a thousand words' (Mitchell 1995, p. 180, note 28). Broadband generally refers to transmission speeds above 64 kbps, the base normal speed of a voice call (Huston 1999a, pp. 160–71). Higher bandwidths generally are made possible by multiplexing the base line. In many regards bandwidth is what makes communications – and specifically Internet Protocol (IP) – networks different from transport networks. The limiting factor of IP networks is not distance, but the capacity of the bandwidth available on the network from one location to another. The amount of bandwidth available to locations (nodes) connected to communications networks is not equal, and there are resulting different (uneven) levels of service available to locations across space (Moss 1998). Mitchell (1995, p. 17) makes the point that:

> A low band-rate (bandwidth) connection puts you in the boonies, where the flow of information reduces to a trickle, where you cannot make so many connections, and where interactions are less intense. The bondage of bandwidth is replacing the tyranny of distance. . . . Since the high cost of bandwidth cable connections grows with distance, information hot-spots often develop around high-capacity data sources, much as oases grow up around wells.

The lack of empirical research on telecommunications networks that measures the agglomeration of advanced telecommunication services and infrastructure in metropolitan areas results in misleading conclusions. For example, Atkinson (1998, p. 140) says: 'Information technology on the WWW does not take place at the nodes, which are passive switching stations. Instead the action occurs at the extremities among dispersed users. . . . Nodes have little meaning.' To conclude that nodes are unimportant fails to take into consideration that bandwidth capacity is installed to serve major cities. This is nowhere more true than of producer services and other intangibles that can be provided via telecommunications, thereby having become an engine of economic growth (Beyers and Lindahl 1997; Wood and Marshall 1995). Information about the physical and software infrastructure is among the principal data needs for measuring and understanding the digital economy (Haltiwanger and Jarmin 2000).

THE PHYSICAL STRUCTURE OF THE INTERNET

Communications is often lumped with transportation as just another network and type of infrastructure. Transport networks and communications networks share the commonality that they are networks – composed of nodes and links – and they can be analyzed as such. Outside of network analysis, however, communications networks operate very differently from transportation networks. To 'rethink communications geography', as Hillis (1998, p. 558) suggests, requires understanding how communications networks operate and how information is carried; these are significantly different from the movements of tangible goods on transportation networks. The Internet greatly challenges a rethinking of the geography of communications.

The Internet commonly is depicted by Internet engineers as an amorphous cloud (Bailey 1997; Cavanagh 1998), ignoring the fact that it has a physical and hierarchical structure. The Internet is composed of a wide variety of small, medium, and large networks that all interconnect to different degrees to give the impression to the user of a single machine or system. Since the Internet is composed of a wide range of different networks, owners, operators and technologies, it relies on a structured hierarchy and protocol to operate. This hierarchy of network interconnectedness divides into five levels (Table 5.1). The first level is the network access points, or NAPs, the public hub points where all networks can exchange data. Data (such as e-mail) sent from a user of one Internet service provider (ISP) to a friend connected through a different ISP must be transferred between the two proprietary networks. This is done at NAPs or at other private transfer points in a process called peering; private peering will be dealt with in greater detail below.

Table 5.1   *The hierarchy of Internet network interconnections*

Level	Providers	Example
Level 1: Interconnect level	Network Access Points (NAPs), private peering points	Ameritech Chicago NAP
Level 2: National backbone	National backbone operators	SprintLink, MCI
Level 3: Regional networks	Regional network operators	Erols, Rocky Mountain Internet Inc. (RMII)
Level 4: ISPs	Internet Service Providers	DialNet, bright.net
Level 5: Users	Business and consumer market	

Level two is comprised of backbone providers, which make available transit services for data between city nodes across the USA and the world. If a Sprint user sends an e-mail from his computer in New York to a friend's computer in Washington, DC, the e-mail would traverse a Sprint backbone connecting these two cities. It is important to note that not all cities are directly connected, and perhaps not connected at all, by a given transit backbone.

Regional network providers comprise the third level of connection in the hierarchy. If the recipient of the Sprint e-mail in the Washington, DC, area, actually lives in Springfield, VA, the e-mail must 'hop' onto a regional network, such as Erols, in order to access the suburbs of northern Virginia. Small cities generally are not served directly by national backbone providers, necessitating this switch from backbone to regional network, or access through a point-of-presence (POP). Regional networks may be a dying breed as they are replaced by national providers, whether through their POPs or by acquisition of regional networks.

The ISP is the fourth level of service. Some consolidation is occurring in ISPs, but there remain over 3500 of them in the USA, generally operating either nationally or only in local areas (Greenstein 1998). The e-mail from New York would hop off the Erols regional network onto Springfield Net to be delivered through a dial-up analog modem to the user's home or business, the fifth level of the hierarchy. This example is hypothetical and simplified, but is typical of how the Internet operates as a network.

Downes and Greenstein (1998) and Greenstein (1998) have distinguished between national, regional, and local ISPs in the US on the basis of the number of counties in which they have a local telephone number or POP. Most of the nearly 12 000 POPs for 3531 ISPs are concentrated in the counties of large metropolitan statistical areas (MSAs). Of 3115 counties, 1742 do not have a single POP; at the other end of the hierarchy, 307 metropolitan counties each have over 10 ISPs with local POPs. The largest national ISP is America Online (AOL) with 22 million customers in early 2000, far ahead of all other ISPs.

NATIONAL BACKBONE PROVIDERS

For geographic analysis, the national backbone provider, or transit level, is perhaps the most interesting network level. The backbone providers furnish the infrastructure – the network of networks – in the Internet. The transit network connects city nodes and transports data across long-haul geographic distance. Forty-eight private providers currently operate the national backbone transit layer. These backbone providers include the Who's Who of telecommunication firms, such as AT&T, MCI WorldCom, Sprint, IBM, and Cable & Wireless, as well as several small start-up firms. Of the 48 national backbone operators in the US, just three firms – MCI WorldCom (which includes UUNET, ANS, and CompuServe), Cable & Wireless (which acquired MCI's backbone), and Sprint – together provide backbone service for 86 percent of all ISPs in the USA. ISPs frequently have redundant links, but 58 percent of ISPs link with MCI WorldCom (Boardwatch 1999). Details on the Internet network outside the US is sketchier, since not all firms provide detailed data on their operations. Among the largest is MCI WorldCom subsidiary,

UUNET Technologies, which has acquired several Internet providers in Canada and Europe.

Each backbone provider is called, in network terms, an autonomous system, or AS, which means that each operates independently of the other systems and sets its own policies and network structure. Huitema (1995) suggests that the national transit backbone providers are the best indicators of the geography of the Internet. Where the transit backbones are located has become increasingly important as technology develops. The fiber-optic (transit) backbone is the medium for point-to-point, long-haul backbone telecommunications service. Current projections set worldwide deployment of fiber-optic cable to reach 65.7 million kilometers (NSA 1998, p. 12).

PEERING

Only through peering do two networks interconnect to form what we know as the Internet. Peering is one of the most controversial aspects of today's Internet. Peering is the transfer of data between two proprietary networks, but it is also more than simply the transfer of data. It also allows a peer access to a network's routing tables and thereby its topology. Originally, peering was to be done mainly at the four network access points (NAPs) established by the National Science Foundation (NSF) in 1994 (in San Francisco, Chicago, New York – actually located in Pennsauken, NJ, just east of Philadelphia, and Washington). Several additional Internet exchange points serve as de facto NAPs: the Commercial Internet Exchange (CIX) in Santa Clara, two federal Internet exchanges (FIX-West in Mountain View, CA and FIX-East in College Park, MD), and three metropolitan area exchanges (MAEs) – in San Jose (MAE-West) and two in Washington (MAE-East and MAE-East +). Additional Tier-2 MAEs are Los Angeles (MAE-LA), MAE-Dallas, MAE-Chicago, and MAE-Houston (Rickard 1998; WorldCom 1999). The MAEs are owned and operated by Metropolitan Fiber Systems (MFS), which is now owned by MCI-WorldCom. The NAPs and de facto NAPs are shown in Figure 5.1. A number of other Internet traffic exchange (IX) points have been established, mainly to facilitate exchange between regional ISPs (Paltridge 1998a; TeleGeography, Inc. 1999). Three NAPs or de facto NAPs have the largest numbers of ISPs connected (MAE-East, Washington – 92, Chicago NAP – 83, and MAE-West, San Jose – 83). However, the fourth-ranked internationally is LINX, the London Internet Exchange, with 82 ISPs (TeleGeography, Inc. 1999).

The growth of the Internet in the early 1990s overburdened the NAPs, and resulted in packet loss rates as high as 20–30 percent (Cukier 1998, p. 6). Lost packets must be sent again, causing further congestion of both the network and the NAPs as well as delay for users (Paxson 1997). The four original NAPs, created and still subsidized by the US government through the National Science Foundation, allow any ISP to peer with other ISPs for a set monthly fee (currently $5000). This means that there is complete interconnectivity of the Internet, but only at the four NAPs. At the other exchange points, including MAEs, private peering dominates (Huston 1999b).

In private peering, two or more backbone providers, with their routers located in close proximity (usually in the same building) share data and routing tables (that list destinations on each network) between the two firms and no one else on the Internet

Figure 5.1   *Network access points (NAPs) and metropolitan area exchanges (MAEs)*

network. To provide the quality of service demanded by their business customers, large backbone providers began peering privately – sharing routing tables – with each other, initially through the private MAEs that operated parallel to the NAPs. Exodus Communications, Inc. (1999) makes the following generalization about peering: 'Peering relationships between Internet communications providers have become the most versatile solutions to readily resolve issues of packet loss and latency resulting from an overburdened global infrastructure.' Peering and financial settlements are the core of interconnection. An ISP must pay for knowledge of the routes that can take data onward or upstream in the Internet. 'Routing information is not uniformly available' (Huston 1999a, p. 561). Peer-to-peer bilateral interconnections are private peering points established between large firms that see themselves as equals (thus the term 'peers') (Bailey 1997).

Private peering has become so common that many backbone providers are leaving the NAPs entirely and are refusing to peer with smaller network providers. In order for small companies to get their data to a nonpeering provider, they must pay transit fees (financial settlement) to stay connected. The two-party contracts define a hierarchical bilateral interconnection, the most common interconnection model in today's Internet. In general, the large networks do not make public the terms of their peering arrangements, citing nondisclosure agreements – nor are they required to – keeping smaller ISP's at a disadvantage (Bailey 1997). ISPs that interconnect exchange routing entries that enable traffic. Upstream routes are learned from upstream ISPs, such as backbone providers, only as part of a transit service contract executed between the ISP and the upstream provider (Frieden 1998; Huston 1999a, pp. 555–6). An example of the advantage of private peering is the plan by Digital Entertainment Network to send streaming video, which requires continuous transmission, on the backbone of Exodus from one of two data centers (in California and Virginia). Transit to users would use private peering points instead of congested public peering points, staying on Exodus's backbone until the closest point to the end user (Frauenfelder 1999).

Hierarchical peering acknowledges the power wielded by the backbone providers. In early 1997, UUNET informed 14 ISPs that their peering agreements would be terminated, and that new bilateral transit agreements must be struck, or they would be disconnected from the Internet (Cuckier 1998; Paltridge 1998a). UUNET's market power is such that, when UUNET threatened disconnection from the Internet, it was considered a serious threat. As a result, there has been discussion of possible federal regulation of the peering process to avoid the monopoly power that backbone providers are able to wield (Farrell and Katz 1998; Rickard 1998). At present, however, the Internet remains largely unregulated (Kennard 1999; Leo and Huber 1997).

NETWORK ANALYSIS OF THE INTERNET'S GEOGRAPHY

Data on 40 proprietary networks are made available by the Cooperative Association for Internet Data Analysis (CAIDA), a public–private partnership between the Internet industry and the federal government formed to make Internet data available. The CAIDA data in early 1998 included 33 backbone networks: Agis, ANS, ATMnet, AT&T Worldnet, Cais.net, CERFnet, Compuserve Network Services, CRL Network Services, CWIX, DataXchange Network, DIGEX, EPOCH, Exodus, Genuity, GeoNet, GetNet, Global center, GoodNet, GridNet, IBM global Network, IDT, ipf.net, iStar Internet, InternetMCI, Nap.Net, Netrail, PSINet, Saavis Comm., Sprint IP, UUNet/MFS/WorldCom, Verio, and VisiNet. The CAIDA web site (at www.caida.org) contains a variety of information and tools for Internet data analysis, including Mapnet: A Macroscopic Internet Visualization Tool, which allows interactive viewing of multiple backbone provider maps. Backbone provider maps can also be found in Boardwatch's Directory of Internet Service Providers (Boardwatch 1999). The Boardwatch maps provide a second source of data on these networks, and are the source of most of the CAIDA backbone data.

The CAIDA raw backbone data from Mapnet, with cities as nodes and fiber-optic cables of each backbone as links, were put into a connectivity matrix for analysis using graph theoretical network measures. Network analysis is a well-established branch of mathematics (Harary *et al.* 1965). Analyses of transportation and telephone networks were common during the 1960s, and remain a part of transportation geography (Haggett and Chorley 1969; Kansky 1963; Taaffe *et al.* 1996). Network analysis is well suited to the study of flows in communication networks (Nystuen and Dacey 1961). Although analysts of telecommunications utilize the terminology of networks, sometimes little more is presented than the topology of the nodes and links within a corporate network (Hepworth 1990; Kellerman 1993). Thus, while the concept of a network remains central to the study of the geography of telecommunications, network analysis itself has been largely absent from recent accounts. Using a connectivity matrix for Internet analysis is even more suitable than for past transportation network analysis, since distance is essentially irrelevant. Among the few network analyses of the Internet is the work of Wheeler and O'Kelly (1999) and of Gorman and Malecki (2000).

In the CAIDA data set, the Internet connects 100 city nodes spanning the continental USA. The initial data, which listed city nodes at different levels of geographic accuracy, were aggregated into metropolitan statistical areas (MSAs) or consolidated metropolitan statistical areas (CMSAs). This aggregation also reflects the existence of metropolitan fiber rings that surround the majority of metropolitan areas. Packets routed to the city node hop onto a metropolitan fiber ring to be distributed throughout the urban area. The aggregation of the city nodes into MSAs and CMSAs reduced the number of nodes to 58 (Figure 5.2). These include most of the 46 MSAs with over 1 million population as well as 14 smaller MSAs.

CONNECTIVITY MATRICES

The interconnection of a multitude of proprietary networks into a global network of networks can be analyzed by means of the connectivity matrix, in which locations are placed in both a row i and a column j. The (i,j) cell is given a value of 1 if there is a connection between locations i and j, and a 0 otherwise. In analyzing the US domestic Internet, three different types of matrices will be utilized. These include a binary connectivity matrix, a weighted connectivity matrix to show link redundancy, and a bandwidth-weighted matrix to show differences in technological link capacity. Comparing our approach to that of Wheeler and O'Kelly (1999), our connectivity matrix is the same as their matrix C_1, and our weighted connectivity matrix is their T-matrix. Wheeler and O'Kelly did not analyze a bandwidth-weighted matrix. We do not analyze a shortest-path matrix, or D-matrix.

The binary connectivity matrix is the simplest, but it also gives the least accurate

Figure 5.2   *Metropolitan areas analyzed*

image of the state of the Internet network. A binary matrix indicates only whether or not there is a connection between two city nodes, and ignores the number of connections and the capacity of connections. However, a binary matrix identifies the pure network value of a node – is it connected or not – regardless of redundancy or technological level. When the Internet network, as characterized by the CAIDA data, is put into a binary connectivity matrix, a clear urban hierarchy results, with six urban areas connected to 20 or more cities: Washington, Chicago, San Francisco, Atlanta, New York, and Dallas–Fort Worth. Location quotients shown in Figure 5.3 indicate whether a city has less than the average connectivity (of the 58 MSAs studied) when compared to its population (value less than 1.0), or more than the US average (value greater than 1.0). Especially low values (e.g. less than 0.50) suggest that a place is very underserved by Internet backbones; Portland and Cincinnati are prominent examples. Likewise, values greater than 2.0 suggest that a city has more than twice the connectivity of the average city. Several cities have more than twice the number of binary connections expected for their population: Atlanta, Phoenix, Kansas City, Columbus, Albuquerque, Stockton, and Toledo (Figure 5.3). Of the 58 urban areas, 20 are poorly connected, having links on backbone networks to three or fewer cities.

The steady decrease in binary connectivity suggests a four-tier hierarchy. The top tier includes Washington, DC, Chicago, and San Francisco, each with direct connections to more than 25 of the 58 major urban areas. The second tier includes Atlanta, New York, and Dallas, each with connections to between 20 and 24 other urban areas. A noticeable gap appears after the top six cities, all of which connect to 20 or more other urban areas. The third tier includes 10 cities with direct connections to between 10 and 16 of the 58 areas: Phoenix, Seattle, Cleveland, Houston, Los Angeles, Minneapolis, Columbus, Kansas City, Denver, and Pittsburgh. The fourth tier includes 11 cities with links to between 6 and 9 of the 58 cities in our research. The four tiers

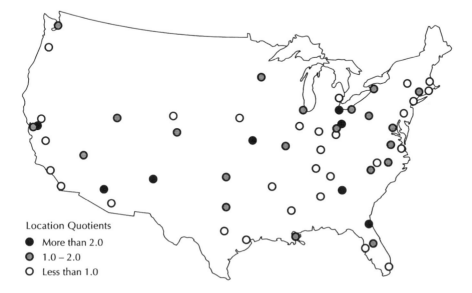

Figure 5.3 *Binary links (number of other urban areas connected on 33 internet backbones)*

include only 27 of the 58 urban areas; the other 31 MSAs have direct connections to no more than 5 (or less than 10 percent) of the other cities in that set. What is immediately apparent, then, is that not all places are equal on the Internet. A hierarchy exists within the network, with a small core of places being much better connected on the network. Chicago, as a central location in the network, is a very important access point connecting cities in the continental interior of the USA, while San Francisco and Washington, DC, serve as network hubs for each of their respective coasts. Finally, it becomes apparent that relatively few urban areas are pivotal locations on the Internet network. Only 27 areas have connections to 6 or more other areas. This could be considered the set of cities with adequate Internet connectivity; Moss and Townsend (1998) similarly delimit their analysis to just 21 urban areas, and Wheeler and O'Kelly (1999) list the top 30 cities, after which city accessibility falls off dramatically.

LINKS ON MORE THAN ONE BACKBONE: REDUNDANT LINKS

Binary matrices give only a partial picture of the importance of urban area nodes, since they do not incorporate the redundant paths that are vital to the network and congestion control. Redundant paths are a result of concern about congestion and of the fact that there are multiple providers, each of which has its own separate connections between cities. The high level of redundancy is particularly large among the top 18 city nodes, all of which have more than 30 links to other cities. Accounting for redundant paths between cities not only increases the number of connections but also changes the places of cities in the hierarchy. Even more important than the shifting of places is the greater difference between the core network cities and the periphery.

As the redundancy in the Internet is taken into account, the gap between the network core and network periphery grows. At the core, six metro areas dominate: Washington, DC, Chicago, Dallas–Fort Worth, San Francisco, New York, and Atlanta. Los Angeles, with 83 links to other cities, remains outside the set of core cities in the redundant-path matrix, if we consider only the areas with 125 or more links as core cities. All of the six core cities, except New York, rank higher than their rank in population, and only five cities (Washington, Dallas–Fort Worth, Atlanta, Kansas City, and Stockton) have more than twice the number of links expected for their population (Figure 5.4).

These redundant-path Internet accessibility levels are similar to those in Wheeler and O'Kelly's (1999) study of 31 Internet backbones in 1997 – with one exception. Because Wheeler and O'Kelly retained city nodes as they were identified by their sources, without aggregating them into MSAs and CMSAs, the San Francisco Bay area (San Francisco–Oakland–San Jose CMSA) loses its true position in the network of the Internet. San Jose, San Francisco, Palo Alto, and Santa Clara are listed (separately) among the 20 most accessible cities; the highest-ranked are San Jose at sixth and San Francisco at ninth. As a CMSA, the San Francisco CMSA ranks fourth, above its fifth-place ranking in population. Finally, having a NAP or an MAE is no guarantee of core status: while this is the case for Chicago, Washington, San Francisco, New York and Dallas, MAE locations Los Angeles and Houston rank only seventh and eighth, respectively, behind fourth-ranked Atlanta.

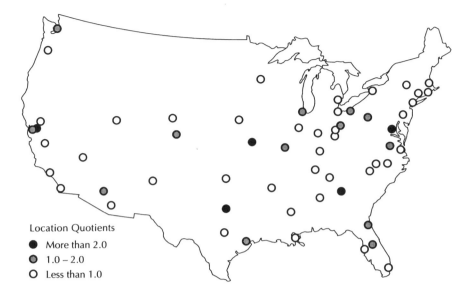

Figure 5.4 *Redundant links (number of other urban areas connected on 33 internet backbones)*

Moss and Townsend's (1998, 1999) analysis of 29 Internet backbones, using data from Boardwatch, also aggregated to MSA and CMSA. Their ranking of 'links to other metros' places San Francisco at the top, followed by Washington, Chicago, New York, Dallas, and Los Angeles. A consistent pattern in their analysis and in ours reported here is the fact that New York and Los Angeles fall well below their 1–2 ranking in CMSA population. Also noteworthy is the Boston area's rank of 15 (Moss and Townsend 1998), 11 (Wheeler and O'Kelly 1999), and 11 in this study of redundant connections – all of which are well below the area's number seven ranking in population. It appears that the Boston area's technological importance and Route 128 image has lagged in Internet technologies. Urban area population remains relevant in the location of Internet domain registrations. Both Moss and Townsend (1998) and Zook (2000) rank the New York region well in the lead in domain names, followed by San Francisco, Los Angeles, and Chicago.

Bandwidth and Internet Connectivity

The redundant-path matrix does not give a complete view of the domestic Internet, however. This matrix treats each connection equally, with a weight of one, and does not take into account levels of technology in various links. All fiber-optic links are not equal. The industry standard had been until recently 45 Mbps (DS-3) fiber-optic cables, but recent advances with asynchronous transfer mode (ATM) technology has allowed 155 Mbps (OC-3) and 622 Mbps (OC-12) lines. The bandwidth-weighted matrix further affects city rank and the core–periphery gap. The inclusion of bandwidth in the connectivity matrix segregates further the four-tier hierarchy seen in the binary matrix, and widens the gap between the core and the periphery of the network.

The top three tiers of the hierarchy stand out: (1) San Francisco, Chicago, and Washington are well ahead of other cities; (2) Dallas, New York, and Los Angeles comprise a second tier, (3) Denver, Atlanta, Seattle, and Philadelphia form a third group. All other MSAs are connected within the Internet at far lower levels of bandwidth. Cleveland, Houston, Boston, Kansas City, and Phoenix comprise a possible fourth tier, all with over 2000 Mbps in total bandwidth (Table 5.2).

The core cities in total bandwidth are a small group indeed. The most disproportionately served with Internet bandwidth, at more than twice the level for their population, are Washington, San Francisco, Dallas–Fort Worth, and Denver (Figure 5.5). No small cities such as Stockton or Toledo are included in the bandwidth-weighted core group, as occurred in the case of binary redundant-path connectivity (Figures 5.3 and 5.4). The diffusion of new technology has continued to reinforce the prominence of the core cities and to increase the gap between cities peripheral (in network terms) from cities in the core (Moss and Townsend 1999), similar to the market-oriented diffusion of the early US long-distance telephone competitors (Langdale 1983).

It should be noted that some CMSAs have a large number of links and considerable bandwidth connecting distinct nodes within the urban region. For example, the San Francisco CMSA has 3260 Mbps among its four nodes, Washington has 1852 Mbps, and New York has 1215. After these cities, multiple nodes are fewer, usually being

Table 5.2   Top US urban areas in total bandwidth of Internet backbone links

MSA or CMSA	Total bandwidth connecting to the 57 MSAs (Mbps)
San Francisco	14 924
Chicago	14 809
Washington–Baltimore	14 174
Dallas–Fort Worth	10 985
New York	9543
Los Angeles	9397
Denver	5942
Atlanta	5426
Seattle	5409
Philadelphia	5045
Cleveland	3461
Houston	3061
Boston	2785
Kansas City	2715
Phoenix	2565
Pittsburgh	1930
St Louis	1800
Columbus	1702
Miami–Ft Lauderdale	1575
Minneapolis–St Paul	1570
Austin	1522
San Diego	1495
Detroit	1309

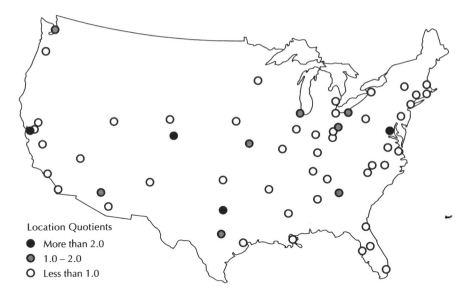

Figure 5.5 *Total bandwidth connecting to other urban areas*

private, rather than public, peering points; the next in line is Los Angeles with 415 Mbps.

The increasing concentration of Internet connectivity in the top-ranked cities can be seen in Figure 5.6, which compares the concentration of Internet links in the top-ranked, top five, and top 10 urban areas. Although the binary links are less concentrated in the leading cities than is population, both redundant links and bandwidth-weighted links are noticeably more concentrated in the top five and top 10 cities than is the population. Moreover, there is a steady increase in the degree of concentration as we consider more comprehensive measures of Internet connectivity (i.e. from binary links to redundant links to bandwidth-weighted links).

In some cases, a city's apparent lack of connectivity in binary terms (i.e. connections to few other cities) is compensated by additional (redundant) links or by additional

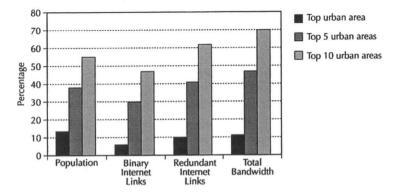

Figure 5.6 *Percentage of 58-city total accounted for by top-ranked urban areas*

bandwidth. Most of the cities near the top of Table 5.2 fall into this category, including Los Angeles. A few cities, however, show increasing weakness as the network measure reflects the greater detail of redundancy and bandwidth. Miami, Minneapolis, Phoenix, Pittsburgh, and Tampa all have poorer connectivity as redundant links and total bandwidth are taken into account. Overall, then, the set of well-connected cities becomes quite small when we consider above-average bandwidth connectivity.

Even the bandwidth-weighted matrix does not account for all the network characteristics that affect nodes in the network. Because of the routing-determined 'hop' nature of the Internet, direct connections do not tell the whole story. A data packet rarely goes from point A to point B in a single hop. As traceroutes invariably show, a packet takes multiple hops, often in a very circuitous path (Carl 1999; Rickard 1996). To get a clear picture of how cities operate as nodes in the network, it is necessary to know how they interrelate in multiple-hop routes. Matrix powering is a useful tool for Internet network analysis, as Wheeler and O'Kelly (1999) have shown. Powering matrices gives the number of two-hop, three-hop, and *n*-hop routes available between any two places. Further, values along the diagonal of the matrix are the total number of *n*-hop routes between a node and all other nodes. Any two points on the network will connect in no more than five hops (called the network's diameter).

The largest variation in city rankings occurs between the one-hop and two-hop path matrices. Why would the rank of city nodes be so greatly affected by the two-hop powering? In two hops, nodes are more restricted to accessing places that are geographically and topographically proximate. To get an idea of how geographic location was reflected in the powering, nodes were categorized into coastal and interior (Table 5.3).

In the ranking of the number of two-hop paths, New York replaces Chicago as second ranked, making coastal locations the top three nodes in the network. Interior, centrally located nodes follow, but coastal Los Angeles and Boston also rise in rank. Cities on the east and west coasts can be better-connected to each other than they are to the interior of the United States. The density of nodes on each coast makes a large number of the 58 places reachable through other nodes along either coast in only two hops. Centrally located nodes, by contrast, cannot reach as many coastal cities in only two hops. Individual backbone networks do not necessarily adhere to this or any other generalization. An analysis of the backbone of Cable & Wireless following its acquisition of MCI's network produced the highest rankings for nodes located in the US interior (Gorman and Malecki 2000). Moss and Townsend (1999) have found increasing concentration of Internet backbone infrastructure in several mid-sized but interior locations.

If cities on the the east and west coasts are nearer to each other on the Internet than to all but a few nodes in the US interior, the general pattern can be imagined as a type of 'coastal wrapping'. New York, Los Angeles, Washington, DC, and San Francisco are functionally and topographically nearer to each other than to most interior cities. The major exceptions in the interior are the major public and private NAPs: Chicago, Dallas, and Atlanta.

Finding the number of different routes from a city node also has implications for the ever-increasing problem of congestion on the Internet. Since time and distance are collapsed in telecommunication networks, taking longer paths to avoid congested

Table 5.3 *Comparison of urban areas by location*

MSA/CMSA	Number of 1-hop links	Location	MSA/CMSA	Number 2-hop links	Location
Washington, DC	195	Coastal	Washington, DC	2685	Coastal
Chicago	174	Interior	New York	2074	Coastal
San Francisco	148	Coastal	San Francisco	1948	Coastal
Dallas	143	Interior	Dallas	1941	Interior
New York	136	Coastal	Los Angeles	1775	Coastal
Atlanta	127	Interior	Chicago	1576	Interior
Los Angeles	107	Coastal	Atlanta	1565	Interior
Houston	68	Interior	Houston	1156	Interior
Seattle	59	Coastal	Boston	803	Coastal
Phoenix	53	Interior	Philadelphia	448	Coastal
Kansas City	52	Interior	Seattle	429	Coastal
Philadelphia	50	Coastal	Denver	418	Interior
Boston	49	Coastal	Norfolk	406	Coastal
Cleveland	46	Interior	Kansas City	346	Interior
Denver	46	Interior	St Louis	301	Interior
St Louis	39	Interior	Phoenix	289	Interior

routes is a feasible option, especially when the longer route has greater bandwidth (Cukier 1999). Nodes with higher rankings in the two-hop (and *n*-hop) matrices have more possible routes to other nodes throughout the network. The more routing options that a node has, the more likely that it will be able to avoid congestion and guarantee quality of service. The nodes and links in this research, and in all other network studies of the Internet to date, are unable to take into account the various peering agreements among the dozens of backbone operators. In addition, as Paxson (1997) has noted, packets tend to follow the same routes repeatedly even when utilizing public peering points such as the NAPs.

New technologies, such as the provider-based addressing hierarchy in IPv6, will allow users to select backbone providers on a per-connection basis, maybe even on a per-packet basis (Huitema 1997, p. 67). This, along with Internet 2 (http://www. Internet2.edu/) will allow routers to route traffic efficiently among a wide variety of providers and, to some extent, to avoid congested peering points. A second problem also is being overcome through technological developments (Paxson 1997). Internet engineers have developed and deployed adaptive routing systems that utilize load sharing to reduce congestion and increase quality of service. Although much attention focuses on congestion, Odlyzko (1998) estimates that there is only a 10–15 percent utilization rate of Internet backbones. This suggests that there is plenty of bandwidth available at the backbone level; it just has to be utilized efficiently. City nodes that are positioned to take advantage of increased routing alternatives will continue to enjoy the greatest economic and network growth associated with the Internet.

IMPLICATIONS AND CONCLUSIONS

Network analysis of the Internet illustrates both old and new geographies. The use of connectivity matrices underscores the Internet's strong spatial bias and hierarchical structure – one that differs from the conventional population-based hierarchy. In particular, New York and Los Angeles fall behind other cities, such as Washington and San Francisco, in an Internet-based hierarchy. Overall, however, the major cities in the economy are the major nodes on the Internet.

The Internet also has changed the meaning of distance, space, and the geographical significance of places (Adams 1997, 1998; Batty 1997; Kitchin 1998a,b). 'Wrapping' the east and west coasts onto each other is possible because distance is not measured in miles or kilometers on the Internet, but in topological distance of 'hops' along routes. The technologies of fiber optics make standard distance measurements irrelevant. Instead, proximity and distance depend on connectivity: the most connected places (Washington and New York in the east and San Francisco in the west) are, in effect, a cluster of proximate nodes. Their relative proximity accurately reflects Internet geography, although radically different from their absolute locations.

A related impact is the progressive peripheralization of small, less connected locations. The same connectivity that places Washington, DC, and San Francisco near one another also increasingly isolates locations at the periphery of the network. The problem for such places is that the growth of the Internet, increasing network size with more links and nodes, does not help their connectivity, but only makes them more distant, at least in part because of the global trend to increase connectivity on high traffic routes between, high-density urban areas rather than to connect smaller places (Cukier 1999).

The research reported here leaves unanswered the question of what causes some locations to be more connected than others. The prominence of the cities with NAPs and MAEs in the early (pre-1995) Internet (Figure 5.1) persists, to the disadvantage of cities outside that core network. In other cases, it is the 'cherry-picking' behavior identified by Graham and Marvin (1996) that attracts many backbone providers to the same locations. The agglomeration of connections also seems to be a response to the high-tech potential of the MSA as an indicator of demand for Internet connection. Thus, Seattle benefits from the presence of Microsoft. Other cities benefit by being intermediate opportunities on long-distance routes (Moss and Townsend 1999). It remains to be seen if private peering will alter the core set of best-connected cities. However, together with the introduction of differential quality of service, the best-connected cities may be those locations with private peering points – a group likely to include the core set of best-connected cities.

The backbone providers' domination since the commercialization of the Internet is based on profit as the primary impetus of network growth and resource allocation (Thomas and Wyatt 1999). The Internet is, and will continue to be, at higher levels of quality where money and demand justify. As this chapter has illustrated, that demand is in the large urban core cities of the network. The Internet is not a utopian public good available to everyone, whether core or periphery. Perhaps more importantly, it is not available at the same level of technology and service to all locations (Harpold 1999).

The disparity is further reinforced by the latest technological developments such as dense wave dimension multiplexing (DWDM), which allows networks to increase the bandwidth of fiber-optic cables by increasing the numbers of data-carrying light-waves that can be carried at once. A network can be upgraded in bandwidth merely by changing the amplifiers at the cable ends without the necessity to dig up or lay new cable. This may further reinforce the current network topology by making it increasingly costly to connect new locations. Rural, remote, and peripheral areas will lack connectivity – other than minimal, low-bandwidth connectivity – and the level of service/technology to be competitive in the marketplace. Such geographic disparities raise the possibility of increased government involvement in the operation of the network. The lack of any direction towards universal service and the current peering debacle could prove to be a growing incentive for government intervention (Farrell and Katz 1998; Frieden 1998).

The relative connectivity of cities on the Internet network is likely increasingly to affect business location, as businesses seek to locate in the locations where information can be most efficiently gathered and distributed. Businesses also can gain a significant economic advantage by establishing their corporate network through the public Internet instead of creating and maintaining a private network. Private networks can cost several times more than using the public Internet in monthly maintenance alone, in addition to the investment costs of creating the private network to begin with (Cavanagh 1998). This research into hierarchical and routing characteristics of city nodes on the Internet network is a preliminary attempt to analyze the available data at one point in time, already supplanted by new backbone installation, mergers, and acquisitions. Further research will be required before the Internet network's impacts can begin to be fully understood, and will be hard-pressed to keep up with the evolving Internet.

1) Network and. of Internet backbones

2) Peering

3) Inequalities between cities /DD.

4) End of distance P/meaning f distance

PART II

E–COMMERCE IN FIRM, REGIONAL, AND INTERNATIONAL CONTEXT

6

The Information Society, Japanese Style: Corner Stores as Hubs for E-Commerce Access

YUKO AOYAMA

Clark University, Worcester, MA, USA

INTRODUCTION

Japan is identified as a technologically advanced nation, with industries that are known for aggressively adopting information technologies (ITs) in production processes. It is somewhat surprising, therefore, that the technological adoption in consumption processes has lagged far behind that of other advanced economies.

Japan might be characterized as suffering from 'keyboard allergy', that is, it has one of the lowest household personal computer ownership rates among industrialized countries.[1] Only about 20 percent of Japanese households have computers, while almost 50 percent of American households have them (TCA 2000). This lack of household computer ownership has deeper implications and, for example, places Japan far behind the USA in terms of computer technology, and also behind Singapore, Hong Kong, and the European Union. In fact, Japan has not adopted the Internet as quickly as others, and ranks among the lowest ranking countries in number of Internet connections. Furthermore, even though Japan is the second largest economy, it has the lowest number of Internet domains per capita among OECD countries (Zook 2001). Also while the USA has 90 electronic commerce web sites per million people, Japan has only 10 per million.

The current delay in the adoption of IT by the Japanese economy and society has important theoretical as well as policy implications. The dominance of Internet technologies has reconfigured the global political economy during the past decade. The US economy is currently the forerunner of the digital economy, and sets the standards for the process of informatization. The US leadership has led to a single, technology-deterministic view in which electronic information transfer is assumed to be the global dominance of US technologies and business practices. Individual PC

ownership and Internet connectivity are considered to be the prerequisites in participating in the process of global technological revolution. This position of dominance
poses a number of challenges for policy makers in other countries, including Japan,
that cannot realistically and efficiently adopt the practices of the USA (Zysman 1999).
A result is that both in the realm of theory building as well as in policy making,
alternative and equally successful models of highly networked economies are being
sought for non-US economies.

This chapter examines obstacles and opportunities in Japan's adoption of e-commerce. By examining the institutional, social, and cultural factors that affect the
consumers' propensity to adopt e-commerce in their daily consumption activities, my
aim is to highlight the complexities of technological adoption and societal variance,
and also to suggest an alternative to the currently widespread technology-deterministic view of informationalism. In Japan, corner shops known as konbini (convenience
stores) are taking the lead in e-commerce adoption. This particular form of partnership
between traditional retailing and e-commerce provides a possibility for an entirely new
way of e-commerce adoption. Konbini chains serve as access points to e-commerce for
the majority of Japanese consumers who are without home-based Internet access. This
model suggests that efficiency derived from technological adoption can vary greatly
among societies.

E-COMMERCE, TECHNOLOGICAL ADOPTION, AND CONSUMER BEHAVIOR

Technological adoption is widely assumed to correlate with an economy's share of
'knowledge workers' who possess the skills to operate new technologies (Gregerman
1981; Cortada 1998). In part because of this assumption, Japan's delay in the informatization is particularly surprising, and sits uncomfortably with the conventional theories of technological diffusion. In a country where the number of industrial robots per
manufacturing worker is more than five times that of the USA,[2] what explains the
delay in technological adoption for an advanced economy with sufficient digital
literacy?

Issues and obstacles that Japanese consumers encounter in adopting e-commerce
reflect structural issues, both formal and informal, which influence their choice of
technologies. These reveal that the relationship between information economy (economic activities facilitated by ITs) and information society (social process of transformations facilitated by ITs) is hardly linear, and they are by no means closely correlated
with one another. The confusion between social and economic processes in analyzing
technological diffusion is attributed to initial works on post-industrialism (Touraine
1971; Bell 1973; Toffler 1980), which were presented as futuristic views that juxtaposed
simultaneous processes of both a social and economic nature. However, as stage
theories became increasingly insufficient in explaining the processes of technological
adoption, it became clear that societies differ in social processes even if similar
technologies are adopted. In the case of Japan, although its economy is highly
informational, its society can still be considered as noninformational (Castells and
Aoyama 1993, 1994; Castells 1996).

As in any technology, e-commerce adoption varies across society in terms of the degree and speed of adoption. Technologically, e-commerce can be understood as an application, rather than the platform technology itself (such as the PC or the LAN) (Jimeniz and Greenstein 1998). As a result, the development of e-commerce has been considered highly reliant on the performance of the platform technologies. Declines in price of the platform technology, or expanded capability (faster modem speed) may greatly affect the use of e-commerce. These applications (including e-commerce) are considered 'co-innovation', and are characterized by a high degree of dependence on the fate of the platform technologies for adoption and diffusion. As a result, the rate of growth for co-innovations is typically highly uncertain.

As an economic activity, e-commerce is a form of long-distance retailing in which the Internet serves as a medium of exchange.[3] The diffusion of e-commerce as an economic activity is a highly society-specific process because it involves changing consumer behavior. Although there is a general lack of literature on the comparative analysis of technological adoption and specifically its relationship to consumer behavior,[4] we can assume that technological adoption by consumers may also be delayed by a discontinuity between the previous and the future technological trajectory. Abundant literature exists on the importance of historical trajectory in technology adoption (Nelson and Winter 1982; David 1985; Arthur 1989). Then, technological adoptions, particularly those that involve consumer behavior, evolve through a certain technological trajectory, which is also determined largely by historically accumulated knowledge.

There are of course differences between businesses and consumers in the manner in which they respond to innovations. While businesses alter their behavior as a result of competitive pressures, consumers respond to the need for 'convenience'. In order to get the mainstream customers to alter their behavior, changes are best accepted when they are logical extensions of preexisting practices. In other words, continuous innovation is more likely to be accepted readily by consumers than discontinuous innovation (Moore 1999; Jimeniz and Greenstein 1998). If an innovation calls for a behavior alteration of a drastic degree, consumers may consider the learning cost too high for the convenience it offers. As I shall explain later, for the majority of Japanese consumers, e-commerce has not only been a largely foreign concept, but also a technologically cumbersome activity that requires significant additional investment and behavioral adjustments.

In part because e-commerce began as a dominantly North American phenomenon (OECD 1999) emanating from US-based economic and social institutions, it is this form of e-commerce which has been transmitted worldwide. As a result, it has been assumed that the diffusion of e-commerce is dependent on the particular set of institutional and infrastructural requirements observed in North America, namely, the diffusion of PCs, on-line network services, and the pool of knowledge workers with related skills (at minimum, the use of the keyboard, personal computers). For other industrialized economies with low ownership of PCs and low purchase of Internet services, instituting e-commerce would require a significant up-front cost. Strategies adopted by Japan's corner stores to grow as hubs of information networks and access points for consumers to access e-commerce are unique solution which not only circumvent issues of infrastructural requirements, but also positions e-commerce under continuous innovation with few behavioral changes required for Japan's aver-age consumers.

The US model of e-commerce adoption also assumes that access is considered to be unequally distributed between information 'haves' and 'have nots'. Such assumption is based on the notion that PC ownership, Internet access, and sufficient digital literacy are limited to the more affluent groups of the population. Most agree that Internet access is not uniformly distributed across the population in the USA, and those who engage in e-commerce are likely to be highly educated and from the high-income groups (Jiminez and Bernstein 1998; Wheeler *et al.* 2000). The Japanese model of e-commerce adoption, however, suggests an alternative model that offers access regardless of PC ownership, or income groups. It suggests that the technology and medium of e-commerce need not dictate nor promote further inequality, and the diffusion of e-commerce does not necessitate the consequence of social marginalization. As Castells (1999) noted, technologies are the medium of expression of already existing political forces and social hierarchy rather than the primary drivers of greater inequality.

OBSTACLES TO E-COMMERCE DEVELOPMENT IN JAPAN

MITI estimates that Japan's e-commerce development over the next several decades will continue to lag far behind that of the United States (Figure 6.1). The projected e-commerce figures for year 2003 for both the USA and Japan show that business-to-business transactions continue to dominate e-commerce, and the growth in business-to-consumer transactions are also expected to grow dramatically, although they will still comprise a fraction each of total commercial transactions. In Japan, business-to-consumer e-commerce is projected to occupy 1 percent of the total commercial transactions by 2003, and even for the USA the figure is 3.2 percent.

In Japan, the privatization of Internet access began as recently as 1995, and the

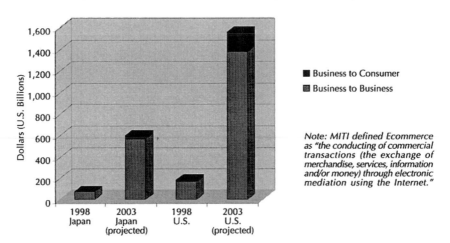

Figure 6.1   *E-Commerce in Japan and the United States (Ministry of International Trade and Industry, 1999a)*

commercial Internet service providers (ISPs) grew from 58 firms in July, 1995 to 3659 firms in July, 1999 (TCA 2000). Japan's Internet population was estimated to be 14 million in 1998, and is projected to grow to 58 million by year 2003 (DSA Analytics 1999; MITI 1999a). MITI is optimistic about the positive impact of e-commerce on the overall economy, as projections show a net job gain (MITI 1999b). While the estimate includes a 2.71 million job-loss in the next five years due to various economic restructuring pressures, it also projects 3.67 million jobs during the same period.[5] The job growth includes the estimated 1.05 million jobs to be created by e-commerce, and an additional 1.44 million jobs to be created because of the other types of IT use. The net gain of 130 000 jobs is expected in the Japanese economy, largely because of the introduction and the use of ITs and e-commerce. However, the net gain is not expected to occur until year 2004, but until then the Japanese labor market will undergo significant restructuring and net job loss.

The government's involvement in e-commerce promotion can be characterized as an old institutional framework (a MITI section taking a coordinating role, with multiple agencies and committees duplicating efforts) adopting new neo-liberalistic policies, emphasizing deregulations and public private partnerships. The Electronic Policy Division of the Machinery and Information Industries Bureau under the Ministry of International Trade and Industry (MITI) became the coordinating agency of various initiatives. The Japan Information Processing Development Center (JIPDC) conducts surveys and research on information technology adoption, and provides technological assistance, policy recommendations, and training. The JIPDC also functions jointly with numerous other agencies, such as the Center for the Informatization of Industry (CII) to provide guidelines to industry on the use of electronic data exchange, Research Institute for Advanced Information Technology (AITEC) for information dissemination, and Japan e-commerce and Central Academy of Information Agency (CAIT) for training (Figure 6.2).

The Committee for the Promotion of an Advanced Information and Telecommunications Society was set up in 1995 to deal with various policy-related issues, such as security and privacy issues, and the Y2K problems most recently. The Committee's three basic pillars are: (1) private sector-led initiatives, (2) deregulation, and (3) participation in a global regulatory framework building and setting up technology standards (Government of Japan 1998a). As part of this Committee, a working group on e-commerce was established to deal with issues that affect e-commerce development (Government of Japan 1998b).

Two primary criticisms on government involvement so far have been (1) deregulation measures that have been unable to keep pace with rapid technological changes, and (2) the emphasis on large firm-driven promotion of business-to-business e-commerce which has brought a neglect of business-to-consumer e-commerce and small startups. In response, the government has launched a campaign to generate digital economy entrepreneurs by providing financial assistance, training, and incubators. These initiatives so far have not fundamentally reconfigured Japan's established postwar business organizations. Indeed, OECD (1999) reports while business-to-business transactions can be promoted as a means of encouraging corporate efficiency, business-to-consumer transactions require a different set of drivers. These are the ease and cost of access, convenience, and the appeal of mass customization. While

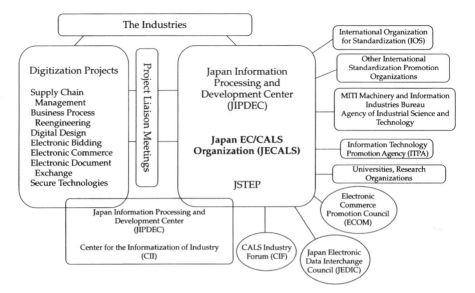

Figure 6.2 *Organizational chart of informatization promotion in Japan (JECAL.< http:// www.jecals.jipdec.or.jp/wwwE/organizationhtm.htm >)*

technologies are used to maximize profits and optimize efficiency on the production side, consumer behavior is historically shaped, socially instituted, and geographically determined. Therefore, issues that surround business-to-business e-commerce are similar across countries than are those associated with business to consumer e-commerce.

The stark contrast between the production and consumption uses of ITs observed in Japan suggests that technological adoption is not simply based on the skill levels of society. MITI's survey (1999c) showed that, unlike business-to-business e-commerce, the growth of business-to-consumer e-commerce use would be best facilitated by certain improvements. These are the availability of more user-friendly web-based transactions, better product information on the web, better search functions, greater availability of product reviews by other customers, improved payment security, and the competitive pricing of products/services offered. In the case of Japan's business-to-consumer e-commerce, the following obstacles were noted: cost of Internet access, security concerns for electronic payments, supporting business practices, urban spatial form, language barrier, and substitute technologies.

The Cost of Access

A comparison of Internet cost conducted by OECD shows that at off-peak times (when individuals are likely to use the Internet), access cost is estimated to be the highest in Japan (Figure 6.3). Cost of access is determined by (1) the cost of phone-calls and (2) an access fee to be paid to the Internet Access Provider (ISP). In terms of the cost of telephone calls, flat rate local calling areas did not exist in Japan until November, 1999. Nippon Telecom and Telegraph (NTT), which had a virtual monop-

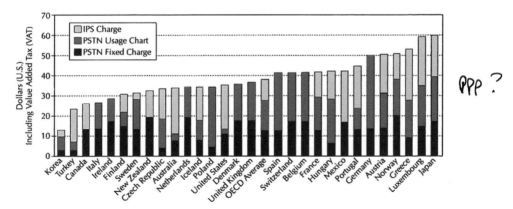

Figure 6.3   *OECD Internet access basket for 20 hours at off-peak times using discounted PSTN rates, 1999* (OECD. See < http://www.oecd.org/dsti/sti/it/cm/>)*

* Basket includes 20 one-hour calls. Off-peak is taken at 8 p.m. PSTN fixed charges include monthly rental fee and additional monthly charges related to discount plans, if applicable.

oly on Japan's communication industry for a long time, controlled prices particularly until 1986, when NTT was privatized and deregulation followed. This prompted the subsequent dramatic drop in telephone call costs. Before 1981, a three-minute daytime call between Tokyo and Osaka (approximately 300 miles apart) cost as much as 600 yen (roughly $1.81 per minute).[6] By 1988, the price went down to 400 yen ($1.20 per minute), then to 90 yen (27 cents per minute) 10 years later. As for the fees to ISPs, the cost structure used in Japan typically adds per-minute surcharges, in addition to the initial setup cost.[7] Combined with no flat-rate calling area, consumers would have to pay per minute fees to both the telephone company and the ISP.

In 1999, NTT began an experimental flat rate service for those customers (1) who already subscribe to home ISDN service, and (2) who are located in Tokyo's three wards (Shinjuku, Shibuya, and Ota) or Osaka's urban core (Chuo-ku, Kita-ku, and Suita-city). At 8000 yen (US$73) per month, this rate does not include the initial installation cost for ISDN lines, nor service charges by ISP. Thus, the cost of home Internet access in Japan can still be as high as four times the US average.

However, the current cost structure will most likely be altered in the near future. NTT's most recent announcement in early February revealed the plan to further slash the cost of the above-mentioned flat-rate service by one-fourth, starting May, 2000, and also expand the service to all 23-ward areas of Tokyo and all incorporated cities in Osaka Prefecture (*Nippon Keizai Shimbun* 2000a). The current trend toward lower access fees is likely to continue through heightened competition. Policy makers are eager to ensure that the cost structure will be equivalent to that of the USA in the near future. Thus, while the current rates are far higher than the USA, it is unlikely that the cost structure will continue to be an obstacle to the development of e-commerce in Japan over the long term.

Security Concerns and Cost of Electronic Payments

Although credit cards are held widely, credit card usage is limited in Japan, due to reluctance by both the sellers and buyers. Japan's retail sector is highly fragmented with numerous 'mom-and-pop' stores that operate on tiny margins, and they are particularly reluctant to cope with high percentage fees (5–7 percent) and delayed payments associated with the use of credit cards. In part because the retail sector has been highly regulated, protected, and is mostly localized, Japan's retail sector has not experienced the pressure to induce retail innovation, including the aggressive use of credit cards to lure more customers.

In comparison to American or European consumers, Japanese consumers are far more reluctant to use credit cards out of fear of fraud (*The Economist* 2000). Most purchases over the Internet still require bank transfers necessitating additional trips during bank hours (9:00 a.m.–3:00 p.m., weekdays) and paying for the bank transfer fee.[8] Consequently, e-commerce neither reduces trips to the commercial district nor does it provide convenience for customers.

Some Japanese scholars suggest that alternatives to credit cards are in development, such as prepaid cards which are now widely offered for pay-phones and for public transit. In late 1999, Sony announced the establishment of an e-bank, providing services that allow consumers to settle online transactions, pay public utility bills, and even get a small loan (Inoue 1999). With rapidly emerging new services and a growing number of entries by traditional giant manufacturers to the Internet business, a more efficient payment system will likely be developed in the near future.

Supporting Business Practices

In the USA long-distance retailing has a long and established tradition that began in the colonial period. Rural populations without direct retail access to nearby stores relied on mail order for tools, farm equipment, and household items. In 1872 Montgomery Ward was the first to publish the mail order catalog, a single sheet listing 150 items, with a money-back guarantee. The Sears Roebuck catalog in 1895 featured 532 pages of apparel, tools, and other merchandise, and quickly became a lifeline for people in remote areas (Gattuso 1993). In fact, Sears drew the majority of its revenue from the mail-order business until 1931, when the emphasis shifted to chain stores serving America's increasing urban population.[9] The US mail-order industries therefore have a century-long accumulation of experience and know-how in factual catalog writing (correspondence between catalog representation and actual products), product quality assurances, accuracy and timeliness in delivery (time-scheduling method), and institutionalized return and exchange policies. Such experience has arguably facilitated the transition to e-commerce, both on the supply side (retailers accumulated know-how in successful long-distance retailing), and on the demand side (consumer familiarity with long-distance retailing).

Unlike US consumers, the Japanese have had little experience in long-distance retailing in general. Although mail-order business also existed in Japan a century ago, it never took off as a major source of consumption. In a densely populated country where commercial zones with retail outlets have always been in easy reach, mail-order businesses did not compete well with traditional retailing. There were also a number of other obstacles, including cost of access (high telephone bills which made both sellers and buyers reluctant to bear the cost), and an inconvenient payment system. Even today, only 16 percent of payments are conducted using credit cards, as over half of mail-order purchases in Japan are done via postal/bank transfer (Dempster 1999). Lack of price competitiveness, and lack of consumer trust are additional obstacles. Retailing without store-fronts was, and still is, viewed in the same category as informal, door-to-door salesmen/women, who were viewed as having no community-base to earn customer trust (Kurozumi 1993).

In part due to the lack of experience in distance-retailing, the Japanese retail sector never developed the necessary institutional structure to support the development of e-commerce either. For example, a money-back guarantee is almost non-existent, and return and exchange policies are rarely taken at face value. Japan's department stores commonly refuse requests for try-ons by customers for certain clothing items, claiming such practice can damage the merchandise. The lack of these policies can easily lead already reluctant customers to become even more unwilling to engage in distance-retailing of any sort. Thus, just as in any distance-retailing, e-commerce requires a set of business practices that effectively support its development. Without it consumers are faced with a discontinuous innovation and adoption will either be delayed or will not take place.

Furthermore, different regional shopping practices may also have an effect on e-commerce use. In Osaka, where bargaining for the right price is still very much a part of shopping experience, e-commerce is seen as rigid and therefore not a cost-competitive option for consumers. In Tokyo, the practice of bargaining has disappeared and now consumers are far more willing to purchase goods online. The emergence of Internet auction sites in Japanese would provide consumers in Osaka an opportunity to bargain on the Internet. It is unclear whether Internet auctions would actually induce more e-commerce in Osaka. However, regional-specific shopping practices may eventually be accommodated by various new services.

Urban Spatial Patterns

Existing consumption patterns are shaped by spatial patterns of cities and retail outlets. In a country such as Japan, where cities are densely populated and real estate costs prohibitively high, decentralized ownership of small real estate lots have been serious obstacles for coordinated city planning. Since the Meiji Restoration in 1868, the Japanese government's overall priority on industrial policy and rapid industrialization over ensuring quality of life for urban residents further undermined infrastructure provision efforts to meet housing needs. The combined result was an inadequate public infrastructure development, private-sector driven housing development along the privately owned commuter trains, and small and fragmented residential lots.

These factors also led to the development of mixed land use patterns, with commercial districts in close proximity to residential areas. This spatial pattern, associated with contemporary dietary preferences for raw fish and fresh vegetables, shape Japan's dominant consumption patterns today. Japan's typical urban consumers shop small volumes far more frequently than their American counterparts. Commercial districts typically surround most train stations, and urban residents, who mostly rely on public transit to get to work, can easily pick up groceries and other daily necessities by dropping by stores near train/bus stations on the way home. Owing to limited housing size and high energy costs, most households did not own large-size refrigerators until recently, thus necessitating frequent restocking. Lack of storage space provided no incentives for customers to cater to large-volume, discount stores that are popular in the USA.[10] This traditional shopping pattern has implications for new ways to introduce e-commerce in Japan.

Language Barriers

Language barriers can affect the development of e-commerce both from the supply and demand side. While an Internet site can be accessed globally, language barriers still prevent an average consumer from accessing and using services in foreign languages. A recent survey conducted by an Asahi newspaper cited potential disputes as being one of the major barriers in using e-commerce offered by companies abroad. While dispute resolution experiences were rated largely positive (most customers stated that they eventually received the product and were satisfied), most described the time and efforts required to engage in international e-commerce as not worth repeating. Composing a series of e-mails describing a problem with an order in detail is not a task that any consumer would prefer to conduct in one's own language, but doing so in a foreign language is well beyond the willingness of average consumers in any country. The language issues would be resolved in time by the growth of multilingualism in cyberspace, particularly with multilingual and local customer support and the emergence of the Japanese e-commerce sites.

Substitute Technologies

Cellular telephones are the major competitor to the PC-based Internet access as the mode of communication. The number of traditional telephone line subscribers began declining for the first time in Japan, starting in 1998. The demand is being replaced by cellular telephones and ISDN (InfoCom Research 2000). Clearly, voice-only telephone is rapidly becoming the technology of the past in Japan. The penetration ratio of cellular telephones in Japan is higher than the USA, the UK, and Germany (Figure 6.4). As of January 2000, there were 55 million cell phone subscribers in Japan, which means one in two Japanese over age 10 owns a cell phone (Telecommunications Carriers Association 2000). Rather than purchasing a costly, space-hogging PC, the cell phone is a cost-effective, space-saving device, which all daily communication needs are met. Cell phones function not only as a telephone, but also as an address book, a watch, a pager, an answering machine, and an e-mail receiver/transmitter. Further, the keyboard allergy worked to the advantage of cell-phone adoption. Using Japanese characters with an English keyboard was already a complex task that required some practice, learning the trick of using the 10-number pads to type Japanese characters did not add much to the already complex input operation.

Cell phones have become a cultural icon of independence among Japan's college students. For Japan's many live-at-home urban college students, cell phones help protect privacy and are the important medium to stay in touch with friends without interference from parents and other family members. For students living away from home, cell phones have become a cost-effective alternative to traditional telephones,

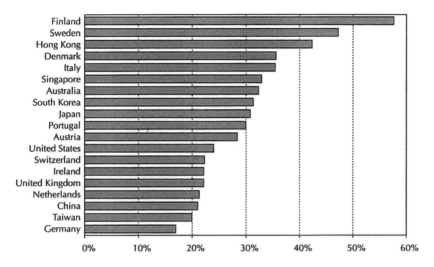

Figure 6.4 *Penetration ratio of cellular phones by number of contracts, January 1 1999. Source: Telecommunications Carriers Association 2000*

which are useful only when one is phoning from home. They also come with hefty initial setup costs (currently approximately US$700 per new line, excluding the cost of new wiring).[11] In fact, it has been predicted that if the current trend continues, cell phone subscriptions will exceed traditional telephone subscriptions by March 2000 (InfoCom).

With a widespread use of cellular telephones by Japanese consumers, companies are devising new means of providing easy access to the Internet via the cellular telephone. Japan's previously government-owned NTT's new service called 'i-mode', launched in February 1999, is a prime example. The service provides Internet access via its own i-mode center, through which customers can not only exchange e-mails, but also offers online information services (news, weather, transportation, city information, apartment rentals), banking functions (payments, balance information, trading, life insurance purchase), database access (restaurant search, dictionary, recipes, telephone number search), as well as entertainment (games, fortune tellers, karaoke, radio). Seventeen months later, the service had attracted over 10 million subscribers. Other companies are entering the market with technologies to display color and graphic images on the tiny window on cell phones. Thus, Japan's consumers may have had a slow start in PC purchase, but they have been fast adopting other means of ITs. And, with the integration of cell phone technology and the Internet, this situation might quickly change in the future.

ALTERNATIVE DEVELOPMENT OF THE DIGITAL ECONOMY: CONVENIENCE STORES AS NODES OF E-COMMERCE ACCESS

The recent and unlikely partnership between e-commerce and convenience stores in Japan has functioned to resolve three major obstacles for e-commerce diffusion: online access, distribution, and e-payments for goods. With convenience stores almost at

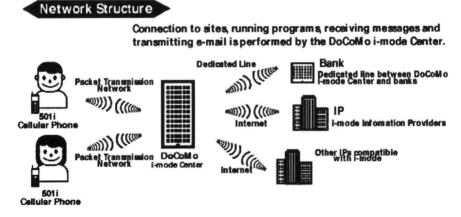

Figure 6.5   *The network structure of i-mode operations [http://www.nttdocomo.com/ser.htm]*

every major urban corner, consumers can use e-commerce without purchasing PCs or using credit cards. This mode of retail innovation suggests a possibility for an alternative model of social informatization. Rather than having to connect every household with high-speed networks, Japan has, perhaps inadvertently, adopted a neighborhood approach where Internet access is shared by area residents, using convenience stores as nodal points. E-commerce is being developed as a strategy to generate additional demand by Japan's convenience store chains.

Convenience stores became part of daily life for many Japanese consumers only in the past few decades. They are typically open 24 hours a day, 7 days a week, average around 100 square meters (1076 square feet) in size, and most are franchised operations. Convenience stores are not just the trendsetter in Japan's otherwise highly inefficient distribution sector, but also have become a trailblazer in adopting information technologies, thereby deeply affecting consumption patterns by aggressively making use of the information networks. The combination of convenience stores with e-commerce delivery capabilities has eliminated society-specific constraints. This model has resulted in opportunities by shifting what used to be a 'discontinuous innovation' for Japanese consumers to a 'continuous innovation'.

A walk around any major Japanese city today gives one the impression that every major street corner is occupied by a convenience store. Examples shown in Figure 6.6 support such observation: the convenience stores are ubiquitous, both in office/ commercial districts near the terminal train station (JR Yokohama Station), as well as in high-density urban neighborhoods (Ohta-Ward, Tokyo). As these areas indicate, 16 or 17 convenience stores are located within almost any randomly selected 1 square kilometer block (0.3861 square mile). For urban residents, this means that a trip to the nearest convenience store is shorter than a trip to the nearest train/subway station.

Tokyo's 23 wards, which together form the urban core, are the location of nearly 4000 convenience stores. Ohta-Ward alone, which is roughly one-third the size of Washington, DC, has more than 250 convenience stores, while Washington, DC, has just 83. There are 1182 convenience stores in the city of Yokohama, which is about three times the size of Washington, DC. Yokohama, the nation's second most

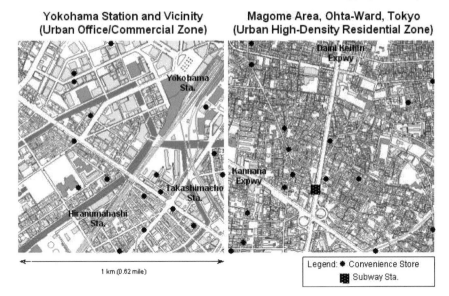

Yokohama Station and Vicinity
(Urban Office/Commercial Zone)

Magome Area, Ohta-Ward, Tokyo
(Urban High-Density Residential Zone)

1 km (0.62 mile)

Legend: ◆ Convenience Store
▦ Subway Sta.

Figure 6.6 *Convenience store locations, 1999. Source: Based on information provided by NTT Townpage, 1999–2000. Map reproduced by permission from Zenrin Co. Ltd*

populous city, also serves as a satellite business district, high-tech manufacturing area, and a residential suburb of Tokyo.

In terms of store density, Yokohama has seven convenience stores per square mile, while Washington, DC, has roughly 1.4 stores per square mile (Table 6.1). There are 16 convenience stores per square mile for Yokohama's central business district and Tokyo's ward areas. There are as many as 32 convenience stores per square mile for Tokyo's central business district (Chuo-Ward in this case). Even taking the different population densities into account (e.g. Tokyo's ward area is on average four times as dense as Washington, DC), the convenience stores are far more ubiquitous in Japan. There is one convenience store for over 6000 people in Washington, DC, as opposed to one for 2000–3000 people in urban Japan.

Factors Behind Success of Convenience Stores in Japan

Convenience stores began appearing in Japan in 1969, but grew rapidly only after 1973, when Ito-Yokado acquired a license from Southland (US) to open Seven-Eleven stores in Japan. Other retail chains followed suit and established their own franchises of convenience stores (Table 6.2). Subsequently, the number of convenience stores grew dramatically from 500 in 1973 to 36 631 in 1997. Despite depressed consumer demand through much of the 1990s, during which the total number of establishments in the retail sector declined in Japan, the number of convenience stores actually grew by 24 percent (MITI 1999d). Today, roughly one in five supermarkets in Japan is classified as a convenience store.[12] In terms of sales, convenience stores grew by 67.1 percent between 1991 and 1997, an impressive rate of growth when the total growth for the retail sector was at 3.8 percent.

Table 6.1 *Comparison of convenience store densities, 1999*

	Tokyo (23 wards)	Ohta-Ward	Yokohama	Washington DC
Area (square miles)	237.9	23.0	168.3	61.4
Population	8 052 396	641 523	3 351 612	519 000*
Population density (per sq. mile)	33 848	27 892	19 915	8453
Number of convenience stores	3856	258	1182	83**
Convenience Stores per sq. mile	16.21	11.22	7.02	1.35
Area average CBD***	31.64	—	16.00	—
Population per convenience store	2088	2487	2836	6253

*Population for Washington DC is an estimate for July 1, 1999.
**Number of convenience stores for Washington, DC reflects 1997 data.
***CBDs used for this table are: Chuo-Ward for Tokyo, and Nishi-Ward was used for Yokohama.
(US Economic Census of Retail Trade 1997; US Census Population Estimates 1999; Tokyo Prefecture 1999; Ministry of Construction Area Survey 1994; Tokyo Keizai 1999; NTT Town Page 1999–2000).

Table 6.2 *Major convenience store chains in Japan*

Name	Owner	Year established	Number of stores*	Sales (in billions) Yen	Sales (in billions) US dollars**
Seven Eleven Japan	Ito Yokado	1973	7924	1950	18.1
Lawson	Daiei	1975	7016	1157	10.8
Family Mart	Seibu	1981	6799	758	7.0
Circle K	Uni	1984	2530	407	3.8
Sunkus	Uni	1980	2371	410	3.8
Daily Yamazaki	Yamazaki	1977	2872	381	3.5
Mini Stop	Jusco	1980	1343	173	1.6
am/pm	Japan Energy	1990	1003	139	1.3

*Dates vary from April 1998 to October 1999.
**US dollar amounts are based on the conversion rate for February 2000.
(Compiled with data provided by official web pages of companies, 1999.)

While most are franchise operations, the top three chains control nearly three-fifths of the convenience store establishments in Japan (Jutaku Shimpo 1999). Japan's largest convenience store chain, Seven-Eleven Japan, franchises nearly 8000 stores nationwide (almost one out of every five stores), with the estimated annual sales of US$2 trillion (1999 fiscal year). This equals 31 percent of the total net sales of convenience stores in Japan. The firm's market value in 1999 exceeded that of Walgreens and Safeway, both major US retail chains (Seven-Eleven Japan, Annual Report 1999b, estimated using the exchange rate on March 31, 1999). Seven-Eleven Japan has been so successful that, together with its parent firm Ito-Yokado, it bailed out the original licenser Southland from bankruptcy in 1991, earning a 70 percent share (Kotabe 1995; Bernstein 1997).

The major reasons for the success of convenience stores in Japan is partly structural; they were created in part by the regulatory framework, and in part due to their innovative strategies (Bernstein 1997; Hashimoto 1999). In 1973, the national Large

Scale Retail Law was enacted to protect small retailers by restricting hours of operation for most large-scale grocery stores. Additionally, prefectures restrict floor size of new grocery stores. Although the Large Scale Retail Law was designed to protect Japan's numerous mom-and-pop stores and preserve inner city commercial districts, it instead provided incentives for large retailers to seek loopholes. Large retailers turned to franchising as an option, which effectively combined large-scale capital with small-size, independently owned operations that are in reality managed and controlled by large capital.[13]

Convenience stores have been characterized by their focused locational strategies, unique marketing strategies, and investment in IT infrastructure that resulted in new service delivery far beyond initial intentions. The locational strategies of Japan's convenience stores were decidedly urban: the chains initially focused on opening stores in close proximity to each other in Tokyo and Osaka. This was done in order to maximize distribution efficiency and minimize delivery routes. Reduction in delivery routes was achieved by bundling product delivery by required storage temperatures. For example, Seven-Eleven Japan currently owns 250 distribution centers, which are classified by product's storage temperatures: 55 centers for refrigerated items (at $5\,°C$), 56 centers for rice dishes (at $20\,°C$), 47 centers for frozen items (at $-20\,°C$), and 92 centers for miscellaneous temperature-insensitive items such as beverages and canned food items. Through restructuring the delivery routes, Seven-Eleven Japan reduced the daily restocking trips per store from an average of 70 in 1974 to nine by the early 1990s, thereby dramatically reducing delivery costs (Seven-Eleven Japan Annual Report 1999b).

The smaller floor space of convenience stores enabled them to locate stores strategically in high-density urban areas, thus providing advantages over supermarkets in terms of access. This strategy was also better suited to the consumer behavior and shopping patterns in Japan, as described earlier. Since urban residents are more likely to walk or bicycle to a nearby grocery store or drop by a store after work en route from a nearby train or subway station, occupying strategic urban locations is the single most important factor for successful retail performance in Japan. Today, an average Tokyo commuter is estimated to walk past three convenience stores on his/her way to work (Landers 1999). Although suburban supermarkets are also thriving in Japan, small stores still dominate the retail sector in Japan, which still occupy 55 percent of the total food and beverage market (MITI 1999d).

In addition to the implementation of a deliberate locational strategy, convenience stores employed a strategic marketing focus. Unlike convenience stores in the USA, which rely heavily on the sale of gasoline, alcohol, and tobacco products, Japan's convenience stores rely upon sales from deli, dairy, bakery, and lunch boxes (Bernstein 1997). For Japan's post-bubble, economy-minded office workers, shopping for a lunch box at a convenience store has become an economical option over having lunch at restaurants. Also, individual-size food items were developed in order to respond to the demand from growing numbers of single-person households in urban areas. The customer profile made available by Seven-Eleven Japan (1999b) indicates that, in 1984, 69 percent of their clients were under age 30. Customer base has diversified since then, and the share of clients under 30 declined to 52 percent in 1998. Yet, convenience stores today serve as a one-stop shop for single-person households of all ages from the yuppies to the elderly. In a country where three-quarters of Japan's retail stores are open less than 11 hours a day (MITI 1999d), the sight of a brightly lit convenience store at odd hours and during holiday seasons has become a lifesaver for many urban residents. Also, while picking up one's necessities, customers can use their coin-operated copy machines, and send a parcel or fax.[14]

This type of multisectoral retailing was new in Japan, where manufacturers and wholesalers have dictated the behavior of retailers and have sanctioned retailers who break exclusive distribution rights. Japan's retail sector was therefore discouraged from diversifying the distribution network and conducting businesses that crossed various traditional retail borders. The wholesalers control the retailers by providing the rights to distribute, and retailers are at the mercy of the wholesalers. Under such a structure, small retailers have been largely prevented from innovation. Retail trade experts argue that Japan's sectoral division of power is characterized by the dominance of manufacturers, and the wholesalers and retailers are regarded simply as distribution arms of the manufacturers.

Building the Information Networks and Services Offered

Japan's convenience stores are known for disproportionately large investments in ITs per floor space when compared with other forms of retail outlets. Convenience stores initially invested heavily in ITs with the sole purpose of improving delivery efficiency (Hashimoto 1998). To shorten the time required for restocking, the point-of-sale (POS) system was conceived. Introduced by Seven-Eleven Japan in 1982, the system allowed just-in-time production and delivery. At this stage, the information network was used simply as an instrument for delivery trip rationalization and cost reduction.

Once the information infrastructure was in place, however, convenience stores quickly realized that the same network could be used to gather valuable customer information. The second stage of informatization thus involved the use of the network for market research purposes. Such research aims to determine the variety and the amount of products on the shelf for each store. They developed coding systems at cash registers that require cashiers to press buttons representing gender and the estimated age bracket of the customer in order to open the cash register drawer and provide change and a receipt. The information, which includes the item of purchase, the gender/age of the customer, and time of purchase, is then relayed back to headquarters and used to order restocking and to add to the database on consumption patterns for different stores. In part because of this system, convenience stores have also served as experimental grounds for a variety of new products (typically prepared food items), which results in their reputation as trend-setters in Japan's consumer market.

It was only during the third stage of informatization when the convenience stores realized the potential of offering e-commerce through the network. By using their already present information network, convenience stores began delivery of new services that can be accessed online (Hashimoto 1999). Today, Seven-Eleven Japan not only provides such services as parcel delivery, ATM access, and life insurance packages, but also an online utility bill payment system (with bills payable to 126 utility companies including telephones, gas, electricity, water, as well as catalog shopping) (Seven-Eleven Japan). In a country where personal checks are nonexistent and credit cards are rarely used, utility bill payments were made exclusively through bank transfers until convenience store chain began offering this service. In early 2000, Seven-Eleven Japan entered the banking industry by setting up its own bank.

New functions are being added so that customers can purchase a variety of electronically transmittable products, including game software, music, and books. Seven-Eleven Japan spearheaded the move by announcing a triangle alliance between an Internet firm and book wholesaler in June, 1999. Together they plan to set up a book-delivery service, called e-books (Seven-Eleven Japan 1999). Since the proportion of convenience stores which sell books is very small, entry into this market offers a potential for growth. Following this move, FamilyMart announced a consortium of five firms to develop its own e-commerce web site in January, 2000. Lawson, which already has its own e-commerce web site, also announced during the same month an alliance with Mitsubishi trading company to solidify its investment in e-commerce.

Multiple alliances between convenience stores and e-commerce vendors further increase the product variety. Convenience stores have already begun performing the functions of a travel agency by allowing customers to book flights, purchase domestic or international package tours, and reserve at the last minute hotel rooms at discount rates. Seven-Eleven Japan has done so by setting up an alliance with Arukikata.com, Japan's major travel guidebook company. Customers can purchase discount airline tickets via the Internet and pay cash at a local convenience store. The flight coupon is then delivered to the store for pick-up. Seven-Eleven Japan also announced a joint venture between Sony Corp., called 7dream.com, that offers travel packages, music, books, and other goods online, starting fall, 2000. It has also forged an alliance with CarPoint, the world's largest Internet automobile dealer (Landers 2000).

Traditional retailers are also seeking alliances with convenience stores. Realizing that consumers frequent convenience stores, even if they have kept away from more expensive specialized retailers, department stores began courting convenience stores as an intermediary to attract more customers for annual year-end gift sending practices. Instead of traveling to a department store in urban centers, customers can avoid the lines, the crowd, and traffic congestion by picking out a department store-grade gift package from a catalog and order it at a neighborhood convenience store and pay cash. The order is relayed via their information network.

With the use of the information networks and their strategic locations, convenience stores have become a one-stop neighborhood shop for consumers of all ages. It is a store where you can pick up, not only a variety of household items and prepared food items, but also order and pick up electronically available products and services. The convenience store functions as a financial as well as distribution intermediary, providing easy access, legitimacy to online retailers and bypassing all security concerns that surround online transactions. For Japanese consumers who are not accustomed to the practice of long-distance shopping, convenience stores provide face-to-face interactions at each of their local store-fronts, thereby reducing consumer anxiety and making the services far more user-friendly.

Convenience stores have therefore become an effective intermediary between traditional retailing and e-commerce in a manner that has not been observed to the same degree in the USA. Combining retail store-fronts with e-commerce in this manner provides the option that can overcome existing social and institutional constraints and simultaneously offer new possibilities for further growth in the retail sector. Convenience stores in Japan are therefore well positioned to adopt other businesses available online. They represent a truly private-sector initiative toward informatization.

CONCLUSION: ALTERNATIVE PATHS TO THE INFORMATION SOCIETY?

The partnership between convenience stores and e-commerce provides an alternative model of IT use. The Japanese example suggests that e-commerce can develop without instituting all elements of support structures necessary to promote home-based e-commerce use. For Japanese consumers, using e-commerce means adopting new business practices and consumer behaviors that come with the technology, and having to institute the necessary infrastructure and regulations that facilitate this mode of exchange.

The role of convenience stores in e-commerce has numerous implications and suggests alternatives to the model of e-commerce used in the USA. Accessing e-commerce through neighborhood corner stores eliminates the issue of unequal access. By making e-commerce an activity combined with the other functions of a neighborhood store, it provides a greater access to consumers regardless of economic status, technological knowledge, and home PC ownership.

Furthermore, the combination of convenience stores and e-commerce not only offers better services to customers across various economic and social backgrounds, but also offers a new way of complementing traditional face-to-face retailing, by offering new magnets for the emerging urban cultural landscape. The partnership between corner stores and e-commerce can not only benefit overall economic growth by stimulating consumer demand, but also ensures the survival of the existing urban life and the sense of community that arises from frequent, face-to-face retailing. It also facilitates the survival of many urban commercial districts whose livelihood has been endangered in recent decades by competition from large suburban retailers. The decline of traditional commercial zones has become an issue especially after 1988 (MITI 1999d). By having convenience stores serving as magnets of pedestrian traffic, some commercial zones in inner-city areas may have been saved from near-death. The partnership would not only impact the youth culture, but can also help improve the quality of life for those without access to automobiles, particularly those raising young children, and Japan's elderly population, many who live alone in urban areas.

However, we need to recognize the benefits and issues that surround franchising. On the one hand, the partnership provided innovation that Japan's retail sector desperately needed. It can function as a catalyst to further innovation and a long-overdue retail revolution, by injecting competition in the retail sector. Also, those mom-and-pop stores that can no longer survive on their own (especially those which had exclusive rice or liquor licenses before deregulation) were saved by joining the franchise and being able to retain their businesses. On the other hand, franchising also means less control by individual retailers, as well as increasing standardization of store-fronts across the nation. The presence of convenience stores may therefore involve the risk of accelerating the demise of traditional, independently operated, mom-and-pop stores, which cannot compete with the new and innovative networked chain.

The future of convenience stores and their partnership with e-commerce lies in whether they can effectively mediate with other ongoing forces and capture the majority share of e-commerce activities. Aside from convenience stores, there are two major competitors that provide e-commerce access in Japan: PCs and cell phones. Prompted by newly available low-cost PCs from IBM and others, the PC sales in 1999 were at a record high in Japan.[15] With such new technological developments as 'i-mode', cell phones would also be a major competitor in e-commerce access.

ACKNOWLEDGEMENTS

This chapter benefited from discussions with a number of Japanese academics in geography and retail trade. Special thanks to Professor Kenji Hashimoto of Osaka Gakuin University who generously shared his knowledge of Japan's retail sector. I am also grateful to Thomas Leinbach and Stanley Brunn for providing detailed comments and suggestions.

END NOTES

1. Japan is second after the USA in terms of the absolute number of Internet users, but low on Internet hosts per capita, with only 6.4 percent of the households are Internet users (TCA 2000; InfoCom 2000).
2. Robots per 10 000 persons employed in the manufacturing industry, 1997. Data provided by the United Nations. Japan ranks first with 413.0 robots per 10 000 manufacturing workers, followed by the USA (77.1 robots), Germany (66.8 robots), and South Korea (30.2 robots) (*The Economist* 1998).
3. On one hand, e-commerce has generated a number of retail innovations, such as mass customization of services (e.g. Amazon.com's suggestions for next purchase), geographical expansion of customer base (e.g. particularly auctions – which used to be largely geographically constrained), and the expansion of the self-service economy (i.e. individual stock-trading on the Internet versus hiring funds managers, or making flight reservations versus using travel agents). On the other hand, the major activities under e-commerce simply represent the digitization of mail-order business, which replaced the use of toll free telephone calls. Thus, the innovativeness of e-commerce varies greatly by the service being provided.
4. This is in part attributed to the lack of appropriate sociological concepts involved in adoption behavior (Rogers 1964).
5. The job-loss figure includes 530 000 jobs to be lost by the introduction of ITs in general, and an additional 270 000 job losses due to e-commerce. Furthermore, MITI predicts that an additional 830 000 jobs are affected by the development of e-commerce due to changing skill requirements.
6. For comparative purposes, all currency conversions have been conducted with the current exchange rate of 110 yen/US dollar (February, 2000).
7. For example, Nifty, Japan's largest Internet service provider and a subsidiary of Fujitsu, offers a $11/month unlimited access through LAN or via other service provider, but charges 10 yen (9 cents) per minute for using their local dial-up access, in addition to $9 initial setup fee. AOL Japan does not charge a setup fee, but has a higher charge ($17.30 for 15 hours LAN or third party access), and also charges 10 yen for the use of local dial-up access.

8. The lack of competition in the banking sector also hinders the promotion of credit cards use. For example, as of January, 2000, most Japanese banks charge a fee for ATM use during nonbusiness hours (after 6:00 p.m. during weekdays and all day during weekends). The ATM surcharge can be as high as US$7 per transaction, especially when interbank transfers are involved.

9. Sears' switch from rural to urban focus corresponds to the changing characteristics of US population from majority rural (1890s) to majority urban (1920s). Sears opened its first store in 1925 adjacent to a mail-order processing plant in Chicago, and by 1927 had 27 stores in operation nationwide. By 1933, Sears operated 400 stores nationwide, and the number grew to over 600 by 1941. Currently, Sears operates 833 stores in the USA (Sears, Roebuck and Co. 1999).

10. This is in stark contrast to the US retail sector, in which wholesale membership clubs saw phenomenal growth in the 1990s.

11. Cultural factors also influence the choice of products in each society. Industry analysts argue that for Japanese consumers to adopt technologies, the equipment needs to be (1) miniaturized so that it is portable, and (2) converted into a consumer electronics equipment, in order to achieve a quick success in the Japanese market (Amaha 1999).

12. Supermarkets include general supermarkets, specialty supermarkets, other supermarkets, and convenience stores (MITI 1999d). Japan's retail census defines convenience stores as those with (1) the opening hours of 14 hours or longer, (2) the store space between 30 and 250 square meters (323 and 2691 square feet), and (3) food items.

13. Coincidentally, franchising was promoted by Japan's Small and Medium-size Enterprise Agency (SMEA) at the time, as policy makers considered it as a strategy to retain small retailers.

14. In part due to the success of convenience stores in providing office services, convenience stores effectively eliminated business opportunities for specialized office service outlets, such as Kinkos and Mailboxes, etc. Kinkos does have about a dozen outlets in Tokyo, but they cater almost exclusively to traveling business professionals by locating in the central business district or near large hotels with international clients.

15. According to *Nippon Keizai Shimbun* (2000b), Dataquest reported that the 1999 domestic shipments for personal computers were 10.54 million units, a growth of 36 percent from the previous year. The household purchase grew by 60 percent, comprising 40 percent of new purchases in 1999.

i) Slow adoption of ecommerce in Japan (+ PCs)

ii) Convenience store approach ⇒ distinctive develt
path

7

Internet Economies and the Online Recruiting Industry

SHARON COBB

University of North Florida, South Jacksonville, FL, USA

INTRODUCTION

'There is a new geography in the making. It is composed of a vast web of telecommunications whose fixed points are computers of many sorts. Its traffic is information. . . . It has no formal organization and is more like an arcane, sprawling underground than a formally constituted system of communications' (Batty and Barr 1994, p. 699).

'The cutting edge for business today is electronic commerce' (Kalakota and Whinston 1996, p. 1).

Further understanding of the sea-change in the global economy heralding tertiarization and the rise in importance of information has become the remit of academicians and policy makers alike. Synergistic growth of the information society and the telecommunications infrastructure – the means by which the information product is disseminated – will be explored here in the context of e-commerce. The way to conceptualize this new mode of communication and economy is a matter of debate and various labels are used to describe it ranging from cyberspace (Gibson 1984; Kitchin 1998a), meganet (Dizard 1997), information superhighway (Mougayar 1998).

This chapter will explore the economies of the Internet using as a case study the online recruiting industry, particularly those firms engaged in the recruitment of highly skilled workers in the IS/IT sector of the economy. Synergistic growth in IS/IT and online job recruiting makes this worthy of study. According to IBN (1998, p. 61), 'five years ago, the notion that an entire electronic industry devoted to the movement of people between jobs was unimaginable. Even the entrepreneurs who began Online businesses in the 1980s couldn't anticipate the extraordinary growth. . . .' The inconsistencies of Internet economies is well evident within the electronic recruiting industry which is itself a dynamic sector constantly self-reinventing and, at times, defying basic laws of economics as many services for job seekers are offered 'for free'. The case study will address differential real space and cyberspace geographies found within the online recruiting industry seeking to answer the following questions:

1. Are there new economies of the Internet as evidenced by the online recruiting industry?
2. Does geography matter at all when participating in the online recruiting process?
3. What are the potential future economic and spatial trends for online recruiting?

For e-commerce, the most critical element of the information society and infrastructure is the Internet and its associated navigation tool for finding information in multimedia format: the World Wide Web (WWW). The beginnings of the Internet as a child of the US Department of Defense's Advanced Research Projects Agency (ARPA), known as Arpanet, is well documented (Kalakota and Whinston 1996; Castells 1996). The WWW had its origins in 1989 as a collaborative project of CERN (a research and development group of European high-energy physics researchers). According to Kalakota and Whinston (1996, p. 228), 'the initial proposal outlined a simple system of using networked hypertext to quickly disseminate documents among colleagues [but] the project quickly expanded beyond all imagination as others understood the potential for global information sharing'. In 1995, the WWW became the largest Internet communication tool (Kitchin 1998a).

The importance of the enabling role of information technology (IT) in the growth of the Internet is widely recognized (US Department of Commerce 1998; Gilder 1997). Moreover, the explosion of the Internet and the WWW in the mid-1990s has drawn considerable attention from a variety of disciplines including social theory (Pritchard 1999; Gibson 1999; Warf and Grimes 1997); economics (Klopfenstein 1998; McKnight and Bailey 1998; Shapiro and Varian 1998); labor economics (Lee 1997); business (Watson *et al.* 1998); political economy (Schiller 1999); engineering (Nielsen 1995); and communications (Dizard 1997; Gilder 1997; Lindstrom 1997). Theoretical and conceptual understanding of the Internet is an epistemological challenge for economic geographers as a new understanding of space (or cyberspace) is in the process of being defined – evidenced in part by this book's remit.

Recently, the role played by the Information Technology and Information Services (IS/IT) sector in the growth and sophistication of the global economy has been the subject of considerable attention by government bodies, business executives, and academe. The IS/IT sector is defined by the US government in terms of industry (SIC codes) and occupation. Information services (IS) include the provision of software, computer programming and processing, information retrieval services. IT involves microelectronic technologies including manufacture and trade of microprocessors, computers, robotics, satellites, and fiber-optic cables.

Kitchin (1998a, p. 131) argues that ITs can be seen as fundamental 'agents of change' in the late 20th century's structural change of economy and society. Acknowledgment of the enabling role of IT in the phenomenal growth of the Internet – partially evidenced by the synergistic growth patterns of the IS/IT sector and the Internet in recent years – is now commonplace (US Department of Commerce 1998; IBN 1998; Batty 1993).

Current estimates of worldwide access to the Internet are 148 million people with 88 million of those residing in the USA and Canada[1] (Nua Internet Surveys September

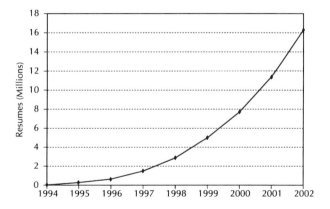

Figure 7.1 *Estimated number of résumés posted on the Internet, 1994–2002. Source: NUA, 1999 [www.nua.ie/surveys]*

1998). Phenomenal growth of the number of web sites on the Internet – from 74 000 sites in January 1996 to 1.8 million sites in January 1998[2] is reported by Iconocast (1999). Nua (1999) reports that there is now an estimated 3.6 million sites on the web, of which 2.2 million are publicly accessible. The NEC Research Institute estimates that the WWW contains at least 320 million pages (Lawrence and Giles 1998).

Exhibiting similar growth patterns, the online (or electronic) recruiting industry comprises one piece of the complex jigsaw of cyberspace. The much heralded – but increasingly controversial – notion that the global economy is suffering a critical shortage of qualified, skilled IS/IT workers is being played out on the Internet. Increasing numbers of electronic job boards and résumé banks are appearing on the WWW disproportionately servicing the IS/IT sector (IBN 1998). The recruiting element of the IS/IT job market increasingly is being played out in electronic space, as evidenced by the exponential increase in number of résumés posted on Internet recruiting sites (Figure 7.1), but does this also hold true for the job market itself? In other words, is the performance of IS/IT services increasingly occurring through electronic space via telecommuting, or is face-to-face interaction through real space still important? Litan and Niskanen predict that the Internet will facilitate: 'A virtual job market [which] will make it possible to find employment opportunities through a specialized on-line broker, conduct on-line job interviews, and telecommute from one's house to a distant firm with only occasional direct contact' (Litan and Niskanen 1998, p. 14). Telecommuting is defined as 'the substitution of commuting to a worker's employment center by producing work from home via telecommunications innovations such as computers, modems, faxes, and phones' (Stutz and de Souza 1998).

The dynamic nature of the online recruiting industry is as frenzied as its absolute growth making academic publication time-lines almost ridiculously long when compared to the volatile nature of the subject being analyzed. Doing business on the Internet is a constantly evolving process, evidenced in terms of WWW site content and infrastructure, as well as user/client base (personal comments, IGY 1998). The exponential – and sometimes chaotic – growth of the Internet, the WWW, and the online recruiting industry poses a challenge to those seeking to understand it.

INTERNET ECONOMIES

'Electronic commerce appears to be an integrating force that represents the digital convergence of 21st-century business applications and computing technologies' (Kalakota and Whinston 1996, p. 215). 'Academic debate regarding the nature of the economics of the Internet and e-commerce is lively – nowhere more so than within the electronic recruiting industry where attempts to define and quantify the industry and propose new business models are in its infancy' (IBN 1998). More generally, Choi *et al.* (1997, p. 13) assert that 'technology is transforming many aspects of business and market activities . . . electronic commerce refers to the use of electronic means and technologies to conduct commerce, including within-business, business-to-business, and business-to-consumer interactions'. The pervasive nature of e-commerce is recognized by Kalakota and Whinston (1996, p. 7) who argue that e-commerce is associated with 'the convergence of industries centered on information that until today has been isolated – content, storage, networks, business applications, and consumer devices'.

Choi *et al.* (1997) argue that differences exist when analyzing the economics of the Internet versus the economics of e-commerce. The authors assert that the economics of the Internet addresses a logical extension of network and telecommunications analysis focusing upon issues of the efficiencies of the physical network infrastructure, whereas the economics of e-commerce addresses issues of digital commodity (information) markets. Litan and Niskanen (1998, p. 1) define the digital world as a 'discontinuous world in which any type of information and data (voices, pictures, numbers, and letters) is reduced to bits, or strings of just zeros and ones'. It is the nature of such products that poses a challenge to traditional ways of understanding market processes and efficiencies. Choi *et al.* (1997) argue that digital products have three fundamental and synergistic features – indestructibility, transmutability, and reproducibility – which create a myriad of new economic, social, regulatory, and legislative concerns. Creation of a digital product that, by its nature, is infinitely durable (indestructible) and easy to change once received by a consumer (transmutable), producers have to develop new strategies of pricing that usually involve product differentiation through updating or licensing. Regulatory or copyright protection counters the ease of reproducibility of digital products and the initial problem for producers of zero marginal costs of production.

According to Batty (1993, p. 616), 'it is no longer clear whether existing theories and principles of economic management can be applied to these new types of space and network'. Adherents to this view argue that classical economic principles of cost and pricing may not be directly applicable to a medium is perceived by many as being 'free' (Lamberton 1992). More detailed analysis of the spatial location of Internet users and the methods by which Internet access is obtained illustrates that the majority of users of this so-called 'free' medium are in the USA, Western Europe, and Japan. These users have sufficient disposable income to purchase the hardware and software needed to use the Internet and WWW (Iconocast 1999). Hof (1999) argues that electronic business means discarding old business models and reinventing the way firms do business. Indeed, the loss-making activities of many so-called e-merchants has been subject to speculation in both business and financial institutions (The Economist 1998a,b).

In contrast, Shapiro and Varian (1998, p. 2) argue that the information age still functions within basic economic principles by asserting that managers should not 'ignore basic economic principles. . . . Technology changes. Economic laws do not.' Choi *et al.* (1997, p. 45) point out that 'the Internet resembles a preindustrial market where sellers and buyers meet at one place at the same time thus promoting market efficiencies through the elimination of intermediaries'. The notion of 'dynamic pricing' through online auction houses takes this process to the extreme: in this way any good is instantly priced according to what the market will bear (*Business Week* 1999a). Critically, Watson *et al.* (1998) assert that the WWW has changed the nature of communication and knowledge diffusion rather than the economic principles by which Internet commerce takes place.

The rationale for corporate presence on the Internet is varied:

- to reduce costs of matching buyers and sellers;
- to promote the image of a leading-edge corporation and increase visibility;
- to improve customer service;
- to enable market expansion;
- to lower stakeholder communication costs through online transactions and global information distribution (Watson *et al.* 1998, p. 36).

The issue of product pricing in e-commerce has received little attention by academicians. Choi *et al.* (1997) argue that traditional methods used in pricing products are inappropriate for digital informational products because the majority of the production costs are fixed costs of the first unit (or copy) and virtually no marginal costs exist for further replication. Debate exists, however, as to the true marginal cost structure with some arguing that marginal costs exist due to per-copy copyright payments. Copyright and Intellectual Property issues are, however, extremely difficult both to measure and enforce. Furthermore, most digital products are customized and consist of numerous components. As a result neither the seller nor the market can be expected to operate with one price for all differentiated products and for all consumers. Rather, pricing strategies become as complex as the products themselves (Chou *et al.* 1997, p. 348).

Choi *et al.* note that the marginal cost to consider is the cost of production, rather than distribution, due to the existence of positive network externalities. Externalities arise when one market player affects others without any form of compensation being paid (Shapiro and Varian 1999).[3] In the context of the Internet, network externalities are positive because, in general, the greater the number of participants in the network, the greater the benefit to all. Of course, the 'network' can be defined as the Internet itself or this case study: the online recruiting-industry. However, due to the lack of regulation and control of the Internet, the cost of distributing information products via the Internet or WWW falls on the provider rather than the recipient of the product, further complicating the informational pricing issue.

Difficulties occurring in pricing digital products lead to consideration of the types of competitive strategies needed for success in the production of information products. Shapiro and Varian (1999) argue that only two models exist for successful production of digital informational products:

- The dominant firm model where size and economies of scale result in cost advantages for one large firm even though the (informational) product may not necessarily be the best.
- The differentiated product market where several firms produce varieties of the same information, i.e. create a market niche.

Martin's (1997, p. 1) conceptualization of the WWW is as the Digital Estate whereby 'the marriage of technology to content . . . and the immediate nature of the Internet and the electronic transfer of data means that individuals no longer need wait for information . . . to filter through intermediaries'. According to Martin (1997, pp. 4–6), Digital Estate companies exhibit the following characteristics:

- willingness to create and embrace new concepts;
- creation of opportunity through the establishment of distinct vertical niches;
- consideration of the market as communities of interactive audiences;
- lack of geographical limitations and resulting adoption of a global platform;
- creation of products and services to empower users.

Many of the issues highlighted in the consideration of the economies of the Internet and e-commerce will be further explored in the next section, which addresses a case study of the online recruiting industry.

ONLINE RECRUITING INDUSTRY

'Labor shortages, often reported in the press in the IT sector, are widespread. . . . We are at the very beginnings of a shift in the way that work is understood and accomplished. . . . Recruiting becomes a question of managing scarcity. As such, the rules of the new game are 180 degrees different from techniques that worked as recently as five years ago. Recruiting is changing into a discipline of labor supply management' (IBN 1998).

A small, but growing piece of the Internet and e-commerce jigsaw is the online (or electronic) recruiting industry, which, in 1998, had an estimated worth of $4.5 billion (Vesely 1999). This segment of e-commerce has been driven by growth in the IS/IT sector and the concomitant need for qualified workers to efficiently match with the increasing number of job vacancies (US Department of Commerce 1998; IBN 1998). The majority of clients (either employers with vacancies to fill, or potential employees looking for work) served by the online recruiting industry are part of the IS/IT sector. (See *The Electronic Recruiting News* at http://www.interbiznet.com for a listing of the major recruiting sites on the Internet.) Kitchin (1998b) asserts, however, that this relationship between information/communication technologies and employment is complex, but recognizes the importance of using cyberspatial technologies to manage a company's workforce in the context of the corporate value chain and the labor supply management chain.

Much of the Internet recruiting industry services the IS/IT sector – one of the most rapidly growing segments of the global economy (US Department of Commerce 1998;

Business Week 1998b; Daniels 1993). Definitional difficulties as to the nature of services and the associated problems of measurement pose a challenge for empirical research (Nunn *et al.* 1998); however, the importance of spatial proximity for information-based services has been recognized by many (Hepworth 1989; Malecki 1997). Illeris (1996, p. 118) asserts that, 'to quote an anecdote from the computer service field: you get more new ideas from spending a night in Silicon Valley than from reading and telephoning a whole year'.

Internet recruiting facilitates the match between job seekers who announce their availability for employment by submitting a résumé to one or more electronic résumé banks, and employers who advertise job vacancies or, using the industry jargon, 'post' jobs on electronic job boards (Kennedy and Morrow 1995). Over 2500 job boards are present on the WWW that, according to IBN (1998, p. 69), 'offer job hunters the opportunity to sort through numbers of job opportunities in online databases'. In addition to individual job seekers looking for employment using the Internet, recruiting firms use the same electronic interface with the aim of placing their clients with prospective employers.

Tensions may exist between those searching for employees using their own corporate recruiting web site, and recruiters who are trying to place qualified candidates – in some instances for those very same corporations – for a substantial fee. A major concern of recruiters is that they will be squeezed out of the electronic marketplace as the online job-match process becomes more user friendly and cost efficient both for individual users and prospective employers (*The Economist* 1998c; IBN 1998).

According to IBN (1998), the electronic recruiting marketplace is quite complex, being comprised of the following elements:

- web site development, maintenance and improvement;
- job posting process involving value-added activities generating marketing and administration costs which are then priced through fees and subscriptions collected by job boards;
- traffic development activities or 'eyeball acquisition';
- pro-active sourcing activities involving technical development using the Internet as a résumé database;
- integration with other existing administrative and information systems, often large search engines and portal sites;
- candidate pool development through the use of mailing lists, web site content, and other visitor retention strategies (IBN 1998, p. 72).

Prospective employers who post jobs onto one of the hundreds of job boards normally are charged a fee to post jobs and a fee to review all résumés contained in the résumé bank – some online recruiting sites offer both services; some one, or the other. Recruiting companies are most usually concerned with the latter element of the job match process – access to résumé banks. Prospective employees, however, are generally offered access to job boards and e-mail notification of job matching services free of charge. Disparate pricing structures both between prospective employer and employee, and within the 'employer' segment – such as differences between direct corporate interest and recruiting firm, or between all firms depending on size of account –

support Choi *et al.*'s (1997) assertions that pricing structures are as complex as electronic information products themselves. Indeed, pricing structures used by those engaged in the online recruiting industry embody some of the issues highlighted by those who argue that electronic commerce requires new business models and new theoretical and conceptual frameworks (Batty 1993; Donovan 1997; Mougayar 1998).

Recruiting facilitators add value to the job search process through efficiencies of information collection (providing large numbers of new, quality résumés); information manipulation through key-word matching of specific résumés and jobs; and daily information dissemination of matches to both prospective employers and employees. The willingness of recruiting firms and prospective employers to pay a fixed fee each month is absolutely conditional upon the frequent receipt of fresh, high-quality résumés. Usually, the costs of Internet recruiting is offset by the value generated by the employee once recruited (IBN 1998).

The challenge for recruiting facilitators is to both attract new résumés to the facilitator's own web site, and to retrieve résumés from the WWW. Although both of these tasks are completed electronically, quality and reputational issues of the service provider often necessitates manual inspection of each résumé to ensure quality and relevancy.

Although much research has addressed the relationship between services and regional growth (Clark 1981; Coe 1998; Garcia-Mia and McGuire 1998; Harrington 1995), spatial analysis of the online recruiting industry has been largely ignored. However, spatial concentrations of online recruiting activity do exist (Tyner 1998). Many of the jobs advertised on Internet job sites and résumés electronically posted to those same sites or other résumé banks are located in the widely recognized IS/IT leading areas of innovation such as Silicon Valley, Boston, and new centers such as Austin, TX, and Atlanta (Hamilton 1999). Findings of spatial patterns of activity are in contrast to the assertion of Martin (1997) that geography (or real space) does not matter when participating in cyberspace. Indeed, Kitchin (1998b) asserts that spatiality is essential to understanding cyberspace. In a broader context, spatial divisions of high-tech labor have been documented at global and regional levels, where it is argued that such divisions have comprised a huge driving force in the sustenance of agglomerations of IS/IT activity (Massey 1995; Saxenian 1994).

Recent research has explored the relationship between the computer services sector and regional economic growth in North America (Nunn *et al.* 1998; Cornish 1996). The computer services sector (SIC Code 737) is one that is characterized by rapid growth, increasing sophistication, and unequal geographical distribution (Pollard and Storper 1996). The online recruiting industry is generally involved in the job search–job match process for highly skilled professionals demanding high salaries within this sector. Often, the job description is project-based, taking the form of a limited time contract for completion of a specific task. The increasing number of highly skilled computer professionals choosing to work on a contract-to-contract basis is reflected in recruiting industry jargon—contract professionals – and in the creation of an industry journal of the same name specifically addressing their needs. Furthermore, current research has begun to address some spatial patterns associated with both contract services firms and temporary services employment (see Reimer 1999; Segal and Sullivan 1997).

The spatial complexity of the IS/IT sector results in a paradox of simultaneous forces promoting both concentration and de-concentration. For example, much evidence exists to document the concentration of information intensive industries and occupations in large metropolitan areas in the USA (Drennan 1989; O hUallachain and Reid 1991). Yet, at the same time, flexibility in work practices enabled by modern telecommunications technology supporting telecommuting and the creation of telework, teleports, and electronic cottages, particularly (although not exclusively) for the IS/IT sector is recognized (Christopherson 1989; Kitchin 1998a).

No doubt exists regarding the growth of the Internet as a successful job search and recruiting medium, but are those employers, willing to use this electronic medium to recruit, also willing to use the Internet and telecommuting as an employment strategy? Previous research addressing the spatial complexity of highly skilled professionals highlighted 'an intensive *localized* dynamic of labor mobility in which engineers move between firms in a series of short term employment contracts' (Angel 1989, p. 99, emphasis added). But does successful completion of job contracts involve work from home, work in the field, or work in the office? The assertion that real space matters, and that face-to-face interaction is an important part of highly skilled activities has been widely acknowledged (Thrift 1994; Malecki 1997). But at the same time, the incidence of telecommuting – facilitated by the Internet and WWW – has increased dramatically in recent years (*The Economist* 1997).

The space-bridging qualities of a sophisticated telecommunications system and the concomitant ability efficiently to produce work at home using computers, modems, faxes, phones, and the Internet has stimulated the rise of telecommuting (Saunders *et al.* 1994). Cost savings through increasing efficiencies of at-home work production, combined with decreases in employee commuting costs savings has resulted in more and more corporations electing to use this work strategy (*The Economist* 1997). However, a major key to success using the telecommuting strategy appears to be the necessity of some face-to-face interaction during the working week leading to the creation of a dual work space. Telecommuting most efficiently promotes employees' work partly at the place of residence using electronic space to interact with others, and partly at the place of employment using real space for face-to-face interaction (*Business Week* 1998c).

CASE STUDY: AN ONLINE RECRUITING FACILITATOR

A segment of the electronic recruiting industry is concerned with developing computer architecture to facilitate the job matching process between recruiter firms (acting on behalf of corporate clients) and the job seeker. (As previously noted, the job matching process is played out on the Internet in other ways – usually by direct corporate recruiting efforts through their own web sites rather than (or as well as) those efforts of recruiting firms working through an Internet facilitator or broker.) Firms developing this particular type of computer and systems architecture may also provide direct recruiting services although many firms do not do this. The remit of the case-study firm, IGY, is to facilitate electronic 'matching' of résumés and job vacancies through the provision of specific Internet database and systems architecture (Figure 7.2).

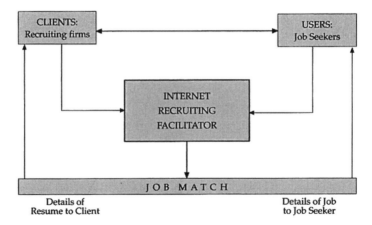

Figure 7.2   *Internet recruiting facilitator. Source: Cobb*

The case study firm is a small, but rapidly growing, member of the dynamic and complex field of online recruiting. IGY has approximately 300 paying clients (mostly recruiting firms); 15 000 job postings; and 90 000 résumés. IGY, and similar competing firms, manage electronic databases of résumés (submitted by those looking for work) and job vacancies (submitted by recruiting firms) and provide the computer programming expertise and systems architecture to 'match' suitable résumés with specific job openings, using keyword parameters. It is important to note though, that the entire electronic recruiting industry is more substantial (and complicated) than this specific case study. Some firms involved in this sector aim to match jobs and résumés for end-users (i.e. corporate clients such as banks, insurance companies, computer services firms) rather than servicing recruiting firms. Furthermore, some Internet recruiting sites offer niche services such as health care, or financial employment opportunities as well some who serve only a particular geographic or regional area (Tessler 1999; Sumser 1998).

Services for those looking for work – potential employees or 'contractors' – are provided free of charge and services for such companies' clients – recruiting companies – are provided for a monthly fee which pays for job postings, access to a résumé database, and electronic matching services linking specific résumés with specific jobs. The value added provided by such recruiting facilitators is directly related to the provision of new, high-quality résumés for their paying clients to view. A number of different strategies to increase the number of quality résumés exist and include:

- use of Internet spidering technology where résumés are electronically captured from the WWW;
- active business relationships with large search engines or portal sites to ensure favorable listings on these web sites, in other words, appearing high on the list of web sites offering requested services, rather than lower on the list;
- the establishment of a user-friendly web site to encourage job seekers to directly submit their résumés to the facilitator's site and résumé bank.

For the second strategy, favorable listings occur through the strategic use of meta-tags – key words about the services provided which are used by search engines to classify and rank sites in their own WWW organizational structure. The latter strategy is dependent upon constantly increasing traffic to the web site and one of the most efficient ways of doing this is to forge good working relationships with major Internet search engines in order to appear close to the top of any Internet search for online job opportunities. This is achieved by working closely with major search engines to create specific key words, meta tags – which closely correspond to the search engine's classification criteria.

In addition to search engine key-word manipulation, word of mouth is – ironically – an important source of increased traffic (IGY 1998). Paradoxically, much word of mouth occurs through the Internet and the specific electronic medium of the Usenet, which is defined as:

A distributed bboard (bulletin board) system supported mainly by UNIX machines. Originally implemented in 1979–80 by Steve Bellovin, Jim Ellis, Tom Truscott, and Steve Daniel at Duke University, it has swiftly grown to become international in scope and is now probably the largest decentralized information utility in existence. As of early 1993, it hosts tens of thousands of news groups and a staggering number of new technical messages, news, discussion, and chatter (see http://www.dejanews.com/info/gloss-ary.shtml#usenet).

According to dejanews.com, discussion groups are so invaluable because they are the only medium that allows disparate groups of people with like interests to communicate on a worldwide scale. Any person in the discussion group can send a message to the entire group, similarly, any of the other members can immediately respond to the entire group. The importance of the Usenet for the online recruiting process is widely recognized within the field (IBN 1998). Of course, the importance of informal information networks has been recognized by many researchers of business and economics systems (MacDonald and Williams 1992; Malecki 1997; Thrift 1994).

The evolving spatial distribution of paying clients of IGY is shown in Figure 7.3. Beginning in spring, 1998, listings of the case-study firm's clients were taken at three six-monthly intervals. These data were made available through personal connections of the author, but for this firm, and many others providing similar services, it would be possible (although cumbersome and time-consuming) to compile similar data from information available on the WWW. Figure 7.3 shows that a distinct spatial distribution of clients exists and did not significantly alter over the 18-month period, although the number of paying clients varied from 281 in February, 1998, to 506 in September, 1988, to 358 in February, 1999.

The largest number of IGY's paying clients are found in those states containing the traditional centers of IS/IT – California, Massachusetts, New York. An important assumption – and one worthy of further study – is that paying clients are recruiting firms trying to fill jobs in their own state. Anecdotal evidence suggests that this is usually the case, but this issue is worthy of further analysis. Furthermore, relatively large numbers of paying clients are located in the Midwest, Colorado, Georgia, and Florida. According to evidence from a vice-president of IGY, this is due to personal links forged by the IGY president. Also, IGY's headquarters is located in Florida.

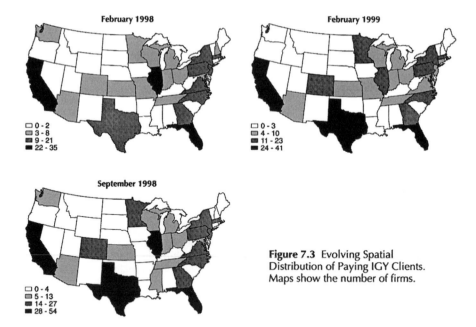

Figure 7.3 Evolving Spatial Distribution of Paying IGY Clients. Maps show the number of firms.

Figure 7.3   *Evolving spatial distribution of paying IGY clients. Source: Author's survey, Cobb*

IGY's spatial marketing strategy evolved approximately halfway through the study period from a state-focused approach to a key metropolitan area-focused approach. Job postings and résumé bank entrées were changed and became classified and ordered in terms of city location rather than state location. This relates to anecdotal evidence, suggesting that employers within the IS/IT sector are willing to embrace cyberspace technologies in the recruiting process but require traditional place-based interaction for the actual work process (Cobb 1998). The flexibility of the employment process within the IS/IT sector is apparent when analyzing specific employment opportunities – many of which are contract-based and time-specific. The opportunities for highly skilled IS/IT contract workers are plentiful if they are located in, or close to, a major metropolitan area.

DISCUSSION

Adequate spatial analysis of the online recruiting industry is greatly hindered by the lack of acceptable occupational and employment definitions of this sector. Unless personal connections afford the luxury of customized manipulation and classification of online recruiting databases, the compilation of industry-wide data is relegated to substitution of unsatisfactory Census-derived secondary aggregate data. For example, IGY is not easily classified using SIC codes: it is not a 'personal supply services' firm per se, but seeks to facilitate the services provided by those firms through the creation of Internet database management techniques. Should the case-study firm therefore be classified as SIC code 7379: 'Computer Related Services, Not Elsewhere Classified'? This study's analysis of the spatiality of the case-study firm was enabled by the use of proprietary data accessible through personal connections, but comparative studies would have to involve the use of other aggregate data unless a personal link could be forged with another, similar, firm.

Second, analysis of the electronic recruiting industry is far more complex than the simplified case study presented here. Companies such as the case-study firm face competition from other services providers with deeper pockets offering job-matching services in addition to other Internet functions. In addition, large corporations (or 'end users') often advertise their own job vacancies on their own web sites as well as through recruiting firms. In some instances such services are offered for free, or for a ridiculously low price, as providers are willing to operate in nonprofit-making mode for months, or even years.

A third problem relates to the speed at which data changes on the Internet. Surely one of the most frustrating aspects of Internet research is that the medium is so temporally, spatially, and structurally dynamic. Most academicians have been trained to recognize and analyze phenomena moving and changing at considerably less than the speed of light. Census data substantially and rigorously changes once every 10 years. A decade is perceived as almost neolithic in Internet time and speed. How can we adequately report on such changes when they happen so fast?

When faced with such (unfair) competition, how can small independent firms even hope to survive? IGY representatives argue that the strategies for success are twofold. First, increasing traffic generation to the site can be achieved through sophisticated use of the Internet portals or gateways such as the major search engines. Second, success in the job-match process can be achieved with a localized or specific city-focus rather than a regional or state focus. In other words, geography does matter and the Internet job-match process – although facilitated by an aspatial medium – is realized through real space.

Further anecdotal evidence suggests that the basic rules of economics still exist for the online recruiting industry. The business and marketing strategy of IGY revolves around the provision of cost minimization solutions for paying clients through a large and appropriate selection of résumés to match with their job vacancies. The only 'free' service is the no-cost to the prospective employee process of posting résumés to the facilitator's web site and the low-cost process of 'web spidering' used to capture résumés posted elsewhere on the WWW. The costs of these so-called 'free' services form, of course, part of the fee paid by IGY's client-recruiting firms.

The concern that recruiting firms will be squeezed out of the job market when both job seekers and those with job vacancies realize that the lowest costs of operation occur when the recruiting 'middleman' is removed from the process, is a valid one for recruiters. The Internet recruiting industry appears to be evolving more into a résumé procurement service that is well served by the electronic medium of the Internet. Moreover, based upon anecdotal evidence from industry players, it is the use of sophisticated computer architecture, programming solutions, and database management, all involving the manipulation of information on the Internet, which will be the key to success in the electronic recruiting industry.

CONCLUSIONS AND FUTURE RESEARCH

Work processes and pricing strategies and indeed general economies of electronic commerce and the Internet as applied to the online recruiting industry embody elements of both old and new. The traditional business tenets of cost minimization and increasing efficiencies are seen as vital to the success of service providers in the online recruiting industry. Possibly the biggest challenge to those engaged in online recruiting is the establishment of a competitive pricing strategy. New network economies and positive network externalities cause small online recruiting service providers, such as IGY, to adopt Shapiro and Varian's differentiated product market model with the aim of creating niche services for which corporate clients would be willing to pay.

The variability of IGY's client base over the 18-month study period suggests that evidence of volatility and a fickle nature of the online recruiting industry. Indeed, anecdotal evidence from IGY suggests that a free or low-cost 'trial basis' service is a necessary competitive strategy within the industry but results in high client turnover. This can be linked to Choi *et al.*'s (1997) work on the unique nature of digital products, particularly the characteristic of low to zero marginal costs of production due to ease of reproducibility. Once a trial basis client has 'mined' the existing résumé bank, all job needs may be filled – at least in the short term – and the desire to pay for continued service considerably lessened. IGY's continued strategy of fresh résumé procurement is the main method to avoid the problem of 'trial basis' attrition.

Although the electronic job search/job match process is facilitated through a new medium, work activity still appears to be constrained by real space. Prospective employers and employees are willing to adopt electronic recruiting as a viable means to an end (successful match of employer demands and employee skills), most jobs advertised in this manner require at least some office presence. Although the incidence of telecommuting is increasing in this country (*Business Week* 1998c), most employers are still looking for some traditional work-space presence.

To gain a greater understanding of the online recruiting industry, further research should:

- establish better measurement indices for Internet services companies in terms of services provided and match with SIC/occupational codes;
- analyze at a more detailed geographic scale – CMSA, PMSA, rather than state.

Finally, a problem challenging the development of substantive research in Internet geography is the fast pace at which raw data for the researcher change – be it numbers of clients, services offered, or basic structure and mission of a web-based enterprise. A temporal mismatch between the rapid evolution of Internet industry and the slower publishing deadlines of those trying to study it seem to challenge the validity of academic analysis – how can this problem be adequately addressed?

END NOTES

1. See [http://www.nua.ie/surveys/how_many_online/index.html] for current estimates and explanation of methodology.
2. See [http://www.iconocast.com] for current estimates.
3. See also Antonelli (1992) for further discussion of network externalities in the information economy.

§ e-recruiting
- space still matters (geog of supply + demand for vacancies; need for F2F)

8

Grounding Global Flows: Constructing an E-Commerce Hub in Singapore

NEIL M. COE

University of Manchester, UK

and

HENRY WAI-CHUNG YEUNG

National University of Singapore, Singapore

INTRODUCTION

The late 20th century has witnessed the emergence of a global economy qualitatively different from its predecessors. This 'new' global economy is characterized by the increased spatial and functional integration of economic activities, facilitated by significant enhancements in transport and communication technologies (Hepworth 1989; Dicken 1998). These globalization tendencies have allegedly produced rather different geographical organizations of economic and social life characterized by the domination of the 'global space of flows' and an emerging 'network society' (Castells 1989, 1996). These concepts allude to the complex interpenetration of people, capital, goods, service, and information flows on a global scale that in turn forms a distinctive space in its own right. Among these penetrating global flows, there is no doubt that information flows via cyberspace are the most fluid, rapid, and dynamic form. These electronic impulses and flows constitute the first layer of material support of the space of flows (Castells 1996). Some writers (e.g. Toffler 1980; Toffler and Toffler 1995) celebrate the so-called 'information revolution' as akin to a new Kondratiev long wave capable of fundamentally transforming the social and institutional organization of the global economy.

In their extreme forms, these futurologists predict that the ease with which information flows through global cyberspace has eroded the power of the nation-state and the role of place as the basic organizing units of the world in which we live. Some ultra-globalists (e.g. Ohmae 1990, 1995; O'Brien 1992; cf. Weiss 1998; Held *et al.* 1999) have conveniently concluded that the 'end of geography' and the 'end of the nation state' are at hand. This is clearly a case of overstating the power and influence of technologies that are seen by these writers as embodying metaphorically 'the very essence of contemporary cultural, economic, geographical and societal change. This brings with it, of course, the attendant dangers of relying on simple technological determinism in thinking about how new technologies are related to social, and spatial, change' (Graham 1998, p. 167). As noted by Thrift (1996), much of the literature on electronic and communications technologies has been infected by the virus of 'new era thinking', a virus that is simply another variant of technological determinism. It seemingly underestimates the extent to which technologically mediated flows are grounded in physical places via material flows and social relations (see a review in Kitchin 1998a).

In this chapter, we use the general concept of 'nodes in global flows' to explore the potential for particular localities to emerge as hubs within the rapidly emerging world of electronic commerce (e-commerce). These nodes and hubs, and their dominant elites (social actors) form the second and third layers of material support for Castells' (1996) notion of the space of flows. We argue that the domination of abstract metaphors in the literature on information and communications technologies tends to obfuscate the intricate relations between these technologies, their social users, and material geographies. It is true that advancement in these technologies has greatly facilitated the emergence of e-commerce and the possibility of participation in global flows for individuals and firms all over the world. It is equally true, however, that these 'virtual flows' on a global scale do not preclude the important role of place in organizing social life. As argued by Castells (1989, p. 170), 'most of these flows are directional, and these directions have a socially specific, place-based component'. Our analytical task in this chapter, therefore, is to show how certain places can enhance their positions as 'nodes' and 'hubs' in the cyberspace of e-commerce through tapping into the social dimensions of global flows, recognizing the need for support infrastructure such as logistics and distribution, and developing suitable policy initiatives. We argue it is possible for specific localities to ground global flows in e-commerce by constructing nodes and hubs of a physical, materialized nature. Thus we conceive of technological change as a highly contested process leading to multiple and overlapping development trajectories, not a set of predetermined social and spatial outcomes: some places and social groups benefit more than others from embracing technological change.

Singapore provides us with an excellent case study through which to explore these conceptual assertions, due to the wide-ranging efforts of the government to establish the city state as a premier e-commerce hub in the Asia–Pacific region (Figure 8.1). To a certain extent, Singapore's fortune is always intertwined with the global economy. However, one distinctive feature of Singapore's urban competitiveness is that it is very much a city (in a territorial sense) coupled with a strong nation-state (in an institutional sense); a state with powers far beyond those of any local state. To an unparalleled extent in Asia, the city-state has relied heavily upon developmentalism to legitimize its political power and control. The state's decision to pursue the strategy of global reach has been relatively uncontested, in part because the state has generated a political discourse of survivalism and ruthless competition; a discourse currently

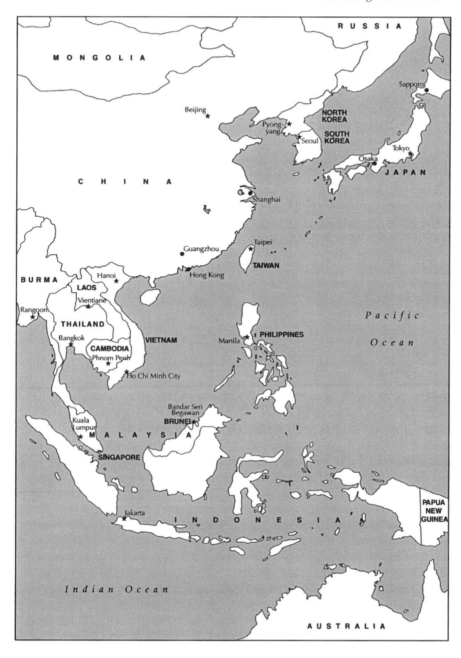

Figure 8.1 *Singapore and other major financial centers in Asia*

propagated in association with the dominant discourses of globalization (Leyshon 1997; Yeung 1998a; Kelly 1999). This discourse of survivalism and competition, backed by strict political control, has sustained Singapore's competitiveness in the face of global competition, thereby legitimizing the state's control over most aspects of social life. It has also enabled the bureaucracy, led by the dominant Peoples' Action Party, to bypass the local politics typical in many urban Western cities (see the case of England in Peck 1995; Jones and MacLeod 1999). Singapore is very much a city-state in which the global scale juxtaposes with the national scale (the city and its national state). It is a unique urban/national formation by virtue of the developmental role of a highly autonomous and sovereign state (Perry *et al.* 1997; Low 1998; Yeung and Olds 1998).

Since the early 1980s, Singapore has implemented a series of well-known national IT initiatives and policies, of which the 1998 Electronic Commerce Masterplan is the latest example. In a typically foresighted move, the first formal step to prepare for e-commerce was the formation of the Electronic Commerce Hotbed Programme in 1996, which instigated the collaborative process that produced the Masterplan by April 1998. The Masterplan takes a broad view of the steps that are necessary to establish Singapore as a premier e-commerce hub, covering issues to do with legal frameworks, the security of online transactions, local and international standards, support and logistics services, e-commerce measurement, and the education of both the private and public sectors, and private individuals. While it is perhaps too early to judge the success of the plan, preliminary evidence suggests that e-commerce levels are growing impressively in Singapore.

TAPPING INTO GLOBAL FLOWS: CONSTRUCTING HUBS AND NODES IN THE VIRTUAL WORLD OF ELECTRONIC COMMERCE

Before we examine the case study of Singapore in more detail, it is useful to establish some conceptual parameters about the nature of constructing an e-commerce hub and how it enables a place to become an important node in the global space of flows. In this section, we first engage critically with the debate on the rise of 'placeless' transactions through e-commerce. We then propose a more materialist view of e-commerce through the so-called 'grounding effect' whereby global flows of information and transactions are conceived as being grounded in specific localities and can only be executed through a well established physical and logistical infrastructure. In this sense, it is possible for specific localities to tap into global flows through the provision of this infrastructure and its concomitant 'software' (i.e. human resources). This possibility, however, is dependent upon the strategic capability of the state (local, regional, or national) and related institutions in these localities in governing the processes of e-commerce adoption.

The Rise of 'Placeless' Transactions Through E-Commerce? The Technological Determinism View

The protagonists of cyberspace rhetoric proclaimed in the 1996 'Manifesto for the digital society' published in *Wired* magazine that 'the Digital Revolution that is sweeping across society is actually a communications revolution which is transforming society. When used by people who understand it, digital technology allows information to be transmitted and transmuted in fundamentally limitless ways. This ability is the basis of economic success around the world' (quoted in Graham 1998, p. 168). This generalized logic of digital technology is seen not only as mediating every aspect of social and cultural life via the global reach of Internet access, but also as an opportunity for the globalization of business and commercial activities via e-commerce. It is argued that as information and communications technologies allow virtual access to all forms of information, social and economic actors are becoming increasingly 'liberated' from the constraints of space or the so-called 'friction of distance'. These technologies enable their users to transcend the tyranny of geography as a major constraint on the global reach of human life. They are also deemed to be eroding the role of place as the central unit of organizing social life. In particular, Castells (1996, p. 394) remarks that '[information technology] futurologists often predict the demise of the city, or at least of cities as we have know them until now, once they are voided of their functional necessity'.

In the ruthless world of business, these essentialist views of information and communications technologies represent transactions via e-commerce as 'placeless' in two ways. First, they argue that from the perspective of consumers, transactions can be conducted via the Internet from anywhere, and by anyone who has access. E-commerce empowers these cyber-consumers to transcend national regulations on products and services, and to make purchases on the basis of much wider access to information and choice. The common vision of e-commerce is an ideal electronic market in which consumers interact directly with producers (Sarkar *et al.* 1998). Traditional retail centers and marketplaces are increasingly threatened, and perhaps replaced, by global competition fostered through the widespread adoption of e-commerce. At the core of this 'informational economy', according to Castells (1993, p. 20), 'the fundamental source of wealth generation lies in an ability to create new knowledge and apply it to every realm of human activity by means of enhanced technological and organizational procedures of information processing'.

Second, the recent rise of the 'Amazon.com' phenomenon adds further support to the deterministic views held by essentialists because online companies are often perceived as embedded in cyberspace rather than in real physical places. Participation in online business or e-commerce has been hailed as a passport to instantaneous access to a repertoire of global customers, thereby defying spatial constraints as the logical limit to capital. A natural outcome of this despatialization and decentralization of business and economic activities via e-commerce is interpreted as the effective dissolution of the city itself as a place for geographical agglomeration of activities. Graham (1998, p. 168) argues that this view toward urban dissolution is based on the false assumption that 'networks of large metropolitan cities will gradually emerge to be some technological anachronism, as propinquity, concentration, place-based relations and transportation flows are gradually substituted by some universalized, interactive, broadband communications medium (the ultimate 'Information Superhighway')'.

Cities as Important Places in Global Spaces of Flows

Notwithstanding the above universalizing assertions by technological determinists, there is another rich strand of research in urban studies that has 'rediscovered' the city as the powerhouse of the globalizing world economy. Cities are perceived as being relatively more important as the key creative, control, and cultural centers within globalizing economic, cultural, and social dynamics (Amin and Graham 1997). In particular, this literature is associated with the development and dynamics of the 'world city' or 'global city' (see, for example, Friedmann and Wolff 1982; Friedmann 1986; Sassen 1991, 1996; Knox and Taylor 1995). One of the main contributions of these studies has been to relate dominant socioeconomic trends within these cities (e.g. deindustrialization, the geography of capital flows, the expansion and spatial concentration of financial and producer services industries, labor market segmentation, class and ethnic conflict, sociospatial polarization) to an evolving urban hierarchy and the global economic forces that underlie it (Brenner 1997, 1998). World cities are conceptualized as key strategic governance centers in national and international urban systems. Their importance is measured by their functions (in terms of economic activities and extent of control) and performance (in terms of competitiveness and market share). These urban regions are said to be hierarchically arranged on a global scale according to their differential mode of integration and articulation into the global economy. They act as 'a collective "brain", as centers of excellence in a given industry, offering for collective consumption local contact networks, knowledge structures and a plethora of institutions underwriting individual entrepreneurship' (Amin and Thrift 1992, p. 577; see also Scott 1988, 1996).

The location and concentration of information-intensive industries in these 'informational cities' has enabled them to exploit global flows; they perform a range of roles in evolving spatial divisions of labor. Some cities act, therefore, as key sites of understanding and coordination among flows of energy and labor, commodities and capital, information and images, even though surplus value is increasingly being realized within more deterritorialized circuits of money and finance (Castells 1989; Lefebvre 1991; Sassen 1991). Place remains highly important in facilitating capital accumulation and social (re)production in an era of intensified technologically mediated flows on a global scale (Amin and Graham 1997; Yeung 1998a). In theoretical terms, capital depends on place for material conditions (e.g. infrastructure and resources) and social relations (e.g. business networks and labor processes) in order to reproduce successfully in an era of global competition. For example, although telematics has made possible the spatial decentralization of economic activities and the overriding of conventional jurisdiction and boundaries, Sassen (1995, p. 31) argues that 'there is also a space economy which reveals the need for strategic sites with vast concentrations of resources and infrastructure, sites that are situated in national territories and are far less mobile than much of the general commentary on the global economy suggests'.

Materializing Global Flows Through Hubs and Nodes

How then does this 'grounding effect' of e-commerce take place within specific nodes in the global space of flows? We focus here on three specific dimensions: (1) the social and symbolic dimensions of global flows; (2) the role of logistics and distribution in e-commerce; (3) the role of state initiatives. These dimensions not only show that the physical size and location of companies continue to be major attributes accounting for their success when conducting business on the Internet (cf. Angelides 1997), but also demonstrate the possibility for specific localities to create sustainable competitive advantage through consciously constructing hubs and nodes in the world of e-commerce. First, while it is true that e-commerce is not as restricted by geographic barriers vis-à-vis their wholesale and retail predecessors, the operationalization of e-commerce requires significant social and symbolic capital in specific localities. This is because 'the human construction of space and place is seen actually to ground and conceptualize applications and uses of new technologies' (Graham 1998: 172). Nodes in the world of technologically mediated flows exist as places of reflexivity, trust, and reciprocity. These nodes have a material dimension because they are embedded in specific physical locations. As such, the social relations of e-commerce cannot exist in cyberspace alone; they need to be grounded in places and localities in which social actors have invested significant meaning through face-to-face interactions and material flows. For example, whereas they may be able to provide specialized services for consumers, it is questionable whether e-commerce service providers (e.g. online reservation by airlines) can offer the social atmosphere and support that consumers expect from many traditional channels (e.g. travel agents). A recent survey of 23 small businesses in Australia has shown that while the gain of these firms from e-commerce can only be described as 'perceived benefits', such benefits are marginal, and often circumstantial (e.g. inconsistent sales). Many sampled firms believed that either their offerings were not easily purchased over the Internet, or that they required some form of face-to-face interaction (e.g. consultations) in addition to their Internet presence (Poon and Swatman 1999).

Second, the role of specific localities in the provision of logistics and distribution of e-commerce products and services further enhances the importance of place in conducting cyberspace transactions. Despite the recent fervor with the 'Amazon.com' phenomenon, it is hard to believe that such a highly globalized virtual e-commerce bookstore operation can be viable without concomitant support through physical infrastructure in the form of logistical and distribution facilities. For every Amazon.com to excel in the world of global business, we need more of the services of global credit companies (e.g. Visa and American Express), global distribution companies (e.g. Federal Express and DHL), global producers (e.g. publishers and entertainment companies), local warehousing and Internet service providers. This, however, does not necessarily imply that every locality can become an important node in global spaces of flows via e-commerce. Two factors explain why certain localities are better equipped than others in engaging e-commerce activities and thus becoming an important hub for such activities. On the one hand, geography continues to shape the e-commerce trajectories of specific localities. This is the issue of path-dependency well explained in the existing literature on urban and regional development (see, for example Storper 1995). Information and communications technologies are not evenly distributed over space and e-commerce still requires the physical transportation of goods and services (Kitchin 1998b). To a large extent, the effectiveness of e-commerce as a developmental strategy for specific localities depends on the efficiency of existing and future communications and transportation infrastructure of a given locality.

On the other hand, e-commerce allows the decoupling of different functions in a given production chain (e.g. publishing industry) because electronic markets consist of both physical and information, or virtual, channels for marketing and distribution. Sarkar *et al.* (1998) have argued that the e-commerce lowers supply chain coordination costs and thus contributes to the separation of physical distribution from other 'cybermediary' functions. In the early stages of the electronic market, many e-commerce companies are unlikely to integrate forward or backward along the production chain. Instead, they may make use of services provided by other cybermediaries (e.g. gateways, directories, search services, online malls, and electronic publishers) as an efficient mechanism for supporting electronic exchanges and achieving economies of scale and scope. E-commerce opens up more opportunities for small entrepreneurial producers to start their business by outsourcing channel functions to specialized cybermediaries. Though their physical distribution channel may be shortened, however, these e-commerce companies are likely to continue to depend on integrated logistics companies (e.g. Federal Express) as their distribution systems. This decoupling process also produces complex and longer networks of information-specific intermediaries (e.g. some firms may locate products, others provide evaluations of related products, training, and settlement services, and so on). Localities can strive to become an important node if they are able to provide favorable social and institutional contexts for the development of these interfaces of physical and cyber networks bringing together consumers, producers, and their intermediaries.

Third, there is clearly a case for policy and developmental initiatives because nodes and hubs in the e-commerce world do not develop randomly in specific places. Similar to much of the literature on networks, innovation, and regional development (Saxenian 1994; Storper 1997; Cooke and Morgan 1998; Scott 1998; for a review, see Yeung, 2000a), the development of e-commerce nodes and hubs requires sustainable initiatives by various actors from institutions at different spatial scales. These actors may come from business and trade associations, labor unions, civil and voluntary associations, and local, regional, and national government agencies which are empowered to foster social and economic development and political stability. Together, they constitute an 'associational economy' based upon collaborative networking between institutions, which for some authors defines the coming shape of global production, competition, and political order, and thereby determines the success of places in generating self-sustaining growth at the local level (Amin 1999; cf. Lovering 1999).

How then do these institutions explain the rise of certain places as important nodes in the global flows of e-commerce? As noted earlier, world cities tend to have a 'first-mover' advantage in constructing e-commerce hubs by virtue of their well-established positions in the global economy. The advantages possessed by world cities, however, cannot be successfully reaped if they are not accompanied by a favorable institutional context. In this regard, the political economy of the institutional context becomes highly important because certain world cities have a unique configuration of state–business relations such that an enormous amount of resources can be mobilized and deployed for a common objective of developing a competitive node in the global economy. As e-commerce has the potential to bypass specific localities in its global reach, and an e-commerce hub requires substantial social capital endowments, and physical and logistical infrastructure, 'holding down' global e-commerce flows in specific localities becomes a political initiative that necessitates intense collaboration among public agencies, private business, and social actors. To understand the evolution and success of certain e-commerce nodes, we need to go beyond an analysis of their economic functions and interconnectedness. More importantly, we need to examine the ways in which these economic dimensions are woven together with local politics and institutional relations to form complex power geometries. It is these power geometries that explain the success and failure of specific localities in constructing e-commerce hubs as important nodes in global spaces of information and transactional flows. In the next section, we look into the experience of Singapore in constructing an e-commerce hub in the Asia–Pacific region.

THE EXPERIENCE OF SINGAPORE IN DEVELOPING CAPABILITIES IN INFORMATION TECHNOLOGY AND ELECTRONIC COMMERCE

'Singapore is now a world city whose fate is dependent on events in New York, London, Tokyo, and connected nodes in the international economy. Its trading, investment and information links to distant countries are far more important than those to its immediate regional neighbors' (Perry *et al.* 1997, p. 1).

We concur that Singapore's experience in developing its IT and e-commerce capabilities is perhaps quite unique. As a city-state in Southeast Asia (see Figure 8.1), Singapore has been highly proactive in creating and sustaining its competitiveness as a strategic node in global spaces of flows (Yeung and Olds 1998). Over time, different sets of national development strategies have evolved and significantly shaped its competitiveness as a world city (in Singapore's case, 'national' is also 'urban' as the majority of the 623 square kilometer city is urbanized). We argue that the creation of city competitiveness in Singapore via constructing an e-commerce hub is highly contingent upon the (national) state's capabilities to exercise power in the implementation of national development strategies, strategies that situate the city-state in a beneficial manner to global spaces of flows. In other words, Singapore's experience in constructing an e-commerce hub represents an extreme combination of political economy and city-state advantages to sustain particular national initiatives that are unlikely to be found in many other world cities (see Corey 1993). Given that Singapore is a large Southeast Asian city and a relatively recent independent state, Singapore's experience is unique in its historical and geopolitical contexts, and it may not be used in a straightforward manner to derive lessons for the planning and management of other Asian cities (or nations). Lessons based upon Singapore's experience cannot, we would argue, be necessarily replicated elsewhere. In this sense, we want to avoid the problem of constructing paradigmatic examples for policy innovation elsewhere (e.g. the new urbanism literature). Amin and Graham (1997, p. 416; our emphasis) note that 'an inevitable outcome of the rediscovery of the city within so many research strands and discourses has been the elevation of single or small groups of urban examples to be paradigmatic; that is, to offer apparent lessons for all other urban areas'. In this section, we first discuss the political economy of creating sustainable national competitiveness in Singapore. We then examine Singapore's recent drive to become an IT and e-commerce hub in the Asia–Pacific region. We also provide an assessment of the current state of e-commerce in Singapore today, and consider some of the social and cultural constraints to the adoption of e-commerce that may be underestimated by optimistic growth projections.

Creating Sustainable National Competitiveness in Singapore

⌈Ever since its independence in 1965, Singapore has relentlessly pursued a national development strategy that depends heavily on the influx of foreign capital in the form of direct investment and on the leading role of state-owned enterprises⌋ This reliance on foreign capital worked very well in the first two decades of Singapore's industrialization by plugging into the so-called 'new international division of labor' (Rodan 1989; Huff 1994; Chiu *et al.* 1997). By the late 1970s and early 1980s, Singapore was no longer competitive in attracting low-cost manufacturing assembly investment because cheaper production locations could be found throughout the world, notably in neighboring Asian developing countries. The strategy of low labor cost pursued since independence had also backfired when systematic distortions in the labor market resulted in severe labor shortage. The lack of investment in indigenous technological capabilities also contributed to low value-added activities by domestic enterprises. By the late 1970s, Singapore faced a 'competitiveness crunch' in the changing international division of labor. To regain its competitiveness in the global space of flows, the state revised its national strategies in favor of promoting high-tech and high value-added manufacturing and business services. The state initiated a major industrial restructuring, the so-called 'Second Industrial Revolution', through which labor wages were increased substantially to drive out labor-intensive manufacturing activities, and labor productivity and skills were upgraded to attract world-class high-tech manufacturing investments. The Second Industrial Revolution resulted in a shift in Singapore's industrialization strategy from an offshore production location to a center for the spatial agglomeration of high value-added and high-tech investments.

⌈Since the mid-1980s, Singapore has also been actively seeking to attract the control and coordination functions of leading global corporations in order to develop the city into a truly international business hub, serving countries within and beyond the Southeast Asian region.⌋Regional offices and regional headquarters of major global corporations are actively sought after and promoted. The intention is that these regional operational headquarters bring in high value-added jobs and skills to the aspiring white-collar workforce in Singapore. The state has again taken the initiative to attract these regional offices and regional headquarters through a clearly defined set of strategies (see Perry 1992, 1995; Perry *et al.* 1998a,b; Yeung 1998b). More recently in the 1990s, the state has begun to realize that to remain competitive in the global economy, it is insufficient for Singapore to be just a nodal point for the influx of capital, skills and knowledge, but it is also vital to the future of Singapore to spread its 'external wing' (Yeung 1998c, 1999, 2000b). In its recognition of the need to generate intra- and interregional interdependencies for the domestic economy, Singapore has clearly learnt from the experience of Switzerland and the Netherlands. The state aims to implement certain policies to enable Singapore to be less vulnerable to sudden downturns in its major markets in the Triad regions of Western Europe, North America, and Japan and East Asia. A well-developed external economy can also sustain Singapore's long-term competitiveness by tapping into business opportunities and a world-class pool of knowledge, skills, and capital. Together, these three national development strategies are being implemented over time and in different phases to sustain the competitiveness of Singapore as a leading megacity in Southeast Asia.

National IT Policy and the Recent E-Commerce Drive in Singapore

There can be little doubt about the state's determination to make Singapore an IT hub within Southeast Asia. Since the establishment of the National Computer Board (NCB) in 1981, Singapore has implemented a progressive series of national IT policies and initiatives. This evolution can usefully be divided into four phases (Choo 1997; Corey 1997: Table 1). The first, from 1981 to 1985, saw the initiation of the Civil Service Computerization Programme, designed to computerize the activities of government ministries and thereby improve productivity and service quality, while simultaneously starting to develop a pool of computer professionals in Singapore. The second period, from 1986 to 1991, was shaped by the National IT Plan of 1986 (NCB 1986), which detailed the twin goals of developing an export-oriented IT industry, and improving

Table 8.1   *Four phases of national information technology policy in Singapore*

Period	IT plan	Target groups	Strategic goals	Enabling technologies
1980 to 1985	Civil Service Computerization program	Public sector: Government ministries Departments	Raise productivity Improve service Develop IT manpower	Transaction processing Data modelling Database management systems
1986 to 1991	National IT Plan	Private sector: IT industry Local companies	Develop local IT industry Promote business use of IT IT R&D	Software engineering Expert systems Electronic data interchange
1992 to 1995	IT2000	Industry sectors Communities Individuals	Increase national competitiveness Improve quality of life Personal development Community development Develop global hub role	Broadband networks Multimedia Telecomputing
1996 to date	Restructuring for IT2000	Industry clusters Government General population	Public–private partnerships Strategic alliances Hub development IT goods/services exports	Internet

(Adapted from Choo, 1997: 50, and Corey, 1997: 192.)

business productivity through the application of IT, thereby representing a shift in policy focus from the public to the private sector. This plan was constructed around seven key 'building blocks' (Corey 1993, 1998): upgrading the telecommunications infrastructure, developing IT manpower, promoting an IT culture, building IT applications, fostering a local IT industry, engendering IT creativity and innovation, and encouraging coordination and collaboration in the implementation of the plan. Critical assessments by authors such as Corey (1993) suggest that the collaborative interagency approach coordinated by the NCB was highly effective in promoting and realizing the strategies contained in the National IT Plan.

The third phase began in March 1992 with the publication of the IT2000 report, *A Vision of an Intelligent Island* (NCB 1992). This new strategy drew on Singapore's previous IT achievements, and sought to integrate them with new applications of IT that would enhance the working, living, and leisure environments of society as a whole. At the heart of this new vision was the idea of the 'intelligent island' built upon a National Information Infrastructure (NII) interconnecting computers in homes, schools, and workplaces. In this phase, the policy emphasis shifted from the public and private sectors, toward the well-being of the population as a whole. Five strategic themes were contained in the initial report, including improving the quality of life of Singaporeans, linking local and global communities, enhancing the potential of individuals, and upgrading economic competitiveness. Most important in this context, however, is the explicit aim of developing Singapore into a 'global hub' (cf. Ministry of Trade and Industry 1998). As Choo (1997, p. 52) relates with respect to this part of IT2000: 'Singapore is repositioning itself as a nerve center and switching node for staging international and business operations. Its competitive assets will be an efficient and versatile information infrastructure and a workforce equipped with the skills and expertise to operate, manage and get the most out of the infrastructure.' Singapore entered the fourth and current phase of its IT planning in 1996 when the IT2000 framework was reviewed under the 'Restructuring for IT2000' initiative. The key dynamic here is the corporatization of NCB functions that lend themselves to private sector adoption through public–private partnerships and strategic alliances (Corey 1997). This shift in emphasis means that the NCB will no longer be the sole source of expertise for developing IT policy, and reflects the accumulated size and maturity of Singapore's contemporary IT industry. As a result, the NCB's promotional efforts for IT in Singapore will increasingly be focused on specific industry clusters.

The Electronic Commerce Masterplan, announced in September 1998, is part of this latest generation of national level strategies. The Masterplan aims to develop Singapore into a hub for electronically transacted business through a series of policy interventions, incentive schemes, and education initiatives (*The Straits Times* 1998). The target is to have S$4 (US$2.4) billion worth of products and services transacted electronically through Singapore, and 50 percent of businesses to use some form of e-commerce by the year 2003. The first formal move to prepare for an era of e-commerce was, however, taken in 1996, when the NCB established the Electronic Commerce Hotbed (ECH) Programme, with the aim of 'jump-starting' e-commerce in Singapore. The ECH initiative brought together 38 founding parties, ranging from financial institutions to academic, telecommunications, and IT organizations, to pursue two broad objectives; firstly, to make e-commerce widely available, and secondly, to position Singapore as an e-commerce hub. The main thrusts of the program were fourfold: to establish and deploy common services such as secure payment systems, to showcase new and promising e-commerce applications, to raise awareness and acceptance of e-commerce among industry and the general public, and to address legal and policy issues. In January 1997, the E-commerce Policy Committee was established to further explore these legal and policy issues. Chaired by the Monetary Authority of Singapore (MAS), the E-commerce Policy Committee comprised members from 15 agencies, with the NCB providing secretarial support. In April 1998, the Committee completed its review and made its recommendation to the government, listing six guiding principles with regard to e-commerce development:

1. The private sector should take the lead.
2. The government should put in place a legal framework to provide certainty and predictability.
3. The government should provide a secure and safe environment for electronic transactions.
4. The government should use joint venture pilots and experiments to expedite e-commerce growth and development.
5. The government should be proactive in pursuing innovative, liberal, and transparent policies.
6. International consistency, cooperation, and interoperability should be encouraged (NCB 1998).

After a period of public consultation, these policy recommendations were passed to the Electronic Commerce Coordinating Committee (EC3), which formulated the Electronic Commerce Masterplan of late 1998. To give some indication of the institutional support that lies behind this initiative, EC3 comprised the Attorney General's Chambers, the Ministry of Finance, the Ministry of Law, the Ministry of Trade and Industry, the Monetary Authority of Singapore, the National Computer Board, the Public Service 21 Office, and the Trade Development Board. The Economic Development Board, the Singapore Tourism Board, and the Department of Statistics were also consulted during the planning process. Interestingly, the Masterplan explicitly recognizes one of the grounding effects we described earlier with respect to the e-commerce services sector. According to the plan, this will comprise business strategists, creative designers, system integrators, network operators, and other 'cybermediaries'. It also notes the important contribution of the additional activity that can be generated for Singapore's port, logistics, financial, and telecommunications services due to the multiplier effects of e-commerce transactions. Overall, the plan has five main thrusts, accompanied by various implementation programs, which we will now consider in turn.

1. *To develop an internationally linked EC infrastructure*. This is seen as crucial to strengthening Singapore's position as an e-commerce hub, with the financial and logistics sectors being given a key role. The plan aims to develop and deploy, in partnership with industry, an efficient settlement system for Internet transactions between businesses, covering international trade payment and multi-currency payment, within two years (i.e. by late 2000). Certain areas of e-commerce infrastructure development are also singled out for special attention, including trust management,

rights management, business-to-business trading platforms, and business-to-consumer payment systems. Efforts will be made to link local infrastructure services to those overseas, for example through the cross-certification of certification authorities.

2. *To jump-start Singapore as an e-commerce hub*. This part of the plan focuses on the sectors in which Singapore already has an inherent advantage as a hub, including the financial, transport and logistics industries, and telecommunications infrastructure providers. In particular, the government aims to attract 25 of the world's top logistics, manufacturing, and service companies to set up their e-commerce operations in Singapore by 2003 (Compaq and Dell were early successes). Incentive schemes will be implemented to attract international and local companies to base their e-commerce hub activities in Singapore. International publicity will be increased to create awareness of Singapore as an e-commerce hub, in particular through promotion at trade shows. Certain innovative e-commerce services will be actively identified and supported as 'flagship' success stories. For example, two companies (Kian Ann Engineering, a local engineering firm, and EXCA, a Japan–US electronics joint venture) were recently the first to be granted tax concessions under the Trade Development Board's Approved Cyber Trader Scheme, under which firms pay just 10 percent corporation tax instead of the normal 26 percent (*The Straits Times* 2000).

3. *To encourage businesses to use e-commerce strategically*. In this thrust, education and other support programs are seen as essential to helping businesses exploit e-commerce to enhance their productivity and competitiveness. This will be facilitated in several ways: large-scale training schemes for business people to use simple e-commerce platforms; a usage promotion drive and financial incentives to improve adoption levels among SMEs; manpower development through retraining schemes and new tertiary level courses; and support to help leading local e-commerce providers succeed internationally.

4. *To promote usage of e-commerce by the public and businesses*. This thrust aims to extend the benefits of e-commerce to the general public. Firstly, the government itself will help to promote the use of e-commerce in Singapore through its electronic public services initiatives, with key public services being delivered electronically by the year 2001. Secondly, mass education schemes will provide training for the public. Thirdly, mass media schemes will be used to improve general awareness of e-commerce and its implications.

5. *To harmonize cross-border e-commerce laws and policies*. This final thrust is designed to develop Singapore as a 'trusted node' for e-commerce. The necessary legislation will be developed and periodically reviewed to ensure that Singapore laws are competitive, congruent, and internationally consistent. Areas to be considered include intellectual property rights, data protection, consumer protection, and taxation. Bilateral agreements will be sought with key trading partners, and efforts have already been initiated with Canada, Australia, and Germany. Singapore will also participate actively in international fora such as ASEAN, APEC, UN, and WTO to promote the harmonization of e-commerce frameworks.

Assessing Singapore's Progress Toward Becoming an E-Commerce Hub

On paper at least, there can be no doubt that the Electronic Commerce Masterplan represents a thorough, comprehensive, and wide-ranging policy intervention in the drive to develop e-commerce in Singapore. We now move on to consider how far Singapore has progressed thus far in its bid to become an e-commerce hub. Figure 8.2 presents a stylized depiction of the e-commerce environment in Singapore, reflecting the all-encompassing policy approach that has been adopted. In this section, we will use the components of this diagram as a framework for assessing e-commerce developments. Next, we briefly consider some preliminary evidence from large-scale surveys that attempt to quantify levels of e-commerce in Singapore.

At the level of the general e-commerce environment, largely associated with government policy, Singapore has made significant progress in developing legal frameworks, technical standards, and incentive schemes for e-commerce. In terms of legal frameworks, a major step was the enactment of the Electronic Transactions Act, an Electronic Commerce Policy Committee recommendation, which came into force in July 1998. This Act covers a broad range of issues pertaining to e-commerce, including the authentication of the originator of electronic messages, the legal recognition of electronic signatures, the retention of records by electronic means, the formation and validity of electronic contracts, and the legal liability of service providers. Other developments include amendments to the Computer Misuse Act to give greater protection to critical computer systems, and an updating of copyright laws to protect multimedia works. With regard to standards, Singapore has established a set of open, industry-led standards in the areas of network protocols, security, e-mail and directories, e-commerce, and information sources and exchange, all designed to facilitate the interconnection and interoperability of businesses via computer networks. The drive to establish standards is becoming increasingly international: in June 1998, the NCB signed the world's first international cross-certification agreement with a transaction certification authority in Canada. Singapore has also instituted a range of incentive schemes to promote e-commerce. For example, the Cluster Development Fund and Innovation Development Scheme (through the Economic Development Board) can provide funds for qualifying companies to develop their e-commerce projects. The

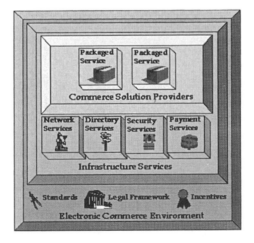

Figure 8.2 *Graphic representation of Singapore's e-commerce infrastructure. Source: [http://www.ec.gov.sg]*

Approved Cyber Trader Scheme targets companies that use Singapore as a base from which to undertake international trading activities via e-commerce. In a scheme targeted specifically at SMEs, an S$9 million (US$5.4 million) extension of the NCB's Local Enterprise Computerization Programme offers grants of up to S$20 000 (US$12 000) for the first 500 SMEs that make the move into e-commerce. In order to assist businesses in gaining information on the evolving plethora of e-commerce policies and schemes, in August 1999 the NCB established a 'one-stop' help desk to coordinate the dissemination of information (NCB 1999). Again reflective of the breadth of institutions mobilized in Singapore's e-commerce drive, some 14 ministries and statutory boards were listed as partners in the help desk initiative. In addition to financial incentives, a range of educational programs has been initiated to raise awareness both among local businesses (such as the 'eVision' workshop for CEOs and 'ec.Think' think tank set up by Andersen Consulting and the NCB) and the general public (through 'eSales' and road shows to encourage online shopping).

The next domain presented in Figure 8.2 is that of infrastructure services, which is characterized by a high level of collaboration between government and business. Infrastructure services can usefully be subdivided into four components. First, network services provide the networks that enable e-commerce. Such services are provided by private sector Internet service providers, of which there are three in Singapore (Pacific Internet – part of the Sembawang Group, Singnet – an arm of Singapore Telecom, and Starhub – a joint venture involving Singapore Technologies) and broadband network access providers such as Singapore Telecom's Magix service and Singapore Cable Vision's cable modem service. It is perhaps worth noting that infrastructure providers are tightly regulated in Singapore, with all these services being controlled by Government Linked Corporations detailed above (GLCs – privatized, formerly state-owned corporations, over which the state still holds significant managerial control). In addition, there are a wide variety of companies providing value-added network services (both local and foreign). Singapore's actual physical infrastructure is very advanced. Singapore currently has a direct Internet connection to the US Internet backbone (45 Mbps as of mid-1999), and through the Singapore Telecom Internet eXchange (STIX) acts as an Asian Internet hub, connecting to over 20 countries in the Asia–Pacific region. Singapore's renowned 'Singapore ONE' network provides for broadband access to homes, businesses, libraries, and kiosks across Singapore. Second, there are also a wide variety of directory services on offer in Singapore, allowing customers to search for information and web sites. Some general-purpose search engines such as Yahoo! have Singapore sites (http://www.yahoo.com.sg), and there are also a range of directory services that serve the local context, such as the Shopping Village which covers over 180 online retailers (http://www.shoppingvillage.com.sg), and the National Contact Information Service which provides contact information of people and organizations in Singapore (http://www.ncis.ncb.gov.sg/). The 'Singapore Infomap' provides a useful compilation of such directory services (http://www.sg).

The third infrastructure services component is that of security services. While many tools are available commercially from vendors such as Microsoft and Netscape, the NCB's Infrastructure for Electronic Identification initiative (IEI) is a local initiative seeking to provide secure communication and identification through digital certificates and signatures. A company, Netrust, was established in July 1997 as a joint venture between the NCB and the Network for Electronic Transfers (Singapore) (NETS) to issue and manage digital keys and certificates. At the time this was Southeast Asia's first Certification Authority set up to provide a complete online identification and security infrastructure. Payments services constitute the fourth and final element of infrastructure services. Several secure online payment systems are already in place in Singapore. For example, consumers can make low-value online payments using a stored-value smart card through NETS C-ONE service. Another NETS service, the Financial Electronic Data Interchange (FEDI) allows payment and collection instructions to be sent electronically in a manner similar to an inter-bank GIRO. An Electronic Commerce Hotbed initiative started in 1996 has made significant progress towards developing a Secure Electronic Transactions (SET) protocol to support secure credit card payments. In April 1997, the NCB, in partnership with Visa International, Citibank and IBM, Brel Software, and Mentor Internet Solutions announced the world's first secure Visa card payment over the Internet. It is hoped that SET will become the global standard for credit card transactions, and an increasing number of banks and businesses are becoming involved in piloting the protocol in Singapore. In addition to these moves to develop open standards, a range of companies now offer secure payment system solutions for the particular requirements of their clients.

The third level of the e-commerce infrastructure (Figure 8.2) is that of commerce solution providers (CSPs), of which there are a wide variety in Singapore. Such CSPs offer complete e-commerce solutions to businesses that do not have the capability, or choose not to, implement their own e-commerce services. Some CSPs create and host e-commerce web sites for merchants that sell directly to consumers (see for example, AsiaOne Commerce – http://www.ecomz.com/), while others provide services for electronic transactions between businesses (see BookNet for example – http://www.booknet.com.sg/). Overall, there already appears to be a well-developed and sophisticated infrastructure for e-commerce in Singapore, supporting a wide range of specific e-commerce applications, ranging from the government sector (e.g. electronic filing of tax returns), through retailing and leisure (e.g. online shopping with Cold Storage supermarkets) to the financial sector (e.g. Internet banking and share trading). This growing infrastructure not only provides ever-increasing levels of high-skill, high-wage employment in itself, but is also designed to make Singapore an attractive location for companies to establish their own e-commerce operations.

E-Commerce Implementation Progress?

The central test of Singapore's e-commerce drive will be to see how the developing infrastructure stimulates actual levels of e-commerce. Results from an NCB survey conducted in early 1999 provide some indication of the current level of business-to-business e-commerce in Singapore (see http://www.ec.gov.sg). Over 1000 companies of varying sizes were surveyed across three manufacturing and five service sectors. Overall, just 9 percent of companies were currently using some kind of Internet-based e-commerce, with a further 28 percent expressing an interest in doing so in the following six months. However, the level of usage varied between different sectors and size categories. While 15 percent of manufacturers of electronic products were already using e-commerce, less than 5 percent of firms in other sectors such as aircraft manufacturing, courier services, chemical and chemical products manufacturing, and storing and warehousing services were doing so (Figure 8.3). In terms of firm size, 17 percent of companies with over 100 employees were using e-commerce, compared with only 8 percent of small and medium-sized firms with less than 100 staff (Figure 8.4). The volumes of business undertaken electronically by firms are still quite small, with over 90 percent of firms undertaking less than S$100 000 (US$60 000) of business each month in terms of both Internet sales and procurement. Interestingly, some 45 percent of the firms already using e-commerce procured over 50 percent of purchases from overseas suppliers. Of the firms planning to adopt e-commerce in the next six months, only 6.5 percent thought they would procure over 50 percent of electronic purchases overseas. Taken together with anecdotal evidence from the press, the survey suggests

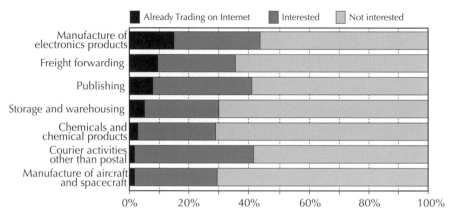

Figure 8.3   *Interest and usage of business-to-business e-commerce in Singapore by industry. Source: NCB Business-to-business EC Survey 1999 [http://www/ec/gov.sg]*

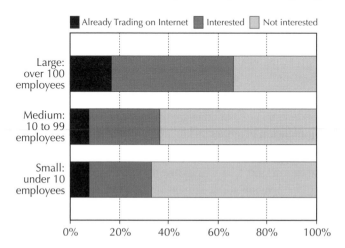

Figure 8.4   *Interest and usage of business-to-business e-commerce in Singapore by company size. Source: NCB Business-to-business EC Survey 1999 [http://www/ec/gov.sg]*

that e-commerce is entering a transitionary stage in Singapore: while the level of penetration among large multinational companies in certain manufacturing sectors (namely electronics) is quite high, e-commerce is now starting to attract the attention of small and medium-sized local firms in a variety of sectors.

Preliminary research by Saw (1999) into the uptake of e-commerce by insurance and computer product SMEs in Singapore illustrates some of the social and cultural constraints that may make the 50 percent penetration target of the Masterplan difficult to achieve. Saw categorizes these constraints under eight interrelated headings, ranging from issues such as individual preference and awareness, to factors such as need, cost, and corporate culture (see Table 8.2 for a summary). More generally, the local press has reported anecdotal evidence that the high bank charges and security problems associated with online credit transactions are slowing the uptake of e-commerce in the SME sector (*The Straits Times* 1999a). For instance, while the SET protocol described above is available to ensure security, it requires all individual customers to install certain software on their computers. These findings add more detail to the conclusions of the large-scale e-commerce survey that of the companies already or planning to use e-commerce, security issues were seen as the main barrier to uptake, while for those with no current plans to adopt e-commerce, the lack of need for electronic transactions was the main factor. A 1999 Department of Statistics survey of 2000 companies suggested that e-commerce transactions in Singapore in 1998 were

Table 8.2   *Constraints on the uptake of e-commerce by SME's in Singapore*

Factor	Characteristics
Individual preference	Personal unfamiliarity with IT and electronic networks
	Personal preference for other forms of communication
	Personal concerns over reliability and security of electronic networks
Company culture	Resistance to change in dominant forms of communication
	Collective preference for more traditional forms of communication
	Continued preference for paper based systems of communication
Awareness	Lack of awareness of different types of electronic networks
	Lack of awareness of potential uses of e-commerce
Need	Business not deemed to require e-commerce
	E-commerce not used by competitors or customers
Social factors	Personal touch deemed crucial to business
	Face-to-face contact more important than electronic networks
	E-commerce not seen to build trust in relationships
Cost	High cost of installing relevant hardware
	High cost of hiring qualified staff to maintain and update networks
	Widespread availability of cheaper alternative communications
Purpose	Perceived as only being useful for non-urgent functions
	Perceived as only being useful for large volumes of information
	Perceived as only being useful in long-standing relations where trust has been established
Compatibility	Concerns over compatibility with customers and suppliers
	Concerns over compatibility with overseas parties

(Adapted from Saw (1999, pp. 86–7.)

worth S$1.2 billion (US$0.72 billion), up from S$723 million (US$434 million) in 1997, with a projection of S$1.5 billion (US$0.9 billion) for 1999. Such data suggests that e-commerce growth was not hit badly by the Asian economic crisis, and indeed many companies may have started switching to online transactions as a cost-reduction measure. Overall, however, the survey found that only 4 percent of businesses were engaging in e-commerce with their suppliers and partners, and only 2 percent with end consumers (*The Straits Times* 1999b). Business-to-business e-commerce accounted for 97 percent of total transactions by value, which chimes well with a consumer survey of 1500 adults in Singapore that found only 2 percent had ever made a purchase over the Internet (see http://www.ec.gov.sg). Such regular surveys, themselves another element of the Masterplan, will continue to provide the best guide as to how the implementation of e-commerce policy is proceeding in Singapore, and whether adoption is effectively permeating the consumer and SME marketplaces as planned.

Of course, Singapore's ultimate success as an e-commerce hub will also depend on the extent to which other cities in the competitive environment of the Asia–Pacific can themselves emerge and progress as important nodes in the space of electronic flows. A plethora of consultancy reports predict explosive growth in Asia–Pacific e-commerce over the next few years – Dataquest, for example suggests that business-to-business e-commerce will increase from US$18 billion in 1999 to US$280 billion in 2003 – but it is difficult to predict how much of this business will be transacted in particular centers. Many countries other than Singapore are now pursuing initiatives to tap into this growth (for example the Multimedia Super Corridor (MSC) in Malaysia, the Cyberport in Hong Kong, and Jakarta's Cybercity). In addition to the social, infrastructural, and policy considerations outlined in this chapter, other comparative considerations such as telecommunications costs and perceived political stability will also come into play. However, while competition will undoubtedly continue to increase, initial evidence seems to suggest that Singapore will gain a significant proportion (in relation to its size) of Asia–Pacific e-commerce. A 1998 survey of SSL web server densities (SSL web servers support web payments with Secure Sockets Layer protocol) in Asia gives an indication of Singapore's favorable level of e-commerce hub development: while Singapore had 22.33 servers per 1 million inhabitants, Hong Kong had 9.86, Japan 3.40, Taiwan 1.95, Malaysia 1.14, South Korea 0.83, Thailand 0.10, Indonesia 0.06, and the Philippines 0.04 (*Asia Computer Weekly* 1999). Another survey in 1999 (*Business Times*, 1999) found approximately 1400 web sites in the Asia–Pacific selling online to consumers, of which some 100 were in Singapore. In volume terms, the markets of Japan and South Korea, and in the longer term, China and India, will dominate the structure of e-commerce in the region, and much of this business will be enacted through companies and cybermediaries within those national economies. In Southeast Asian terms, however, Singapore has a substantial lead over its neighbors in terms of both policy implementation and current e-commerce levels, and seems ideally placed to fulfill its aim of emerging as an influential hub city.

CONCLUSION

We propose that the emergent global trend toward e-commerce will not have the spatially homogenizing effects that some ultra-technologists predict. Instead, as with previous technoeconomic systems, the world of e-commerce will be characterized by distinctive and constantly evolving patterns of uneven development. Place, in the abstract sense, and cities, in their material form, will remain of the utmost importance, as there will continue to be a need for centers of coordination and control, or hubs and nodes, in the intensifying world of electronic flows. At a conceptual level, we have proposed three arguments why this is so. First, there are sociocultural aspects to e-commerce that are embedded in particular places and contexts. Second, the effective operationalization of e-commerce does not simply require an electronic link between two parties, but in many cases also relies upon a whole range of e-commerce service providers (logistics, distribution, etc.) and cybermediaries (online gateways, search services, etc.). Third, the development of e-commerce also requires a particular policy context that ensures stability, reliability, security, and transparency. Thus, there may be significant 'first mover' advantages for cities (or regions) that are able to combine their existing IT knowledge base and logistics and distribution functions with an institutional and policy framework that is supportive of e-commerce.

As we stated earlier, due to its unique political economy, there may be problems associated with using Singapore as any kind of transferable role model. However, as our analysis of Singapore's policy drive to become an e-commerce hub has shown, several aspects of policy formulation and implementation may be suggested as being indicative to 'best practice' (see also Choo 1997). We make four main points in this regard. First, and most simply, we argue that there is a powerful argument for coordinated national policy intervention to stimulate and facilitate e-commerce development, and that increasingly such policies will need to be oriented toward international harmonization and standardization. Although some will see any kind of policy intervention as unnecessary and distortive, without some form of central coordination e-commerce markets may develop in a piecemeal and ineffectual manner. While Singapore is peculiarly well placed to implement such schemes, these are issues that all states will have to address in the near future. Second, the Singaporean case illustrates that a broad-based and integrated set of e-commerce policies is desirable. This goes way beyond providing a legal and regulatory framework for electronic transactions, and includes areas such as developing secure payment systems, coordinating standards, nurturing IT skills, building business and public awareness, attracting both foreign investors and local uptake through incentive schemes, and fostering support services. The Singaporean idea is to develop the complete environment from which an e-commerce hub may emerge. Third, we suggest that Singapore illustrates the kind of progressive institutional support that is necessary to mobilize such initiatives. While the NCB has played a crucial coordinating role, the success of e-commerce policy formation in Singapore arguably rests on the large number of parties that have been consulted, covering a broad range of ministries, statutory boards, foreign multinationals, local businesses, and educational establishments. This pluralistic approach, although undeniably strongly marshaled by state institutions, has speedily produced a coherent policy framework well in advance of other countries in the region. Finally, we suggest that the Singapore case indicates that e-commerce hub development should not purely be left to either state institutions or the private sector, but ultimately relies on sustained and effective collaboration between the two domains. Thus, while it may well turn out that Singapore has already gained an unassailable head start in e-commerce development in the Asia–Pacific region, there are elements of policy 'best practice' that authorities in other states may do well to emulate.

ACKNOWLEDGEMENTS

Neil Coe would like to acknowledge the financial support of NUS Academic Research Grant RP3982090, entitled: 'High-tech hubs and knowledge flows: IT sector linkages between Southeast Asia and the USA'.

How do nodes survive in e-commerce
- Place-based nature of transactions/mutuality
- State regulation (Singapore)
- Provision of related IT services
    - credit services
    - warehousing + distn
    - security of IT transactions

(?)

Place

9

Finding the Source of Amazon.com: Examining the Store with the 'Earth's Biggest Selection'

MARTIN DODGE

University College London, UK

INTRODUCTION

Amazon.com is an archetype of the emerging e-commerce, heralded by many as a paragon of the bright future of retailing. But what is the real story behind the hype? How did it come to be, how has it grown in its five-year history, how has it established such a strong brand on the Internet and beyond, what is its strategy to build a loyal customer base, and what might its impacts be on 'bricks-and-mortar' retailers? Amazon.com had net sales revenue of $1.64 billion in 1999 and a customer base of over 17 million people. It is consistently the most popular e-commerce web site on the Internet and has enjoyed spectacular growth in every year of operation. For example, sales grew by 169 percent from 1998 to 1999, but significantly it has not yet made any profits. The company has also expanded rapidly in terms of the range of goods sold, moving beyond books to sell music, videos, toys, and tools, and thereby making the grand claim of offering consumers the 'Earth's biggest selection'. The company was founded and is led by the ebullient Jeff Bezos, who was named 'person of the year' by *Time Magazine* for 1999.

HISTORY OF AMAZON.COM

Few companies in recent history have enjoyed such a successful birth as Amazon.com. In the space of five years, Amazon.com has built a powerful brand in the USA and internationally that rivals many established corporations. It is widely recognized as the largest and most high-profile online retailer in the world. This position is more remarkable when you consider that Amazon.com lacks the physical presence of stores of the conventional retailers. It has also expanded the range of goods it stocks through internal expansion and an aggressive strategy of acquisitions and investments. The history of these developments from the opening of the first public web site on July 16, 1995 through January, 2000 is plotted in the timeline (Table 9.1).

The core ethos of the company rests firmly on the shoulders of one man, Jeffrey P. Bezos, the founder, chief executive, and largest shareholder in the company. Bezos is Amazon.com and Amazon.com is Bezos. The success of the company has also made him a multi-billionaire, on paper at least, and led to him being named *Time*'s 'person of

Table 9.1   *Timeline of Amazon.com*

Date	Event
July 16, 1995	Amazon.com website opens for business
December 1995	Net sales of $0.51 million
December 1996	Net sales of $15.75 million and 0.18 million customers
October 14, 1997	One millionth customer account
November 18, 1997	Second distribution center in Delaware opens
December 1997	Net sales of $147.8 million and 1.5 million customers
April 1998	Acquires Bookpages Ltd in UK and ABC Burcherdient in Germany
May 15, 1998	IPO. Initial stock price: $18.00
June 11, 1998	Music store opens at Amazon.com
August 4, 1998	Acquires Junglee and PlanetAll.com
October 15, 1998	Amazon.co.uk and Amazon.de open
November 17, 1998	Video and gift stores open at Amazon.com
December 1998	Net sales of $610 million and 6.2 million customers
January 7, 1999	Nevada distribution center opens
February 24, 1999	Investment in and alliance with Drugstore.com (46% stake)
March 29, 1999	Investment in Pets.com (54% stake)
March 30, 1999	Online auction site opens at Amazon.com
April 12, 1999	Acquires Livebid.com, Accept.com and Alexa Internet
April 13, 1999	Kansas distribution center opens
April 26, 1999	Acquires Exchange.com
May 18, 1999	Investment in Homegrocer.com (35% stake)
May 25, 1999	Two distribution centers in Kentucky open
June 7, 1999	Ten millionth customer account
June 8, 1999	Georgia distribution center opens
June 16, 1999	Alliance with Sotheby's auction house ($45 million investment)
July 14, 1999	Investment in Gear.com (49% stake)
October 4, 1999	'Amazon.com Anywhere' launched
October 15, 1999	Tacoma customer-service center opens
October 27, 1999	Toys, electronics and zShops stores open at Amazon.com
November 9, 1999	Home improvement, software, video games, gift ideas stores open
November 10, 1999	Alliance with NextCard credit card (9.9% stake)
November 11, 1999	Grand Forks customer-service center expands
December 1, 1999	Alliance with Ashford.com (16.6% stake)
December 1999	Net sales of $1.64 billion and 17 million customers
January 13, 2000	Huntington, West Virginia, customer-service center opens
January 21, 2000	Investment in Greenlight.com (5% stake)
January 31, 2000	Investment in Audible.com (5% stake)

(Amazon.com company reports & press releases.)

the year' in 1999. His face is one of the key visual motifs used to represent the company in the media. Bezos is one of the archetypal 1990s relaxed, media-friendly chief executive officers (CEO) (Figure 9.1). He enjoys a good personal profile in the press and media. De Jonge describes him as a '. . . brilliant, charming, hyper and misleadingly goofy mastermind' (De Jonge 1999, p. 36). His persona is typical of the jovial 'tech-nerd' millionaires, with his informal dress sense and attitude. His ability and drive have also been underestimated by competitors, to their cost. One pundit famously predicted the failure of the company, terming it 'Amazon.toast' (Kotha and Rindova 1998). Bezos is hard-working and hard-driving on his employees, injecting an almost missionary zeal in the company, whose motto is 'work hard, have fun, make history'. He passionately believes Amazon.com will lead a revolution in the way the world shops. De Jonge, again, tellingly comments that, '. . . Bezos is one of the world's most ascendant capitalists, with apparently boundless ambition' (De Jonge 1999, p. 68). However, the company came in for more criticism in 1999, as worries surfaced about increasingly heavy losses, future growth, and profitability.

It is widely understood that the idea for forming an e-commerce company came to Bezos in an almost revelationary moment in the summer of 1994, when working at an investment bank on Wall Street. He is reported to have seen the statistic that the Internet was growing at 2300 percent a year. His oft-quoted response was that 'It was my wake-up call' (Kotha and Rindova 1999; Quittner 1999). Bezos's choice of books as the initial target market for an online shopping venture was prudent, because databases of books in print were readily available and could easily be linked to a web site for customers to interactively search. Also, the mammoth book superstores of Borders and Barnes & Noble could only stock a fraction of the books in print. This feature is perhaps the key advantage that online retailers have over store-based ones, that is, being able to offer customers a huge, easily searchable selection of goods that cannot be stocked in even the largest stores. In addition, the two dominant players in the US book market, Barnes & Noble and Borders, only held about 12 percent of the market, meaning there were not any '800-pound gorillas' that controlled the territory. Bezos clearly saw the book market as ripe for a new style of aggressive competitor and he was proved right.

Figure 9.1 *Jeff Bezos, founder and CEO of Amazon.com. Source: Amazon.com*

The prototype Amazon.com web site was built on workstations in the garage of the house Bezos rented in Seattle, very much fitting the myths of other successful technology start-ups like Apple and Microsoft (Cringely 1996). The web site went live in July 1995 and within a couple of months the company was doing $20 000 worth of business a week. The Amazon.com name quickly spread by word of mouth, clever marketing and an increasingly large advertising budget. Expansion has been rapid ever since.

In the beginning of the company's history there was the idea of Amazon.com as the 'David' figure, in the 'David v Goliath' battles with established retailers. The small upstart Amazon.com presented itself as battling the mighty 'brick-bound' bookstore to offer consumers better service and lower prices. At the beginning of Amazon.com's history there was certainly substance to this 'David' image as it was dwarfed in scale by both Borders and Barnes & Noble (1997 revenues for Borders were $1.9 billion, Barnes & Noble $2.4 billion and Amazon.com only $147 million). Lawsuits launched from the likes of Wal-Mart and Barnes & Noble against Amazon.com in the past helped perpetuate the 'David' myth (Sullivan 1998b). However, Amazon.com has quickly caught up, gaining marketing share and diversifying significantly beyond books, with 1999 sales revenues of $1.64 billion (US) and a market capitalization of over $22 billion (as of January 2000). It is now the 'Goliath' in the retail e-commerce book world.

KEY STRATEGIES IN THE DEVELOPMENT OF AMAZON.COM

Amazon.com has been a pioneer in e-commerce and many of its strategies have become common practice in the industry. There are four key areas of strategy at the core of the company's success over the last five years: infinite selection, technological innovation, customer service ethos, and community.

The power of the web is almost infinite in scope. An online shop, like Amazon.com, can list an almost infinite range of goods. These goods do not require the shelf space of conventional stores, because they only exist as a web page (bits of information) until purchased by the customer. The web page for any given item can be generated from a computer database an infinite number of times at a marginal cost. In the case of books, there are several million titles in print and even the largest superstores can only display a fraction of these, but at Amazon.com customers can quickly search the database and order any of them. Amazon.com claims to offer customers the widest selection of goods in the world, some 18 million as of January 1999. This infinite selection is also available to anyone in the world who is online at any time of day or night.

Commentators have also noted that the choice of name Amazon.com is important in generating a fresh image, differentiating it from existing 'bricks-and-mortar' retailers. It could be argued that the image of the Amazon.com creates a sense in people's minds of a place of vastness, a never-ending river, a store much larger than in the physical world, and thereby being able to offer unrivaled selection (Kotha and Rindova 1999). There is also the conscious decision to add .com to the name, instantly establishing its online credentials. While De Jonge eloquently says of the name, '. . . overflowing with so much third-world, underdog, eco-conscious goodwill that every click on Amazon.com feels like a vote for the rain forest' (De Jonge 1999, p. 40).

In terms of technological innovation Amazon.com has been at the forefront of web site engineering in constructing a scalable infrastructure that can seamlessly handle millions of customers a day, as well as developing distribution and logistics systems to fulfill customer orders quickly and reliably. Much of this innovation is hidden from the public's view. Probably the most visible innovations that Amazon.com customers see are the recommendations system, 1-Click ordering and wish lists. For registered customers the Amazon.com web site will attempt to make intelligent recommendations of goods you might like based on what you have purchased and viewed in the past. 1-Click order was first introduced in September 1997 and allows customers to configure the web site so they can purchase goods with a single click of the mouse, thereby bypassing lengthy form filling. This innovation is viewed by the company as one of its most significant technologies to make online shopping as easy as possible. It received a patent for it in September, 1999 and has since launched litigation to prevent infringement.

A strong customer service ethos is deeply instilled in the Amazon.com corporate culture. In virtually every interview Bezos gives he proudly reiterates the Amazon.com mission that 'Our vision is that we want to be the world's most customer-centric company' (*Business Week* 1999c, p. 54). This customer service commitment costs a significant amount and Amazon has invested considerable financial and human resources during the company's startup. In the second half of 1999 the company opened three new service centers across the USA. This decision appears to be paying dividends as the company reports that during the fourth quarter of 1999 over 70 percent of orders were repeat business from existing customers. Amazon also handles all the packaging and delivery of goods in-house, rather than outsourcing this function. This decision requires significant warehousing facilities (see Geography of Amazon.com section below, p. 177), but allows the company to maintain full control over the product fulfillment processes which are crucial to meeting customers' expectations of online retailing.

To build customer trust and loyalty Amazon.com has also been successful in promoting the communal ethos whereby shoppers become actively involved in the company beyond simply spending money. This feature is seen most obviously in the facility to write and post short book reviews on the web site; it has proved to be popular. Also, thousands of customers have signed up for the Associates program, which has been a particularly successful initiative. It is a form of micro-franchising where other web sites list goods such as books and CDs (usually in a specialized niche) which are linked to Amazon.com for purchasing. The owner of the Associate site earns a small commission of between 5 and 15 percent for every sale generated for Amazon.com. There are more than 350 000 Associate sites and these represent a huge number of virtual storefronts scattered across the web that direct business to Amazon.com (Johnson 1999).

MARKET CAPITALIZATION AND VALUATION ISSUES

The history and strategy of Amazon.com has often been lost in the hyperbole of the company's stock price and market capitalization. Along with AOL, Microsoft,

Yahoo!, eBay, and a handful of other companies, Amazon.com was very much one of the 'it' stocks of the Internet economy at the end of the 1990s. The boom in Internet stocks is one of the key drivers of US economic prosperity at the turn of the millennium. The actual Amazon.com company is truly virtual as its actuality seems to bear little relation to its valuation on the stock market. Many reports on Amazon.com focus on its capitalization and the fact that it is worth so much more than large, established, and profitable corporations. For example, a *Business Week* article from December, 1998 included a table entitled 'Amazon's Amazing Valuation' showing it ahead of firms like Hilton Hotels, Barnes & Noble, Toys 'R' Us and Kmart. Amazon's valuation is based on hope, and one might say dreams, of future returns. To date, Amazon.com has not made a profit and it is not projected to do so for another couple of years, however, in the latest financial results (February 2000) the company reported that the US book segment showed a profit.

As of January 26, 2000, Amazon.com's market capitalization on the Nasdaq stock market was $22.4 billion (US), with a share price of $62. This figure compares to an initial valuation at the initial public offering (IPO) in May, 1997 of $18.00 a share. The fluctuations in Amazon.com stock price from May 1997 to the end of January, 2000 are shown in Figure 9.2. In the later half of 1998 Amazon.com share price increased dramatically, along with many other Internet stocks. A peak valuation of $80 per share was reached in early January, 1999 followed by a significant downward readjustment. 1999 was a dramatic year for Amazon.com's share price, with large swings over relatively short time scales. There were a series of peaks and troughs, with a high-water mark of $106.00 in December, 1999.

Amazon.com has posted some extremely impressive growth figures since opening for business in 1995, which has impressed the stock market. The growth in sales revenues, net losses, customers, and advertising costs over the five years the company has been trading on the web is significant. Amazon.com's net sales have increased dramatically, for example, from 1996 to 1997 they grew by a massive 838 percent from $15.75 million (US) to $147.79. Sales powered ahead by 321 percent in 1998 driven by a growing customer base, the opening of subsidiaries in the UK and Germany, and expanding in music and videos. From 1997 to 1998 the number of customers quadrupled, reaching over 6 million; 1999 saw slower growth in sales of merely 169 percent

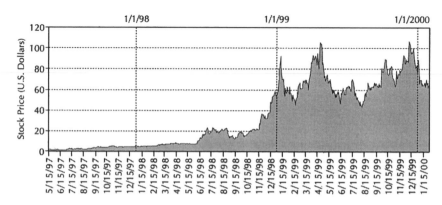

Figure 9.2   *Fluctuating Amazon.com stock price. Source: [http://www.nasdaq.com]*

with the customer base more than doubling. To sustain this level of expansion Amazon.com has invested heavily in acquisitions, marketing, infrastructure, and a deep inventory, all resulting in mounting losses each year. In 1999 the net loss was some $720 million, an increase of 478 percent over 1998.

The crucial question to consider is whether these figures justify the huge expectations of future earnings on which Amazon.com's stock valuation is based. Some critics argue that Amazon and the other high-flying Internet stocks are the result of a classic 'bubble' and are not being judged rationally. Comparisons have been drawn between Internet stocks in the late 1990s and other famous speculative bubbles from history, such as for tulip bulbs[1] in Holland in 1637 (Terkowitz 1999), railway companies in the 1840s and radio stocks in the 1920s (Chancellor 1999). Many analysts are struggling to define new models and parameters that fit the empirical facts of the stock prices, which *Business Week* memorably described as 'Trying to get your arms around the value of an Internet stock is like trying to hug air' (*Business Week* 1998a).

If one accepts that Amazon.com is part of an Internet stocks bubble, the key question is when will it burst? (*The Economist* 1999). There were some sizable readjustments in the stock price in the spring of 1999, but it still remains much higher than when the company went public. Amazon.com shares are also highly volatile, with wild fluctuations at the slightest news or rumor, subject to rampant speculation and sudden panics (Figure 9.2). The massive capitalization is also a powerful distorting lens making it difficult to gauge the real worth of Amazon.com. De Jonge describes the result as '. . . Amazon.com is a $20 billion, 2100-employee company built on the thin membrane of a bubble, and this brings a manic precariousness to the place that no amount of profitless growth can diminish' (De Jonge 1999, p. 39). The bubble has facilitated Amazon.com's rapid expansion in 1998 and especially 1999 through acquisitions and investments. Bezos and other Amazon.com executives have assiduously avoided comment on the swings in stock value. But it is certainly a key motivating factor for many employees who enjoy stock options. Bezos is a paper multibillionaire from the stock value, but has reportedly only sold one small block of shares, netting himself around $23 million (Bayers 1999).

THE GEOGRAPHY OF AMAZON.COM

Amazon.com has several important geographical dimensions, both real and virtual. For any Internet company the principal public face is their web site. Amazon.com's web site is vital, it is its store-front to the world, accessible to tens of millions of potential customers. Web sites are a form of geography – geography of the screen. Amazon.com's home page screen design is simple and functional, almost to the point of being plain (Figure 9.3). It is easy to use and, crucially, fast loading over home modems with only a few small graphics. The site is also backed up with technical innovations such as 1-Click ordering. To explore the virtual space of Amazon's web site one either browses or uses keyword searching. Web pages are generated from databases of the 18 million books, CDs, videos, toys, tools, and gifts that the company currently sells.

Figure 9.3 *Amazon.com home page, February 2000. Source: Amazon.com*

The geography of the screen is a world in miniature, totally under the control of the designers (Johnson 1997). The design and usability of web sites is an area of increasing concern given the growing number of people who are accessing information and services via this medium. This is not necessarily an area for geographical concern, as it is more at the scale of architecture (Wurman 1997) and graphic design (Nielsen 1999). The major reasons people shop online is the speed and convenience of the experience; however, too many web site designs fail seriously to meet these requirements (Chaplin 1999; Lohse and Spiller 1999). Key problems remain – difficulties with site navigation, confusion over how to order, and most especially slow loading pages. These difficulties all impact directly the experience of shopping online. Amazon.com is better than many e-commerce sites and this is reflected in its growing number of customers (see Table 9.1) and the high volume of repeat business. For some customers, usability is also an issue of accessibility, for example, when sites are rendered completely unusable for people with disabilities (Waddell 1999).

In addition to screen space, domain name space is a vital commodity in today's Internet. The history of the domain name system means there is an artificial scarcity of names in the prized .com portion, with people launching a 'land-grab' for the short, memorable name (Shaw 1997). A good domain name is vital to the establishment of an online presence. It is as equally as important as having the right retail locations in the real world. Domain names are a combination of brands and virtual locations. Their importance is illustrated by the high prices companies are willing to pay to secure the most appropriate and memorable name for their business, for example the BBC buying bbc.com or Compaq paying over $3 million for altavista.com (Bicknell 1999). Amazon.com is clearly synonymous with its domain name, but beyond its core web sites (amazon.com, amazon.co.uk and amazon.de), it has also made a land grab of its own, registering over 40 additional names under .com alone (as of summer, 1999). Many of these names are clearly related to its core retailing areas of books, videos, and music, while other names have been registered for future expansion and also to lock out 'carpetbaggers'.

Another important geographical dimension is the geography of growth, expansion, and diversification. This has certainly been rapid, as can be seen from the growth in revenues shown in Table 9.1. The growth is evident in both new online stores, major investments in other companies and new physical facilities. Figure 9.4 maps out the extent and landmarks of the Amazon.com empire as of January 2000, showing the results of both internal expansion and external diversification through acquisition. At the core of the map is Amazon.com itself, represented by the solid rectangle, which in the real world is spatially represented at the headquarters address at 1516 Second Avenue, Seattle, but it is more meaningfully mapped by its web site location at http://www.amazon.com. Surrounding Amazon are all the associated properties and facilities, both real and virtual.

It is obvious that Amazon.com does not have physical, 'bricks and mortar' retail stores. Instead it has a growing number of virtual stores on its web site. Amazon.com started with books and has moved into music, videos, and gifts in 1998, and auctions, toys, software, video games, electronics, tools, and zShops in 1999. These virtual stores are mapped as small ellipses physically connected to the Amazon.com core. In some senses these represent natural, evolutionary growth as the main Amazon.com web site becomes a vast virtual department store.

The company, as noted above, expanded and diversified, particularly in 1999, through investments and acquisitions. These additions are shown as small, rounded rectangles arranged along the bottom half of the map. They fall into three broad categories, web retailing properties, strategic technologies, and auction related. (The timeline in Table 9.1 provides details on the dates of these investments and acquisitions.) They represent a sizable outlay of capital and also highlight the considerable ambition of Bezos to expand Amazon.com beyond books. In terms of online retailing Amazon.com has invested in a range of corporations that operate their own consumer web sites, the most important being a pharmacy (Drugstore.com), pet products (Pets.com), brand sports goods (Gear.com), luxury gifts (Ashford.com), and grocery shopping (Homegrocer.com). There has also been investment in terms of online auctions with a major alliance with the world leading auction house, Sothebys, and the purchase of LiveBid.com. Amazon.com has purchased a number of companies with innovative Internet technologies as well in order to keep it ahead of the competition. For example, Alexa.com is a leading company in data-mining web traffic to find how people navigate and shop online. A recent initiative called zShops provides a sort of virtual flea market, whereby small firms and individual traders can sell to the mass of Amazon.com customers.

Despite the globalization rhetoric of the 'Earth's biggest selection', Amazon.com still felt it necessary to expand overseas by opening subsidiaries for 'local' markets. This decision was achieved with the national Amazon web sites in the UK (www.amazon.co.uk) and Germany (www.amazon.de), which both opened in October 1998. These are represented on the map in Figure 9.4 as emboldened ellipses. At present (March 2000), they do not have the range of the parent web site, only selling books and music. It may appear strange to open local stores as consumers from around the world, including the UK and Germany, can purchase at the main Amazon.com stores. At issue is to build trust with consumers outside the USA to shop with Amazon.com, when many customers perceive the store as being American, with prices in US dollars and high overseas shipping charges. The logic is that customers will be happier buying from a 'local' store, charged in local currency. (And in the case of Amazon.de the site is in German, of course.) Local distinctiveness comes from the domain names, the site design, the language employed, and unique editorial content (Steinfield and Klein 1999). Another key advantage is faster and cheaper shipping costs for books that can be sourced locally. These two new national Amazon.com subsidiaries have been successful since their launching and are the leading online bookstores in their respective countries. It will be interesting to see if and where Amazon.com opens further national branches in the near future.

Despite the localization efforts in these national branches, the reality is that true power still resides in the head office in Seattle. Like many global operations they are arguably fooling the public into thinking they are buying locally when in fact the money flows out of the country. In the case of Amazon, this can easily be revealed because the web sites of Amazon.co.uk and Amazon.de are hosted on the powerful Internet servers back in Seattle, despite the appearance of the national domain. Thus,

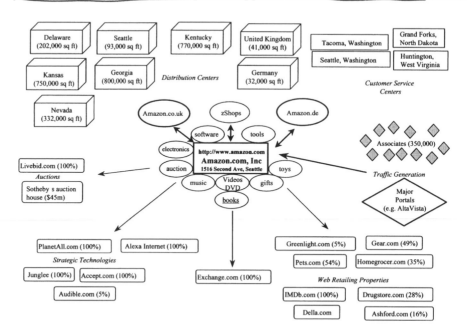

Figure 9.4 *Map of the expanding Amazon.com Empire, as of January 2000. Source: Amazon.com corporate reports*

the sales, revenues, and customer information are automatically transferred back to the USA.

Although Amazon.com is an online company, its principal activity is still shipping real goods to customers, rather than dealing purely with bits of information. To support this activity it needs facilities to store and pack goods. Amazon has had to invest significantly in warehousing, particularly in 1999, and the company currently has seven major distribution centers strategically placed throughout the USA to serve different regions. In addition there are two distribution centers in Europe to serve the UK and German subsidiaries. These are represented by cubes on Figure 9.4 and are labeled with their location and size. In 1999 Amazon.com has also greatly expanded its customer service infrastructure, opening three new centers, in addition to the one in Seattle.

The final components of the map of the Amazon.com empire is the vital 'traffic generation' infrastructure to lure visitors into their web site to buy items. The two key components of this infrastructure are the thousands of small-scale Associate sites and the links from major search engines and portals. These features are shown as diamond-shaped symbols on the right-hand side of Figure 9.4. Amazon spends millions of dollars each year for prominent links and recommendations from major search engines and portals, including, AOL, Excite, and AltaVista. This investment is very much like prominent advertising in the real world to get customers through the doors and into a store. (Amazon.com also invests heavily in 'off-line' advertising on television and in print.) Amazon.com has been very successful and is the most visited retail web site on the Internet. Web site popularity measures (like television audience figures) show Amazon.com in or around the top 10 most popular sites. Media Metrix[2] data, show that Amazon.com received an estimated 16.6 million unique visitors in December 1999.

EXPLORING THE GEOGRAPHY OF E-COMMERCE

The use and impact of e-commerce varies greatly across space and at various scales. But in the absence of firm sales/customer figures from the online companies themselves, it is very difficult to obtain an empirical handle on the differential and evolving global geography of e-commerce. (Amazon.com has not provided any data to the public on sales or customers segmented by region.) Governments and regional organizations like the EU and OECD are beginning to prepare for serious measurement (US Department of Commerce 1999; OECD 1999d), particularly as there is increasing interest in taxing e-commerce activity. In the absence of comprehensive, representative and reliable statistics on the Internet economy, there is an over-reliance of the dubious projections (speculations) from pundits and consultants, as well as high-priced research reports based on small samples, often with little geographic discrimination.

Although the Internet has diffused around the world with remarkable rapidity, there are still significant variations in access to the online world across space and within different segments of society, including the costs of getting online, which vary greatly (Hoffman and Novak 1998; McConnaughey and Lader 1999; Petrazzini and Kibati 1999). Despite the growing numbers of users outside of the USA, North America is still the overwhelmingly powerful force in the online world. Not surprisingly, the USA is leveraging this power to dominate global e-commerce. While the structure of the Internet's network infrastructure and bandwidth costs continue to give the USA unfair advantages, or what the telecom's commentator Kenneth Cukier has memorably termed 'bandwidth colonialism' (Cukier 1999). The USA also has the early adopter benefits so that all the most popular web sites are owned and located within its borders. The OECD found in 1997 that 94 of the top 100 sites were based in the USA, with 40 of these being in California (Cukier 1999). Figures from Matthew Zook's analysis of the geography of domain names ownership[3] show that 67 percent of .com domains (favored by e-commerce sites) are registered to US businesses and individuals. Other countries are developing their Internet infrastructure rapidly, but they have much to do to catch up with the USA.

Strong evidence of America's dominance of e-commerce is provided by the OECD's analysis of the geography of secure web servers used for electronic commerce (OECD 1999c). Figure 9.5 shows a bar graph of secure web servers per capita for the OECD countries in August 1999. Some 22 000 secure web servers were located in OECD countries, but 16 000 of these were in the USA, yielding a per capita measure of 6.1. This was three times the OECD average and considerably ahead of the second placed country – Iceland.

CONCLUSIONS

A key question of interest to planners and geographers is what will be the spatial impacts of e-commerce,[4] pioneered by Amazon.com, on retailing in real shops and malls. Will Amazon.com replace malls? A corollary is whether Amazon will still be in the vanguard of change in two or five years' time. Not surprisingly, Bezos is very positive about the prospects for his company and also the impacts of online retailing. For example he is quoted as saying that 'strip malls are history' (Bayers 1999, p. 116).

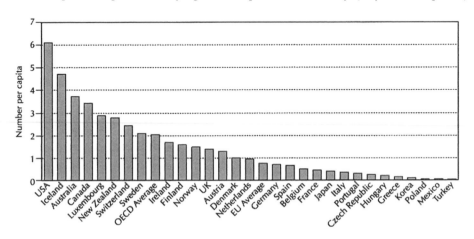

Figure 9.5 *Secure web servers used in e-commerce per capita for OECD countries, August 1999. Source: OECD 1999c*

The argument is that the convenience, wider selection, and lower prices offered by online merchants will drive the older, general purposes shopping malls to the wall as increasing market share is taken by cyberspace. However, online shopping is not likely to destroy all retailing in bricks and mortar stores, as even the most ardent virtual advocates acknowledge that the web cannot replace the physical, emotional experience of shopping in the hustle and bustle of the real world. For many people shopping is a leisure activity, where holding the goods in one's hand and the instant gratification of walking out of the store are significant. The point-and-click of web shopping cannot match this. The physical retailers that will continue to flourish are likely to be at two ends of the spectrum – the high-quality 'shoptainment' stores that provide personal service and/or an entertainment experience and the 24 × 7 convenience store. Retail space in the middle will be increasing squeezed by the online world, although the degree of impact will vary from product to product. More recently commentators have begun to argue for the advantages of a combination of web site and stores, in a strategy dubbed 'clicks-and-bricks' (Greenfeld 1999). The dominant retailers will be those who can offer an integrated shopping experience by combining the best of online and offline.

Empirical evidence on the these impacts and changes at the local scale is difficult to gather (Steinfield and Whitten 1999). It is probably still too early in the restructuring to discern boarded-up shops and closed malls as a direct consequence of virtual retailing. At present, online shopping only constitutes a small percentage of total retail spend in the USA, although it has been shown that for one market segment, the travel agency, that online merchants are dramatically affecting physical agencies (Wilson 1999). Investors' perceptions do not necessarily wait for empirical evidence as the mark down in the stock value of big corporate mall owners has shown. During 1999, the stock price of the four biggest owners of US malls fell by 14 percent (*Wired* 1999). Clearly in all the speculation on the impacts of online retailing, we need to be careful not to fall into the utopian, 'death of cities' fantasies that lurk behind much of the writing about telecommunications and the Internet (Graham 1997; Gillespie 1998).

Another important question is whether Amazon.com will suffer the fate of the hare in the race with the tortoise. Amazon.com was ahead of the curve and has grown impressively, but the question is can it fight off increasingly stiff competition from other large corporations or nibbler startups? How long will its 'first mover' advantages last? For example, the German media giant Bertelsmann AG has aggressively entered the online book market with a large investment in barnesandnoble.com and the development of the bol.com (book online) web stores in six main European countries. Amazon.com is saddled with heavy debts and the worry is that other companies with deeper pockets will wait them out in a long game and undercut them with heavier discounts. There is also an interesting new area of emerging competition from consumers who can use agent technologies for powerful comparative shopping. A good example in the field of books is the Deal Pilot comparative shopping site (Sullivan 1999a), which is powerful and easy to use, enabling one to find the best price deal from 20 plus online retailers. There are also the dangers of weakening the Amazon.com brand through too rapid and diverse expansion. Amazon.com may be just like the department stores that try to cover too much of the retail market and become vulnerable to companies that focus on just one niche.

Some have argued that despite the early lead of the online pioneers such as Amazon.com, they are inherently vulnerable because the barriers to entry are supposedly much lower than in the material world. This observation is in fact far from true. It is relatively easy and cheap to set up an e-commerce web site, but crucially it is difficult and very costly to get customers through the door (Rosenberg 1999). Getting people to visit your web site is harder than it might look. The majority of web users, like consumers in the real world, take the path of least resistance, which means they will end up at the doors of the online retailer who pays the portals and search engines the highest amount for prominent advertising and links. Only the largest will survive and make a profit online.

END NOTES

1. At the height of the legendary tulip price bubble, one bulb sold for 4200 guilders, around $1.5 million today.
2. Media Metrix are one of the leading companies undertaking web site popularity measurement. [http://www.mediametrix.com/].
3. Further details are available at [http://socrates.berkeley.edu/~zook/domain_names/index.html].
4. Of course online shopping is only a small component of e-commerce, with many predictions that the most dramatic impacts will be in the business-to-business side of things, rather than consumer retail.

· Geog of amazon in e- + geogr. space
· Reasons for success
· Hiding the 'real' loch in Seattle

10

Electronic Banking and the City System in the Netherlands

MARINA van GEENHUIZEN

Technical University of Delft, the Netherlands

and

PETER NIJKAMP

Free University of Amsterdam, the Netherlands

SETTING THE SCENE

Recent years have witnessed a rapid introduction and worldwide penetration of information and communication technologies (ICTs). The full benefits of ICTs can only be reaped if there are commonly accepted standards within institutional frameworks that ensure cooperation in a state of competition (Swann 1996). This observation is clearly reflected in recent European policies which seek to exploit benefits through a double-track approach: liberalization and harmonization of trade, financial services, and telecommunication (Sandholtz and Sweet 1998). In this context, the ICT sector will have an increasingly important role for the economic, social, and cultural development of Europe. In a directive of a decade ago (see EU Council Directive 1990) the European Commission argued that '. . . the improvement of telecommunications in the Community is an essential condition for the harmonious development of economic activities and a competitive market in the Community'. Or as Thord (1993) claims: 'A smoothly functioning system of communications is a prerequisite for social and economic integration between separate geographical regions'. Clearly, such integration efforts do not necessarily lead to more interregional balances in the EU (Fischer and Nijkamp 1999; van Geenhuizen 2000); and may reinforce competition between regions and between cities, leading to a strengthening (or weakening) of their current hierarchical status.

Historically, the application of ICTs in manufacturing and services shows a development from use in administrative processes via a broad support of primary and secondary processes and logistic organization (inventory control) to ultimately facilitating direct transactions between business and customers. Clearly, the unprecedented acceptance of ICTs has not only been propelled by technological developments, but also by dramatic cost declines in information-processing industries that were the offspring of the microelectronics revolution (Warf 1999). The result has been a massive rise in the volumes of trade in data and capital services. The financial system world-wide, for example, is entirely dependent upon the Internet connecting all countries in real time all over the world, so that 24-hour trading, banking, and stock exchange is possible (see also Shapiro and Varian 1999; Vervest and Dunn 2000).

A proper explanation for the emergence and rapidly increasing popularity of Internet and e-commerce services can be found in network externality theory (see Katz and Shapiro 1985; Farrell and Saloner 1986; Capello 1994; Economides 1996). According to van Hove (1999) there are several driving forces for the economic importance of these services, namely the existence of a critical mass of customers, the importance of the installed user base, the possibility of a first-comer advantage, the need for compatible technologies in case of market uncertainty, and the possibility of carrying out differential pricing strategies at a worldwide level. The strong point of these new services is that they offer simultaneously economies of scale and of scope in virtual network configurations.

Internet services have generated new types of advanced ICT services which will have drastic implications for the economic functioning of business activities as they create a decentralized package of opportunities; this trend is in contrast to the separate infrastructure facilities offered in the past (e.g. broadcasting, voice telephony, and online computer services). The fusion of telecommunication, data processing, and electronic applications is leading to further advances in the ICT field. In addition, mobile telecommunication means that we can access the Internet from anywhere. The gradual replacement of the old-fashioned telecommunications infrastructure in Europe, with broadband ISDN telephone cables, means that within the near future we have a range of interactive services at our disposal in our homes and workplaces. This development has undoubtedly important impacts on the way businesses interact with each other, as well as with customers.

The past few years have seen the emergence of widely different views about the future of cities as influenced by the rapidly converging computing, communication, and media technologies (Graham and Marvin 1996). One extreme scenario is that of the 'death of distance' in which place and location no longer matter and as a consequence, large industrial cities weaken their hold over economic and social life (Cairncross 1997). Urban meeting places, markets, entertainment, etc. will give way to virtual gathering, e-commerce, information exchanges, and entertainment spots for plugged-in customers. Planners and designers will structure the electronic channels, resources, interfaces, and delivery systems without constraints of physical space (Mitchell 1995). In this situation, urban functions are allowed to spread into a world where space and time converge. Already indicated by Toffler in 1980, there will be an era of widely spread 'electronic cottages', i.e., homes (re)designed to be physical access nodes for households acting as labor, producers, and consumers through multifaceted telecommunication with the outside world. Electronic cottages are freed from the need for proximity in cities, and people can therefore find a living place in rural areas. The other extreme scenario says that large cities strengthen their position at the expense of smaller ones. This scenario recognizes the role of large corporations in decision making in the global economic system, as well as the fact that their specialized decision making based on the need for face-to-face contact may hinder any trend for spread. Most probably there are only a few of such 'global urban command centers' that create pools of highly qualified professional workers (see Gillespie and Williams 1988; Graham and Marvin 1996; Sassen 1996). ICTs help to extend their dominance of other cities, by allowing for action at a distance and remote control of smaller towns and rural places. A third alternative of a more moderate nature is that ICTs enable the access of a selected number of medium-sized towns and smaller settlements to global decision-making networks. Thus far, however, the Internet age seems not to have drastically changed the economic–geographic landscape of our world; urban and regional inequalities, with a few exceptions, have largely remained the same (cf. Malecki 1999).

We take the position that ICTs have no deterministic impacts but merely work through the ways in which they are constructed by society in complex processes of institutional and personal interaction. Once technologies are available, socioeconomic actions can direct their application and change their effects in each case, including those on cities. The relation between cities and ICTs therefore, seems complex, nonlinear (e.g. the pace of technology change is not necessarily coupled with the pace of urban change) leading to different results in different places and times (Graham and Marvin 1996). In this vein this study attempts to go beyond simple dichotomous concepts, such as the 'death or rise of cities', and tries to discern the differentiation within the city system. To this end, it presents a partially retrospective empirical analysis of financial services in the Netherlands. The study focuses on the banking industry because the largest banks work in the domestic market through hierarchically built office networks, with national headquarters at the top of regional offices and local offices. The large banks in the Netherlands have changed the functional and spatial organization of their domestic office networks various times in recent decades (van Geenhuizen and van der Knaap 1998). There has been a great extension of the number of local offices since the mid-1960s in response to retail banking, with a concomitant establishment of regional coordination centers. Since the early 1980s this has been followed by a progressive rationalization and concomitant downsizing, and currently, there is an acceleration of this process due to electronic banking.

In this chapter we discuss the influence of the use of ICTs, in particular electronic banking and e-commerce in a broader sense, on the reorganization of banks and on the location of these firms in the Dutch city system. The structure is as follows. The next section is concerned with theory, explaining the location of services that operate in complex and uncertain environments. The chapter proceeds with a discussion of the development of the Dutch banking industry by focusing on headquarter functions in the city system. This is followed by an analysis of the penetration of electronic banking and its impacts on the supply of retail services lower in the city system, i.e., local and regional bank branch offices. The final section is devoted to e-commerce in the Netherlands and wider implications of the rising e-economy on banking organizations.

AGGLOMERATION ECONOMIES AND INFORMATION SPILLOVERS

The banking industry currently operates in a highly uncertain environment. Uncertainty rests on a growing competition from new entrants from other sectors and from other countries, opportunities, and threats from the penetration of new technologies and new applications, such as the Internet, and cycles of financial boom and bust, as experienced during the 1980s and 1990s. In addition, financial services at the (inter)national level need a continuously new and varied knowledge input to perform satisfactorily, and related with these services is a need for the input from highly specialized intermediate services and labor markets (e.g. Ter Hart and Piersma 1990; Porteous 1999; Leyson and Thrift 1997). This pattern holds, for example, for the lead management of syndicates, deposit taking, leading mergers, management buy-outs, portfolio management for investors, swap transactions, and stock trade in large amounts and in locally listed shares. Several theoretical notions contribute to an explanation of the location of such services, particularly the relationship with urban size.

The general arguments can be described as a reduction of costs of uncertainty and benefits from increasing returns of scale in production and technology (Arthur 1994, 1996). Following Marshall in the recognition of positive externalities at the level of individual firms, the notions of agglomeration economies and information spillovers are especially useful. Agglomeration economies include, first, cost reductions of firms in the same industry located in the same area based upon the larger scale and a more efficient division of labor, and second, cost reductions based upon a differentiated structure of economic activity and a differentiated labor market. Accordingly, agglomeration economies point to scale and differentiation (scope) as favorable attributes of production environments, and thus to large cities. The notion of increasing returns is closely related to that of agglomeration economies in that it refers to the dynamic and cumulative advantages of spatial proximity. In terms of scale of production it means decreasing unit costs related to production increase. In terms of adoption of technology, it means that the adoption of new technology is easier (cheaper) in places where other firms (have) experience(d) a similar learning curve (Arthur 1996). In particular, the latter type is important for firms that face continuously nonroutine problem solving and the need for innovation of their portfolio. This development is included within the concept of knowledge spillovers.

Knowledge spillovers refer to the phenomenon that knowledge, as a nonrivaling and nonexcluding good, generates benefits for third parties. The uses of modern ICTs have definitely increased these spillovers. In this context a distinction needs to be made between two fundamentally different types of knowledge, i.e., codified knowledge and implicit (tacit) knowledge. The former includes, for example, facts, figures, and laws, and can be transferred by documents, databases, formulas, etc. Marginal costs of transfer of codified knowledge over distance seem to decrease due to technical developments in ICTs. Thus, transactions including codified knowledge lend themselves increasingly and easily to electronic transfer. By contrast, the latter type of knowledge, implicit knowledge, cannot be easily stored and transferred, because it refers to 'know how' and 'know who' in specific situations, for example, the way to operate complex machinery or apply customized software, and knowledge about informal networks (van Geenhuizen and Nijkamp 1999). This type of knowledge which is typically specific for individuals and firms seems increasingly important in problem solving and innovation (e.g. von Hippel 1994; Nonaka and Takeuchi 1996). Implicit or tacit knowledge is often a condition that enables one to work with codified knowledge and, more importantly, it is used to discover new combinations and new applications (also named serendipity). The more important implicit knowledge is for an adequate performance; the more important spatial proximity; that is knowledge as embodied in persons, can only be transferred in close human interaction (e.g. Audretsch 1998). The previous reasoning suggests large cities as attractive locations or nodes for nonroutine production and innovation. Cities with the highest hierarchical rank are generally in the best position for a spatial concentration of these activities (e.g. Daniels 1993; Noyelle and Stanback 1983). These conditions are especially instructive in looking at the labor market, intermediate services, and knowledge inputs of financial resources.

In regards to labor market externalities, financial services at the (inter)national level are particularly dependent on highly skilled labor, meaning a quicker filling of vacancies and a greater choice of applicants. Highly specialized financial workers prefer to be in financial centers because of the abundance of career opportunities. As for the concerns of intermediate services, financial firms at the (inter)national level use specialized producer services, such as hardware and software services and sophisticated legal advice (Porteous 1999). Proximity may cause better (timely) services and lower prices. A more recent factor is the availability of access to global communications networks (Graham 1999). Due to the influence of privatization and liberalization, advanced telecommunication infrastructure is increasingly made available only where the market demand is high, i.e., in the largest cities and in the economic core areas of countries.

In terms of knowledge spillovers, proximity of financial firms means the following. Localized innovation may be a source of positive externalities, both in the sense of new financial products and new ways of completing tasks. More importantly, there are spillovers of implicit or tacit knowledge, including knowledge about what other firms are doing and what is going on in the sector. Knowledge becomes a basic input for nonroutine and complex problem-solving (Illeris 1994; Porteous 1999). From a sociocultural perspective, financial centers typically operate through rules and norms of behavior of the participants. These rules are often institutionalized and direct the daily business practices of the markets involved. They also act as the conduits along which mutual trust is established and non-routine (tacit) knowledge flows through networks. Processes like these are essential in financial center formation and continuation. But there are also decentralizing forces at work strengthened by information and communication technology. These include the high costs of operation in financial centers, congestion costs, and disamenities of life in large cities (Moulaert and Gallouj 1993; Porteous 1999).

DEVELOPMENT OF THE BANKING INDUSTRY IN THE NETHERLANDS

The adoption of information technology in Dutch banking took off in the early 1960s with head office automation of data processing (first and second generation computers) (Diederen *et al.* 1991). This was followed in the early 1970s by the establishment of separate computer centers (with third generation computers) at good suburban sites that were accessible from the headquarters for the physical transport of magnetic tapes, and diskettes, like Amstelveen at the edge of Amsterdam and Zeist at the edge of the city of Utrecht. Decentralized automation and data transmission networks were established in the late 1970s, followed by important improvements in the 1980s.[1] We also observe then a further decentralization of administrative and computer work to localities at a distance of 200–300 km from the headquarters (e.g. medium-sized towns like Zwolle and Leeuwarden).

At the same time that suburban sites were emerging, forces were at work that strengthened the nonroutine headquarter functions in the largest city, Amsterdam. This development is strongly related to the relatively high level of market concentration in the Dutch banking industry. Today, the five largest banks account for approximately 85 percent of national assets in banking (Bikker and Groeneveld 1998). By contrast, the level in Germany is close to 50 percent and that in the UK 40 percent. The situation in the Netherlands is completely different from the one in Italy where the banking industry is dominated by the presence of many small local banks operating in restricted territorial areas and a few relatively small national banks (Alessandrini and Zazzaro 1999). The strong market concentration in the Netherlands is the end result of a long-lasting and systematic acquisition and merging by large banks in the past decades[2] (van Geenhuizen 1999). Mergers and acquisitions were clearly evident at different layers in the city system, i.e., 50 percent of all mergers and takeovers from 1950 to 1985 were undertaken by banks headquartered in Amsterdam and were concerned with banks in smaller cities. In addition, almost 20 percent of all takeovers took place within Amsterdam. The second largest city, Rotterdam, was much less important in this process. Thus, large and medium-sized banks in the largest city strengthened their position and increased their size at the expense of banks located lower in the city system. The acquired banks were subsequently incorporated and integrated. As a consequence, this process has strongly contributed to a spatial concentration of headquarters and national control functions in Amsterdam from the 1950s to the 1980s (van Geenhuizen 1993; van Geenhuizen and van der Knaap 1998). A second phenomenon in banking has reinforced this spatial pattern, i.e., the entry of foreign banks in the Dutch market. In the first decades of foreign banking, Amsterdam received an overwhelming preference for location in the Netherlands. Between 1960 and 1985 almost all foreign banks (83 percent) located there (van Geenhuizen 1993).

Also 61.5 percent of the headquarters of the 40 largest banks were in Amsterdam by the end of the 1980s. At this point it needs to be mentioned that there are no large cities comparable to London or Paris in the Netherlands. Instead there are four 'relatively small' cities located near each other that act as a network of cities (Figure 10.1). Each has a certain economic specialization: Amsterdam, Rotterdam, The Hague, and Utrecht (e.g. Lambooy 1998). These four cities form the backbone of what is named the Core (or Randstad) in the western part of the country. There are also various larger medium-sized towns, all located outside the Core. This size category is increasing in number. The relatively high concentration quotient (see note 3) for headquarters in the banking industry in Amsterdam (615) underlines a remarkable asymmetry in distribution, with the next largest cities Rotterdam, The Hague, and Utrecht far behind Amsterdam.

1998 City Population

150,000 - 200,000	*Apeldoorn**
200,000 - 300,000	Utrecht
400,000 - 600,000	**Rotterdam**
More than 600,000	**AMSTERDAM**

* not included in this class in 1988

Number of Bank HQs
(40 largest banks only)

City Size (by inhabitants 1988 and 1998)	1988 Percent of Cities	1998 Percent of Cities	Location of Bank Headquarters 1988 Percent Share of HQ	1998 Percent Share of HQ
Less than 50,000	92.7	89.4	0	2.5
50,000 - 100,000	5.1	6.2	5.1	7.5
100,000 - 150,000	1.4	2.6	0	5.0
150,000 - 200,000	0.4	1.1	2.6	2.5
200,000 - 300,000	0.1	0.2	12.8	7.5
400,000 - 600,000	0.2	0.4	17.9	20.0
More than 600,000	0.1	0.2	61.5	55.0

Figure 10.1 *Distribution of bank headquarters in the Netherlands. Source: NIBE 1998, 1999/2000; Netherlands Central Bureau of Statistics*

In the 1990s several new developments have started to slightly affect the location of headquarters in the city system including withdrawal of some banks from Amsterdam and the emergence of banking headquarters in smaller towns. These developments can be summarized as follows:

- A rapid integration of banks in Amsterdam based upon previous mergers and acquisitions.
- A withdrawal of some large foreign banks from the Netherlands, i.e., from Amsterdam especially Japanese banks due to an internal reorganization of the mother bank.
- The emergence of various new banks with origins in the domestic insurance and savings sector which are often located in smaller towns.

The distribution pattern for 1998 indicated a small move down the urban hierarchy. This is most clearly evident in the share of headquarters in smaller towns (less than 150 000 inhabitants), i.e., an increase from about 5 to 15 percent. But the presence of headquarters in Amsterdam remains relatively strong with 55 percent (Figure 10.1). In this context it is difficult to disentangle the role of ICTs and specifically that of electronic banking. We argue that ICTs enable new head offices of banks to operate at some distance from Amsterdam. But there is also evidence that most newcomer banks have no strong links with the prime financial functions in Amsterdam, i.e., the stock exchange for shares and bonds, options and futures and an array of specialized supporting services (van Geenhuizen and van der Knaap 1998).

The latter observation ties into the international financial center function and standing of Amsterdam. The Amsterdam Exchanges (AEX) substantially lost activity to London in the late 1980s. In 1986 a full automated screen-based trade system was introduced at the London Exchange enabling Dutch institutional investors to avoid fees charged by Amsterdam intermediaries by trading in Dutch shares via the London Exchange (NRC-Handelsblad, September 29, 1994). But Amsterdam responded to this situation by a significant move towards specialization, i.e., trade in options and futures. Today Amsterdam has the second largest exchange in this particular segment in Europe, following German exchanges (mainly Frankfurt). What this development illustrates is that particular banking firms do not feel the necessity to be in Amsterdam, because they may run their routine exchange activity by screen in alternative places, i.e., the cheapest locations.

We conclude this section with the observation that in accordance with our theoretical views, headquarter functions remain concentrated in the largest city, Amsterdam. Some spread is nevertheless possible, but this is based upon loose connections of newcomer banks with the core financial activity in Amsterdam. We next examine another key feature of the banking industry, the penetration of electronic banking.

ELECTRONIC BANKING IN THE NETHERLANDS

Use of Electronic Banking

Electronic banking includes simple electronic payments as well as more advanced forms like PC banking for ordering trade in shares and for portfolio management.

Data on the use of cash dispensers and automated teller machines (ATMs) indicate that the Netherlands is ahead of many small and larger economies in Europe (Table 10.1). Only Sweden has a higher use level of these modes. When considering the pace of increase in European countries during the past five years, Italy and Belgium are ahead due to a relatively low level in 1993. The level of use of cash dispensers and ATMs in the Netherlands was already high in 1993, but this was not true for the use of Electronic Funds Transfer Point of Sale (EFTPOS). There has been a considerable increase in the use of this channel in the past years (by 605 percent). At the end of 1997 the Netherlands was ahead of many small and large economies in Europe. Only France showed a higher level of use of these electronic media. Thus, the Netherlands is among the leaders in accepting these forms of electronic banking.

Internet connectivity is an important condition for continued growth in electronic banking. Internet connectivity at the national level can be measured as number of hosts per 1000 inhabitants, where hosts are individual computers with network access. Because multiple users may use a single host computer, this is not a measure of number of users, but can be regarded as a measure of Internet presence in a country. Figure 10.2 indicates the intermediate position of the Netherlands compared with various small and large economies in Europe. There is a gap with the Scandinavian countries, particularly Finland. Outside Europe, the USA is clearly ahead. The penetration in terms of regular use of the Internet as a percentage of the population shows a similar pattern (Figure 10.2).

Potential Growth of Electronic Banking

The question that arises is whether the pace of adoption of these electronic modes, including Internet as a channel, will continue to increase or level off in the near future. Answers to this question shift our attention to the perceived advantages of electronic

Table 10.1   *Relative importance of electronic bank transactions in selected countries*

Country	Cash dispensers and ATMs			EFTPOS		
	1993	1997	(Index)	1993	1997	(Index)
Netherlands	20.5	33.3	(162)	4.4	31.0	(705)
Belgium	9.1	15.7	(173)	14.2	27.2	(192)
Switzerland	8.3	11.4	(137)	4.0	13.6	(340)
Sweden	28.3	35.3	(125)	6.5	15.9	(245)
Germany	11.5	15.3	(133)	0.9	2.8	(311)
France	13.3	19.9	(150)	24.3	39.2	(161)
United Kingdom	21.3	29.6	(139)	n.a.	n.a.	
Italy	3.8	7.2	(190)	1.0	4.4	(440)
United States	29.8	40.7	(137)	1.7	5.4	(318)
Canada	37.4	52.7	(141)	2.6	34.2	(1315)
Japan	3.3	5.0	(152)	0.005	0.004	(80)

Notes: Index figures are shown in parentheses (1993 = 100). Germany: for cash dispensers and ATMS: end of 1994 and end of 1996; for EFTPOS: end of 1997 is concerned with electronic cash only.
(Bank for International Settlements, 1999.)

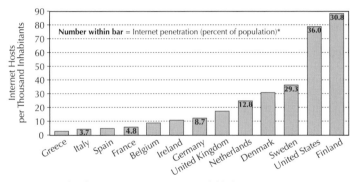

Figure 10.2   Internet use indicators in selected countries. Source: OECD 1999a; Hargittai 1999

banking and electronic money on the supply side (see Singh 1999; Struye de Swielande 2000).

In the analysis of future adoption of electronic banking and electronic money, the perspective of providers often dominates (Singh 1999). In this perspective, the arguments that point to a large-scale future adoption are based on the principle of economic efficiency. In the USA operating expenses of electronic banking services are estimated to be only 25–30 percent of the cost of providing traditional banking services using existing bank branch offices (Westland and Clark 1999). More specifically, in the case of the Internet, there is a decrease of costs of developing, implementation (testing) and first use of new services, because these new services may make use of already known standard interfaces and network infrastructure. There are also lower costs for the supply of tailor-made services, the control of customer relationships, and cross-selling strategies (Struye de Swielande 2000). A second factor is the disappearance of access barriers in the sector. One important access barrier has been the capital-intensive establishment and maintenance of physical distribution networks, both domestic ones and those abroad. These developments would indicate a severe down-sizing of local bank branch offices, as well as the emergence of branchless banks. What this also means is that financial services are cheaper. This development can be illustrated by the Bank of Scotland (BoS), which most recently entered the Dutch market using a web site to sell mortgages. Price differences are not large, but one point is clear: BoS does not charge provision which is often 1 percent of the mortgage sum.

Impacts on Local Bank Branch Offices

Downsizing the banking organization at the local level is certainly not a new strategy in the industry in the Netherlands. Following the saturation of the retail market since the late 1970s and the restructuring of the global banking system, large banks system-atically rationalized their networks in the 1980s. A second force in favor of closure was the overlap of local branch offices in particular localities after the merging of banking organizations. Today, it seems that the increased penetration of electronic banking accelerates the closure of local branch offices. Figure 10.3 shows a downsizing for the

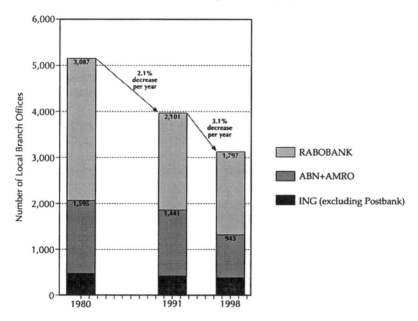

Figure 10.3   *Local offices of the largest banks in the Netherlands. Source: Rabobank and ABN-AMRO Annual Reports*

three largest banks in the Netherlands by 2.1 percent per year for 1980–91 and by 3.1 percent per year for 1991–98. In absolute terms almost 1200 and another 800 local branch offices were closed in the two periods respectively. For the UK, Leyson and Thrift (1997) suggest a similar or slightly smaller contraction in the 1980s and an acceleration since then.

ABN–AMRO and Rabobank have recently introduced important new plans to adjust their branch office networks to the new conditions of electronic banking and new customer demands. Further closures of local branch offices are envisaged, while the staff at remaining local offices will be reduced drastically. Three ICT related conditions enable such development. First, administrative processing of transactions can be disconnected from local branches and, second, advisors of financial products have become footloose in the sense that they can give personal advice to customers at any place by using a computer for support. A third condition is the reduction of back-office workers. In the near future there will likely be one back-office worker for each front-office worker (Rabobank Press Release, December 8, 1999).

In a transformation towards a 'market-oriented' organization since the early 1980s, large bank corporations have introduced a new tier of regional branch offices (Figure 10.4). In this way, the supply of competence and specialist know-how has been spread or diffused to some degree from headquarters in Amsterdam to smaller cities. It needs to be mentioned that Rabobank is different from the other large banks in that the cooperative structure gives autonomy to local (affiliated) banks in determining the range of services. In other words, there is no formal structure of service levels.

During the past several years, the contraction at the local level has caused a transfer of functions previously located in local branch offices to a smaller number of regional

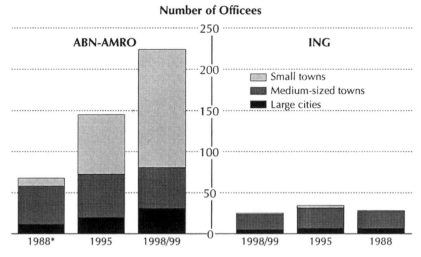

* Includes totals for ABN and AMRO, which were separate banks at that time.

Figure 10.4   *Number and location of regional bank branch offices. Source: Rabobank and ABN-AMRO Annual Reports*

branch offices. This observation complies with what Marshall and Bachtler (1984) and Marshall and Richardson (1996) see as impacts of the use of IT, i.e., the closing of smaller local bank branches, but at the same time an increased importance of activities of market-oriented regional branch offices. In essence, the latter development represents a compensation of some disadvantages for electronic banking. Electronic banking reduces the opportunities of banks to talk with their customers and to support the latter's bank loyalty in a situation in which new suppliers emerge in the market. Established banks feel the need to provide more attractive specialist customer services based on face-to-face contact at regional branch offices (*The Banker*, September, 1997).

In their policy to upgrade regional branch offices, ABN–AMRO and ING Bank have adjusted their organization in a somewhat different way. ABN–AMRO has moved to a relatively large network, with more than 200 regional offices, in which medium-sized towns are giving way to small towns. In contrast, ING Bank, with an overall much smaller number of regional offices, has a consistently strong presence in medium-sized towns. On closer investigation, it can be observed that the location of these towns in the Netherlands is mainly outside the Core (68 percent), including all large and medium-sized towns here: Eindhoven, Tilburg, Groningen, Breda, Apeldoorn en Nijmegen. This picture is confirmed by the regional spread of a type of financial services that is its by nature nonroutine and knowledge intensive, i.e., venture capital activity (van Geenhuizen and van der Knaap 1998). Venture capital activity operates with a strong input of nonroutine information and nonroutine personal contact between supplier and client. The decision to provide venture capital is a high-risk decision and the follow-up role in monitoring the quality of the venture, its management, and its networks clearly ask for face-to-face contacts, particularly in the process of building mutual trust and commitment (Illeris 1994). We may conclude that the above developments signal the emergence of new regional marketplaces in financial services, based on face-to-face contact between suppliers and their customers.

The above development ties into the 'other side of the coin' of electronic banking in which an emphasis is put on the importance of habit, comfort, and trust in banking relationships for customers (Pratt 1998; Rogers 1996; Singh 1999). First, customers use a mix of payment modes (electronic, cash, card) dependent on the activity involved such as payments in groceries, cinemas, and gift shops, and periodic payment of fees (like utilities). Second, particular customer segments are excluded from electronic modes because they have no PC or credit card. Third, an important attribute of modes of payment is the information provided. This information is mainly concerned with a record of the money spent and the money still in account, as well as with the context of payment (personal face-to-face, physical, or virtual). Payments using the Internet, for example, can be qualified as impersonal and virtual. Related to information needs is the demand for trust that the payment is safe, the personal information is safe, and the account is safe. Another not well resolved issue related to the penetration of web site banking is the ultimate responsibility for operations on the Internet, such as the failure and delay of transactions (Westland and Clark 1999). Thus, a poor performance in terms of perceived information attributes and control may prohibit a further quick adoption of electronic banking and may render regional 'meeting places' necessary as a counterbalance.

We conclude that in line with our theoretical perspectives, electronic banking has caused dramatic changes in banking organizations at the level where financial transactions are mostly routine in nature, i.e., at the local level. Accordingly, the closing down of local bank branch offices underwent an acceleration in the 1990s. At the same time we have seen as a counter movement the supply of high order services based on face-to face contact in regional offices.

E-COMMERCE AND CHANGING FINANCIAL SERVICES

E-commerce in the Netherlands

With total online sales of 1.27 billion ECU, e-commerce in the Netherlands is at a modest level (Table 10.2).[3] Most online sales are business-to-business (73.2 percent), leaving business-to-consumer sales as a relatively small segment (26.8 percent). This pattern compares with that across Europe; witness the shares of 69 percent and 31 percent respectively (Booz Allen and Hamilton/Ministry of Economic Affairs 2000). Private sales by Internet in the Netherlands are still a small fraction of all retail sales, i.e., only 0.5 percent, with a heavy concentration in a few categories, such as, hardware, software, books, and music (65 percent). According to various estimates future growth in private sales in the Netherlands will increase explosively, i.e., from 0.34 billion ECU in 1999 to 5.8 billion ECU in the next five years (ABN–AMRO 1999).

Despite a small total of online sales in the Netherlands, online sales as spending per user are relatively high compared with other members of the European Union (Table 10.3). Likewise, the figure for Denmark is clearly above the average in Europe and far above figures for Germany and the UK. However, as we have seen for Internet

Table 10.2   *E-commerce key figures in the Netherlands*

	Billions of European Currency Units		
	1998	1999	Est. 2004
Total online sales	0.36	1.27	
Business sales	0.20	0.93	
Share of total online services	56.3%	73.2%	
Private sales	0.16	0.34	5.8
Share of total online sales	43.7%	26.8%	
Share of total retail sales		0.5%	
Share of hardware, software, books, CDs (in retail)		65.0%	

(National Internet Monitor, Pro-Active International, 2000.)

Table 10.3   *Online spending per user*

Country	ECU dollars spent per year
United States	148
Denmark	76
Netherlands	75
Finland	70
Sweden	67
France	64
Belgium	64
Germany	57
United Kingdom	56

(Booz Allen & Hamilton, Ministry of Economic Affairs, 2000.)

connectivity and Internet use, the difference between the Netherlands and the USA is substantial.

How Financial Services Tie Into E-commerce

E-commerce has created a new role for traditional banks as 'trusted parties', that is, an intermediary role in which payments are checked inter alia by authentication of source and destination of payments (Westland and Clark 1999). Connected with this role is the participation of banks in shared payment programs, such as in the Netherlands I-Pay coupled with the international standard SET (secure electronic transaction). But individual banks may also develop bank-specific payment systems (Sonnemans 1996). By offering payment programs banks attract new customers with their accounts.

E-commerce is not only about Internet, web sites, and payment systems; there is a larger and more important transformation going on, specifically the dawn of the e-economy (*The Banker*, July 1999a). The basic change in e-economy is the customer- or buyer-driven approach. The Internet allows powerful search agents which save customers time and money. These new Internet-based intermediaries (agents) fundamentally change the relationships between customers and suppliers. Consumers search the Internet for the cheapest price, e.g. of a book or an airline ticket; but they search also for offerings that satisfy a bottom line given by the customer or set by an independent referral agent in the case of financial loans (mortgages). It goes even further in that intelligent search agents offer packages of financial services tailored to customers' stages in the life cycle. In this situation, services are not supplied by one financial firm but out-sourced from different ones, while the customer is 'in the driver's seat' demanding personalized offerings tailored to his/her requirements (*The Banker*, July 1999b). Related to this basic change is the emergence of new roles of banks in the new business processes, connected with portals, interest communities, request for proposals (buyer driven auctions), or 'infomediaries'. In other words, the positions of banks now are defined in terms of providing electronic access and information and providing electronic devices for selection and connection of customers with suppliers. The short- and long-term implications for the strategy of established banks cannot easily be predicted, but we suggest a few important ones:

- 'Brick and mortar banks' as one-channel banks will be transformed into multichannel banks in which a range of channels, including mobile phones, cash dispensers, Internet, and others which are offered that work to support a different customer segment.
- Banks will form alliances with specialized financial suppliers to be able to add innovative elements to their set of services.
- Banks will define new roles for themselves in the new customer-driven value chain, running from simple information supply to connecting customer segments' demand with selected supply (e.g., Radecki 1997).
- Banks will become involved in a 'web' of alliances, acquisitions, and newly established firms in order to secure the roles they want to play in the e-economy, such as with Internet firms (providers, portals, etc.) and online banks.
- In regard to customer segmentation, traditional banks are not currently used to this strategy because they are largely product or product-channel oriented. But they have all the necessary ingredients in house, i.e., a large customer base, a stockpile of customer data, deep and long-term relationships with customers, and a trusted brand.

In daily life the above developments are clearly visible in the growth of 'webs' of different financial online parties. Thus, banks acquire stakes in existing Internet firms or develop such firms by themselves. For example, UK's Prudential (insurance) has established Egg and German Commerzbank has established Comdirect. In addition, Internet firms try to acquire online banks, like American E*trade. And traditional banks establish online banks, like Bank24 by Deutsche Bank together with telecom firm Mannesmann (later British Vodafone). Dutch ABN–AMRO recently entered into cooperation with Bluestone Capital's Internet portal for financial services TRADE.COM. This portal enables the bank to supply online brokerage services worldwide with other products and services to follow later. The agreement is the first of this kind for Dutch banks. We next illustrate the developments mentioned above using Dutch Rabobank as an example.

Rabobank

Rabobank is the largest retail bank in the Netherlands. Originally a 'brick and mortar type', today it operates more than 1700 local branch offices. In addition, it has developed strong roles in food-producing industries and in agribusiness. It is therefore, a good example to trace the growth of electronic banking and to identify new strategies with regard to electronic banking and the e-economy in the private and business segment. It is clearly a traditional bank which is now moving toward another approach. First, we discuss the development of electronic banking in the past years, then we move to the current channel approach of Rabobank. This discussion is followed by a much broader reflection on online competition and the new conditions of the e-economy with potentially new roles for the bank. Finally, we discuss how Rabobank is actually involved in e-commerce.

When considering the penetration of various types of electronic banking that have emerged during the past decade, it becomes clear that banking by telephone and payment transactions by EFTPOS has grown explosively, particularly in the late 1990s (Table 10.4). This trend also holds for PC banking by private persons and to a smaller extent for PC banking in the business segment. By using shares in giro transfers as a measure for penetration of PC banking by private persons, it becomes clear that there remains a large part of the segment to be gained (88 percent). This situation is true for the basic payment product but different for other products, such as tele-saving which is 100 percent online.

The present channels of the bank clearly indicate a multichannel approach, including alongside traditional desk services the supply of cashing machines and a large number of services by phone and by PC (Internet) (Table 10.5). Rabobank is the first Dutch bank to offer Internet (WAP) services by mobile telephone (Press Release, February 9, 2000). There is also some flexibility in a choice of services. Thus, customers can create a package based on their personal preferences. Rabobank's supply of Internet services by mobile phone use (GSM) touches upon a broader theme that has attracted the attention of the European ministers involved in e-commerce policy, i.e., the already mentioned laggard position in Internet use of Europe compared with the

Table 10.4   *Rabobank payment systems (index numbers)*

	1992*	1995	1999
Number of cash dispensers	100	130	176
Number of transactions (using cash dispensers)	100	131	167
Number of EFTPOS	100	442	828
Number of transaction by Rabo clients (using EFTPOS)	100	749	2442
Number of Rabofoon users	100	490	2692
Number of PC banking *firms*	100	288	704
Share of PC banking in giro transfers (of firms)	9%	31%	61%
Number of PC banking *private persons*	100	407	1624
Share of PC banking in giro transfers (of private persons)	0.7%	2.9%	12.1%

*1992 is the index year. 1995 and 1999 should be compared to this index year when 1992=100. (Personal communication.)

Table 10.5   *Current channels and approaches by Rabobank*

Channels	Functions	Comments
Cashing machines	Cashing and loading of Chipknip, a stored valued card	
PC banking using Rabo-specific software or Internet (www.rabobank.nl)	Payment, savings, and investment, including information and advice	Internet clients can create their personal home page and subscribe to information services. *Optional*: manage portfolio
Rabofoon	Balance information, savings, money transfer, and various services	
Other phone lines	Shares and options orders; information and offers on consumptive credits, mortgages, holiday-related financial services	
Rabofoon using GSM-WAP (Wireless Application Protocol) Total package	Information on exchange rates and indices, advice on investment and equity and options markets A flexible package of services: a. *Core*: account, credit card and Chipknip b. *Optional*: (1) Phone for savings, money transfer and information on account balance; (2) PC telebanking; (3) Discounts on travel insurance and credit cards for partners	Internet via mobile phone; available 24 hours Price: 27 ECU per year

(Press Release Rabobank Nederland, February 9, 2000.)

USA. The latter situation causes e-commerce players from the more advanced US market to rapidly occupy the best positions in major European markets (Booz Allen and Hamilton and Ministry of Economic Affairs 1999). The barriers in Europe include the impact of an incomplete deregulation, i.e., Internet access costs remain too high, there is an absence of a comprehensive regulatory framework for e-commerce leading to small consumer confidence in e-commerce, and there are less favorable conditions for entrepreneurship in the field. Against this background, the guiding vision would be for Europe to become the world leader in mobile e-commerce (m-commerce) by building on existing strengths in mobile communications (Booz Allen and Hamilton and Ministry of Economic Affairs 1999). It needs to be mentioned that today security is still a major issue in m-commerce, preventing Rabobank from offering integrated transactional services through WAP.

Like many other traditional banks, Rabobank faces competition from online banks and from new types of parties, such as these financial portals offering price and service comparisons for a range of financial firms with access to home pages of these firms, target group and event intermediaries, and direct banks like Deutsche Bank. In the new online circumstances, in which markets tend to be divided by parties involved in providing access and intermediation, the response of Rabobank is to establish access and intermediation by itself. In addition, Rabobank sees an important role for itself as an 'infomediary', that is, an information intermediary. This role is based on the relevance of client profiles in the new customer-driven approach to business and because it has extensive client data at its disposal, and because it enjoys the trust of clients. As an 'infomediary' the bank connects customers' demand with supply.

The e-commerce strategy consists of three tiers: (1) improved access and intermediation, (2) a complete online virtual bank (together with the offices), and (3) new products. In access and intermediation one can expect both new portals and more Internet presence on other portals. Similar changes will happen in telephony (both WAP and voice). In the virtual bank area, it is foreseen that the products that can be bought, used and maintained online will include almost all of the consumer products. This move is also needed to reduce costs of local offices while keeping services for customers on the necessary level. In the business area Rabobank will accommodate ease-of-use and proliferate into the administration of the clients' business. With regard to new products, there is no limit so far, which opens the way to innovation. V-TRACTION (to be discussed in the next paragraph) is a good example of this strategy.

Direct involvement of Rabobank in e-commerce is limited to date (Table 10.6). It does offer Internet access to consumers and advertising/shop facilities to a number of shops in the Netherlands under the name of Trefpunt. Further, Rabobank has established a business-to-business e-commerce company in food and agriculture based on co-operative principles; these features make it the first in the world. The leading thought behind this initiative was that within a few years more than 10 percent of the world market in food and agricultural products will be traded via online markets using the Internet. vTRACTION.COM facilitates the development of virtual business-to-business auctions and markets that potentially lead to dominant electronic market-places in various food and agriculture sectors. Since its establishment a few months ago, vTRACTION.COM entered into alliances with a number of important players, such as concerning e-markets for the pork industry and for vegetables and fruit, through electronic auctions. These firms will be supported by Rabobank's knowhow in the field of food and agribusiness and by financial services tailored to meet the specific conditions in these sectors.

It is difficult to evaluate the strategies and roles of Rabobank because fast changes in

Table 10.6   *Rabobank E-commerce*

Service name	Comments
Virtual Shopping Plaza	Internet access to a number of virtual and physical shops in the Netherlands (to date on a modest scale).
vTraction.com	A business-to-business e-commerce company based on cooperative principles. It facilitates the development of business-to-business food and agricultural vertical exchanges. The cooperative approach gives the vTraction.com family of vertical exchanges the traction, or liquidity, to lead the way in their respective markets.

(Press Release of February 9, 2000 and personal communication.)

the environment go hand in hand with equally fast changes in strategies and roles. Nevertheless, it remains clear that Rabobank establishes its strategies in a playing field that has basically changed due to the rise of the e-economy, i.e., in particular with the recognition of new parties, new roles (in terms of electronic access and intermediation) and a major role for customers. Rabobank places an emphasis on the development of its potential as an information intermediary besides putting its complete business online. What matters in a new and competitive environment is how quickly the bank responds to all these changes by concrete actions.

SUMMARY AND CONCLUSIONS

This chapter has shown that e-banking and the e-economy today are placing heavy pressure on traditional banking organizations. First, there is an increased price competition from suppliers, from other sectors, and from abroad. Banks without the heavy burden of an office network may eat into the retail market shares of traditional banks. The operating costs of the former are much lower and, therefore, they can offer better services for a certain range of products, and they can charge less. As a consequence of these developments, national headquarter functions at the top of the traditional domestic retail organizations will decline. Electronic banking has already caused an increase in the number of closures at the base of these organizations, i.e., local branch offices. Second, there is heavy competition in the division of new roles in the emerging online markets between banks and other parties. We believe that some traditional banks that cannot adapt themselves in a timely manner to the new online conditions will be forced to merge or they will disappear, leading to smaller headquarter functions in the largest city. Connected with this is a potential erosion of activity in the largest city as an international financial center. A part of the exchange trade may become footloose because there is a growing preference for using screen-based exchanges in the cheapest trading place on the globe. What will remain in Amsterdam is the important activity for which the accumulated specialized experience, interpersonal relationships, and potentials for continuous innovation are a condition sine qua non.

There is also a phenomenon at work that may erode or, conversely, strengthen the position of Amsterdam, but this is only related to the e-economy in an indirect way. If large Dutch banks get involved in cross-border mergers, (inter)national control functions may move from the headquarters in the city of the other party, or conversely they may be located in Amsterdam. Of course, this development depends on the terms of the merger, whereas the relative strength of the city may also play a role, such as the strength of a first tier financial center (London) compared with second and third tier centers (Frankfurt, Zurich, Paris, etc.). In this respect it is interesting to see that the Amsterdam Exchange has most recently merged with Paris and Brussels, the latter two operating on a similar or lower tier in global finance compared with Amsterdam.

By examining medium-sized and small towns in the analysis, we observed indications for the rise of new regional marketplaces which served mainly as a counterbalance against the increasing closure of local bank branch offices, in the 1990s at a rate of 3 percent per year for large banks. What these regional market-places have in common is the supply of services that are nonroutine and complex in character, and need face-to-face contact between bank employee or banker and customer. There are still shortcomings of electronic banking or perceived shortcomings in the eyes of customers, mainly around safety (trust) of sensitive information and around the lack of control over the Internet itself and responsibility for failure and congestion. In addition, banks themselves need to remain in personal contact with their clients in order to 'feed' the latter's loyalty with the bank. However, there are signs that over time a part of these shortcomings of electronic banking will disappear, namely when banks are able to offer attractive (cheaper) packages online in a transparent way and when they are sufficiently tailored to customers' needs based on an accurate listening to them by electronic means, and when regulation of the Internet has improved.

The above analysis suggests a number of future research opportunities. On the urban side of the theme, there is a need for research on the design of urban policies that help to improve the quality of knowledge attributes of cities. Such policies include, of course, more than advancing the use of ICTs and inserting cities with cables and transfer points into global communication networks. Returning to the different nature of codified and tacit knowledge, such a policy needs to advance the growth of socioeconomic networks in knowledge-based activity and the formation of institutions that support the functioning of such networks, including keeping the city attractive as a working and living place for major actors in these networks. The overall objective is to advance the creation and use of tacit knowledge. There are, however, no blueprints and no standard recipes for such policy. The 'glue' that holds the networks and makes them productive and innovative differs between economic sectors and between localities. But there is one feature in common, i.e., urban knowledge policy needs to be based on an integrated approach, including fields like education and culture, physical planning for office locations and urban architecture, and labor market and housing market policies in order to satisfy the needs of knowledge workers (e.g. Knight 1995).

On the side of electronic banking there is a need for research on progress in ICT technology. We cannot exclude the possibility of new or improved ways of electronic communication in which shortcomings of current electronic media in terms of personal face-to-face contact and information attributes can be reduced or compensated. To be more specific: would it be possible in the future to create an 'electronic, nonphysical' version of implicit knowledge and concomitant knowledge spillovers? We might extend this issue with the question on the repercussions of such development for physical marketplaces on the longer term. A final research opportunity is of a similar basic nature. It is concerned with the question as to whether dominant positions in physical space (large cities) are maintained (reinforced) in electronic space. Although access in electronic space is not determined by distance and economic functions are not filtered, for example by land rent gradients, the mechanisms at work in creating barriers and thresholds in networks in electronic space and the power to open new electronic space may be connected with that of historical ones in physical space. In the Netherlands, institutional forces enabled a continuous merging and acquisition of banks in the past decades leading to a concentration of them in Amsterdam. It remains to be seen whether institutions and power in electronic space will enable a continuation of this situation in the next decade.

END NOTES

1. There have also been important developments in interbank transfer systems, for example, the Society of Worldwide Interbank Financial Telecommunications (SWIFT), set up in 1977.
2. ABN–AMRO is typically the 'product' of merging and acquisition that culminated in the birth merger of the two predecessors (each in 1964) and in a second birth merger leading to the present bank (1990). There are three other important mergers in recent history, i.e., between two central cooperative banks in 1972 (leading to Rabobank Nederland), between NMB and Postbank in 1989 (later ING Bank Group), and between Belgium AG group and Dutch AMEV and Dutch Verenigde Spaarbank (leading to Fortis Banking Group). In early 2000, ABN–AMRO was the largest bank in the Netherlands, ranking sixth in the world based on size (assets) (*The Banker*, July, 1999). The second largest bank in the Netherlands is ING Bank Group, 26th on the world list. The third largest bank is Rabobank Nederland, 32nd on the world list based on assets. Fortis Banking Group, a joint Belgium-Dutch bank, holds 27th position in the world.
3. The concentration quotient indicates the level of concentration in the urban hierarchy. A quotient value of 1 indicates a perfectly even distribution, i.e. each city-size class locates a share of offices at a given tier (national head office, regional office) equal to its share in all cities. The concentration quotient is defined as follows:

$$O_{is}/C_s,$$

where O_i is offices (as a share) at a given tier i and C_s are cities (as a share) in a given size class s.
4. There are different definitions of e-commerce, i.e., broad ones and narrow ones, which sometimes hamper a comparison of figures.

1) E-banking + shifting of routine fns out of local (small places + non-routine fns to large places
∴ → (agglom (spillover effects)

2) Slight decline in centrality of Amsterdam ∴ ↑ growth of regional hubs

3) Closure of local branches (DD not addressed)

4) ∇ banking related to growth of e-commerce

11

Global Electronic Spaces: Singapore's Role in the Foreign Exchange Market in the Asia–Pacific Region

JOHN LANGDALE

Maquarie University, North Ryde, Australia

The foreign exchange (FX) market is the most highly globalized industry relying heavily on information and communications technologies (ICTs). Major fluctuations in countries' currencies may occur at any time of the day. The FX market is thus a truly global electronic space operating on a 24-hour basis.

Most financial firms trading in the FX market operate a number of dealing rooms in global cities scattered around the world. These dealing rooms may range in size from the very small (e.g. two or three traders) to the very large (e.g. several hundred traders). Each trader or dealer is electronically connected to traders in other firms in the FX market. In addition, the dealing room has numerous sales and marketing staff whose primary role is to liaise with customers of the firm, whether they be individuals or corporations.

The Asia–Pacific region occupies a key role in 24-hour trading in the global FX market, partly because firms need dealing rooms which are open to cover the hours between the New York market closing and London's opening. The Asia–Pacific region is also important in the FX market because the region acquired a much greater role in the global economy as a result of rapid economic growth in the post-1970s. While the Asian economic crisis of 1997–99 had a negative impact on growth in some East Asian countries (Indonesia, Thailand, Malaysia, and South Korea) and Japan remains locked in low growth, most Asian countries returned to positive growth rates by 2000. These rapid shifts in growth rates have created a significant demand for FX in the region.

This chapter focuses on Singapore's role in the globalization of the Asia–Pacific region's FX market. Singapore emerged during the 1990s as a major FX center for the region, even though it is smaller than Tokyo in terms of FX turnover. Tokyo's FX role is primarily as a yen trading center, whereas Singapore functions as a global and Asia–Pacific regional hub.

The role of global and regional information flows is of critical importance since these flows are critical in the FX market. Successful FX firms are able to efficiently and effectively collect and analyze information on factors which influence the value of currencies. Major FX firms include global commercial banks such as Citibank, Chase Manhattan, and Deutsche Bank, as well as investment banks such as Goldman Sachs and Merrill Lynch. Cities which are major FX trading centers are also simultaneously global, regional, and national information hubs. Singapore's FX market performs a dual information function, since it is a global information hub linked to London and New York as well as a regional information hub for Asia–Pacific countries.

Singapore's regional information hub role was clearly illustrated during the most recent Asian economic crisis. Asian currencies fluctuated violently and it was vital for market participants to have up-to-date information on developments in these countries. The information relationships between Singapore and Indonesia during the crisis provides an illustration of Singapore's global and regional hub role. Indonesia's economy and society are particularly affected in this period, with political disturbances and economic dislocation bringing the economy to a virtual standstill. Rioting and looting in Indonesia occurred in May 1998 and culminated in the resignation of President Suharto.

A clear illustration of the importance of Singapore's regional information hub role occurred during interviews. A meeting was scheduled with a global investment bank on the afternoon of the May 19, 1998, which is when President Suharto offered to hold new elections to dampen discontent over his handling of the Indonesian economy. The meeting was rescheduled to a later time, because my respondent needed to be on the telephone to his London head office informing them of the implications of these political developments for the value of the Indonesian rupiah and for the rest of the region. The market had anticipated that Suharto's speech would have some good news and that the Indonesian rupiah had improved in value from its disastrously low values. The crisis in Indonesia by itself was not that important for the global FX market, since the country represents only a very small percentage of the overall FX market. A crash on the Indonesian market, however, would have had a potentially significant contagion impact on other ASEAN currencies and, to a lesser extent, on the Asia–Pacific region.

The Indonesian crisis of May 1998 illustrated the use by foreign financial services firms of Singapore as a regional information hub: the city has strong links within the Southeast Asian region and to global cities. The regional FX headquarters of global financial services firms in Singapore collected information from the firm's offices in the region, from the mass media, and, very importantly, from the firm's contacts in business and government in different countries. It used this information in its FX trading during Singapore's trading day and passed it on at the close of its trading day to London in the global 24-hour trading cycle.

GLOBAL–LOCAL INTERRELATIONSHIPS

The nature of global–local interrelationships is a central issue in understanding the changing nature of global, national and local economies (Dicken 1994; Gertler 1997). The complexity of the interdependencies in the processes operating at different geographical scales makes the global–local issue difficult to deal with.

Spaces of Flows

The term 'spaces of flows' may be seen in terms of the range and size of interconnections which link the global economy (Castells 1996, 1998). They are incredibly diverse and include economic (e.g. international trade and foreign direct investment), social (e.g. migration) and political (e.g. membership of intergovernmental organizations) flows. Furthermore, illegal transactions are of growing importance in this global spaces of flows, including illegal trade in drugs, people smuggling, and arms (Castells 1998; Findlay 1999). Little information exists on the volume and geography of these spaces of flows, particularly those taking place by electronic means. Most research on the spaces of flows has concentrated on the flows of goods (international trade), investment and of people (e.g. migration and tourism), because information is readily available in these areas.

Globalization may be conceived as having two interrelated dimensions: scope (or stretching) and intensity (or deepening). Social, political, and economic activities are becoming stretched across the globe (McGrew and Lewis 1992). More countries than ever before are involved in global activities. Transnational corporations (TNCs) operate in many countries throughout the world. In political terms, a growing number of countries have signed international agreements covering a wide range of issues. For example, countries have agreed to harmonize regulations concerning the environment and labor relations. These developments are leading to global information flows linking more countries and regions together.

The second component of globalization is intensification or deepening, reflecting a much deeper or more intense set of relationships between countries. Thus countries are connected via an increasing variety of economic, social, and political linkages in complex spaces of flows. New ICTs are a key factor in shaping these spaces of flows. This is partly because the cost of distance is being reduced as a result of cheaper telecommunications charges, but also because a vastly greater range of services (e.g. telephone, Internet, mobile and fax) are available to users. Not only are more countries being connected to these global information spaces, but the range and intensity of information transmitted is increasing rapidly. Thus, barriers of time and space are being overcome by these new ICTs (Cairncross 1997; Westland and Clark 1999, p. 55).

Twenty-four Hour Markets

Globalization is leading to an almost instantaneous awareness of events on a 24-hour basis. The emergence of 24-hour news reporting provides a clear illustration of this. Reports on political, economic, sport, and popular cultural events are broadcast around the clock via radio, television, and the Internet. In particular, the adoption of new mobile telephone and hand-held computer technologies means that individuals are able to access, process, and transmit information at any time of day or in any location.

The rise of 24-hour financial markets is associated with globalization, the growing importance of ICTs and the deregulation of financial services. Major political and economic events have almost instantaneous repercussions on financial markets in industrialized countries. The FX market is probably the most visible 24-hour market, since the value of nations' currencies are prominently displayed in the world's media and fluctuations are extensively commented upon by the media.

The emergence of 24-hour trading in global financial markets represents a significant component of the spaces of flows. Demand and supply factors underpin this trend. On the demand side, organizations need to respond quickly to events occurring at any time of day, given that such events may have a significant impact on their overall operations. A war or major political upheaval in a country is likely to lead to significant repercussions on that currency's value. The FX and other financial markets will react instantaneously to such events. On the supply side, the ease of transmitting and accessing information on a global basis has improved with the IT revolution. Traders in global financial markets now have on their desktop terminal access to a huge amount of information, whether it be from the information vendors such as Reuters and Bloomberg, or from their own firm's sources.

Countries' equities markets have also been integrated into the 24-hour trading cycle (Langdale 1999, 2000). While few stocks are traded on a 24-hour basis, a crash or a sharp rise on Wall Street in the USA has ripple effects throughout the world. While each national market interprets Wall Street news in the light of its own local developments, most countries' markets are affected by major shifts on Wall Street (OTA 1990). Major brokerage firms such as Merrill Lynch and Schwab as well as online rivals such as E*Trade and TD Waterhouse are planning to establish global broking firms able to execute trading 24 hours a day in stock markets around the world (Mackintosh 2000).

Spaces of Places and Global Cities

The local perspective, or spaces of places in Castells's terms, is closely interrelated with the global spaces of flows. Global cities, which function as global, national, and local centers for the collection, processing, management, and dissemination of information, are critically important nodes in worldwide financial markets. The role of information provision is especially important and is a key reason for large corporations, producer or business services, and governmental agencies clustering or agglomerating in these cities.

Global cities are centers which exert control over significant parts of the rest of the world. They play two key roles (Hamnett 1995; Beaverstock *et al.* 2000). First, they function as command centers for TNCs. The globalization of economic activity and the emergence of manufacturing plants and service industries in different countries creates a need for greater central control and coordination. New ICTs provide greater possibilities for dispersal of control functions; however, firms use the flexibility in different ways. Some have centralized control in global cities, while others have decentralized power to subsidiaries. Thus, while global cities retain important control functions, significant decentralization trends have also taken place.

A second function is that global cities have a concentration of specialized financial and business services (Sassen 1994). A central reason for the clustering of specialized service industry firms in banking and finance, accountancy, and law in global cities is the need to have regular face-to-face meetings with clients and with other service industry professionals. It is not a matter of face-to-face meeting versus electronic communications; professionals in these industries make heavy use of many forms of communication and the range and intensity of information which is collected, processed, and transmitted is substantial. New ICTs have allowed them to conduct their business from a 'mobile' office, with 24-hour access to voice, text, and data.

The local is still very important for these service industry professionals (Sassen 1999). Places such as Wall Street and the City of London are not simply aggregations of people and institutions who carry out specialist tasks; they are information nodes, with large volumes of messages and social contacts (Hamnett 1995). This dense clustering of people and information in a small area is crucial to the efficient functioning of global cities.

It is commonly argued that geography is less important in an era of cheap global telecommunications and Internet access (Cairncross 1997). While the cost of distance is lower, particular places have acquired enormous significance in the global economy. This is especially true for major global cities such as London and New York. A key component of this information hub role in global cities is the need for expertise in interpreting changes. These cities have a key role in the creation and maintenance of a specific culture, a set of contacts, and a body of carefully built-up knowledge and expertise which cannot be electronically duplicated (Hamnett 1995, p. 120). Personal or informal business networks remain a very important means of disseminating and receiving such information.

Regional Hubs in the Asia–Pacific Region

Cities such as Hong Kong and Singapore function as regional hubs for the Asia–Pacific region. These cities are also key centers in the emerging global and regional division of production. They occupy a central role in the Asia–Pacific region as the regional headquarters for major TNCs; they also coordinate and control firms' activities (e.g. manufacturing and sales offices) and act as intermediaries between the global corporate headquarters and the firms' affiliates in the region (Dicken 1998, p. 209). This global and regional division of production is particularly important in high technology manufacturing industries such as electronics. Low-wage countries (e.g. China and Indonesia) concentrate on basic assembly operations, whereas countries with a more sophisticated infrastructure and skilled workforce (e.g. Japan and Taiwan) specialize in higher value-added manufacturing activities. This headquarters' role has significant implications for banking and finance as well as for specialized business-oriented services, since these headquarters require such services to manage their regional operations. Furthermore, new ICTs play an important role in enhancing these cities' roles, since they lower the costs of communications within the region (Langdale 1999).

Singapore and Hong Kong also have a concentration of specialized financial and business services. While these services are not as large or as specialized as those in

London and New York, they perform a connecting role between the dominant global cities and the Asia–Pacific region. The two Asian cities are active competitors for these financial and business services, but their economies also complement each other (Ridding 1998; Handley 1998). Hong Kong has considerable expertise in funds management, loan syndication, and equities and has very strong linkages with the booming southern China (Guangdong and Fujian provinces) and with Taiwan. Singapore, on the other hand, has strengths in money market activities and is the regional hub for Southeast Asia.

GLOBALIZATION OF THE FOREIGN EXCHANGE MARKET

FX is the world's most highly globalized industry, with the market operating 24 hours a day. The globalized market relies on the extensive adoption of ICTs and a deregulated operating environment. The FX market, however, needs to be seen in the context of global–local relationships. The local is important in that a large percentage of global FX turnover takes place in three cities and market participants are geographically clustered in the financial districts of these cities. In addition, local informal business networks are very significant for FX dealers and sales/marketing staff. Many participants in the FX market rely on these information networks to complement the information obtained from more formal information sources.

Role of Global Cities in the FX Market

Turnover in the FX market is geographically concentrated in a small number of global cities, with London accounting for 32 percent of global turnover in 1998 and New York 18 percent (Figure 11.1). The dominance of these two cities increased from 43 percent in 1992 to 50 percent in 1998.

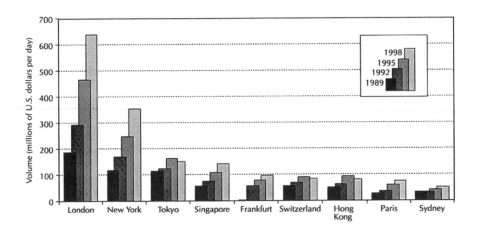

Figure 11.1   *Volume of foreign exchange trading by City, 1989–98. Source: Bank for International Settlements, Basel, Switzerland various surveys*

London

London's growing dominance in the global FX market during the 1990s reflected the growing trend for FX firms to centralize their FX operations in a region and adopt a regional hub-and-spoke strategy. Many FX firms rationalized European dealing rooms during the 1990s and centralized their dealing operations in London, although sales/marketing offices were still located in major European cities. London was selected as the European FX center given its existing dominance in financial services and in FX. European FX customers increasingly want to deal through London because of its superior liquidity and because the large London dealing rooms see heavy FX trading flows which customers want to know about.

London's global dominance in FX trading also reflects its overall role as a global city and world financial center. London has a number of strengths in FX. Its time zone is a major advantage, since it covers the same time zone as Europe and afternoon trading in London overlaps with morning trading in New York. Historically, London has had an important position as an international banking and finance center, reflecting the UK's role as a dominant international trading nation in the 18th and 19th centuries. Furthermore, the UK government adopted relatively liberal regulations in financial markets, whereas most European governments strictly regulated their respective national markets.

While London dominates the European time zone, other major European cities such as Frankfurt and Paris have retained a significant presence in FX, largely because of the size of their domestic economies and the presence of a large number of headquarters of national banks. It is likely, however, that with the introduction of the euro in 1999, the volume of intra-European currency trading will have substantially declined as would the role of these European FX centers.

New York

New York's strong FX role reflects the city's dominance over the massive US domestic market. New York is the headquarters of many US commercial and investment banks, a number of which play a dominant role in the global FX market. For example, commercial banks (e.g. Citibank and Chase Manhattan) and investment banks (e.g. Merrill Lynch and Goldman Sachs) have major global FX operations. New York also functions as the regional hub for North America (particularly Canada) and South America.

New York's key competitive strength in FX in the 1990s is that the US is the headquarters for many large institutional investors. Institutional investors include such firms as hedge funds and funds managers (e.g. pension, superannuation, and mutual funds). Hedge funds are private investment pools, often domiciled offshore to capitalize on tax and regulatory advantages. In the US they typically offer their shares in private placements (i.e. they are not listed on the Stock Exchange) and have fewer than 100 high net worth investors in order to avoid government regulatory restrictions (IMF 1998).

Hedge funds have been very active in the FX market, often with spectacular impacts on the value of currencies, although they have been less active since the financial crises in 1998, involving Russia and the near crash of a major hedge fund (Long Term Credit

Management). Many large institutional investors have close relationships with US-based investment and major commercial banks; thus, New York-based FX firms have a major competitive advantage in terms of 'seeing the flows'. New York-based investment and commercial banks often follow the hedge funds in their speculative 'raids' on different countries' currencies, thus compounding the impact of these funds on currency values.

The Role of 24-hour Trading

Until the early 1990s, banks and financial firms traded FX in a relatively large number of countries, with each dealing room trading a wide spectrum of currencies. While major cities such as London, New York, and Tokyo dominated FX trading, little coordination existed between different dealing rooms and costs were relatively high.

By the early 1990s most FX firms moved to a more globally integrated network based on a regional hub-and-spoke model. Global cities were selected as the hubs for major regions: London was the center for Europe, Africa, and the Middle East, and New York for the Americas. In the Asia–Pacific region the hub location varied depending on the organization; Singapore was a dominant location (Figure 11.2), although some firms used Hong Kong, Sydney, or Tokyo as their regional hub. In particular, Japanese banks used Tokyo as their hub for the Asia–Pacific region (Figure 11.3).

A number of financial services firms, particularly large ones such as Citibank, Chase Manhattan, and Deutsche Bank, adopted a more complex global trading model in this period, although it was still based on the regional hub-and-spoke model. The more complex global trading model reflected the size of their operations in different countries. In the Asia–Pacific region they have included Sydney in their 24-hour trading activities to operate between New York market's closing and Asia's opening. One firm, for example, transferred its global order book from New York to Sydney for three or

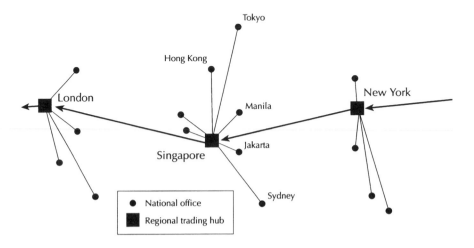

Figure 11.2   *Regional hub-and-spoke FX operations in Singapore. Source: Langdale*

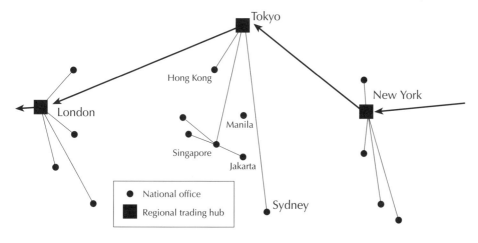

Figure 11.3   *Regional hub-and-spoke FX operations in Tokyo. Source: Langdale*

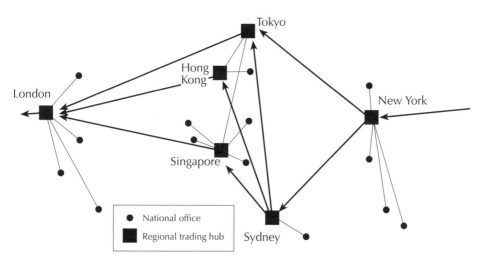

Figure 11.4   *Regional hub-and-spoke FX operations in a major global commercial bank. Source: Langdale*

four hours, but when the Asian markets opened, split the orders to various Asian centers: yen trading went to Japan; Hong Kong dollar and sterling to Hong Kong; and euro, US dollar and Southeast Asian currencies to Singapore (Figure 11.4).

Rationalization of Dealing Rooms

Firms reduced the number of FX dealing rooms located in different countries in the early 1990s. The reduction affected all countries, but was particularly apparent in Europe where many firms cut back their dealing rooms to a single center. This rationalization occurred for a number of reasons:

- risks associated with FX transactions could be better managed from a small number of centers;
- IT had improved, which allowed sales/marketing staff and customers to quickly and cheaply access the regional hub dealing room;
- dealing rooms are expensive and firms found that they could more effectively utilize traders and terminals in a smaller number of dealing centers;
- FX was becoming less profitable in the 1990s and firms were forced to reduce costs.

While firms adopted a regional hub-and-spoke strategy for their dealing rooms in the early 1990s, sales and marketing offices are still decentralized. Firms need a physical presence in each country to deal directly with customers on a regular basis. Thus FX firms have adopted a global–local strategy in their operations.

Electronic Trading

The FX market has always been heavily reliant on ICTs, but a number of other financial services (e.g. retail banking, trade finance, stock, and futures trading) were also adopting electronic commerce by the late 1990s, although the role of electronic trading is less well developed than in the FX market (Biederman 1998; Langdale 2000; Wenninger 2000; Westland and Clark 1999). Heavy use of electronic trading has facilitated rapid globalization of the FX market. This rapid adoption of electronic trading, in conjunction with the industry's declining profitability, has altered the geography of the industry, with a rationalization of dealing rooms among the firms.

A number of different electronic systems are used. Dealers use Reuters 2000-1 for interbank trading and making deals with other industry participants. In addition, Reuters (Reuters 2000-2) and Electronic Broking Services (EBS) offer electronic broking services: financial firms use computer screens to display the best available bid and offer prices in a number of currency pairs. Either price can be hit at the touch of a button and a ticket is printed automatically. Trading currencies electronically has brought much greater transparency to the market. Electronic broking also enables large and small banks to deal directly with each other, bypassing the voice brokers. The industry rapidly adopted electronic broking during the 1990s, with voice brokers occupying a much less important role. For example, electronic brokers increased their share of total FX turnover in London from 5 percent in 1995 to 11 percent in 1998. Electronic brokers are particularly strong in the major currencies (euro, yen, and US dollar) (Bank for International Settlements 1999a, p. 15).

EBS dominates electronic broking in heavily traded currencies (euro, US dollar, and yen) in the Asia–Pacific region. Most Asian currencies, however, are not on electronic broking systems, primarily because governments in the region fear that their currencies will be more vulnerable to rapid fluctuations as a result of 'raids' by hedge funds.

More recently, a number of banks have adopted Internet-based FX trading, particularly for customers from small and medium-sized enterprises. While the volume of Internet FX trading is still small, it is likely to grow rapidly in the future, reflecting the overall growth of Internet-based trading. This trend will further reduce the number of FX staff, since the handling of small FX customer orders is relatively labor intensive and Internet trading is a much more cost-effective approach.

Some firms centralized their FX trading in a single city and used their dealing room 24 hours a day. Sales/marketing offices, on the other hand, continue to be decentralized and operate during normal business hours in various countries around the world. In effect, sales/marketing offices function as intermediaries between the customer and the global dealing room and provide local face-to-face contacts.

It is technological feasible for a more widespread adoption of the geographically centralized hub approach, but most firms found that it has significant disadvantages. One is that good dealers do not want to work late in the evenings or in the early mornings on a regular basis. In addition, such a dealing room is 'artificial' in the sense that the active FX market and business day is on the other side of the world; also a centralized dealing room inevitably has limited awareness of political and business events occurring in the rest of the world, despite being electronically connected to Reuters and Bloomberg screens.

Most FX firms argued that the regional hub-and-spoke model was more desirable than the single centralized hub. As we have already seen, the former model often has three dealing rooms: Europe, the Americas and the Asia–Pacific region, with each covering eight-hour shifts in the trading day. Thus each dealing room is open during the region's business day and trading 'follows the sun' on a 24-hour cycle.

SINGAPORE'S ROLE IN THE ASIA–PACIFIC FOREIGN EXCHANGE MARKET

FX Trading in Singapore and Other Asia–Pacific Centers

Singapore has grown rapidly as a global and Asia–Pacific FX center. This role is closely related to its function as a financial and general service industry hub for the Asia–Pacific region. In contrast, Tokyo and Hong Kong, Singapore's chief regional FX rivals, have shown either a much slower growth rate or a decline in the volume of trading (Figure 11.1).

While FX trading has undoubtedly grown in Singapore, a problem with interpretations of the volume of FX trading figures is that they rely on a survey conducted every three years by the central banks of each country on behalf of the Bank for International Settlements (BIS). The survey provides the only reliable statistical base for the FX market. The BIS survey results unfortunately provide a snapshot of the market's development for a single month (Bank for International Settlements 1999a). The first half of 1998 was a period of major Asian currency volatility. Sharp increases were recorded in the volume of trading in Singapore dollars, Malaysian ringgit, Indonesia rupiah, and Thai baht, much of which was transacted in Singapore. Since then the volume of trading in these currencies has fallen sharply and Singapore's turnover also has fallen (Holland 1998).

The composition of currency trading changed quite significantly in Singapore in the 1990s (Figure 11.5). The US dollar dominated trading slightly increased in importance over this period. In contrast, the next two heavily traded currencies (Japanese yen and German Deutschmark) declined in importance. The remaining currencies relatively increased, reflecting the onset of the Asian economic crisis and heavy trading of Asian

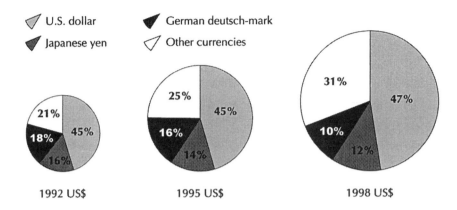

Figure 11.5   *Top three currencies traded in Singapore. Source: BIS Surveys 1992, 1995, 1998*

currencies in 1997 and early 1998 (Holland 1998). For example, transactions involving US and Singapore dollars in April 1998 averaged US$17.6 billion daily to account for 12.7 percent of total turnover in the Singapore market, a growth of 213 percent as compared to April, 1995 (Singapore 1998).

FX Firms in Singapore

Respondents from 30 FX firms were interviewed in Singapore in the period from May, 1998 to January, 1999 in order to provide an understanding of the role of the Singapore FX office in the firms' global operations. It is difficult to assess the representativeness of the sample, since no overall statistics on the size of each firm's turnover exists for the market. It was felt that the responses reflected the broader population of firms. The sample was biased toward the large firms in the market, mainly because they are increasingly dominating the FX market. The interviews were semi-structured and were conducted with the head of FX or with a senior dealer. The interviews averaged about one hour in duration.

The survey responses suggest that rapid growth in Singapore's FX turnover in the early 1990s was the result of a number of interrelated factors. Many respondents mentioned that they were attracted to Singapore on the basis of the profits they made out of trading with Bank Negara, the Malaysian central bank, which at that time engaged in very speculative currency trading. The Singapore government also encouraged firms in locate in Singapore by providing them with FX business from the Singapore Government Investment Corporation (SGIC). Furthermore, as we have already seen, firms were adopting a regional hub-and-spoke strategy globally in the early-1990s; Singapore was seen as a desirable location for these Asia–Pacific regional hub activities.

Many foreign TNCs established regional operations in Singapore during the 1990s. The chief factors attracting these operations were the political and social stability and quality of telecommunications infrastructure (Table 11.1). Of somewhat less importance are Singapore's reputation as an FX center and its strong regulatory framework. These regional operations make heavy use of Singapore's FX market and a number of

Table 11.1 *Factors in foreign TNCs establishing regional treasury operations in Singapore*

Factor	Rating 1 = not important 5 = important
Political and social stability	4.5
Developed telecommunications infrastructure	4.4
Singapore's reputation as a leading center of foreign exchange trading	4.1
Strong regulatory framework of the financial industry	4.0
Presence of high quality financial institutions offering sophisticated financial products	4.0
Favorable taxation policies	3.7
Presence of international institutions	3.7
Singapore's geographical location	3.5
Domestic economy	2.9
Wage costs	2.9

Source: Singapore Foreign Exchange Market Committee, 1997 Annual Report.

respondents pointed out that they are sophisticated users of the FX market. The presence of these regional treasury operations was also a factor in FX firms expanding their regional hub activities in Singapore.

Large FX turnover in a city does not necessarily mean higher profits for firms. While a number of large global FX banks and financial firms, as well as those with good regional information networks, made large profits at the onset of the Asian crisis, turnover in many Asian currencies has been quite low in recent years. Two examples illustrate this trend. The political and economic difficulties in Indonesia led to a slowdown in rupiah trading and few Indonesian banks were sufficiently creditworthy after the crisis to be FX counterparties for global FX firms. In addition, the Malaysian government pegged the ringgit to the US dollar in September 1998, which led to little trading taking place in this currency. Furthermore, global hedge funds have been less active in the Asian FX market recently, partly because of the credit restrictions imposed by banks, but also because it is difficult to speculate on Asian currencies given their lack of liquidity.

The Singapore FX operations of a number of foreign banks suffered from other problems by the late 1990s. Singapore functions as a major Southeast Asian regional hub for Japanese banks, but in mid-2000 they contracted their global FX activities as a result of the collapse of the 'bubble economy' in Japan. Furthermore, a number of European banks relied on being specialists in their domestic currency (e.g. Italian lira or French franc). The onset of the euro has cut out this advantage and they now must compete with major global FX banks (e.g. Citibank, Chase Manhattan, and Deutsche). These two developments have affected the global FX operations of Japanese and European banks, but Singapore has been particularly affected because of its regional hub status.

Despite these problems, most major global FX firms have not changed their regional hub-and-spoke strategy. One reason was that they invested considerable management time and expense setting up the regional hub in the early 1990s and are unwilling to reorganize the firm without good reasons. The Singapore-based regional management is unlikely to initiate a corporate reorganization which led to a reduction in their power.

Singapore's Role in 24-hour Trading

Singapore has a key role in the 24-hour FX trading cycle. The Singapore market has, in effect, two opening times. The first is from 6 a.m. to 7 a.m. in which some firms take over trading directly from New York, cutting Sydney out of the global order loop. The second is the normal start at 8 a.m. (9 a.m. Tokyo time) to the Asian market. One respondent pointed out a burst of activity in the market takes place from 8 a.m. to 8:15 a.m. when Tokyo starts trading yen heavily.

The market effectively closes down between 11 a.m. and 12:30 p.m. Singapore time (12 noon–1:30 p.m. Tokyo time) for the Tokyo lunch break. It then picks up in the afternoon when Europe comes in between 2 p.m. and 2:30 p.m., with firms passing their orders through to London about 3 p.m. Singapore time.

Key components of the westward transfer of information are the informal links between dealers in different centers. Dealers in the center that is closing pass on their views on what they had seen in currency trading for the day and overall trends in the market. Major FX firms have gone to considerable lengths to ensure that information was passed effectively on a 24-hour basis. Despite the sophistication of electronic information on the Reuters and Bloomberg screens and the firms' internal information sources, virtually all major FX firms interviewed mentioned that informal information exchange was quite significant. Voice communications thus still plays an important role in these global electronic spaces.

We have seen earlier that Singapore performs an important regional role in collecting, processing, and transmitting information from the surrounding region. Singapore has significant strengths as a regional information hub for Southeast Asia, because of its traditional trade and finance role for the region. Its dependence on Asian regional linkages proved to be a handicap in the Asian economic crisis of 1997–99. While it survived the Asian economic crisis of 1997 much better than its neighbors, ongoing political, economic, and social disruptions in the region led to limited regional FX activity. FX trading, although on a limited basis, is again taking place in Singapore in the Malaysian ringgit and in the Indonesian rupiah. While some recovery took place in 1999 in Thailand and the Philippines, economic growth is still fragile and the volume of FX trading in these currencies remains quite small. Consequently, Singapore's regional FX function for Southeast Asia has been severely affected over the past few years.

One component of Singapore's regional function is that a number of foreign banks use their Singapore office to maintain a regional network of links with local banks throughout the region. For example, a European bank with a regional dealing room centralized in Singapore pointed out that 'we are also maintaining our relationships with Thai, Korean, and Philippine banks to have domestic news and information with them. It is quite important to trade a bit with them to maintain our relationships'. Later on he pointed out that 'it is too expensive to have an office in Bangkok; it is much better to have this network of informal contacts and relationships business' (personal interview, January, 1999).

Information on political and economic developments in countries in the region is vital for FX firms with regional dealing operations in Singapore. Some of this information is obtained via information vendors (e.g. Reuters and Bloomberg) and from official government sources. More importantly, a number of firms emphasized that they built up their own network of political and economic contacts in different countries who could give them an 'insider's view' of developments; thus the FX firm would have knowledge before the market did. These informal information sources were particularly important in Asian developing countries' markets. As one respondent from a US bank pointed out that 'it is creating one's own efficient information channels when the market norm is inefficiency' (personal interview, May, 1998).

One difficulty for firms hubbing their Asia–Pacific FX operations in Singapore is that it is distant from the large Northeast Asian economies of Japan, Korea, China, and Taiwan. Japan has traditionally functioned as a yen market and while a few firms trade other currencies in Tokyo, its strength is primarily as a yen center. Hong Kong is the natural information hub for Northeast Asia and still retains a significant, albeit diminished, role in FX. One respondent pointed out that there was a marked information divide between Northeast and Southeast Asia and that Singapore was often poorly placed to access Northeast Asian information.

SUMMARY AND CONCLUSIONS

The FX market provides an illustration of the complexity of global–local relationships. The global information spaces in FX are comprised of regular and irregular flows. The regular component is the 24-hour transfer of information in a westward direction anchored in three global cities: London (for Europe, Africa, and the Middle East), New York (for the Americas) and primarily, but not exclusively, Singapore (for the Asia–Pacific).

Superimposed on this regular 24-hour cycle are unpredictable and massive swings in the volume and geography of information flows associated with currencies that are suddenly 'in play' with currency speculators. The major participants in the FX market in recent years have been the large institutional investors (particularly the large hedge funds) and their associated commercial and investment banks. If these firms target a particular currency (e.g. the Thai baht in May, 1997), such activity engenders a major increase in information flows within the targeted country, as well as between key cities in the global FX system. More importantly, such currency crises often lead to contagion effects on other vulnerable economies, further adding to the complexity in the geography of global information flows.

The global spaces of flows in the FX market are primarily electronic in nature and take place on Reuters and EBS screens. The telephone is also used by dealers to talk to other dealers, or by sales/marketing staff to talk to clients. The importance of electronic brokers, particularly in heavily traded currencies (e.g. euro, US dollar, and the yen) rose sharply during the 1990s. This trend is likely to continue in the future. In addition, many FX firms provide Internet-based FX services for small and medium-sized enterprises; these services are expanding as a result of the rising importance of global e-commerce.

The role of place, particularly in the major global cities of London and New York, is of vital importance in the FX market. Turnover is dominated by these global cities. Participants in the FX market are tightly geographically clustered in very high office rental districts, despite the fact that they rely very heavily on electronic information. This clustering is partly related to the close interrelationships between FX and other financial services. FX dealers and sales/marketing staff also rely on local informal networks, which make it important to be close to other FX firms.

The growing electronic nature of the business will lead to a further decline in the number of dealers and a shift of the business into more sophisticated areas of derivatives trading. Thus cities that are FX dealing centers will become even stronger electronic hubs of information. The personal information networks of dealers and sales/marketing staff will continue to play an important role in the market. At the same time, sales/marketing offices, which are locationally decentralized to be near customers, will lose some staff as routine FX transactions are shifted to the Internet. Fewer opportunities, however, exist for firms to automate client relations, since most FX firms want to be able to retain close linkages with their corporate clients in order to sell them a range of other financial services.

The FX case study raises a number of issues regarding the nature of global information spaces. While the FX market is the most highly globalized industry operating on a 24-hour basis, a number of manufacturing (particularly in the high technology area) and service industries are moving toward 24-hour operations. This trend is being accelerated by the shift into e-commerce and the rapid decrease in international telecommunications costs. For example, design teams in major automobile companies working in different countries and in different time zones are jointly designing cars. Generally, these global information spaces involve regular information flows on a 24-hour basis.

At the same time, massive surges of irregular information flows have been associated with financial crises involving the global stock and bond markets or with particular countries (e.g. Russia, Thailand, Indonesia, and Mexico). These irregular information flows represent in a sense 'panic attacks' in international financial markets, which in turn engenders new surges of global, regional, and national information flows. Considerable concern exists on the part of regulators of banking and financial markets about the ability of the financial system to cope with such 'shocks'. Growing complexity in global information spaces combined with the emergence of 24-hour markets make the international financial system extremely difficult to regulate (OTA 1990).

We have seen from the FX case study that most of the global information flows are generated from a small number of global cities. This is likely to be true in other activities which generate significant global information flows, although other cities may be prominent in some financial markets: for example, the Chicago futures exchanges dominated global futures markets with 41 percent of turnover in 1997 (Sarkar and Tozzi 1998).

The interrelationships between the global and the local are also likely to change quite significantly with rapid adoption of e-commerce. It is difficult to forecast the likely implications for the role of global cities, but it is clear that those cities and countries that have poor telecommunications and IT infrastructures will be uncompetitive as e-commerce hubs. Certainly, Singapore has made e-commerce the cornerstone of its international competitiveness strategy and sees its role developing as a global and regional information hub (Coe and Yeung 2000; Langdale 1997; Wong 1998). Singapore's emergence as a key global and regional hub in the FX market thus fits in with its broader international strategy; the difficulty the city-state faces is to maintain its position given the rapid technological and market changes taking place.

ACKNOWLEDGEMENTS

I would like to thank the Australian Research Council for its funding support for the trips to Singapore. In addition, discussions with Pierre Agnes on a parallel project on Sydney's FX market have greatly assisted my work on the Singapore project.

· Imp of place in globaliz- (global cities)
· Singapore as an Asian place in 24hr trading
     — hub + spoke system, but need for local faces for f2f
        + for connection to regional banks w/ local knowledge
· Importance of transferring informal judgments/predictions/observations
     westward from one node to next at close of business

PART III
E-COMMERCE: FINANCIAL, LEGAL, AND STATE DIMENSIONS

12

The Currency of Currency: Speed, Sovereignty, and Electronic Finance

BARNEY WARF and DARREN PURCELL

Florida State University, Tallahassee, FL, USA

'What goes around faster comes around faster, but then it also goes around faster again' (Friedman 1999: p. 110).

Floating exchange rates, electronic funds transfer systems, and digital money in the late 20th century radically altered the mechanisms of global finance and governance. This chapter explores the economic and spatial implications of foreign currency exchanges. It opens by reviewing the stability of currencies during the heyday of the Bretton Woods system. Second, it turns to the forces that have freed money from its traditional geographic restraints, including deregulation and technological change, emphasizing how digital money was freed to roam the world at the speed of light. Third, it focuses on the challenge to national sovereignty that electronic money poses by progressively undermining the capacity of national governments and central banks to control their own currencies. Fourth and fifth, it reviews the recent East Asian and Russian financial crises, respectively, to demonstrate how global money wrought havoc in two important regional contexts, imposing the neoliberal logic of the global market on varying national financial systems.

Geography and money are no strangers to each other. A sizable literature has documented the complex, often contradictory ways in which finance and space are shot through with each other (Corbridge *et al.* 1994; Leyshon and Thrift 1997; Laulajainen 1998; Martin 1999). Capitalism without complex systems of finance to lubricate investment and trade is unthinkable; global capitalism today without neural networks of glass wires to transfer money electronically across national borders is equally unimaginable. The rise of electronic money in the wake of floating exchange rates and the microelectronics revolution fundamentally undermined the role of national monetary policy. In the process, it has also radically reconfigured the relationships between capital and space.

This chapter explores the implications of electronic money as it relates to international currency fluctuations. In an age of hypermobile, global capital, national borders, and national controls over the money supply have been significantly eroded as obstacles to the flow of funds. Deregulation and the microelectronics revolution allow vast quantities of digital money to change hands with ease, existing now as yen, then yuan, then francs, and finally pesos, generating havoc with exchange rates. These transactions have powerful consequences. Currency fluctuations are important in several respects, including their impacts upon national interest and inflation rates, as well as the ways they determine exchange rates, which in turn heavily affect the relative prices of imports and exports among nations. Because exports are critical to national economic competitiveness, especially given the worldwide hegemony of neoliberal programs designed to encourage export promotion over import substitution, exchange rates are important factors in determining not only trade balances, but foreign revenues and domestic employment. Thus, the currency of currency lies in its multiple linkages to other parts of the economy.

The chapter opens with a brief review of the Bretton Woods agreement, under which currency fluctuations were the exception, not the norm. It then explores the nature of electronic money, trade in which greatly eclipses all other economic activities. As national borders and national monetary controls have gone the way of the passenger pigeon, local political structures have often been plunged into chaos; in the post-Cold War era, currency fluctuations have dramatic political implications as well. To shed light on this issue, the chapter turns to the impacts of the financial crises in East Asia and Russia during the 1990s, which were largely driven by rapid changes in the values of their currencies. Far from homogenizing the world into some vast isotropic plain, the intersections of global money and the nation-state play out in different ways in geographically specific contexts.

BRETTON WOODS AND THE STABLE EXCHANGE RATE REGIME

Currencies have not always gyrated so wildly. Under the Bretton Woods agreement, from 1947 to 1971, there was relatively little exchange rate fluctuation; most currencies were pegged to the US dollar, fluctuating only within 2 percent in a given year without International Monetary Fund (IMF) intervention (Williamson 1983). The dollar, in turn, was pegged to gold, at \$35/ounce. The fixed exchange rate system required the free international movement of gold as well as minimal government interventions to offset its effects, such as changes in the money supply designed to change real interest rates. The regulations on exchange rates imposed by Bretton Woods were largely designed to avoid the rounds of depreciations that accompanied, and were deepened by, the Depression of the 1930s.

Under this system of international regulation, currency appreciations or depreciations reflected government fiscal and monetary policies within a system of relatively nationally contained financial markets in which central bank intervention was effective. Trade balances and foreign exchange markets tended to be strongly connected: rising imports caused a currency to decline in value as domestic buyers needed more foreign currency to finance purchases. Rising exports had the opposite effect, raising the price of domestic currencies on the international market. Devaluations made exports cheaper and imports more expensive; appreciations, conversely, made exports more expensive and imports cheaper. Thus currency fluctuations figured prominently in rectifying trade imbalances. The relative stability of exchange rates during the post-war Fordist–Keynesian boom was further enhanced by a series of other measures, including multilateral clearing policies for different currencies through the IMF, short-term borrowing from the IMF (which treated any disequilibrium in exchange rates as temporary), and the use of special drawing rights (SDRs) from the IMF. Loans drawn against members' contributions could be converted to foreign currencies (but not used domestically) to stabilize exchange rates.

The system of stable currencies ended abruptly with the collapse of the Bretton Woods agreement in 1971 and the shift to floating exchange rates in 1973 (Strange 1994). This change reflected US trade imbalances with its European partners and the overvaluation of the dollar, whose strength was maintained only through a steady outflow of gold. Despite the repeated efforts of the Exchange Stabilization Fund, which the US erected to mitigate such problems, the accumulation of dollars overseas, which significantly enhanced the growing Euromarket in the 1960s, contributed to an increasingly unviable trade imbalance. Finally, President Nixon announced the USA would no longer abide by the Bretton Woods rules governing the dollar's convertibility to gold, forcing a global switch to flexible exchange rates. Hereafter, supply and demand would dictate the value of a nation's currency, and currency trading became big business.

CURRENCY UNBOUND: THE BIRTH AND GROWTH OF FREE-FLOATING MONEY

The global sea change in capitalism that began with the traumatic petrocrises of the 1970s and massive restructuring of industrialized economies (deindustrialization and the microelectronics revolution) included a fundamental worldwide renegotiation of the relations between financial capital and space (Harvey 1989). Freed from many of the technological and political barriers to movement, capital has become not merely mobile, but hypermobile (Warf 1999). As Castells (1996, 1997) emphasized, all around the world the 'network society', dominated by a 'space of flows' rather than a 'space of places', has generated new political formations, forms of identity, and spatial structures.

A key part of this new order was the emergence of 'stateless money' (Martin 1994), which originated in its contemporary form through the Euromarket. Originally the Euromarket comprised only trade in assets denominated in US dollars, but not located in the USA. Today it has spread far beyond Europe, and includes all trade in financial assets outside of the country of issue (e.g., Eurobonds, Eurocurrencies, etc.). One of the Euromarket's prime advantages was its lack of national regulations. Unfettered by national restrictions, it has been upheld by neoclassical economists as the model of market efficiency. Indeed, US banks invested in the Euromarket in part to escape the restrictions of the Glass–Steagall Act, which prohibits commercial banks from buying and selling stocks. Further, the Euromarket lacked any reserve ratio requirements until 1987, when the world's central bankers met at the Bank for International Settlements in Basel, Switzerland, and agreed on global reserve standards.

Capital markets worldwide were also profoundly affected by the digital revolution.

Banks, insurance companies, and securities firms, which are generally very information-intensive in nature, have been at the forefront of the construction of an extensive network of leased and private telecommunications networks, particularly a skein of fiber-optic lines (Graham 1999). Electronic funds transfer systems, in particular, that form the nerve center of the international financial economy, allow banks to move capital all over at a moment's notice, arbitraging interest rate differentials, taking advantage of favorable exchange rates, and avoiding political unrest (Warf 1995). In the USA the Federal Reserve Bank's Fedwire system transfers the balances among private bank deposits; Fedwire traffic grew from $2.6 trillion in 1977 to $223 trillion in 1997 (Solomon 1997, p. 41). CHIPS (Clearing House Interbank Payments System), a consortium run by private firms to clear international transactions, processes $310 trillion annually (Solomon 1997). In Europe, the Belgian-based SWIFT (Society for Worldwide Interbank Financial Telecommunications) plays a comparable role. Private firms have similar systems. Citicorp, for example, erected its Global Telecommunications Network to allow it to trade $200 billion daily in foreign exchange markets around the world. Such networks give banks an ability to move money – by some estimates more than $3 trillion daily – around the globe at stupendous rates. Reuters, with 200 000 interconnected terminals worldwide linked through systems such as Instinet and Globex, alone accounts for 40 percent of the world's financial trades each day (Kurtzman 1993, p. 47). Other systems include SEAQ in London, Soffex, the Swiss Options and Financial Futures Exchange, the Computer Assisted Order Routing and Execution System at the Tokyo Stock Exchange, and TSE and CATS in Toronto. Such networks provide the ability to move money around the globe almost instantaneously (the average currency trade takes less than 25 seconds); subject to the process of digitization, information and capital become two sides of the same coin.

In the securities markets, global telecommunications systems facilitated the steady integration of national capital markets (Langdale 1985; Hepworth 1991). Electronic trading frees stock analysts from the need for face-to-face interaction to gain information (O'Connell 1995). The National Associated Automated Dealers Quotation System (NASDAQ), the first fully automated electronic marketplace, is now the world's fourth largest stock market; lacking a trading floor, NASDAQ connects half a million traders worldwide through telephone and fiber-optic lines, processing 2000 transactions per second (Nairn 1998). EASDAQ, the European version of NASDAQ launched in 1996, operates similarly, albeit on a smaller scale. Facing the challenge of online trading head-on, Paris, Belgium, Spain, Vancouver, and Toronto all recently abolished their trading floors. Online trading allows small investors to trawl the Internet for information, including real-time prices, eroding the advantage once held by specialists such as Reuters, and execute trades by pushing a few buttons. With 40 percent of US households now owning both stocks and personal computers, the current surge in trading may be just the beginning.

The ascendancy of electronic money shifted the function of finance from investing to speculation, institutionalizing volatility in the process. Foreign investments, for example, have increasingly changed from foreign direct investment (FDI) to intangible portfolio investments such as stocks and bonds, a process that reflects the securitization of global finance (Kahler 1998). Unlike FDI, which generates employment, technology transfer, and alters the material landscape, financial investments tend to create few jobs and are invisible to all but a few agents. Furthermore, such funds are provided by nontraditional suppliers. A large and rapidly rising share of private capital flows worldwide no longer intermediated by banks. Thus, not only has the volume of capital flows increased, but the composition and institutions involved have changed as well. As we shall see below, these facts are critical in understanding recent financial crises in Asia and Russia.

Traveling at the speed of light, as nothing but assemblages of zeros and ones, global money dances through the world's fiber-optic networks in astonishing volumes. For example, every two weeks the sum of funds that passes through New York's fiber-optic lines surpasses the annual product of the entire world (Kurtzman 1993, p. 17). Salomon Brothers, which routinely buys 35 percent of US government bonds, runs the equivalent of the nation's total bank holdings through its computers every year. CS First Boston, the world's leading bond trader, trades more money each year than the entire GNP of the USA. The total volume of electronic financial transactions worldwide exceeds $516 billion annually, including the vast system organized through SWIFT, the Society for Worldwide Interbank Financial Telecommunications, which now extends into 130 countries (Teitelman and Davis 1996). National boundaries mean little in this context: it is much easier to move $1 billion from London to New York than a truckload of grapes from California to Nevada (Figure 12.1).

The volume of capital movements around the world cannot be ascertained with much certainty; attempts to measure it have never proved to be very successful, showing up as the 'errors and omissions' part of IMF reports. Capital flight also remains a perpetual problem for developing countries in which political instability frequently shakes investor confidence, a chronic condition augmented by corrupt dictatorships (e.g., the Philippines' Marcos, Zaire's Mobutu). Even in economically advanced countries the mobility of capital has profound impacts on domestic markets. For example, capital outflows often discourage excessive reliance on short-term foreign borrowing. In this sense, exchange rate risk can cause banks and governments to hedge their exposure to foreign debt.

Globalization and electronic money have had particularly important impacts on currency markets. Since the shift to floating exchange rates, trading in currencies has become a big business, driven by the need for foreign currency associated with rising levels of international trade, the abolition of exchange controls, and the growth of pension and mutual funds, insurance companies, and institutional investors. The world's currency markets trade roughly $1.6 trillion every day, dwarfing the $25 billion that changes hands daily to cover global trade in goods and services (Solomon 1997). The vast bulk (72 percent) of foreign exchange transactions occurs in only three currencies, the US dollar, German mark, and Japanese yen (Laulajainen 1998, p. 104). London remains the premier world center for this practice, exchanging $465 billion in currencies annually, followed by New York ($250 billion), Tokyo ($185 billion), and Paris ($75 billion). The market opens each day in East Asia while it is evening in North America; funds then travel west, bouncing from city to city over fiber-optic lines, typically from Tokyo to Hong Kong to Singapore to Bahrain to Frankfurt or Paris to London. Changes in the structure of institutional investing have had profound impacts on this market: rapid movement of funds worldwide has meant that under- or

Figure 12.1   *Money and the evaporating national border. Source: Kobrin 1997 (Illustration by William Bramhall)*

overvalued currencies are likely to be subjected to speculative attacks from large hedge funds or financial institutions. Electronic funds transfer systems increased the velocity of money considerably, i.e., the rate at which it turns over and triggers successive rounds of purchases.

Electronic money can be exchanged an infinite number of times without leaving a trace, making it difficult for regulatory authorities to track down transactions both legal and illegal. The intermediaries that now serve as checkpoints for recording such transactions are eliminated by peer-to-peer transactions (Kobrin 1997). The opportunities for money laundering, a staple of the drug trade, are thus made all the more attractive. Tax evasion has become increasingly serious as electronic money has become the norm; moreover, the jurisdictional question, 'who gets to tax what', is vastly complicated. Digital counterfeiters can also take advantage of this situation, working anywhere and using the Internet to spend currencies in any other place. Encryption offers one route to limit such activity; secure e-cash transactions require strong encryption technology, but make it as difficult for authorities to identify criminal activities as much as legitimate ones.

The classic (i.e. neoclassical) case for capital mobility holds that such fluidity allows countries with limited savings to attract financing for domestic investments, that it allows investors to diversify their portfolios, that it spreads risk more broadly, and that it promotes intertemporal trade. Capital mobility implies that firms can smooth consumption by borrowing money from abroad when domestic resources are limited and dampen business cycles. Conversely, by investing abroad, firms can reduce their vulnerability to domestic disturbances and achieve higher risk-adjusted rates of return. The major problems concerning capital mobility in this view center around the asymmetry of information in financial markets and a 'moral hazard', reliance upon the state (or IMF) to bail them out during crises. Yet neoclassical theory is flawed in several respects, not the least of which is an inadequate appreciation of politics and space, the ways in which national, class, gender, and other nonmarket relations shape and constrain flows of money, even electronic money, and how the intersections of global capital and nation-states play out unevenly across the globe. Capital flight, as will be seen below, can generate financial chaos as much as it harmonizes investments. Central to this issue is the relative degree of influence and power that global capital and individual nation-states exhibit at varying historical conjunctures.

SOVEREIGNTY AT BAY: ELECTRONIC MONEY VERSUS THE NATION-STATE

Raymond Vernon's (1971) classic work *Sovereignty at Bay* argued convincingly that the nation-state as classically conceived, sovereignty, and the national economy were on their death-bed, victims of multinational corporations and international capital. Advocates of this perspective, of course, have long exaggerated claims that the nation-state was dying. A fully integrated world of digital finance, however, lent credence to Vernon's predictions in ways he or his advocates may not have anticipated.

Classic interpretations of the nation-state rested heavily upon a clear distinction between the domestic and international spheres, a world carved into mutually exclusive geographic jurisdictions. State control in this context implies control over territory. (It is worth noting parenthetically that there is no necessary correspondence between capitalism and the nation-state. For centuries, capitalism relied upon city-states, and the nation-state itself is a fairly recent Enlightenment institution.) In contrast, the rise of electronic money has generated a fundamental asymmetry between the world's economic and political systems. World-systems theorists (e.g. Chase-Dunn 1998) have argued that the fundamental political geography of capitalism is not the nation-state but the interstate system, which allows capital great leverage by flowing across borders in ways that the reach of regulatory authorities cannot.

Because finance has become so inextricably intertwined with electronic transfers of funds worldwide, it presents the global system of nation-states with unprecedented difficulties in attempting to reap the benefits of international finance while simultaneously attempting to avoid its risks. Friedman (1999, p. 90) writes of the 'Electronic Herd', which consists of 'all the faceless stock, bond and currency traders sitting behind computer screens all over the globe, moving their money around with the click of a mouse from mutual funds to pension funds to emerging market funds, or trading from their basements on the Internet'. For better or worse, global finance today is dominated by this vast assembly of large and small investors. Advocates of unfettered capital flows hold that such mobility creates opportunities for portfolio diversification, risk sharing, and intertemporal trade, all important criteria for the IMF. In the context of electronic money, Kobrin (1997, p. 75) notes:

> E-cash is one manifestation of a global economy that is constructed in cyberspace rather than geographic space. The fundamental problems that e-cash poses for governance result from this disconnect between electronic markets and political geography. The very idea of controlling the money supply, for example, assumes that geography provides a relevant means of defining the scope of the market. It assumes that economic borders are effective, that the flow of money across them can be monitored and controlled, and that the volume of money within a fixed geographic area is important. All of those assumptions are increasingly questionable in a digital world economy.

As large sums of funds flow with mounting ease across countries' borders, national monetary policies have become increasingly ineffective, making monetary controls over exchange, interest, and inflation rates progressively difficult to sustain. In the USA, for example, the Federal Reserve, ever vigilant about the prospect of inflation, raised the reserve ratio of banks multiple times during the 1990s, only to find that its control over the national money supply had diminished severely. The New York Federal Reserve's Foreign Exchange Office, the operational arm of the Treasury Department's Exchange Stabilization Fund, has likewise attempted repeatedly to stabilize the dollar against other currencies, with mounting difficulty. As Peck and Tickell (1994, p. 291) note: 'As private capital began increasingly to circuit globally on a deregulated basis, Keynesian nation states progressively lost control of one of the most important macroeconomic levers – the setting of interest rates'. This is not to say nation-states enjoy no leverage whatsoever over such factors, but the steady convergence of short-term interest (but not profit) rates globally undoubtedly reflects the mounting ease with which capital transcends national borders.

When currency speculators mount an attack on a given currency, nation-states have tools at their disposal, although their effectiveness may be questionable. 'The attackers can be held at bay by only one condition – that central banks are willing to subordinate most normal goals of monetary policy' (Solomon 1997, p. 165). Central banks can buy back their base from the speculators or draw on 'swap-line' agreements with other banks to borrow currency quickly. Political authorities can attempt to manipulate exchange rates where the currency remains shackled by a 'managed float' or 'crawling peg' system, usually harnessed to the US dollar and usually creating internal and external price distortions. Capital controls offer short-term benefits but discourage long-run investments such as infrastructure development, and often get mired in corruption (Kristof 1998). More drastically, they can raise interest rates. The goal in such situations is to convince speculators that the bank will stay the course and commit whatever reserves are necessary to shore up its currency by using the same leveraging tools as their private adversaries. As discussed below, however, few nations possess the resources to maintain such a defense for long. To confront such trends, a digital world economy requires unprecedented international cooperation, harmonized national legislation, and much stronger global institutions. Attempts to control global money, the necessity for which becomes obvious during crises, have increasingly shifted the scale of regulation from individual nation-states to international regulatory bodies, particularly the IMF.

In short, Vernon's predictions, however premature, may have considerably more validity at present than they did in the past. This is not to say that the nation-state is obsolete, or event that it will be in the near future. But electronic money, as one of the central dimensions of a new global order that emerged in the late 20th century, has markedly shifted the nature of international finance and investment, undermining the effectiveness of national monetary controls. Much of contemporary political geography has made precisely this point. Taylor (1994) and Agnew and Corbridge (1995), for example, stress notions of hegemony and territoriality at various spatial levels, particularly the 'power container' of the nation-state and its mounting 'leakages' to and from the world system. The interactions of global money on the rampage and the rapidly evaporating borders of the nation-state are evident in the case to two regional economic crises, East Asia and Russia.

MELTDOWN: THE ASIAN FINANCIAL CRISIS

The East Asian newly industrializing countries (NICs), following the historical experience of Japan in the famous 'flying geese formation', experienced the most rapid, sustained rates of economic growth in the world following World War II (Cummings 1984; Jenkins 1991; Brohman 1996). Productivity, GNP per capita, and real incomes grew by significant margins, uplifting the lives of tens of millions. Sustained capital inflows into the region implicitly guaranteed stable exchange rates. This trajectory, which was driven both by the geopolitics of the Cold War in the region as well as various internal factors, inspired many developing countries around the world with regard to the possibility of economic development.

Asia's rapid economic growth attracted a multitude of foreign investors in telecommunications, seeking profits from lucrative markets in mass media and producer services, leading to a substantial upgrading of telephone networks, fiber-optic lines, and satellite facilities. Somewhat surprisingly, Japan's IT system is poorly developed in comparison to the USA or Europe (McIntyre 1994; Warf 2000). Singapore, conversely, which has moved aggressively up the global chain of value-added functions into producer services, exhibits an extremely well developed telecommunications system that allows it to rival Hong Kong and Tokyo in the foreign exchange markets (Corey 1991), and Malaysia is currently building a technology corridor in hopes of attracting some of this growth (Jussawalla 1995). Connecting these hubs is a grid of fiber lines recently laid down by an international consortium of firms. AT&T and Japan's Kokusai Denshin Denwa (KDD) are building the Fiberoptic Link Around the Globe (FLAG), a 27 300-kilometer cable connecting Asia, Europe, and Africa (Warf 1998), as well as the Asia Pacific Cable Network, a 12 000-kilometer system linking Japan, South Korea, Taiwan, Hong Kong, the Philippines, Thailand, Vietnam, and Indonesia. Information flows within the region are, not surprisingly, dominated by movements between Tokyo, Hong Kong, and Singapore, and to a lesser extent, Bangkok, Manila, and Taiwan (Telegeography 1998).

The death of the 'Asian model' of development began with the deterioration of
Japan. Following the Plaza Accord of 1985, which forced down the US dollar, Japan
suffered a round of *endaka* (yen shock) forcing Japanese banks to hedge by selling more
dollars, a move that Leyshon (1994) insists was part of a broader American
geoeconomic offensive against Japan in the 1980s. Japanese capital and technology
have long served as one of the major motors of growth in the region, and as Japan
went, so has Asia. With an economy mired in prolonged recession and corporate
earnings flat and its 'bubble economy' burst, Japan's travails in the 1990s set the stage
for the region-wide catastrophe that followed. In bust times as well as boom, the 'flying
geese formation' proved, cruelly, to be all too true. In 1997 the East Asian 'miracle'
came to an abrupt end.

The origins of the Asian crisis have been attributed to several factors, most of which
revolved around the region's intersections with global finance, particularly in the
domain of exchange rates. The decline of the yen against the US dollar in 1996 and
1997 forced an appreciation of Southeast Asian currencies pegged to the dollar
(Feldstein 1998). Pegged currencies encouraged capital inflows because investors were
not deterred by exchange rate risks, which led to the deterioration of asset quality for
foreign-owned portfolios. In addition, Asian financial markets suffered from insufficient regulation, leading to political considerations in credit allocation based heavily
upon corrupt, cronyist ties to ruling families (Henderson 1998). Institutional restraints
to excessive risk taking, including disclosure rules and safeguards against hedge
speculators, were often absent (Lee 1998). Often badly managed and poorly audited,
banks and other lending agencies engaged in excessively risky lending practices, with
assets exaggerated by inflation rates, leading to high debt-to-equity ratios (Henderson
1998). Poor record keeping masked a deterioration of 'fundamentals', the primary
measures of economic health that attract or repel capital on a global basis. When
exposed to sudden onsets of illiquidity or bankruptcy, the Asian financial system
turned out to be highly fragile.

The Asian crisis found its genesis in Thailand, which offers a textbook example of a
small country confronted with large capital flows. In July 1997 the saturated Thai
commercial property market bubble burst. The baht, pegged to the dollar (a move that
had been proclaimed as providing stability), should have weakened along with the
banks and property markets, but the Thai government, determined to avoid the
embarrassment of devaluation, stubbornly supported the baht. Thai money market
managers, knowing their currency was overvalued, sought to make a quick killing by
selling baht. When Thailand's investors began buying dollars, they attracted the
attention of foreign speculators, particularly foreign hedge funds who, sensing the
nation's difficulty, bet heavily against the baht. Fresh from the Mexican currency crisis
of 1995, American speculators in particular sought greater returns in the economically
greener pastures of the Asian NICs. Determined to preserve its currency at all costs,
the Bank of Thailand risked everything to protect the nation's currency against the
foreign onslaught, until it was finally forced to let go, which sent the baht into a free-fall
of devaluation.

The Thai 'blood baht' soon spiraled into a vortex of financial instability that
included all of East Asia except China, with secondary effects on Australia, North
America, and Europe. Poon and Perry (1999) trace the geography of the 'Asian flu' as it

leapfrogged in 1997–98 from Thailand to Malaysia to Indonesia to South Korea to Taiwan to Hong Kong. A massive reversal of capital flows, which had swept into the region for decades, saw tens of billions of dollars leave for the US and Europe; in 1997 alone, net capital flows out of Thailand were equivalent to 10.7 percent of its GDP (Lee 1998, p. 21). Ratings agencies such as Moody's and Standard & Poor, which provide the international financial community with much of their information on the health of economies, issued increasingly bleak outlooks for Asia's economies, which in turn drove down their credit ratings and increased the cost of their debts. Exporters were in no hurry to convert falling local currencies to US dollars, while importers were anxious to do so immediately. Interest rates rose throughout the region, stimulating a banking crisis. Decreased earnings led to deflationary shock. Corporate bankruptcies soared, especially among firms with the most debt exposure and highest debt-to-equity ratios. Stock exchanges throughout Asia suffered a repeated series of drubbings, falling as much as 75 percent by the end of 1998 (Figure 12.2). Manufacturing firms, ranging from Korean steel to Indonesian electronics, tried to take advantage of devaluations to export their way out of misery, engaging in price slashing that affected clients around the world. Unemployment rates, generally below 5 percent before the crisis, typically doubled or tripled. Rising poverty rates for many meant severe deprivation, including

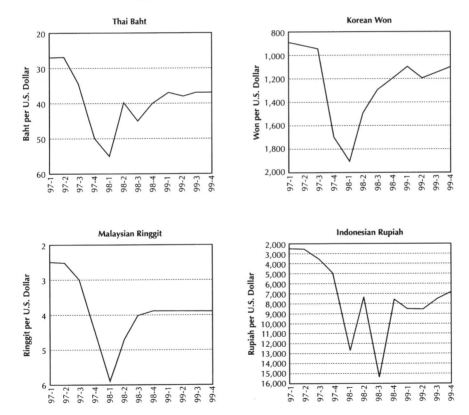

Figure 12.2 Exchange rates of East Asian currencies. Source: New York Times, 12 July 1999, p. A6

hunger and malnutrition. Indonesia, beset by 60 percent inflation in 1998 (particularly in staples such as rice and cooking oil), witnessed 40 million people, or 20 percent of the populace, sink into poverty (Lee 1998). Poor people, frequently peasants attracted to urban areas by the presence of foreign firms and jobs, often took the brunt of the burden, forced into deeper poverty or a return to subsistence agriculture in the hinterlands. Notably, those economies least connected to the international financial markets, such as Vietnam and the Philippines, proved to be the least susceptible. The economic turmoil also had political repercussions, leading to new, more democratic governments in South Korea and Indonesia, where the Electronic Herd deposed reigning corrupt despots such as Suharto.

Currency fluctuations played a pivotal role in the unfolding Asian drama. The vast majority of foreign exchange transactions in East Asia are concentrated in Tokyo, Hong Kong, and Singapore (Laulajainen 1998, p. 108). Considerable variability exists in the degree of exchange rate flexibility among nations in the region. In the wake of the spreading crisis, Asian currencies plummeted like ripe fruit as speculators dumped increasingly worthless monies, many of which had been freed from pegs to the dollar and allowed to drop unrestrained (Figure 12.3). The Indonesian rupiah suffered particularly dramatic declines, dropping from 4000 to 15 000 per dollar despite massive Bank of Indonesia intervention in the form of purchases of billions of US dollars to shore up the currency before they gave up and sought IMF assistance. National differences in production regimes, international reserves, current account balances, debt accumulation, and strategies to cope with the crisis produced varying degrees of devaluation (Henderson 1998). Whereas Thailand and Indonesia saw their currencies fall disastrously, others, such as Singapore and Taiwan, suffered less than a 20 percent decline. Hong Kong, with a dollar pegged at a fixed rate to that of the US, buttressed by large reserves, and regulated by a currency board, saw a mere 14 percent decline. The Chinese yuan emerged unscathed altogether. Despite repeated interventions by

Figure 12.3 *East Asian stock market indicators: composite index. Source: New York Times, 12 July 1999, p. A6*

central banks, nothing slowed the exodus of funds until 1999. Malaysia's Prime Minister Mahathir Mohammed complained to the IMF that: 'Currency trading is unnecessary, unproductive and immoral! It should be stopped. It should be made illegal! Currency traders have become rich – very, very rich – through making other people poor! (quoted in Henderson 1998, p. xi)'. Of course, politicians frequently blame 'speculators' when in need of a convenient scapegoat.

The role of the IMF in this context is worth emphasizing. Short-term IMF interventions included a $40 billion bailout in Thailand, $23 billion in Indonesia, and $57 billion in South Korea (the largest rescue in IMF history). Under heavy pressure from the US since the 1980s to liberalize capital flows worldwide, the IMF often tied currency stabilization, financial support packages, and debt restructuring to removals of statutory restrictions on capital account transactions, tax reforms, and bank restructuring and privatization. In Indonesia, IMF intervention was exceptionally strong, including the closure of 16 insolvent banks, establishment of the Indonesia Bank Restructuring Agency, the removal of limits on private ownership of banks, among other actions (Robison and Rosser 1998). Often IMF rescue packages included precipitous demands, such as the closure of bankrupt firms, reduced government expenditures, increased minimum capital requirements for banks, new deposit insurance funds, or increased interest rates, which, it argued, would stem the capital flight from the region (Feldstein 1998). Often, such measures attempted to prevent a crisis of liquidity from converting into insolvency; however, whether IMF intervention reduced rather than enhanced investor confidence is debatable. Krugman (1994) argued the IMF's intervention in Asia represented a 'moral hazard', a risk that investors expected to be bailed out. Longer-term measures included closure of weak institutions and write-downs of shareholder's capital, improved supervisory and regulatory systems, and recapitalization of undercapitalized institutions, often with foreign funds.

More broadly, the Asian crisis demonstrated that unfettered capital mobility has its costs, that liberalizing capital accounts without safeguarding the financial system can be catastrophic, and that macroeconomic stability is insufficient to guarantee financial stability. As Henderson (1998, p. 160) notes: 'The ability of capital to move at lightspeed around the world, of necessity, narrows the policy deviations between national financial authorities, whether they like it or not'. The Asian financial crisis, in short, gave ample evidence to Vernon's view of sovereignty at bay. These lessons were hardly learned in time to save another region under assault from foreign capital, Russia.

SAFETY NYET: RUSSIA'S CURRENCY CRISIS

In the wake of the collapse of the Soviet Union in 1991, Russia began the long, painful transition from a wholly state-owned economy to a relatively market-based one, a move supported by the West as well as reformers inside the Russian government. Global finance, increasingly electronic in nature in Russia as elsewhere, played a key role in the unfolding catastrophe that was the Russian economy. The break-up of the ruble zone, for example, saw no fewer than a dozen new currencies emerge (Cohen 1998). Despite desperate attempts to introduce market relations, the Russian economy continued its long slide into chronic crisis. In the late 1990s, the Asian financial crisis, which was widely feared to have contagion possibilities, resurfaced under very different political and economic circumstances.

A multitude of factors contributed to the Russian collapse. The first of these included the decline in international prices of what Russia produced most, raw materials. Oil revenues accounted for nearly 75 percent of Russia's foreign revenues during the 1990s (Cohen 1998; IMF 1999), and the demand for oil plummeted as the formerly expanding economies of Asia retreated (Francis 1998). Second, the Russian government's budget deficit, which reached 9 percent of GDP, caused concern among private and institutional investors. Third, high levels of crime, massive corruption, an inadequate legal system unable to enforce property rights, and crony capitalism gave foreign and domestic investors little reason to place faith in the Russian government's economic policies (Dunford 1998). As Rogers (1998), the head of an international investment company, noted in testimony to the US Congress:

> Since I have constantly warned to avoid Russia politically, economically, and socially, everyone now calls asking whether this is the time to get involved. After all, buying low means getting involved when things appear the bleakest. . . . The answer: Not with my money, time, career, energy or anything else. You ain't seen nothing yet. I would not put a nickel of my money there. I would not put a nickel of other people's money there.

Further evidence of corruption was evident in purchases of government securities (GKOs), which were dominated by a select cadre of Russian banks, all well connected to the central government. This state of affairs effectively shut out domestic as well as foreign investors from these lucrative issues, and did nothing to mollify investor concerns about the environment in which they were investing. Boone *et al.* (1998) argue that the lack of institutional protection and perceptions of managerial theft accelerated capital flight.

In contrast to Asia, in which FDI financed an expanding network of telecommunications, Russia has a poorly developed IT sector; with only 15 telephone lines per 100 people, and a total of 259 Internet hosts in 1997. It lags well behind Japan (46 lines and 1564 hosts, respectively), South Korea (38 and 348), or Taiwan (38 and 376) (Telegeography 1998). Not surprisingly, Russia's volume of international telecommunications traffic (201 million minutes in 1997) was also dwarfed by East Asian countries. Without a well developed IT infrastructure, finance and e-commerce in Russia were poorly positioned for growth.

Such considerations hardly made Russia a favorite of global investors. In 1996, for example, total FDI amounted to a mere $1.6 billion. Most importantly, the lack of a domestic constituency eager to court foreign investments is a major characteristic of the Russian economy (Buyske 1998). In the wave of deregulation and privatization that accompanied the nation's attempts to develop market relations, the nation's powerful banks diversified into the oil, television, telecommunications, and newspaper industries (Blasi *et al.* 1997). Fearing competition, Russia's banks and government ministries related to the military–industrial complex have steadfastly resisted foreign investment, exacerbating a shortage of funds in an already cash-strapped economy. While unable to attract much foreign direct investment, Russia did see an influx of portfolio investments, which reached $7.5 billion in 1998, from foreigners hoping that the nation was the last of the world's undervalued financial markets.

Major forces behind this surge of speculative capital included the booming Moscow stock market and the opening of the government's treasury bill market to foreign investors. The Russian Federal Securities Commission courted such funds as a political counterweight to the banks (Buyske 1998). However, the entrenched power of a conservative bureaucracy left reformers reduced to a core group of liberalizers clustered around the president.

Given the imbalance between Russia's economic fundamentals and the speculative surge of foreign capital, it was only a matter of time before the overvalued ruble, under those economic conditions, would become prey to speculative attacks by speculators. May 27, 1998 saw the concerted selling of rubles, stocks, and Russian government bonds by both foreign and domestic investors (Solomon 1999). The government, insisting that no devaluation would take place, authorized the Central Bank to buy rubles to shore up the currency, expending $1 billion on that day alone, which left a mere $14 billion in foreign currency reserves, a sum that could not sustain extended support of the ruble (Saburov 1998). The inability to maintain the ruble at a rate of six to the US dollar, the goal of the Central Bank, necessitated bond issues at progressively higher interest rates to continue to attract investors. In desperation, the government resorted to using a IMF tranche of $4.8 billion to support the ruble, resulting in huge profits for speculators both foreign and domestic. In August, Prime Minister Kyrienko announced that the government intended to devalue the ruble by 34 percent by the end of December, as well as impose a unilateral moratorium on foreign debt payments and a de facto default on domestic issues (Cohen 1998; Fossato 1998). Six days after the devaluation announcement, Kyrienko was fired and Viktor Chernomyrdin, the choice of the oligarchs, returned to power. Some economists argued that the devaluation of the ruble devastated a reemergent faith in the financial system by the citizenry (Åslund 1998; Blejer 1998). Despite these measures, the crisis continued to worsen. In the fall of 1997, the Central Bank announced that it would cease doing business with 11 major foreign financial institutions because of their failure to honor their securities transactions obligation. Reformers, attempting to stave off default, argued that Russia had to 'live by its own means', a plea ignored by politicians and industry oligarchs set on obtaining state subsidies and votes. Finally, the default materialized at $43 billion, but that declined as the ruble spiraled steadily downward to 21 rubles to the dollar by December 1998 (McKenzie 1998) (Figure 12.4).

As with Asia, Russia's crisis was closely linked to the IMF, which argued that actions such as the debt exchange of Russian treasury bills for dollar-denominated Eurobonds, major fiscal adjustment, actions to address the nonpayment of debts and the promotion of private sector development along with a comprehensive approach to banking sector problems, could have worked with the proper political support. The IMF (1999, p. 33) claimed that:

> From the time of its introduction, the success of the program depended on whether Russia's revenue and expenditure measures received full parliamentary approval and whether interest rates were brought down by a return of investor confidence. The failure of these conditions to be realized, and the authorities' course of action in response – in particular, the unilateral debt restructuring – aggravated the consequences of the program's breakdown.

In its defense, the IMF stepped in at a time when it was highly unlikely that Russia

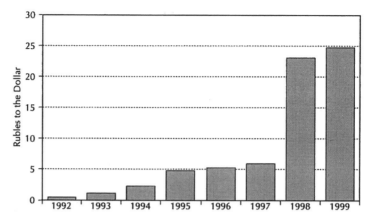

Figure 12.4 *Exchange rate of the ruble. Source: Business Central Europe [http://www.bcemag.com] 20 March 2000*

could have found relief in the international bond markets. Also, the Russian state proved to be an unwilling partner in beginning the clean-up of a Chernobyl-esque financial meltdown. Similar to that environmental catastrophe, estimates of the real costs were vague, donors were in short supply, and the private sector credit and debt markets could not, nor more importantly, would not take on the risk of financing the restructuring. The 'dialogue' between the IMF and Russia was not completed until April 1999, eight months after the collapse, resulting in the issuance of a standby loan of $4.5 billion. The IMF, blamed for the collapse of the Russian Federation, was particularly resistant by banks and other powerful institutions to external intervention in the economy. Even before the collapse, the harsh dictates of the IMF provoked response from various representatives of the state apparatuses and the oligarchs that controlled them. Moscow Mayor Yuri Luzhkov invoked nationalist sentiment when he declared Russian dependence on the IMF a 'national disgrace' (*Radio Free Europe/ Radio Liberty Newsline* 1997). Others observed that perhaps Russia did not even need a government, as the IMF was seemingly in control (Gould-Davies and Woods 1999). The credibility of the IMF was further undermined when the *Los Angeles Times* quoted Anatoly Chubais, one of the negotiators for the Russian Federation, that they 'conned' the IMF for $20 billion (Weisbrot 1998), and that Russia had no choice but to lie about the real conditions of the economy lest global lenders 'would have stopped dealing with us forever' (Paddock 1998). Kagarlitsky (1998), a Russian economist, argued that IMF's assumption that a 'strong currency automatically leads to a stronger economy' was wrong. Thus, using the $4.8 billion tranche turned out to be a mistake, putting money in the hands of speculators when the government found that it could not support the ruble.

It is clear the consequences of the Russian crisis are still being felt in mid-2000. Nominal GDP fell from $462.5 billion in 1997 to $182.9 billion in 1999, average monthly wages fell by two-thirds of their 1997 levels, and FDI is down to one-third of that in 1997 (Figure 12.5). The painful restructuring that occurred at the expense of the Russian people may facilitate economic growth, but even that can be explained by the weak ruble supporting export industries (Bush 2000). One positive aspect of the

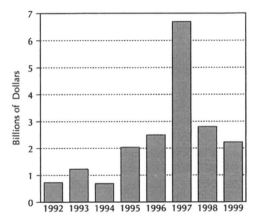

Figure 12.5 *Foreign direct investment levels in Russia. Source: Business Central Europe [http://www.bcemag.com] 20 March 2000*

collapse might be the return of capital to the 'real economy' instead of the profitable but deceptively safe market for Russian domestic debt (Zimine and Bradshaw 1999).

What does the Russian crisis teach us about money in the digital age? Unlike East Asia, whose economies welcomed foreign investments and whose governments generally acceded to IMF intervention, the Russian case reveals a logic in which nationalist politics triumphed over market forces. Unlike Asia, in which FDI continued to surpass portfolio investments even during the height of the crisis, foreign funds in Russia were overwhelmingly speculative. The absence of a dependable legal system and suspicion of foreign economic presence contributed mightily to Russia's long slide into essentially Third World economic status. In the era of global money, however, in which portfolio investments can disappear overnight, xenophobia carries a stiff price. Defending sovereignty, as Vernon (1971) noted, means something altogether different in the face of free-floating capital. Indeed, in both Russia and Asia, the financial crises of the 1990s reflected the power of global capital to discipline unruly, corrupt, or inept political authorities, imposing the harsh logic of the international market.

CONCLUDING COMMENTS

Virtual money, pulses of light gliding through cyberspace, has profoundly reconfigured the world's capital markets. From the arguments put forth above, three major sets of observations can be made. First, it is clear that deregulated, hypermobile, electronic money has changed the ground rules of the global economy. Since the collapse of Bretton Woods and the birth of the global 'casino economy' (Strange 1994, 1998), such funds have grown in magnitude to dwarf world trade in agricultural and manufactured goods. As neoliberal trade and regulatory regimes continue to become ensconced across the planet, a fundamental shift has taken place in the economic role of currency exchange rates. Currency fluctuations have became progressively divorced from trade imbalances and more subject to the whims of global capital markets. Currencies that used to reflect the relative health of a national economy – its balance and terms of trade, inflation, investment, and interest rates – now in large part determine that health. Currency fluctuations, in short, have switched from effect to cause of national economic security. In this context, conventional nationalist monetary tools, particularly raising interest rates, have relatively little impact in terms of restoring market confidence. This observation holds as much for the US Federal Reserve, in its chronic phobia of inflation, as it does for the IMF, which sought to use it for stabilizing currencies.

Second, although currency speculators work in the rarefied office towers of global cities and national capitals, their actions have powerful impacts on the lives of millions, if not billions, of people worldwide. The Asian and Russian crises demonstrate, for example, that the folly of central bankers and the IMF had disastrous effects, including unemployment, inflation, and hunger, for large numbers of poor people. Spikes in interest rates, raids by hedge funds, and rapid capital flows are translated, frequently through IMF austerity programs, into human suffering for those who can afford it the least and politically resist it with the fewest resources. Whereas electronic money may circulate in the netherworld of global finance, as zeros and ones dancing gaily through the fiber-optic lines connecting the world's metropoles, its impacts on the ground, in terms of the quality of life for billions of people, are very real. Harvey (1989) may dismiss finance capital as 'fictitious', but its consequences are anything but.

Third, it is abundantly evident that geography still matters. On the one hand, deregulation and digitization have severely attenuated the linkages between money and space, a theme commonly exaggerated as 'the death of distance' (Cairncross 1997) or 'the end of geography' (O'Brien 1992). Given the enormous increases in volatility and liquidity that financial capital has acquired, the huge quantities of funds that flow freely across national borders, the regulation of national money supplies is highly problematic, leading to diminished control over interest, inflation, and exchange rates. On the other hand, contrary to much received opinion, global money does not presuppose the disappearance of the nation-state, but a rearticulation of its functions. The pool of funds sloshing from one country to another creates speculative bubbles around the globe, leaving behind shattered nations when it leaves. Rather than a simplistic contradiction that views global capital in opposition to the nation-state, a dichotomy that thwarts their integration, the geography of hypermobile capital should be seen in light of the multiple scales at which it unfolds. The impacts of global forces and institutions, whether electronic funds transfer systems or the IMF, are always mediated through regional and national contexts, which both reflect and perpetuate spatial differences in geopolitical and economic status and regulatory policy.

[Handwritten notes:]

- Global banking hist
  ? nation state
- E Asia + Russia crises
- Conclude: Geog still matters: Impacts played out locally
  + affect geog data in uneven devolt
- Reregulation rather than no nation state
- Flows deterior - tho' nat. control less appealing,
  → speculation + uncertainty incos

13

Information and Communication Technologies and the Integration of European Derivatives Markets

DOMINIC POWER

Uppsala University, Sweden

Europe has traditionally trailed behind the USA in its affection for the classic indicators of a thriving e-commerce sector such as business-to-consumer (B2C) online retailing. In 1999 online B2C transactions in the USA totaled an estimated $20 billion compared with $3.6 billion in Europe (*The Economist* March 26, 2000, E-Commerce Survey, 4; 35). In light of such a gap and in the context of the building of the European single market, European industry and government have striven to play catch-up with the successful wiring of the USA's 'new economy'. Rafts of literature and policy initiatives have been produced and the promotion of a vision of a wired e-economy has become something of a holy mantra in European policy and governmental circles. In the UK this fever pitch resulted in 1999 with the Secretary of State for Trade and Industry, Stephen Byers, setting ambitious targets for information and communications technology (ICT) usage by small and medium-sized firms, and the appointment of Patricia Hewitt as 'e-Minister' (Minister for Small Business and E-Commerce) in July 1999. Furthermore, an e-gold-rush fever has hit cities such as London, Stockholm, and Dublin where signs of a rapid expansion in the penetration and profitability of e-commerce abound from omnipresent adverts for web sites to buoyant venture capital markets and Internet millionaires. However, by focusing on the obvious signs of a digital or wired economy such as online retail, the proliferation of web sites or the instance of populations' Internet usage we are in danger of ignoring what is by far the most wired sector of European economies: financial services.

The globalization of banking, finance, and money has been one of the most significant economic phenomena in recent years. Although there have long been international and cross-border flows of finance capital, changes in, among other things, regulatory systems, financial practices, technology, telematics and telecommunications have meant that banking and finance now stand at the cutting-edge of the creation of abstract electronic realms of exchange (O'Brien 1992; Ohmae 1990). An intensely wired world of e-commerce and exchange has been created where firms dealing in global money and finance, created and processed through electronic realms, seem to have little rational need to be tied to high-cost locations in financial centers. It has become a strong possibility that such information reliant sectors will be at the forefront of creating electronic markets that are essentially unfettered by place and geography and that transcend national and regional scales. However, a paradoxical situation has arisen whereby hand-in-hand with the decentering, internationalization, and globalization of money and capital, key centers have remained central to the control of these markets, and in the cases of New York, Tokyo, and London have greatly extended their global preeminence and reach.

The penetration of technology into every aspect of the organization and operation of finance has not meant then the 'end of geography' (O'Brien 1992), but rather it can be seen to have reinforced, in complex and reflexive ways, the dominance of certain geographic places within international finance and capital. This chapter draws upon this observation and seeks to provide a modest contribution to the body of literature that suggests the globalization of finance does not necessarily lead to the annihilation of space or place, but instead that capital must be localized or embedded in certain ways in order for it to be controlled, understood, and made free (Amin and Thrift 1992; Mitchell 1997; Harvey 1982; Scott 1995; Storper and Walker 1989; Thrift and Leyshon 1994). Thrift and Leyshon's work on financial agglomerations in London (Thrift and Leyshon 1994) strongly supports this observation and suggests that in order for contemporary finance to function, space must be made for negotiation, interaction, and exchange so that the complexity of electronic realms of finance can be understood and acted upon. Their analysis suggests that the existence of relatively distinct urban agglomerations of social production networks implies that modern finance stand-alone centers acting as nodes in a global system are the privileged spaces of financial production (see also Thrift 2000).

If we are to better understand contemporary financial production it appears important to attempt empirical verification of such claims. This chapter attempts to contribute to such a verification and draws upon a long-running qualitative research project on London-based financial services. Material for this chapter derives from research and interviews with workers and officials from various London stock and derivatives exchanges, IT consultants, investment brokerages, and banks.

In line with the above, this chapter sets out to examine current attempts to forge entirely electronic pan-European derivatives markets. The chapter argues that while the ICT revolution in finance in the long term may threaten the existence of grounded urban financial centers, we can say that at least in the short to medium term ICTs effect on finance seems to favor the continued existence of financial centers as the privileged places for the production of finance. Research on the recent evolution of the derivatives industry in Europe strongly suggests that tightly packed urban financial agglomerations are necessary to the operational efficiency of the large firms that dominate the European derivatives markets. The competitive advantage of these ICT-reliant firms is strongly determined by the quality of a center's ICT infrastructure, easy access to a wide range of specialist ICT skills, as well as a dynamic and favorable programming and modeling environment. Furthermore, examples of recent moves to create pan-

European and pan-regional derivatives markets show that in addition to issues such as regulation and liquidity, increasingly rivalries between financial centers are being 'fought' and 'forged' through ICT issues. In these ways the ICT environment of European cities cannot be ignored as a determining factor in its prospects as a financial center.

Empirical investigation of European derivatives markets then appears to go some way in verifying Thrift and Leyshon's observations. However, it was found that we must complement their stress on the 'stand-alone' nature of urban financial agglomerations with an understanding that takes account of the extent to which interurban rivalries between existing financial centers help determine the manner markets and centers come together. In derivatives it seems clear that European centers are consciously shaping and negotiating the particular form in which European financial integration takes place. European financial centers are increasingly hybrid forms of agglomeration and globalization and not simply stand-alone agglomerative masses. Technology it seems, rather than threatening their lifeblood, is a key mediator in this hybridization process and is a crucial aspect underlying the shape and form of market integration (see also Power 2000).

The chapter will first treat changes to the trading and production of financial derivatives. Recent attempts to create pan-European electronic derivatives markets are then examined with special attention to the context of technological and institutional change within which these attempts have been made. It is argued that these attempts provide a leading edge example of emerging themes in the social production and the urban centering underlying the construction of even the most open and abstract e-commerce spaces. In particular it is argued that the existing European financial centers stand to gain most from the 'opening-up' and globalization of European finance markets that technological and regulatory change bring and that they are consciously working to ensure this.

FINANCIAL DERIVATIVES: THE ELECTRIFIED ABSTRACT?

Derivatives are financial contracts which specify certain obligations or rights based on, or derivative of, an underlying financial instrument such as a stock, bond, commodity (e.g. pork bellies, wheat), currency, index, or service (for fuller definitions see IOSCO 1996; Chance 1999). These rights and obligations can be a cash settlement, delivery of, or the transfer of rights to the underlying instrument. Derivatives can either be traded in open, regulated exchanges or can be traded as 'over-the-counter' (OTC) products which enjoy no protection or regulation from an exchange.

In a relatively short time derivatives, in particular OTC derivatives, have become extremely important and useful to firms, financial systems, and economies (Berkman *et al.* 1997; Carter and Sinkey 1998; Guay 1999; Howton and Perfect 1998; Krawiec 1998; Miller 1999). From its roots in the 1970s derivatives trading charted a meteoric rise through the 1980s so that by 1991 the amount of outstanding OTC derivative contracts stood at $6 trillion (Budd 1995, p. 357). By the end of June 1999 this figure had risen to $81.5 trillion (source: Bank for International Settlements) making derivatives central to national and international finance. In fact these figures may underestimate the total value of derivatives; it was estimated in April 1995 that daily average turnover in derivatives contracts stood at $880 billion (Group of Thirty cited in Tickell 2000).

Basically put, these financial instruments allow organizations, firms, investors, etc. to unbundle risks and allocate them to those investors most willing and able to take them on. Thus derivatives have been widely embraced as central planks in the profit maximization and risk allocation strategies of both financial and nonfinancial institutions and firms (Bodnar *et al.* 1998). Despite scares associated with large losses incurred by institutional investors in the mid-1990s (Clark 1997; O'Brien 1995; Scholes 1996; Swyngedouw 1996; Tickell 1999a,b) they are now viewed as crucial to the success of both financial and nonfinancial industry profitability and stability.

The most interesting development about derivatives from the perspective of this chapter is that the wide range of derivative products and their increasing complexity makes them perhaps the area of finance most reliant on high technology computing and telecommunications. Derivatives were traditionally traded in open-outcry trading floors operated by exchanges in financial centers such as Chicago, New York, and London. However, as derivatives trading has expanded in both volume and complexity they have become almost entirely technologically mediated financial products.

> Information technology has made possible the creation, valuation, and exchange of complex financial products on a global basis heretofore envisioned only in our textbooks, and even that just in recent years. Derivatives are obviously the most evident of the many products that technology has inspired . . . What is really quite extraordinary is that there is no sign that this process of acceleration in financial technology is approaching an end. We are moving at an exceptionally rapid pace, fueled not only by the enhanced mathematical applications produced by our ever-rising computing capabilities but also by our expanding telecommunications capabilities and the associated substantial broadening of our markets (Alan Greenspan, Chairman of the US Federal Reserve System, before the *Journal of Financial Services Research* and the American Enterprise Institute Conference, Washington, April 14, 2000).

Derivatives have become the technologically leading edge sector in the financial services industry and as such their trading around the world has rapidly moved to electronic trading platforms. In Europe the transition of derivatives to entirely screen-based electronic trading environments was fully completed recently with the closing of the open-outcry trading floors/pits of derivatives exchanges such as France's Matif and the London International Financial Futures Exchange (LIFFE). By the mid to late 1990s most derivatives trading in the world had been transferred to order-driven electronic systems making a variety of routing and remote access options a reality.

As with many sectors of the financial services industry in the same period that traditional exchanges have been moving toward screen-based trading, the emergence of entirely electronic remote access trading platforms have become a serious challenge to the traditional exchanges. The high level of technological input into the trading and creation of derivative products makes them particularly suitable for trading on Internet-based electronic communications networks (ECNs). ECNs are electronic trading systems that offer easy access to markets through the Internet and as such are readily able to transcend national boundaries. The openness and ease of accessibility of ECNs have started attracting new breeds of investors wanting to take increasingly independent, diversified, and varied investment strategies that traditional exchanges and brokerages are ill-suited to serving. In the US stock and securities markets ECNs, often with the backing of leading brokerages and investment banks, have already taken considerable trading and liquidity from established exchanges such as Nasdaq.

ECNs, ease of access and remote access, combined with the ways in which they allow real-time execution of trades, efficient price discovery, easy clearance and settlement, anonymous trading, and greater market transparency make them ideal for adaptation to many types of OTC derivative trading. Numerous firms (such as Tradepoint, BrokerTec, Coredeal, eSpeed, and EuroMTS) are lining up to take a share of these emerging markets. A key feature of ECNs is that they make these products accessible from anywhere in the world and point to the fact that ICT advances pose a serious threat to traditional exchanges and their attendant financial centers. 'To an institutional investor with a Reuters terminal on his desk, a traditional exchange is just one pool of liquidity among many' (*Financial Times*, May 5, 2000).

With a tide of change sweeping through derivatives markets 'traditional' exchanges rooted in existing financial centers have had to rapidly face up to these challenges and opportunities. The dominant way in which most exchanges worldwide have done this has been by attempting to preempt or indeed undercut ECNs on their own ground. To this end exchanges have been engaged for the last five years or more in positioning themselves at the center of integrated electronic markets by moving toward electronic trading structured around global alliances that offer their members access to genuine 24-hour global markets.

GLOBEX is perhaps the prime example of an entirely electronic spatially diffuse challenge to the tradition of derivatives and futures exchanges that are located in and operated out of a single metropolitan area (see also Budd 1995, 1998). GLOBEX is an automated international computerized trading system which allows users from anywhere in the world to enter orders for futures and options which are then matched by the system. GLOBEX was only made possible by technological advances in computing and telecommunications and the alliance itself was secured by technology swaps and the integration of systems. As an enterprise it demonstrates the extent to which technological issues have determined important elements of the speed and shape of change. The challenge GLOBEX, and others like it, pose to more traditional forms of even electronic trading is that they are further pioneering recent advances in open architecture solutions, thereby offering members a common interface to access a growing range of products but with a much greater degree of flexibility. This allows members a degree of technology solution freedom that was not found in the traditional electronic exchanges which involved a more rigid set of solutions. Such flexibility further allows firms to seek out the competitive advantages offered by ever more tailored software and trading. Most importantly, though, the technology allows all participants equal access and nearly continuous price discovery and because it operates outside normal trading hours makes 24-hour trading a reality. This development is especially important to the large globalized finance firms pursuing portfolio investment strategies that are based on a global rather than regional outlook.

Despite being an essentially abstract electronic market, GLOBEX points not just to the globalization of finance but also an apparent tendency in the globalization of finance, not towards the death of geography but rather the bolstering of geographic differentiation and competition aimed at securing certain cities' continued role as trading centers for global finance. The system itself is operated by Reuters utilizing as its core technology the NSC platform originally developed by ParisBourse, and is at present the result of a set of strategic alliances between the Chicago Mercantile Exchange (CME), ParisBourse, and the Singapore Exchange Derivatives Trading (SGX, DT) as well as the Montreal Exchange (ME) and São Paulo's Bolsa de Mercadorias & Futuros (BM&F). The ability to develop alliances enabling cross-exchange and after-hours trading has significantly added to the trading volumes and liquidity of these exchanges.

The GLOBEX example demonstrates that while fully electronic trading platforms offer a single remote electronic access point to a global set of derivatives positions, the structuring of these abstract realms through systems and intermediaries embedded in existing financial centers currently characterizes market activity. Such alliances are not aimed or designed to aid the death of geography, but rather they should be seen as targeted and engineered attempts at strengthening the competitive position of each member's position as a viable financial center.

Taming the Beast: European Derivatives Markets

In Europe too there has been a rapid process of change that has had a great effect on the nature of European derivatives trading. European finance has long been characterized by a high degree of fragmentation by virtue of the existence of a multiplicity of regulatory frameworks, markets allegiances, and a patchwork of nationally oriented exchanges. However, recent rounds of restructuring apparent in the European derivatives markets and exchange system have started to move the European situation closer toward a consolidated pan-European framework of some type. Two main pressures have been especially important to the changes European financial markets, including derivatives, have been going through: European monetary and financial integration and the changing ICT environment.

The creation of the Single European Market has had obviously far-reaching consequences for the evolution of European financial markets. The creation of the euro, the single European currency, stands as testament to a long-running project aimed at the creation of a single financial area with harmonized financial systems and regulation. In the run-up to monetary union in the mid to late 1980s the European Commission (EU) became increasingly aware of the fact that a single market in financial services was absolutely vital both to European industrial competitiveness and to the creation of a wider European integrated economic area. The Commission came to believe that:

> The European financial system was 'inefficient' on a global scale because the presence of a plethora of smaller institutions hampered its ability to compete with US and Japanese institutions and, more importantly, that inefficiencies impacted negatively on the economy more generally (Tickell 1999a, p. 63).
>
> The Eurosystem has an obvious interest in well functioning and efficient financial markets because financial markets are the conduits through which monetary policy decisions are channeled into the economy (Christian Noyer, vice-president of the European Central Bank, at the Cérémonie de remise des Victoires des SICAV, Paris, February 24, 2000).

Harmonization of financial regulation and encouraging integration through alliances and mergers of financial institutions became key EU priorities. Legislation such as the 1988 Directives on Capital Markets, the 1989 Second Banking Directive, and the 1993 Investment Services Directive combined with the introduction of the euro have made financial and market integration not only a governmental desire but a matter of necessity to the competitive position of the banking and finance industry in Europe. Thus the industry's exchanges and investment firms see the creation of pan-European platforms as both necessary for their viability and necessary to access the potentially enormous profits and savings to be gained from pan-European trading.

Derivatives trading in Europe has, as elsewhere in the world, been subject to a second force for change: the evolution of ICT. As has been noted already the rapid growth of Internet-based ECN alternatives, global alliances such as GLOBEX, and more powerful and flexible electronic trading platforms have made a reality the specter of easily accessible electronic markets able to transcend national boundaries.

These pressures and the potential profits to be made from an integrating European financial space have forced since the mid-1990s established exchanges and associated investors and institutions to move quickly to ensure their continued survival at the center. These two pressures, then, are central to the explicit and implicit creation in recent years of a series of mergers and alliances which have been formed with the express aim of creating pan-European derivatives exchanges that will have a powerful place both in Europe and globally (Domowitz 1995).

The most successful example of this development is Eurex (EURopean EXchange) which was formed by the merger of Deutsche Börse's Deutsche Terminbörse and the Swiss Exchange's Soffex derivatives market (Swiss Options and Futures Exchange) to create a pan-regional derivatives exchange. In a relatively short time Eurex has become the dominant exchange in Europe (Tables 13.1 and 13.2) and since January 1999 has overtaken Chicago as the world's largest derivatives market. Its daily average trading volume rose from 907 394 contracts in November 1998 to 1 668 252 contracts in November 1999 and by January 2000 its monthly trading volume had reached 40.2 million contracts and included the world's most heavily traded futures contract, the Bund Future (figures from Eurex and the *Financial Times*, February 1, 2000).

Eurex is an entirely electronic platform that offers consolidated trading and settlement systems based on a harmonized rule book and a single set of standardized products. Its success is due to both its harmonized product range and crucially its highly praised electronic trading technology. In interviews with traders the high quality, speed, and reliability of the electronic platform itself was most often pointed to as being the basis for the exchanges success. However, the international opportunities the exchanges alliance network offered was also underlined as a key element. 'It's a very attractive package presently. Not only do they have a very large volume which naturally draws us in but they have a very advanced system with a really aggressive international outlook' (from an interview with a London-based bond trader in a large French investment bank).

The exchange has been particularly proactive in chasing partners and agreements that extend the reach and scope of its markets not only in Europe but worldwide. International access is currently available through a network of licensed terminals in Amsterdam, Chicago, Helsinki, London, Madrid, and Paris with more planned in Tokyo, Hong Kong, and New York. Terminal access in a variety of cities is further added to by a set of structural alliances and agreements, such as the recent link and joint development package with the Chicago Board of Trade, that bind other centers into the Eurex system.

Once Europe's largest derivatives exchange LIFFE has fallen significantly into the shadow of Eurex (see Tables 13.1 and 13.2). Eurex has successfully poached among other packages the heavily traded European long-term interest rate contract from LIFFE. As a consequence LIFFE's European position has slipped considerably in relative terms. The migration of such contracts and business to Eurex from LIFFE has been consistently blamed on LIFFE's problems in moving smoothly and quickly to a fully electronic system. At the time the European long-term interest rate contract moved, LIFFE was still trading in the traditional manner: open-outcry pits.

LIFFE's European position then has been significantly affected by its relatively slow adaptation to the new realities ICT have forced upon the markets. This demonstrates that while ICT is not the sole reason underlying individual exchanges success the utilization of the latest advances in ICT systems and platforms underlies then the ability of exchanges to retain existing advantages such as capital liquidity, skilled and innovative products and staff and capitalize on structural factors such as favorable regulatory environments. This development is a lesson not lost on LIFFE and in late 1999 and early 2000 the exchange actively tried to reinvent itself and recapture lost

Table 13.1   *Stock and index options and futures: 1999 figures for major European derivatives exchanges*

	Stock option volume (no. of contracts)	Stock option national value (million US$)	Equity index options volume (no. of contracts)	Equity index options national value (million US$)	Equity index futures volume no. of contracts)	Equity index futures national value (million US$)
AEX (Netherlands)	40 653 543	NA	5 615 790	337 865	2 939 564	353 675
BELFOX (Belgium)	530 389	5625	1 151 862	1513	5 711 384	10 846
Eurex (Germany/Switzerland)	64 751 525	428 126	40 479 485	1 319 676	25 129 430	2 376 393
HEX (Finland)	1 263 363	NA	270 133	5328	273 809	5400
FUTOP (Denmark)	3307	33	21 617	668	1 298 360	40 104
IDEM (Italy)	1 946 996	47 860	2 235 197	419 657	5 098 586	957 256
LIFFE (UK)	3 601 383	33 001	5 760 351	503 049	8 972 307	1 035 408
MATIF (France)	NT	NT	NT	NT	NT	NT
MEFF Variable (Spain)	8 091 728	3306	861 255	84 878	5 101 588	502 770
MONEP (France)	68 095 743	4229	83 516 737	413 269	25 699 566	1 058 704
OM (Sweden)	26 824 117	NA	5 734 660	55 310	11 931 586	115 079
Oporto (Portugal)	NT	NT	NT	NT	896 130	11 122
Oslo (Norway)	2 684 038	5377	978 014	12 787	703 105	9192
OTOB (Austria)	802 924	5152	427 411	5719	795 510	9673

NA = Not Available; NT = Not Traded.
Source: Adapted from figures from the International Federation of Stock Exchanges (FIBV) and The Chicago Board Options Exchange.

Table 13.2 *Debt and futures options: 1998 figures for major European derivatives exchanges*

	Gvt debt options volume (no. of contracts)	Gvt debt options national value (million US$)	Gvt debt futures volume (no. of contracts)	Gvt debt futures national value (million US$)
AEX (Netherlands)	208 994	1054	211	26
BELFOX (Belgium)	NT	NT	5189	357
EUREX (Germany/Switzerland)	7 911 988	1 123 936	133 051 383	18 803 174
FUTOP (Denmark)	NT	NT	77 577	11 578
HEX (Finland)	NT	NT	156 455	29 274
IDEM (Italy)	NT	NT	NT	NT
LIFFE (UK)	7 424 736	942 580	39 730 031	4 915 494
MATIF (France)	3 394 735	287 840	26 177 850	2 219 628
MEFF (Spain)	648 539	43 429	15 767 009	1 055 652
MIF (Italy)	45 150	6501	1 293 554	189 803
MONEP (France)	NT	NT	NT	NT
OM (Sweden)	2727	342	9 356 221	1 176 246
Oporto (Portugal)	NT	NT	245 306	27 550
Oslo (Norway)	NT	NT	68 755	9105
OTOB (Austria)	NT	NT	3957	319

NA = Not Available; NT = Not Traded.
Source: Adapted from figures from the International Federation of Stock Exchanges (FIBV) and The Chicago Board Options Exchange.

business by completely overhauling its trading system. Despite its possible existing merits (Berkman and Hayes 2000; Corporation of London and London Business School 1993), LIFFE bowed to member and competitor pressure and moved to take advantage of the benefits screen-based trading can offer (Corporation of London and London Business School 1993; Kempf and Korn 1998). It quickly closed its trading floor and invested heavily in the creation of a trading technology company Liffe.com and a new trading platform 'Liffe Connect'. Through this new system the exchange can now offer seamless direct access to investors in, among other places, Japan and Hong Kong. Furthermore, it is planning to use its flexible new platform and an Internet portal to allow trading across the exchange in products other than its traditional preserve of futures and options. This type of move appears in line with an overall consolidation and networking of European finance that is beginning to blur the distinctions between markets and segments and draw liquidity further into the spheres of influence of the largest financial centers.

Parallel to the emergence of integrated pan-regional derivatives systems, European stock exchanges are in the grips of merger and consolidation fever, giving credence to the idea that what is emerging is a new realm of consolidated European financial markets that are entirely electronically reliant and mediated yet deeply centered (see Power 2000). The prime example of this development is the announcement in April 2000 of a merger between the London Stock Exchange and Deutsche Börse, creating Europe's largest exchange and laying the ground rules for future rounds of consolidation aimed at making possible a single access point to Europe's stocks and securities.

Of more interest in the context of this chapter is that in March 2000 it was announced in London, that the Paris, Amsterdam, and Brussels stock markets are to merge creating Euronext. Euronext will be a single market for all the products that are now traded by its three members: equities, options, derivatives, commodities. At the time of writing (mid-2000) Euronext has presented its plans to LIFFE, as a possible provider of the derivatives trading system. The inclusion of options, derivatives, and commodities as well as equities will unify and consolidate markets further than ever before and no doubt set the tone for the coming years where we may see:

> Well we might see a fully integrated European financial platform where everything comes together. You know, derivatives as well as the traditional stock market stuff all in one. This would be a big cost saving advantage to investors and banks and make everything simpler allowing it to become a lot more, I suppose, dynamic you could say (from an interview with a London-based senior planner in a large German bank).

Despite what may happen in the future, Euronext will be dominated by the Paris exchange, thereby securing it against absolute domination by London and Frankfurt.

The much applauded packaging of Euronext with the clearance system Clearnet and the settlement house Euroclear points to a further dimension in the consolidation and harmonization of European finance. Financial industry officials and analysts interviewed considered the integration of seamless clearance and settlement systems into pan-European markets, be they for derivatives, equities or both, to be absolutely crucial to the delivery of the economies of scale and simplification investment banks and brokers want and expect from any pan-European market.

In contrast to the USA Europe's clearance and settlement system, the costly and complex back-office functions without which financial markets cannot operate, is a patchwork of clearing systems and central securities depositories. This fragmentation not only multiplies the costs involved in pan-European trading but greatly adds to the technical and technological difficulties in running cross-border and pan-regional investment and trading strategies. Disagreement over these systems, among other factors, has long been a barrier to market integration and was a central issue in slowing to a halt the original alliance plans of the London and Frankfurt stock exchanges (see Power 2000).

A series of recent mergers and alliances between Europe's largest clearing and settlement houses has opened the way for consolidation and the creation of more integrated and less costly systems. Changes in the operator and management of the previously mentioned settlement house Euroclear have led to talk of a merger with European clearance house Clearstream (*Financial Times*, March 31, 2000). Clearstream itself is the result of a merger of the German clearance system of Deutsche Börse and CEDEL. Euroclear is also currently creating an alliance with the London Clearing House and the French Clearnet and have agreed to buy the French clearing system Sicovam. The settlement system used by the London Stock Exchange, CREST, is also attempting to forge a single pan-European system by creating a single access point to central securities depositories. All of these moves are only made functionally possible by recent advances in technology and system architecture. In turn, an integrated European settlement and clearance system is basic to all other financial market mergers, alliances and platforms which themselves were only able to be realized with recent advances in technology and telecommunications and the opening-up of European regulatory frameworks.

European derivatives then are in the grips of alliance and merger fever. This process though entirely directed towards the creation of pan-European and even global markets does not seem to herald the end of geography or at least the end of place. The process seems set to assure in the short to medium term the dominance of existing financial centers and exchanges and is the result of a conscious process of using technology to reinforce the role of financial centers. A definite tendency toward monopoly embedded in urban financial agglomerations is apparent.

> In markets with significant economies of scale and scope . . . there is a tendency toward consolidation or even natural monopoly. Throughout much of our history this tendency has been restrained by an inability to communicate information sufficiently quickly, cheaply, and accurately. In recent years, however, this constraint is being essentially eliminated by advances in telecommunications (Alan Greenspan, Chairman of the US Federal Reserve System, testimony before US Senate, February 10, 2000).

In European financial markets this tendency is being seized upon by exchanges located in existing centers of liquidity and points to a system rapidly consolidating toward technologically mediated exchanges anchored to key financial centers.

Working the Markets?

One might say that notwithstanding the actions of exchanges to consolidate their own center's position, the possibility to remotely access these electronic markets offers cost-conscious investment houses no reason to pay the high costs associated with a central city location in the likes of Frankfurt or London. Several factors appear to counter such a suggestion. First, advanced technology and telecoms currently rely upon agglomerative economies and efficiencies that are only presently occurring in Europe's existing financial centers. Second, that trading in even the most abstract and automated financial instruments such as derivatives relies upon the sort of social networks of production and ordering that authors such as Thrift and Leyshon (1994) argue to only arise in the dense and proximate interrelations afforded to firms by large urban financial agglomerations.

The transition to completely electronic trading and settlement systems means that European derivatives markets cannot operate efficiently without high-speed state of the art communications and computer networks and a rich diversity of ICT skills and products. Derivatives is now an industry where slight differences in the speed, quality, and reliability of telecommunications services, systems operation, and software agents determine not only a firm's access to markets but ultimately their competitive advantage within those markets. While ICT may make it possible to ignore space and geography when it comes to the products being traded, the cost effectiveness and mechanics of actualizing the trade are currently only best supported by the ICT environments found in large cities.

In established centers such as London, Paris, and more recently Frankfurt, the high level of spending and demand for ICT and telecommunications products combined with the density and size of their financial services markets supports a highly sophisticated, innovative and dense array of telecommunications services that cannot be found in comparable level in smaller centers. In the case of London this has led to a highly competitive core telecoms provision based on an infrastructural provision in the form of fiber-optic networks, digital exchanges, and a major satellite ground station that is unparalleled in Europe (Graham 1999; Power 2000). The existence of a large densely packed community of heavy telecoms users has also allowed the telecoms systems to be designed specifically with their need for reliability and high security in mind. Density of demand then has led to a high level of tailored service, and in the case of London considerable savings on telecoms products. For the average multinational user telecom costs in 1998 were between 30 and 90 percent higher in other European capitals (London First Centre and British Telecom 1998).

In addition to the ICT advantages provided by agglomeration economies it was found that the realities of successfully creating and running derivatives markets, no matter how abstracted and electronic they may be, are currently highly reliant on the density of interaction and social networks of production concentrated in Europe's leading financial centers. The importance of social production to derivatives can be seen in all aspects of the product cycle, from the development of the instruments and systems to day-to-day trading.

Even in trading arenas deeply penetrated by advanced mathematical modeling and automated trading, there remains a high degree of human input in both the production and use of new methods and instruments, by virtue of the fact that the computer and mathematical models used are creations themselves. The variety and complexity of exchanges, firm investment and hedging strategies, and of modeling and model risk mean that significant differences in such aspects as risk allocation, appreciation, calculation, modeling and regulation characterize current practices and methods (Domowitz 1993; Duffee 1996; Grant *et al.* 1998; Geczy *et al.* 1997; Koski and Pontiff 1999; Scholes 1996; Simons 1997). Interviews carried out with econometricians/product development specialists, known in the industry as 'rocket scientists', working in London's derivatives sector on the complex systems and models used in trading, revealed that as with any modeling or rationalization of events with multiple inputs, data sources, and stimuli, there are inherent problems associated with chaotic events and chains and with the interpretation and weighting of inputs. Aside from these inherent problems, before instruments, trading programs, platforms, etc. are introduced, a high degree of human agency and interpretation can be seen to have entered the 'logic' of this type of e-commerce.

The econometricians interviewed cited multiple factors that affect the products they (re)develop for eventual use by traders. It emerged that the perceived risk profiles of the customer were particularly important and it seems that the econometricians' decision to determine the level of risk adversity of the end users was especially important. Many factors emerged as important to these decisions: their understanding of the objectives of the organization; their interpretation of their briefs; communication between them and end users, etc.; their understanding of the general situation and position of markets and particular products; and their understanding, knowledge of, and skill in economics, applied mathematics, and computer systems. Their level of agency in making judgments crucial to the determination of the product was suggested by both themselves and their customers/colleagues as often heightened by communication barriers and misunderstandings. In short a recognized inability of other parties to understand what the econometricians were doing (and to a lesser extent vice versa) seems to allow them considerable leeway or agency to construct their own motivational contexts. It was also found that these factors, interactions, and agencies differ considerably between different firms in the same sector. It emerged from interviews that participants in the process viewed face-to-face contact and proximate social networks as crucial to counteracting the problems such misunderstandings and communication problems may present. Since in many cases a wide variety of in-house and consultant participants may be engaged in the development process, ready access to a large pool of skills and a central city location were highlighted as a definite advantage.

> It's an ivory tower sort of job in theory but in practice I find that I really need to be here [in central London] to get the best result, meaning one that actually best fits with what the firm needs and what the traders demand. I just couldn't imagine being as able to do what I do without the interaction and contact that I get here. Even if it is a bit of a crazy environment most of the time (from an interview with a 'rocket scientist' employed in London by a large American investment bank).

It seems then that human agency, negotiation, and interaction are of continued importance in processes aimed at even the most 'wired' elements of financial services. However, it is not only the development of software and products that the 'industrial milieu' (Lundvall 1992) best supports. The realities of trading activity can also favor localization within a financial center.

The creation of new and complex financial instruments, rather than simply allowing for the imposition of systematized trading and operational logics, have opened up new and dynamic market areas and possibilities in which flexibility and agency are key to competitive advantage. While many aspects of derivatives trading are now automated and human traders themselves do their job through completely screen-based media, interviews with traders operating on LIFFE markets, suggested that the availability of information of different types was central to their performance in trading new and complex products. The complexity and dynamism of derivatives means that in many instances those working in the sector are still heavily reliant on 'the feel of the market', gossip, organizational cultures, trust, and common understandings that are constantly been reworked and rearranged to make and form decisions.

'Even though we are out of the pits now and in front of a screen all day and night the chat and the camaraderie is still really important to knowing what to do at your desk . . . no man's an island eh?' (from an interview with a screen based LIFFE trader). Other studies also confirm such findings:

> It is widely agreed that locals profit both from the gossip and feel of the market and rely on quick response to market imbalances which may be less easily exploited on screen (Corporation of London and London Business School 1993, p. 7).

In short, the spaces of finance in somewhere like London include not only the electronic spaces where derivatives deals are transacted, but also the interactional spaces, negotiations in offices, streets, bars, etc. where information, prejudices, and the like about firms, individuals, systems, and markets are (re)produced and traded. Traders interviewed noted that the frequency of such contact made both a practical difference when trading and also was very personally important to them. It was frequently pointed out that as professionals the existence of diverse corporate and inter-corporate social networks, or 'networking', is an important factor in building their careers and their job mobility. Thus skilled traders are drawn toward centers with a rich social and firm network in order to progress their careers just as the firms themselves are drawn to such centers in order to locate key personnel.

A further point worth noting is that in the light of losses, publicity and concern over large-scale financial scandals involving derivatives, such as, among others, the Barings 'rogue trader' collapse (Clark 1997; O'Brien 1995; Scholes 1996; Swyngedouw 1996; Tickell 1999a,b), risk management, corporate control, and surveillance are also high on the priority list of the increasingly large investment houses that dominate global and European derivatives business. Interviews confirmed that consolidation of corporate personnel under the one roof and the existence of dense social networks were seen to go some way in guarding against illegal activity that may damage the firm.

The above points offer a degree of reiteration and verification of suggestions made before that the space of finance involves not just the formalized and computerized monetary spaces of global finance but also highly localized and sociospatial systems for the production, reproduction, policing, and exchange of 'capital' (Thrift and Leyshon 1994; Pryke and Lee 1995).

A VERY WIRED EUROPE? NODAL SPACES OF EUROPEAN FINANCE

While the growth of e-commerce may in many sectors of the economy suggests a greatly diminished role for geography in production and exchange, it seems that for financial services such as derivatives the foreseeable future will continue to be dominated by the wiring of e-finance within a limited set of nodal spaces. The existing urban hierarchy is further reinforced by alliances and mergers in this most wired of commercial environments. Thus much of what Budd (1995) said of derivatives trading in the mid-1990s seems to continue to hold true, despite the speed at which the derivatives market has continued to expand, rapid advances in technology, telecommunications, and mathematical applications, and the rise of alternative electronic trading systems such as ECNs.

> Financial derivatives being time instruments, and electronic exchanges challenging the constraint of space, appear to offer an empirical example time-space distanciation; the indispensable condition for the concept of globalization. However, the development of derivatives exchanges and alliances between them around the globe seem to stem from national territorial imperatives, not global ones (Budd 1995, p. 359).

Hand-in-hand with the deterritorialization and abstraction of money there are strong tendencies toward the concentration, centering, and localized territorialization of command and control functions. Under financial globalization there has been a pressure to consolidate, integrate, and concentrate the control, management and mediation of economic processes. However, the 'national' territorial imperative Budd observed since the mid-1990s has increasingly become less national than it has become urban; the focal points and driving institutions of the Europeanization and globalization of derivatives have become less concerned with a nation-based territoriality than an urban-based one. Fieldwork in London confirmed this hypothesis and points to the notion that it is not only by virtue of structural alliances and mergers that existing urban financial agglomerations are best placed to reap the rewards of these changing markets, for the technological and social bases of financial production also currently favor dense urban financial agglomerations.

In addition, this chapter has argued that centers are further reinforced in their centrality due to the fact that social production and network processes, competitiveness and efficiency gains outweigh the costs of geographical centering for even highly wired forms of finance. Urban agglomerations like London and Frankfurt have developed highly adaptive and complex systems of localized information exchange and interaction that offer firms better 'access' to advanced ICT, sociocultural networks, and benefits that add to their competitive advantage and operational abilities. Better 'access' to the necessities of competitive advantage in wired worlds of e-finance involves proximate and efficient systems for the provision of specialized services (Sassen 1991), technological and telecommunications services, and information and knowledge to localized processes of knowledge creation and exchange through a 'social production process' (Pryke and Lee 1995, p. 331). As Thrift and Leyshon (1994, p. 312) note: 'the interdependent connectedness of disembedded electronic networks promotes dependence on just a few places'.

Technological advances in finance then do not necessarily involve a teleology directed away from the importance of spatial concerns. The pace and nature of change, in Europe at least, is being shaped by embedded market realities and strategically conscious institutions. However, technology remains key to the evolution of these markets, and the cities that will reap the highest benefits are those whose institutions successfully position themselves and their markets to best provide for and take advantage of the changing financial spaces ICT may herald. An important final point on the evolution of European centers for derivatives demonstrates is that while financial centers are undoubtedly central to the operation of such markets, the centers themselves should not only respond to the pressures of electronic commerce but also to inter-urban rivalries aimed at securing the enormous rewards accruing from a growing financial services sector. The example of Frankfurt-Eurex's success in taking away London's leading European position in derivatives should stand as a warning not only to exchanges but also to planners, regulators, and politicians.

In conclusion, the example of European derivatives markets generally verifies theoretical claims made about the continued importance of financial centers and points to the fact that a rapidly changing ICT environment does not necessarily involve the death of geography and the decentering of financial space and power. However, much further research needs to be done in this area. Research is needed that further explores the links between the development of derivatives markets and developments in other electronically mediated financial markets that are aimed at the creation of pan-regional and pan-European financial markets. Work is also needed on whether cross-sectorally e-commerce exhibits similar tendencies toward consolidation, monopoly and centering based on embedded systems of social production and industrial milieu. Furthermore, there is a need when analyzing the evolution of e-commerce markets to recognize that inter-urban and inter-institutional competition and cooperation can be crucial in the shaping and determination of the impact, adaptation, and adjustment to new technologies. Such work and perspectives may help analysts, policy-makers, and firms alike to better understand the ways and means through which wired worlds of e-commerce are likely to emerge and evolve.

e- Derivatives trading in EU

- Its evol^n shaped by competition between financial cities/centers seeking to reinforce their pos^n

- Conc of activities in such centers still matters
  - access to skills/related services
  - informal F2F contact

14

'Dry Counties' in Cyberspace: Governance and Enforcement without Geographic Boundaries

PRISCILLA M. REGAN

George Mason University, Fairfax, VA, USA

Internet sites offering home delivery of alcohol and online gambling in the USA have proliferated in the last few years. The sites have spawned commercial opportunities and political debate in county councils, state legislatures, state courts, Congress, and international bodies. The absence of legally defined boundaries in cyberspace makes it difficult to maintain local 'dry counties', state-controlled distributions of alcohol, and state gaming restrictions. Ordering a bottle of wine over the Internet involves a purchase that arguably occurs in cyberspace, but also involves a delivery in a physical space where there are indeed legally defined jurisdictions that contain communities with value preferences and public safety standards, as well as governments with revenue needs. Similarly, gambling in cyberspace results in winnings or losses that appear on credit card accounts that are attached to people in a physical space. These activities in cyberspace, then, do not occur solely in the virtual world. At some point the virtual crosses the boundary to the physical world. At that point the laws and regulations of the physical world may be applied.

Traditionally states and local governments have used their police powers to regulate the behavior of individuals within their jurisdictions. When the behavior being regulated, such as purchasing liquor or placing a bet, occurs within a geographically bounded jurisdiction that coincides with the legal jurisdiction, then state and local regulations can be enforced. When individuals can traverse geographic boundaries to engage in that behavior, the ability of individuals to avoid the law increases and enforcement becomes more problematic. The legitimacy and enforceability of laws has always been dependent upon geographic boundaries. Traditional definitions of the 'nation state' (Weber 1947) are framed in terms of a monopoly of coercive power over inhabitants of a geographic area, and the protection of geographic boundaries is an essential state function. But nation-state boundaries have never been impermeable.

People and goods have moved across borders since at least the Middle Ages while nation-states have struggled to ensure the legitimacy and enforceability of their laws.

From this perspective, several questions ensue. One is whether political power can exist without geographic boundaries. Is it possible to have coercive power without having, real or potential, physical control and is physical control dependent upon geographic borders? Is place-identity, the ability to define an individual as being within your physical control, dependent on geography, or are there other characteristics of identity that are more or equally important in retaining political control? A second question is whether activities in cyberspace pose fundamentally distinct and unique problems for governments, or can these problems be analyzed in terms of established theories of political development and change? (Huntington 1968; Almond and Verba 1963). Finally, there is a question about whether the erosion of borders in cyberspace is being overstated. There are many activities in cyberspace occurring without distinction as to geographic boundaries, including research and personal communication. But as cyberspace activities move from the cerebral sphere and become more commercial, borders reappear and may be impossible to eradicate.

This chapter examines the difficulties of enforcing legal and regulatory regimes in cyberspace, as well as the interdependence of legal and regulatory regimes with technological infrastructures and developments. As will be demonstrated below, the enforcement difficulties appear to reveal something of a paradox: the enforcement of laws and regulations in cyberspace may necessitate the authentication of personal identities, including place-identity. In order to enforce laws regarding activities in cyberspace, information about those activities must be captured, resulting in the establishment of a physical record or legal trail. Thus, this paradox results: a seemingly placeless and disembodied activity in the virtual world may result in a more complete picture of one's identity than would result from the same activity in the physical world. In cyberspace, place and identity may become critical components of determining the applicability of laws and regulations. For example, in order to allow for the enforcement of local or national laws in cyberspace, web sites or service providers may be liable for ensuring age or location.

The technology of the Internet allows for the automatic recording of much information. As people surf the seemingly borderless world of cyberspace, tracking technologies (e.g. cookies) that are embedded in many browsers record where one goes. One can disable the technologies or use anonymizing servers. But if one wishes to purchase wine or engage in online gambling, existing legal restrictions may be relevant and authentication of place-identity may be requested. If authentication of place-identity is not technically possible or politically feasible, many local or national laws will be unenforceable. But authentication of place-identity is likely to pose costs in terms of individual privacy. If the privacy costs are too high, people may not engage in Internet activities that require the revelation of personal information. Moreover, if enforcement of laws occurs on the basis of detailed records of online activities, the logic of such a scheme would be that all offenses would be recorded and all fines apprehended. This situation would be a different standard than what is used in the physical world where law enforcement officials have discretion about when to enforce the laws and against whom. Enforcement of laws based on authentication of place and identity will also impose costs in terms of social trust and social order.

With respect to the enforcement of jurisdictional restrictions regarding the online alcohol sales and online gambling, several policy questions are particularly relevant:

1. What are the goals of the existing jurisdictional laws or regulations, and are they easily applied to cyberspace activities?
2. Are there technical or administrative means to achieve those goals without the revelation of place and identity?
3. Can technology establish meaningful new boundaries in cyberspace?
4. How do various policy alternatives affect privacy, practices of social control, and e-commerce?

Each of these policy questions is addressed below in order to inform a concluding discussion regarding the interdependencies among political power, place-identity, and the character of cyberspace.

THE POLITICS OF INTERNET LIQUOR SALES AND GAMBLING

Before examining the policy questions, some examples of what is occurring in cyberspace may provide an instructive background. California-based Virtual Vineyards is the Internet's leading wine and food retailer. A consumer can browse through its offerings without actively identifying herself or registering (http://www.virtualvin. com). If a consumer wants to make a purchase, he/she can click on the order form link, which switches him/her to a secure (encrypted) commerce server. There are a number of payment methods: Visa, Mastercard, American Express, and Cybercash. If the consumer is not comfortable with using a credit card on the Internet, he/she can select the phone payment method and then phone or fax his/her credit card number. At some point, he/she will be asked to affirm that he/she is 21. Age identity is relevant as the sale of liquor is prohibited to those under 21 throughout the USA.

These online wineries and online breweries are doing a booming business, estimated at over $1 billion in 1998 (Goldman and Armstrong 1999). These are typical entrepreneurial niche businesses, which are often relatively small producers. They are unlikely to attract the attention of the distributors as their products would not fill much retail shelf space. The response from the states to online alcohol sales has not been uniformly positive. Several states, including Florida, Georgia, Kentucky, Tennessee, and North Carolina, have passed, or are resurrecting, laws that make the direct shipment of alcohol to consumers a felony. Supporters of such laws argue that mail and Internet ordering of alcohol encourages underage drinking and deprives states of millions in sales and excise taxes. In addition, wholesale distributors and retailers, especially those from states that have established monopolies on alcoholic beverage distribution, are not happy about losing business. They refer to these small upscale wineries as 'Internet bootleggers' (Woody 1999).

A number of interest groups and coalitions have emerged around this legal controversy. The Wine and Spirits Wholesalers of America has funded a lobbying group called Americans for Responsible Alcohol Access (ARAA) (Virtual Vineyards Press Release 1997). Wineries, service providers, and wine consumers have formed the

Coalition for Free Trade in Licensed Beverages (CFT). The Coalition has proposed a model law by which each state would register out-of-state wineries and wine dealers so that state taxes and registration fees are collected, dry counties are respected, and shipments to minors are prevented (Wawine Home 1997). The CFT has also joined a number of other organizations representing wineries in California and other states to form a group called Free the Grapes. It supports the efforts of the Congressional Wine Caucus, a bipartisan group of House members from wine-growing states, to defeat federal legislation that would limit mail-order and Internet sales of alcohol (Salant 1999).

This conflict between established and emerging commercial interests over e-commerce activity does not occur in a legal or regulatory vacuum. There is a question whether the regulatory framework established with the repeal of Prohibition and the ratification of the Twenty-first Amendment in 1933 will endure in cyberspace. The Twenty-first Amendment allows for states to regulate the distribution and sale of alcoholic beverages within their borders. Some states, and/or counties within states, continued the prohibition on alcohol sales, but most adopted a three-tier system of alcohol sales. This system requires alcohol producers to sell to state-licensed wholesalers, who then sell to retailers, and the retailers alone are permitted to sell alcohol to consumers. In some states, the distributors and retailers are both state government agencies. There is variation in state laws governing online sales of alcoholic beverages (Figure 14.1).

Some of the online wineries argue that it is a violation of the Twenty-first Amendment for a state to discriminate against interstate commerce solely to protect local economic interests. This issue was litigated in Utah in 1999 in *Utah* v. *Amoroso and Beer Across America*. Utah prosecuted Beer Across American (BAA), an Illinois company, for selling and shipping alcoholic beverages directly to consumers in Utah. The Utah Court of Appeals ruled that BAA was subject to criminal prosecution in Utah for conduct committed in Illinois, because that conduct caused an unlawful result in Utah (para. 17). It also ruled that Utah's prosecution was a legitimate exercise

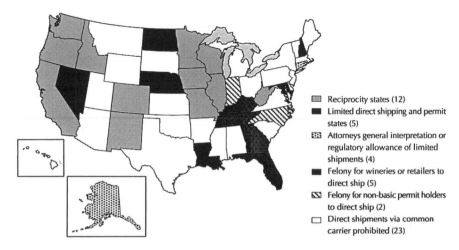

Reciprocity states (12)

Limited direct shipping and permit states (5)

Attorneys general interpretation or regulatory allowance of limited shipments (4)

Felony for wineries or retailers to direct ship (5)

Felony for non-basic permit holders to direct ship (2)

Direct shipments via common carrier prohibited (23)

Figure 14.1   *Direct shipment laws by state for wineries, as of September 1999. Source: Wine Institute [http://www.wineinstitute.org/shipwine/analysis/intro_analysis.htm>]*

of its authority under the Twenty-first Amendment and that it did not conflict with the interstate commerce clause (para. 31). In November 1999, the CFT filed a lawsuit, *Bolick & Heatwole* v. *Virginia Department of Alcoholic Beverage Control*, in the US District Court challenging the constitutionality of Virginia's laws prohibiting adult consumers from purchasing and receiving wine directly from out-of-state businesses. CFT is attempting to use the courts to establish that the interstate commerce clause prohibits states from restricting their residents from purchasing items that flow in interstate commerce. The development of case law is likely to evolve slowly and with many inconsistent rulings given the differences in state laws.

Various bills have been introduced in Congress to address these jurisdictional issues. Receiving the most attention and action in the 106th Congress (1999–2000) was H.R. 2031, the Twenty-First Amendment Enforcement Act, introduced by Representative Joe Scarborough (R-FL). This bill, as amended, passed the House in August 1999 by a bipartisan vote of 310–112. The bill authorizes state attorneys general to bring civil action in federal court to enforce state laws, valid under the Twenty-first Amendment, relating to the interstate transportation of alcoholic beverages. The bill does not supersede the 1998 Internet Tax Freedom Law and does not permit injunctions in federal court against interactive computer services. In 1999, Senator Byrd (D-WV) offered an amendment to the Senate's Juvenile Justice Bill (S.254) that contained language similar to H.R. 2031 requiring for injunctive relief in Federal district court to enforce state laws relating to the interstate transportation of intoxicating liquor. The amended Juvenile Justice Bill passed the Senate in May 1999, but a conference committee reconciling the differences in these bills is unlikely to succeed. The more likely path for the future of legislation is Senator Hatch's (R-UT) S. 577, the Twenty-First Amendment Enforcement Act, which is similar to H.R. 2031. It has been referred to the Committee on the Judiciary.

The emerging politics of cyberspace on this issue appears to be remarkably similar to politics as usual, mirroring identities and interests that are rooted in the physical world. The political resolution of the competing principles and economic interests will likely emerge as a result of bargaining, negotiating, and compromising among the variety of stakeholders, with ongoing political skirmishes in state legislatures, Congress, and the courts. Grassroots involvement is also likely to occur. Some producers and legislators propose a California boycott of Florida orange juice, Florida being one of the states that has made it a felony to ship wine into the state. The Family Winemakers of California have called for a boycott of charity events, competitions, and trade shows in all the states that make it a felony to ship alcoholic beverages directly to residents in those states (Sutton 1997).

The politics of gambling on the Internet are also reminiscent of politics as usual. In 1997 analysts estimated that there were at least 80 live gambling sites on the Internet (most open 24 hours a day, seven days a week) where one can place bets on everything from blackjack to college basketball (Scripps Howard News Service 1997). By mid-1998, that number had increased to more than 200 (Edwards 1998), and by 2000 to 650 sites (Internet Gaming Commission 2000). In most cases, one registers, opens an account with a credit card, and often is required to make a deposit. Winnings are credited to the account and losses are deducted. Some gambling sites operate from outside the USA, for example, Casino on the Net comes from Antigua. Other sites are run by Indian tribes. For example, The US Lottery is run by the Coeur d'Alene Tribe in Idaho.

The legal status of online gambling is somewhat unclear. Most states prohibit gambling except in specific cases, for example state-run lotteries. But the ability of states to enforce existing state statutes has been thwarted by the jurisdictional issues posed by online gambling In one instance, a Pennsylvania judge ordered a Pennsylvania business owner and president of Interactive Gaming and Communications Corporation to surrender to authorities in Missouri so he could be prosecuted on felony charges of violating Missouri laws against online gaming. But a Missouri judge had earlier rejected the attempt by the Missouri attorney general to obtain a court order banning the Pennsylvania-based Interactive Gaming from allowing Missouri residents to gamble on its Internet site. Because the casino operated offshore from Grenada in the Caribbean, it was not subject to US laws (Baker 1997). A New York judge in July 1999 reached the opposite conclusion, ruling that an Antiguan gambling site that can be accessed from New York is subject to the laws of New York (Fleming 1999). Similarly, a Minnesota Appeals Court ruled in 1998 that an Internet operator that advertised to and accepted bets from Minnesota residents was subject to the jurisdiction of the Minnesota Courts (Cabot 1998). Case law will continue to develop but, as is true for online alcohol sales, enforcement difficulties and jurisdictional issues are unlikely to be resolved quickly or easily.

In both state legislatures and Congress, proponents of prohibiting or regulating online gambling are making a number of arguments including: consumer protection against fraud, access by minors, potential for an increase in gambling addictions, and the need to preserve state revenues (Lessani 1998). In mid-2000, several bills were pending in the Congress to ban Internet gambling. The one that received the most attention, and that passed the Senate in November 1999, was the Internet Gambling Prohibition Act (S.692), introduced by Senator Jon Kyl (R-AZ). The congressionally created National Gambling Impact Study Commission recommended a similar prohibition in its June 1999 report. The Kyl bill extends to the Internet the existing federal ban on using telephones or wires to place bets. Businesses running Internet gambling sites would be subject to criminal penalties, as would individuals placing bets through those web sites. In addition, Internet service providers, such as American Online and Erols, would be required to close gambling web sites once notified by state or federal officials that a web site was violating the Act. State laws that permit certain types of gambling, for example, fantasy sports leagues, or that sponsor gambling in the form of lotteries would not be preempted by the Kyl bill. The Internet Gambling Prohibition Act was sent to the House where it was then referred to the Committee on the Judiciary's Subcommittee on Crime.

The politics of the gambling issue have made for some strange bedfellows. Supporters of a ban on Internet gambling include the Christian Coalition, concerned about the effects of gambling on family values; the Las Vegas casino industry, concerned about the loss of revenue; consumer activists like Ralph Nader, who worry about consumer fraud; and major sports leagues, who want to protect their reputations. Opponents include civil libertarians, who fear government officials intruding on the privacy of people's living rooms, and the Internet service providers, who do not want legal responsibility for policing gambling sites (Akers 1998).

PURPOSE AND LANDSCAPE OF JURISDICTIONAL LAWS

In the cases of legal restrictions on liquor purchases and gambling, there are a number of policy goals that state and local governments seek to achieve through regulation. The first has to do with establishment of cultural standards. In many cases, as is true for liquor and gambling regulations, the governments are legislating a moral code of behavior that is deemed acceptable within that particular jurisdiction. Moral views about the depravities associated with drinking or gambling are often codified in local or state statutes. The content of that code may not be broadly acceptable within society at large, but does have, or did at one time have, the approval of the local citizens. The scope and acceptance of such state and local regulations are intrinsically affiliated with geographic place and individuals identified within that place.

The second involves the protection of established economic interests. Many, if not most, online commercial activities compete with similar activities in the physical world. Virtually all products sold online are also sold in stores and through catalogs. For every good and service offered on the World Wide Web (WWW), there is an existing marketing and distribution system in the physical world. In some instances, online offerings complement existing offerings and market structures. But, in other cases there is conflict. The sale of alcohol over the Internet is one case where there is conflict – between new small wineries and microbreweries who sell online, and the wholesalers, distributors, and retailers who have operated for years in a legal and regulatory system that largely complements their interests. The same type of conflict occurs between legal gambling operations in places such as Nevada, New Jersey, and Native American Indian reservations, as well as legal lotteries run by states or horse tracks licensed or run by states, and the online gambling sites operated by entrepreneurs in the USA and/or abroad. The legal and established gambling operations fear that online gambling sites will siphon off their activity. The specifics of these legal and regulatory systems evolved in an environment of economic activity rooted in geographic place and the systems reflect the particular mix of state and/or local economic activity. Different geographic jurisdictions protect their own established economic interests and do so in their own ways.

The third goal is the collection of government revenue. Governments have revenue needs and do not want to see sources of revenue disappear into cyberspace. At this time, a Supreme Court ruling exempts mail order companies, including those selling online, from being required to collect sales taxes for products delivered across state lines. The Court ruled that one state cannot force a company in another state to collect its sale taxes. Technically, consumers are supposed to pay the taxes, but few do. So, if you live in Washington state and buy a book from Seattle-based Amazon.com, you pay Washington state sales tax. But, if you live in New York and do business with Amazon.com, you pay no sales tax. In most states, consumers who purchase goods outside the state are required to report those purchased and pay use taxes on those goods. Few consumers are aware of these requirements and fewer still comply with them (Martie 1999).

Opposition to sales or use taxes on online purchases comes, in part, from consumers, many who expect online prices to be discounted because the overhead costs are lower and shipping/handling costs are added on. They do not want to pay sales or use taxes on top of those costs and online merchants are afraid they will lose business if they are required to charge sales or use taxes. Many online merchants, especially smaller ones, fear the administrative costs associated with maintaining computer systems to assess state and local taxes nationwide, and to then forward the tax payments to governments. The complexity of our tax laws is also a barrier. According to the Sales Tax Institute, there are 77 000 different sales tax rates in the USA and on average 40 changes in these rates occur each month (Crockett 1977). The complexity of these state systems can be captured in a Rube Goldberg caricature (Figure 14.2).

The fourth goal of laws such as gaming restrictions and the establishment of dry counties is the protection of minors. In several areas, the law treats children differently and permits restriction of certain information. But these differences and restrictions are not automatically transferred into cyberspace. In the physical world, age identity is verified visually or by an identification card. For example, children cannot walk into a bookstore and purchase magazines that contain sexually explicit material. But they can visit a web site that contains such material, although they are often warned about the nature of the content. Children cannot walk into a store and buy a six-pack of beer without showing proof of age. But they can visit the web site of a micro-brewery and purchase a six-pack if they have a credit card number and are willing to affirm that they are 21. Similarly, children are checked for proof of age and denied physical entry into gambling casinos. But children can misrepresent themselves and engage in online

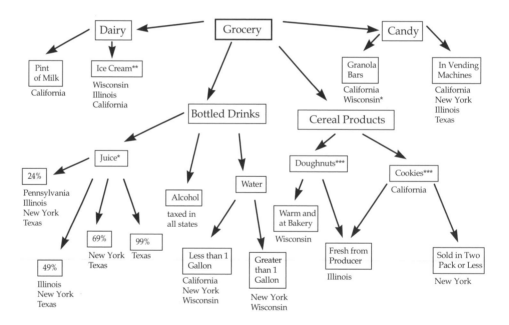

* Wisconsin taxes juice when the label uses the words cocktail, drink, punch, ade or nectar. Granola Bars are taxable in WI only if coated with candy or yogurt coating
** For immediate consumption in a restaurant or parlor.
*** Doughnuts and cookies are taxed in Pennsylvania if they are sold at a carnival

Figure 14.2   *Sales tax treatment of grocery items in six selected states. States that apply sales tax on the item are listed, otherwise the selected states exempt that product. Source: Cline and Neubig, 8 September 1999*

gambling if they have a credit card.

A fifth goal of such laws is consumer protection. State and local governments often supplement federal legislation to protect consumers. With gambling and purchases of alcoholic beverages, governments are concerned about unfair and deceptive advertising and regulate to ensure that gambling operations reveal information about how the 'game' works and expectations of winning and that wholesalers and retailers of alcoholic beverages ensure quality of their products and fair pricing. With gambling operations, consumer protections may also ensure that the operations comply with certain financial requirements and procedures so that the operations are sufficiently solvent to pay anticipated winnings.

In both online gambling and online liquor stores, the effort to impose existing jurisdictional boundaries onto activities in cyberspace reveals two limitations of a simple transfer of legal regimes from physical space to cyberspace. The first is that existing laws are not enforced completely in the physical world; some slack is accepted. For example, it is widely recognized that some underage drinking occurs. Stores and bars are legally responsible for verifying age, but some underage patrons slip by, often by misrepresenting themselves with a false ID card. The amount of underage drinking might be decreased by increasing penalties, surveillance, and reporting requirements. The same holds in the enforcement of gambling prohibitions and sales or use tax laws. Technically 'illegal' gambling occurs quite frequently as people place bets on football games or participate in office pools during March Madness. Society, however, accepts a certain amount of slack in the enforcement as a tradeoff for a less intrusively controlled environment.

This question of slack transfers to the online world. If it becomes a crime to place a bet or to buy wine over the Internet or to access 'indecent' material, how do law enforcement officials discover people violating those laws without violating Fourth Amendment protections against unreasonable searches and seizures? If Internet service providers (ISPs) become legally responsible for not providing certain categories of content or types of services (such as alcohol purchasing or gambling opportunities) to all people, or to certain ages, how do the ISPs determine the quality of content and the identity of the receiver? Should ISPs have that control over the distribution of content? Should a system of authentication be created that all users must adhere to before going anywhere in cyberspace? With such a system, it would be easier to verify age, protect against misrepresentation (identity threat), and hold people accountable. But this would, in effect, be creating in cyberspace a national (or international) identity system that American society has been unwilling to establish in our physical space.

A second limitation is that legal jurisdictions do not easily convey from physical space to cyberspace. Although physical space and cyberspace are not, at this time, parallel universes but intersecting universes, the character of the two universes is fundamentally different. Online gambling and online liquor stores do not conduct the totality of their operations in cyberspace. Liquor is delivered to an identified person in a physical place; winnings are credited, or losses deducted, to an individual account in a physical place. As the online transaction moves into the physical world, the possibilities of enforcing state and local laws increase but are not ensured. Taxes, for example, could be collected at the point of liquor delivery or credit card transaction. Similarly, liquor could be seized if delivery was to an individual living in a dry county or to a minor. But packages can be sent so that their contents are not marked, which would make it difficult to tax or seize. Perhaps even more perplexing questions occur with respect to the intersection of physical spaces and cyberspaces in online gambling. Does the gambling occur in the user's computer where the bet is entered, and hence come under the laws of that jurisdiction, or does the gambling occur in the computer of the gambling operator where the bet is registered, and hence come under those laws?

The intersection of the physical space and cyberspace makes it appear that jurisdictional lines from the physical world can be invoked as activities move from one universe to the other. The reality is somewhat murkier. Although the universes do intersect, there are easy ways of masking that intersection. Enforcement of the laws might then necessitate more surveillance and tracking of cyberspace activities than would be the case for physical activities. Mere observance of cyberspace movements from a distance will not yield relevant information in the way observance would for activities in the physical world. Observance of activities in cyberspace necessitates more intrusion than observance of activities in physical space. 'In plain view' and public space are concepts related to law enforcement in the physical world that do not easily translate into the virtual world.

GEOGRAPHY OF CYBERSPACE: IDENTIFIED OR ANONYMOUS?

The Internet was designed as an open network that provides an essentially public place accessible to many different people who have a range of interests and experiences. One is generally free to wander in and out of web sites much as one would wander in and out of stores in a mall or through the stacks in the public library. One may scan a range of offerings and peruse more closely those that seem interesting. As one wanders around in cyberspace, whether visiting the web sites of Virtual Vineyard, Casino on the Net, the Library of Congress, the National Basketball League, or whatever, one leaves behind a trail of mouse tracks or clickstream data. The Internet service provider has some record of these comings and goings for administrative purposes. Also, there are some online tracking systems that are embedded in Internet browsers. Netscape, for example, has a 'cookies' system that tracks and records information about individual visits to web sites. The webmaster (web site manager) retains this transactional information and automatically consults this information the next time that computer visits that site. These data make it easier and quicker for one to navigate the site on subsequent visits (and assumes you want your activities to be similar each time), but it also provides a historical record of activities and thought processes. The 'cookies' program also collects information on the user's computer regarding prior Internet activities. Although it is possible to disable 'cookies' and also to use anonymous remailers for Internet surfing, many people do not know about these possibilities.

Privacy advocates are concerned about 'cookies' and similar programs that collect personal information on the Internet, because these programs violate what has become known as the 'code of fair information practices'. This code, a component of information privacy laws in the USA and around the world, requires that organizations should limit information collection, provide notice to individuals, allow for individual consent for reuse or exchange of information, and enable individuals to see and correct their personal information (Regan 1995). But, personally identifiable information is routinely and automatically collected at online web sites, most often without the individual's knowledge or consent. Information about an individual's identity, location, and online activities is referred to as 'transactional information'. This transactional information can be bought and sold for marketing and other purposes.

Many web sites require people to register before they can use the site. The *New York Times*, for example, does not charge for its online service, but does require that users register. It also has a privacy statement that one can click on and read about why it collects the information and what it does with it. Other web sites conduct surveys about preferences and demographics. In 1998, for example, the National Conference of State Legislatures asked a visitor to complete a form regarding occupation and interests before entering its online database. On the one hand, the disclosure and retention of this personal information does make it possible for web sites to better serve their visitors. On the other hand, all of this information can enable marketers to prepare detailed personal profiles of online users. In a 1997 survey of 750 families by Family PC, 88 percent of adult respondents said that 'abuse of personal information on the Internet' was one of the most troubling concerns they had about the Internet. When asked about the types of inappropriate behavior they have experienced on the Internet, 64 percent cited having 'to enter personal information to get content' and 63 percent cited being 'solicited to buy goods or services' (Family PC 1997).

In general, most online activities may have the feel or appearance of 'locationlessness'. One may feel anonymous but the reality at this stage of Internet development is different. Tracking of place and identity may not be obvious to the user, but it is occurring. At this point, locational and transactional information is being used for administrative and service purposes, as well as to complete an informational or commercial exchange with a user. It is not being used to enforce laws, because the information is not being passed to state law enforcement or taxation authorities. But, there is nothing inherent in the technology to prevent such disclosures. There are, however, cultural, legal, political, and economic forces that operate against such automatic disclosures.

TECHNOLOGY MEDIATED BORDERS?

Related to the question of tracking individual movements in cyberspace is the question of an individual's ability to negotiate cyberspace on his or her terms. Can individual users have the ability to construct their own boundaries in cyberspace? If network architecture is used as a new geography for cyberspace, or a new paradigm as Joel Reidenberg suggests (1997), technical standards, protocols, and gateways could provide borders on activity. How might such technical borders work and how much control would users have over their arrangement?

One area of online activities where the question of technical borders has been raised involves the control over access to 'indecent' materials on the Internet. In considering the constitutionality of the Communications Decency Act, the Supreme Court noted that although sexually explicit material was widely available on the Internet, users seldom encountered such content accidentally, as they can in the broadcast world. A majority of the Court was also persuaded that there was no reliable way on the Internet to screen users for age. Using credit card possession as a surrogate for proof of age would impose costs on non-commercial sites and an adult password requirement would impose burdens. Neither would be foolproof. The Court agreed that the creation of 'adult zones' on the Internet was more difficult than in the physical world. Justice O'Connor and Chief Justice Rehnquist were more optimistic than the other justices that what they referred to as 'user-based zoning' or 'gateway technology' would in the near future make it possible to create adult zones on the Internet (*Reno* v. *ACLU* 1997).

Many free speech groups, Internet service providers, educators, and parents are optimistic about technical options that give individuals some control over the information they are likely to access on a web site and some choices about what web sites to visit (CDT 1997). These technical options would give individual users, or others, the capability to replicate the equivalent of geographic boundaries in cyberspace. Filtering systems, such as Cyber Patrol, Cybersitter, Netnanny, and others, can be programmed to block access to web sites that parents consider inappropriate for their children. These filtering software can also block the transmission of specific words or phrases from the home computer. Using this software, children could not send their names, addresses, or phone numbers, for example, over the Internet. Labeling systems, such as RSACi and Safe Surf, also provide a warning to children and parents about the information they are likely to encounter on that web site. But these are only warning systems. There is also watchdog software that keeps a record of whatever information has been displayed on a computer. Parents can check to see where their kids have been on the Internet. Time-management systems, such as CYBERtimer, allow parents to limit the total daily or weekly time that children spend on the Internet, as well as the hours during the day and evening when they can surf the Net. Finally, there are family friendly search engines, such as Net Shepherd Family Search and Yahooligans that limit searches of material on the WWW to sites that are reviewed as being appropriate for children.

Such technology offers some means to create boundaries in cyberspace so that users do not access material that they deem 'inappropriate' and do not divulge inappropriate personal information. But technological solutions are not panaceas. There are several problems. The first is who should have the power or authority to set standards, protocols, and gateways. To date, no physical–geographic border is inviolate. Technological borders are not inherently permeable or impermeable. Rather, they are programmed at a certain security level and that level is automatically maintained, although no security system is yet inviolate. Network architecture decisions do not merely have technical implications, but also policy implications. There is a question about whether these technical solutions will become 'user-empowerment tools' or 'censoring' techniques. PICS (the Platform for Internet Content Selection) technology, which is a machine readable labeling system used in blocking and filtering technologies, was developed to give individual recipients control over the materials that they receive over a computer. It was designed as an alternative to sender-centered controls over that information. Civil liberty groups applaud the notion of individual control, but fear the possibility of more centralized controls. So the question becomes who is in

control of the controls, individual users, employers, commercial firms, or governments? (Global Internet Liberty Campaign 1997).

At this stage in Internet evolution, only the most technologically savvy users have
the capability to construct and maintain their own technical borders. Most users
accept the defaults that are set by their Internet service providers and web browsers.
Most users appear to be unaware of and do not challenge the information capture
practices of various web sites. Governments have not been aggressive players in
standards-setting bodies, generally allowing the private sector and telecommunications providers the controlling role. In this environment, commercial firms and technical experts have tacit power over the construction of technical borders.

A result is that the criteria used to construct technical borders are not transparent or
obvious to a potential user, and may be deemed proprietary by the companies making
the software. This point is illustrated by the difficulty of 'objectively' determining
whether content is inappropriate. The statue of David, for example, may be blocked for
full frontal nudity, as may illustrations of condom use for safe sex. Technically, both
meet the criterion of 'full frontal nudity'. Yet in one case the context is art history and in
the other the context is public health information. At this point, much blocking and
filtering software is too crude to incorporate these distinctions. Given the number of
web sites (in the millions, while one labeling group has labeled only 61 000 sites), the
changing nature of web sites, the range of individual preferences about content, and the
necessity of depending upon web sites for information about their practices, rating
systems are unlikely to be 100 percent dependable.

The second problem is that, similar to legal and geographic borders, technological
borders are imperfect. Filters, for example, may block too much material or too little.
The Electronic Privacy Information Center (EPIC) conducted 100 searches using a
traditional search engine (Alta Vista) and a 'family-friendly' search engine (Net Shepherd Family Search) and found that the family-friendly search engine blocked almost
90 percent of the material identified by the traditional search engine (EPIC 1997). For
example, a traditional search for 'American Red Cross' produced almost 40 000 hits
while a family-friendly search produced 77 hits. The family-friendly search effectively
blocked 99.8 percent of the documents available on the Internet. The EPIC report
provoked much discussion among Internet service providers, children's groups, and
software companies. As a result, some product revision took place.

Related to the imperfection of technical borders is that research shows that not all
users will avail themselves of the opportunity to construct borders. For example,
parents do not use the filtering and blocking systems at their disposal. A survey of 750
families conducted by Family PC in November of 1997 revealed that 26 percent used
some form of parental-control software, mainly those built into their web browsers or
offered by their ISP. Only 4 percent used parental-control software that they had to
buy, install, and maintain (Family PC 1997).

Technology may also provide a way around technological borders. In order to
maintain privacy for example, individuals can use anonymizing proxy servers (which
allow one to surf the Internet without revealing a network connection); anonymous
remailers for electronic mail communications; a variety of pseudonyms; and trusted
intermediaries. Privacy labeling and rating systems, similar to those for inappropriate
content, are also being developed. But all of this technology requires knowledge, time,

and a commitment from users, as well as the support of industry and the development of user-friendly interfaces. At this time, no technology option alone provides a dependable way of constructing and maintaining borders.

POLICY ALTERNATIVES FOR ONLINE ENFORCEMENT PROBLEMS

Neither legal nor technical means overcome the difficulties of maintaining borders or enforcing laws in cyberspace. The above analysis reveals that transferring existing geographically-based laws to cyberspace will result in two problems: how to incorporate the slack that exists in geographic enforcement to online enforcement, and how to determine the geographic jurisdiction in which an online activity occurs? Consideration of the creation of technical boundaries also reveals two difficulties: Who should have the authority to set the technical standards, and how to envisage and prepare for the inevitable imperfections of those boundaries?

The policy debates about how best to protect traditional and new policy goals in the online world are similar across a number of issues. The above discussions about online liquor sales and online gambling identify many of those difficulties, as does the current debate about the possible ways which could be used to collect online sales and use taxes (see Table 14.1). Should society depend upon laws, regulation, self-regulation, technology, or some combination? Legal prohibitions on activities such as online gambling or online alcohol sales are difficult to enforce. Jurisdictional questions about where the illegal activity occurs are compounded by the technical possibility of disguising actions. If country A established a ban on an activity such as online gambling and country B regulated but permitted this online activity, it is probable that citizens of country A will avail themselves of the online activities originating in country B. A number of countries, including Australia, New Zealand, Antigua, and Costa Rica, have legalized and licensed Internet gambling services. Principles of international law protecting national sovereignty prohibit another country from extraditing citizens of those countries who conducted legal gambling operations (Bell 1999). Legalization and licensing meet the policy goals of protecting consumers, protecting minors, and ensuring revenue collection. Legalization and licensing may not protect established economic interests, but they will create a managed and predictable environment in which future competition can occur. With legalization and licensing, proponents of cultural standards may be forced to concede the moral high ground, but may be able to lobby for inclusion of some moral or cultural principles. Given a simple choice between prohibition and regulation, this analysis would suggest that regulation will be somewhat more enforceable and more effective at achieving the policy goals sought. Other analyses reach a similar conclusion that prohibition is unwise and that some scheme of regulation should be developed (Bell 1999; Baker 1997; Lessani 1998). Clarke (1998) suggests that to be effective this scheme must be multilateral rather than national.

As in other areas of policy discussion regarding the Internet, most notably perhaps in the area of online privacy, proposals for self-regulation have received serious policy attention. Self-regulation is seen as a solution that avoids the potential dangers that regulation may stifle industry competition and technological innovation. If the indus-

Table 14.1   *Responsibilities for collecting sales and use taxes*

Location of buyer	In-state seller	Out-of-state seller
In-state consumers	Seller collects sales tax	With nexus: seller collects a use tax for the home state. Without nexus: seller does not have liability to collect tax; instead, consumer is responsible for paying use tax directly to home state
Out-of-state consumers	No sales tax collected by the seller if the good is shipped to a state where the in-state seller does not have nexus	Not applicable
In-state businesses	Seller collects the tax on taxable sales to most business purchasers Business purchasers, including direct permit holders, may pay a use tax directly to tax agencies	With nexus: seller collects a use tax for the home state (unless the business pays use tax directly) Without nexus: no sales tax collected by seller; business purchaser pays a use tax to home state
Out-of-state businesses	No sales tax collected by the seller if the good is shipped to a state where the in-state seller does not have nexus or if the tax directly paid	Not applicable

Source: (Cline and Neubig 1999)

try itself can develop and monitor standards or principles that meet the perceived policy problem, then governments need not become directly involved. But, self-regulation does not work unless all sectors providing a good or service have the same interests in adhering to the self-regulatory framework. In the cases of companies selling alcoholic beverages online and those offering gambling opportunities, the companies do not have the same interests. Those companies which also operate in the physical world will have interests that are at odds with those which operate only or predominantly in the online world. Companies based in one jurisdiction, particularly one national jurisdiction, will have different interests and incentives than those in other jurisdictions. In addition, self-regulatory systems alone generally are not effective in overcoming market imperfections and would not work with goals of consumer protection or morality.

The pivotal issue in terms of effectively enforcing legal regulations or voluntary guidelines in cyberspace is the ability to determine what someone is doing in cyberspace. Effective enforcement seems dependent upon constant, but not necessarily intrusive, surveillance. In order to know whether someone is following the law in cyberspace or transgressing that law, enforcement authorities would need to know what that person is doing. Technology makes it possible to monitor cyberspace locations and transactions. The technological prerequisites are in place for effective enforcement. But such monitoring would render the borderless world of cyberspace a maze with multiple and layered borders. Technology does offer the means of identifying a person and location in cyberspace. Technology offers the means of creating a new geography of standards, gateways, and protocols. This geography would not be based on physical characteristics, such as mountain ranges, rivers, or oceans, but on technological interfaces in the communications infrastructure. If such technological monitoring became the norm, place and identity would be more finely calibrated in cyberspace than in physical space.

[One way of phrasing the social and political question that results is whether the benefits of effective enforcement of legal regimes are greater than the costs to individual and economic freedom that would result from such surveillance. There is not an easy answer to such a question.] In some measure, the answer is likely to be that it depends upon the goal of the law, as well as on the configuration of existing interests and governmental institutions. But on a more abstract level, the answer depends upon the perceived or acceptable limits on state or government activity. The question thus returns us to basic issues of political sovereignty and legitimacy – issues that philosophers and political scientists have struggled with for centuries. These issues have undergone metamorphoses at different historical moments, but there may be some enduring elements to the character of these changes.

CYBERSPACE: ANOTHER STATE OF POLITICAL DEVELOPMENT

In the 1960s the Social Science Research Council funded a research effort to understand the universal functions of political systems, as well as the processes of political modernization and political development. In developing cultures, a number of stresses occur including 'a tendency to emphasize the value of words and ideologies and to discount pragmatic considerations' and 'prevailing widespread uncertainty about how existing roles in the political system can be effectively utilized' (Pye pp. 108–109). These stresses bear striking resemblance to the stresses revealed in discussions about the effective governance of cyberspace. Thus, the political development literature and analysis might offer some guidance with respect to the current debate regarding enforcement of state authority in cyberspace.

A number of crises in political development have been identified including crises of identity, legitimacy, participation, penetration, and distribution (Binder *et. al.* 1971). Each will be briefly examined to determine its corollary in the current debate about governing in cyberspace. The identity crisis, which Lucian Pye analyses, involves questions about the basic unity of the society. At a basic level, this concerns a sense of belonging to a particular political community and a territorially defined community (110). Although such a sense involves a psychological dimension, it is also a sense that is rooted in geographical space. Geography offers one important criterion for distinguishing those with one identity from those with another. Pye argues that 'the first step in the building of a polity involves the establishment of its territorial boundaries' (114). A crisis occurs when there is a question as to the definition of such boundaries. The crisis is usually resolved through more sophisticated technological infrastructures that more effectively incorporate outlying geographic areas. Improvements in communication, transportation, and education can be used to resolve identity crises. Resolution of such crises then depends in part on the availability of technological improvements, and in part on the acceptance of the new systems. When we relate this identity crisis to cyberspace issues, a number of parallels appear. Cyberspace challenges traditional community identities, both those that are psychologically defined and those that are territorially defined. Definitions of boundaries of the self are not clear. A more sophisticated use of technology could regenerate existing boundaries or create new ones, but as discussed above/the permeability of boundaries, whether technological or geographic, will continue to be problematic.

The legitimacy crisis concerns questions about what particular structures are considered to be the authoritative ones. This involves both the performance capacity of the system and the sentiments of the population toward governmental authority (136). As with the identity crisis, there is both a technological and a psychological component. Legitimacy crises can occur because the governmental authority is inadequate in addressing political problems. To respond, the total level of power in the system may need to be increased and more institutionalization of power may be necessary (140–1). Again, a crisis of legitimacy appears to be occurring in cyberspace. There is a blurring of authority both within national systems (among different levels and jurisdictions) and at the global level. It is not clear who is or who should be in charge. In democratic systems, there will be understandable resistance, however, to the notion that increasing power will be the answer. More, or different, institutionalizations may be necessary to reestablish legitimacy.

A crisis of participation also accompanies political development and modernization. Participation entails actions to influence the choice of policies, the administration of public affairs, and the choice of political leaders. Fundamentally, crises may occur when there are questions about who can or should participate. In general development and modernization entail a broadening of participation by all groups in society and the creation of institutions that allow for participation. Myron Weiner points out that 'paradoxically, the growth of mass political participation has been primarily associated with the centralization of authority rather than with the growth of local institutions' (177). The crisis of participation in cyberspace appears to be one of democratic participation versus technocratic participation. As knowledge and expertise are required to voice informed opinions, the influence of the technocrats is likely to increase. If issues are defined as technological issues (setting of standards for example), the number of possible participants in those decisions will decrease.

A penetration crisis involves a question about the ability of the central governmental authority to ensure conformance with the policies enunciated by that government. As with the earlier crises, Joseph LaPalobara points out that this has both geographical and sociopsychological dimensions. In earlier stages of political development, the ability to manage this crisis was positively and directly related to technology (210–11). But the relationship does not tend to remain stable as others may be able to utilize the technology to their advantage and contrary to the elite's management of the penetration crisis. Key to a successful resolution of this crisis is the ability to create and institutionalize organizations that provide means for addressing problems before they become crises. The cyberspace parallel to the penetration crisis is the enforcement crisis discussed above. Again, institutionalization appears to be important to resolution.

Finally, a distribution crisis involves the ability of a political system to manage resources within that system. Geographic boundaries, psychological ties, and organizations are pivotal to successful resolutions. Distribution and redistribution of natural and human resources raise questions of fairness as well as system capacity. In cyberspace, the distribution crisis raises questions about the 'information haves' and the 'information have-nots'.

Using the model of political development shows that the crises in cyberspace are not all novel. There are parallels to earlier stages of political development. In those earlier stages, crises were often resolved through institutionalization. One question is whether that is also true for cyberspace. Rather than shying away from new institutions, creatively thinking about how those institutions might be structured, and whether those institutions need to cross traditional geographic jurisdictions, is in order. Indeed new institutions are emerging or being discussed in the areas of online alcohol sales, online gambling, and collection of taxes from e-commerce.

The Internet Gaming Commission (IGC) was established in response to the problems posed by unlicensed and unregulated sites that, according to the IGC home page, 'can do as they wish without regard to you and without responsibility to the government of any country'. The Chair of the IGC describes its work as follows:

> Here's what we do. The staff of the Internet Gaming Commission includes accountants, system engineers, experienced gamblers and statisticians. We comb the web and let you know which gaming establishments are licensed and which ones are not. We warn you of any special conditions the casino may impose on you. We have bulletin boards on all the gaming sites where you can read of the experience others have had with a gaming establishment. We show you how you can learn to gamble more effectively. And we actually show you the odds on the games at most casinos (http://www/Internetcommission.com).

The Chair notes that the IGC is completely independent, does not accept advertising, and will not compromise its integrity. From its web site, it is not clear where the IGC is based, who its members are, or who funds the organization. The Internet Gaming Commission has directories of sites in five categories as shown in Table 14.2. There is also an explicitly industry trade association, the Internet Gaming Council

Table 14.2 *Internet gaming commission's site categories and number of sites in each*

Directory	Number of sites listed, Feb. 23, 2000
Licensed sites	257
Unlicensed sites	129
Licensed, audit in process	61
Licensed, caution urged	47
Extreme caution urged	7

Source: Internet Gaming Commission, 23 Feb 2000, [http://www.Internetcommission.com]

(www.igcouncil.org), formed to self-regulate online gambling sites. With over 80 sites as members, this nonprofit association established a code of conduct to which its members subscribe, provides a forum for discussion, receives complaints about member sites, and runs an online trade journal and newsletter. Its home page describes the Interactive Gaming Council as an 'evolving institution'. It is based in Canada with staff from Canada, Australia, and the USA. Its membership list can be accessed from its home page.

In the case of online liquor sales, the institutional innovation is a new business model, Wineshopper.com, which is to be operational in 2000 and will fill a market niche by working within the existing legal structure. Wineries participating in Wine-shopper.com will present their online offerings to consumers through a single web site, the consumer will make a choice on the Internet, and Wineshopper.com will designate a retailer that delivers the wine to the consumer's home or holds it for pickup by the consumer. Wineshopper.com is attempting to work within the three-tier distribution system that currently governs the sale and distribution of alcoholic beverages in most states. According to Goldman and Armstrong (1999), as of November 1999, 37 states have approved of this method of wine shipment.

In the area of collection of state sales and use taxes resulting from e-commerce, one institutional innovation is a recommendation of the National Conference of State Legislatures (NCSL). The NCSL proposes 'shifting sales tax administration to a technology-oriented business model in which primary responsibility for calculating, collecting, reporting and paying the tax is lodged with "Trusted Third Parties" instead of the seller' (NCSL 2000). This financial clearinghouse would maintain an up-to-date national database of tax rates by jurisdiction and the rates by which products in each state are taxed. When a consumer submits his or her purchase online, the web retailer sends the purchase to the trusted third party (TTP) who would calculate in real time the tax on the purchase and inform the web retailer. The web retailer would calculate the tax into the final purchase price for the consumer and receive the total payment. As envisioned, TTPS will have arrangements with participating vendors and credit card companies to either establish accounts that can periodically be debited for tax payments or establish an electronic-direct system to forward taxes. The TTPs would be responsible for remitting taxes to the states. The NCSL expects that there will be a competitive bidding process to select TTPs, that the nature of TTPs may vary depending on the types of sellers, and that some large online vendors may act as their own TTPs.

Institutional innovations are likely to continue during this period of transition as existing market structures for delivering goods and services move to the online world where they find new entrants to their markets. Similarly, policy debates will persist regarding the opportune degree for enforcing laws, the complementarity of legal and physical borders, the reasonable level of identity required to conduct transactions in cyberspace, and the prudent mix of regulatory, self-regulatory, and technical solutions to policy problems. At this point in the evolution of e-commerce, policy fixes do not exist. Instead, a number of jurisdictional, enforcement, and individual rights issues need to be thoughtfully investigated with an openness to new institutional arrangements that are consistent with changes in place and identity emerging as a result of online commercial activities.

CASES SITED

Bolick and Heatwole v. *Virginia Department of Alcoholic Beverage Control* (filed in US District
Court in Richmond, VA, Nov. 1999).

Janet Reno et al. v. *ACLU et al.* (26 June 1997) No. 96-511. 1997 Lexis 4037.

Mainstream Loudoun et al. and The Safe Sex Page, et al. v. *Board of Trustees of the Loudoun
County Library* (Case No. 97-2049-A) [http://www.aclu.org/court/loudoncomplaint.html].

Melvin I. Urofsky et al. v. *George Allen*, civil complaint filed 8 May 1997 [http://www.aclu.org/
court/urofskyvallencom.html].

Utah v. *Amorso and Beer Across America* (Utah Court of Appeals, 4 March 1999, No. 971712-
CA) [http://attygen.state.ut.us/docs/beersaa.htm].

a) Problems of legal regul^n of Internet   - states as territorial
   - geog / jurisdiction (5 reasons states do this) units vs cyberspace
   - surveillance / privacy problems : closing off access to sites
   - jurisdiction ⇒ enforcement / surveillance

b) Not all new ? Polit develt
        ⇒ institutional mechanisms evolve to
             address the issues

— Liquor, gambling, taxation, sex sites

15

Dot Com Development: Are IT Lines Better Than Tractors?

MARK I. WILSON

Michigan State University, East Lansing, MI, USA

INTRODUCTION

Information technology (IT) and e-commerce are rapidly emerging forces, to which are attributed wondrous powers for generating wealth and growth. Observers of the US economy and its technology-driven stock market may easily see ITs as a panacea for many economic problems. But the further one moves from major corporations, universities, or metropolitan centers, the more elusive the claims for IT success. The adoption and development of ITs has a high priority in many countries, but as the impact is barely understood for the most advanced economies, the role of IT in the developing world requires analysis and evaluation.

Electronic commerce is a rapidly changing phenomenon that leaps ahead of many of our social, political, and legal institutions. To date, little has been written on e-commerce in a development context. The implications of ignoring ITs, however, are great. Lanvin (1995) sees the development of a global information infrastructure as essential if developing countries are to avoid being trapped as commodity producers, and also avoid North–South hostilities caused by the wired world exploiting the poor. For developing economies, ITs certainly can play a significant role in several ways. First, IT is essential for an information- and knowledge-based economy. The generation, management, and transmission of information are most effective through integrated computer and telecommunications systems. Second, IT can be a significant social force through dissemination of information and education, as a source of alternate perspectives and viewpoints, and to streamline the functions of government. Third, an effective set of international electronic links serves to provide efficient trade in services, currency, and to support the internal functions of firms and international organizations. Utilization of IT by exporting organizations can offer cost savings and greater international competitiveness. Fourth, IT can make the physically peripheral closer to the center of an electronic world. In electronic space the issue is not so much distance between locations as it is the cost of electronic access between locations (Arrowsmith and Wilson 1998).

At the same time that IT produces benefits, it can also impose costs. For many developing countries, an advanced communications infrastructure is costly, and must be paid for in commodity exports suffering from deteriorating terms of trade. The use of IT can serve to promote dependency and the extraction of monopoly profits by transnational firms with market power and government influence. As IT is seen as a way for developing countries to reach richer markets, it can also serve the reverse purpose and allow access by sophisticated corporations and organizations to the often fragile markets of less developed countries.

Rather than focus on the cutting edge applications in affluent locations, it is time to consider if and how IT applies to the advance of developing economies. This chapter explores the implications of IT for economic development, and the forces and issues associated with dot com development. After a brief review of the context for IT, the chapter examines the global distribution of ITs, and the spatial patterns of access and use of IT. In part three, the relationship between IT and development is considered, including the issues confronted by developing countries as they expand and modernize their telecommunications infrastructure. The final section investigates the potential roles and impact of e-commerce for the development process.

BACKGROUND

The development of IT is often divided into two spheres that tend not to overlap, the engineering oriented application of hardware and the social impact of new technology. The economic development process, however, represents many social, economic, and political spheres that constantly overlap. The social context of technology and its impact have long been recognized, although often lessons learned from the past are not applied. To provide a framework to investigate IT and development, there are three distinct, but interrelated, facets of IT: technical possibilities, economic viability, and social acceptability. The technical and economic aspects tend to receive most of the attention, yet it is the social context that may well determine the success of the IT choices made in a development context.

The first aspect of IT is the technical possibilities it offers. Primarily, this is an engineering concern, seeking new electronic and scientific advances to improve performance, reduce costs, and produce new applications. Constraints take the form of physics, chemistry, and electrical engineering. IT advances are spurred by basic research in science and engineering and the economic advantages of developing and taking new ideas out of the laboratory. The spectacular gains in processing power (Moore's law) and rapid decline in the cost of computing power are testimony to the speed and technical forces operating to advance IT. The technical possibilities offered by ITs tend to be produced by the world's major research and development centers, which tend to be located in North America, Western Europe, and several Asian nations (Japan, Taiwan, Korea, and Singapore). For the developing world, access to new technologies is filtered through research and economic ties to the core sources of R&D, which tend to be weak linkages.

Technical possibilities alone do not necessarily lead to applications of IT unless those applications also confer some economic advantage. Computer power and telecommunications may be available, but if the cost is too great, then use and impact will be limited. New advances may have to wait until further development reduces costs or increases efficiency. The cost of international telephone calls exemplifies the demand boom associated with drastic cost reductions by telecommunications providers. An application waiting for a technical solution to become economically viable is the international transmission of secure encrypted information over the World Wide Web (WWW). While technically possible, the lack of an efficient and cost-effective way to move information securely (such as credit card details) is a significant barrier to the development of the WWW. Perhaps more important is the social acceptability of such practices.

The social context is perhaps the most powerful force in applications of IT, yet it also tends to receive less attention than technical and economic issues, although all often intersect. The social element of IT use has many dimensions. One important element is the relationship between individuals and technology and the ways different individuals, groups, cultures, and societies perceive, apply, and use IT. Another dimension is the relationship between technology and the state, and the ways in which government affects IT use through industry (subsidy, regulation, standards). A related element is state and society relationships, which introduces technology issues of access, ownership and control, privacy, and security. The challenges here are also significant for development, as the emerging applications of IT have tended to be designed for residents of affluent Western societies, and not developed for the languages, cultures, values, and legal system of developing countries.

THE GEOGRAPHY OF ELECTRONIC INFRASTRUCTURE

The geographic context of the information economy is seen by Hepworth (1990) as the spatial structure of information capital, the physical distribution of computer networks and telecommunications systems. The telecommunications system connects concentrations of population and economic activity to facilitate interaction, with computer networks established on this technical backbone. The significance of this technical infrastructure is the marriage of telecommunications and computer technologies. As Hepworth (1990, p. 68) notes, '. . . the "synergy" arising from technological convergence in telecommunications and computers . . . entails turning our attention to computer networks'. The centrality of the technology directs attention to the individuals, firms, and governments that develop, manage, fund, and control these networks.

The term 'digital divide' is commonly used to refer to the disparity in Internet access and use by residents of a city or country. The digital divide is even more apparent when seen globally. The international disparity in access to ITs such as telecommunications and computers shows a dramatic gap between the developed world and the developing world. One way to capture levels of access is through the scale of the physical telecommunications and Internet infrastructure in each country. Kellerman (1993) notes the uneven distribution of telephones, and that as recently as the mid-1980s,

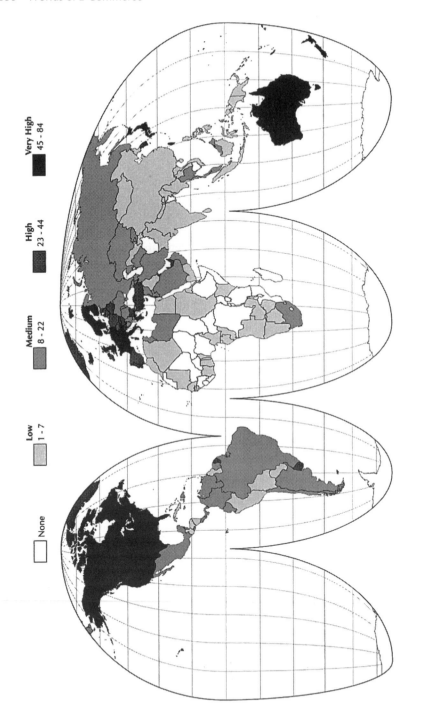

Figure 15.1   *Telephone lines: subscribers per 100 inhabitants. Source: ITU 1999a*

90 percent of the world's telephones were found in 15 percent of the country members of the International Telecommunication Union (ITU).

Patterns of IT Infrastructure

The ITU (1999a) estimates that the world's population of 6 billion people share 832 million telephone lines, or 14 telephone lines per 100 inhabitants. This varies considerably across the world, with a dramatic contrast between affluent and poor countries. The spatial pattern of telephony is illustrated in Figure 15.1, which maps telephone lines per 100 inhabitants for most of the world's countries. The most connected countries are also the richest, such as the USA and Canada (64 telephones per 100 inhabitants); Denmark (66 telephones); Germany (57); France (57); UK (55); Hong Kong (56); Singapore (56); and Australia (51). The highest level of telephone infrastructure is for the financial center of the Channel Islands with 77 telephones per 100 inhabitants.

The wiring of affluent countries contrasts dramatically with the state of telephone infrastructure for developing countries. Overall, Africa averages 2.2 telephone lines per 100 inhabitants, and many of those lines are concentrated in South Africa, which accounts or almost one-third of all telephone lines in Africa. At the lowest levels are the Democratic Republic of the Congo with 0.04 lines per 100 people, Chad (0.12), Niger (0.18), Rwanda (0.16), Somalia (0.14). A number of Asian countries also have low levels of access to telephones, for example Afghanistan (0.14 lines per 100 people), Bangladesh (0.26), Cambodia (0.23), Laos (0.55), and Myanmar (0.52). The poorest countries have less than 1 per cent of the telecommunications lines available to inhabitants of the richest nations.

Different patterns emerge when cellular services are included, although the disparity between rich and poor persists. Figure 15.2 maps cellular subscribers per 100 inhabitants for most countries. The ITU (1999b) estimates that the global rate of cellular subscription is 5.38 per 100 inhabitants. Cellular access is lowest in Africa (0.45 subscriber) and Asia (3.05); the level is far higher in the Americas (12.07) and Europe (13.15). While some countries have no cellular service, such as Chad or Niger, others have a significant cellular base. In Rwanda, more than half of all telephone services are cellular subscriptions. In many countries, cellular services account for more than a quarter of all telephone subscribers, for example: Côte d'Ivoire (35 percent cellular); Guinea (37 percent); South Africa (33 percent); Paraguay (42 percent); Venezuela (43 percent); Cambodia (71 percent); Hong Kong (46 percent); Japan (45 percent); Finland (51 percent). The USA has a cellular rate of 28.6 percent; Germany (23 percent); UK (32 percent); and France (25 percent). Globally 27.8 percent of all telephone subscribers are cellular services, which show significant presence in both the most and least developed nations.

The growth in telecommunications infrastructure has increased dramatically as costs have fallen. As an indicator of potential cost saving through technological advance, the US Federal Communications Commission (1999) reports that the first transatlantic cable, TAT-1 in 1956 had an annual investment cost of US$214000 per circuit, equivalent to US$2.44 per minute used. With the introduction of fiber optics and more advanced telephonic systems, the most recent transatlantic cable, AC-1 in

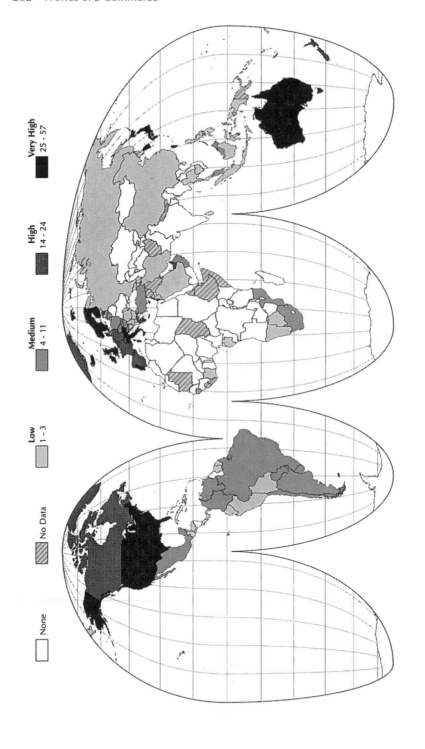

Figure 15.2 *Cell phone: subscribers per 100 inhabitants. Source: ITU 1999b*

1998, carried an annual investment cost of US$304 per circuit equivalent to US$0.003 per minute.

Technological advances and reduced costs have had a significant impact on revenue and traffic internationally. International traffic data for the USA from the US Federal Communications Commission (US FCC 1999) shows that the average revenue per billed international minute has declined from $3.11 in 1964 to $0.76 per minute in 1997. As prices fell, international calls have increased by an average of 17.7 percent annually between 1992 and 1997. World traffic in 1997 was 82 trillion minutes, of which the USA accounted for 27.6 percent. The cost of telecommunications in many countries has declined so much that for businesses and most individuals it is not a significant cost, nor does it exert major influence on operating behavior. Conversely, accessing a telephone can involve considerable expense given the purchasing power of residents of poor countries, especially in rural areas, with limited or no service.

The infrastructure of the Internet is harder to capture due to the very nature of the phenomenon, and the lack of central data gathering forces the use of proxies to capture levels of interaction and commerce. One way to illustrate the presence and scale of the Internet is to measure the density of hosts. The Internet Domain Survey, last conducted in January 2000, counts the number of IP addresses that have been assigned a name. Using hosts as a proxy for Internet presence is limited because it does not take into account the size or significance of each host. In addition, the naming system for domains means that not all hosts can be allocated to a geographic location. While many countries use an identifying suffix (such as .se for Sweden or .jp for Japan), there are also many domain names with nongeographic suffixes, such as .com, .org, and .net. Data will therefore tend to undercount American domains as most US domains do not use the .us identifier. In order to provide some correction for this, the US domains ending in .com, .org, and .net, for which a count is available, were incorporated into the calculations of the number of hosts per million population and presented in Figure 15.3.

[The spatial distribution of hosts follows an even greater level of concentration than the telecommunications infrastructure] with less than a dozen countries accounting for most of the hosts globally. In January 2000, the Internet Domain Survey estimated over 72 million hosts worldwide. Of these, almost 25 million were for .com and almost 17 million were .net. The leading countries in terms of hosts include Japan (2.6 million hosts), UK (1.9 million), Germany and Canada (1.9 million hosts each), and Australia (1.1 million). The level of hosts present in the USA is complicated by the lack of a geographic identification as part of most domain names and the range of alternate domains widely used, such as .edu and .org. The US military (.mil) domain is attached to more than 1.7 million sites, rivaling the level for Canada or Germany. Matthew Zook (2000) estimates that the USA accounts for two-thirds of the world's domains in January 2000, down from three-quarters in mid-1998.

To provide an indicator of host presence, the number of hosts per country is presented in terms of population. The leading countries are Finland (122 572 hosts per million inhabitants), Iceland (105 707), Norway (90 312), New Zealand (69 487), Sweden (67 189), and Denmark (63 571). Many of the largest economies make up in scale for the number of hosts, such as the UK (32 261), Japan (20 843), Germany (20 751) and the USA (24 683).

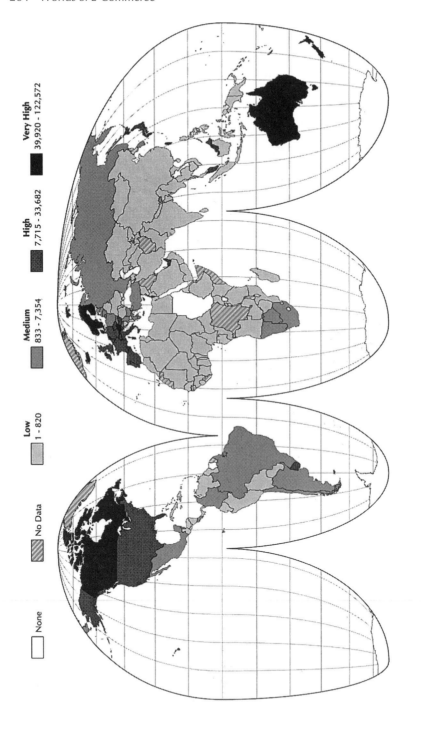

Figure 15.3   *Internet hosts per million inhabitants. Source: ITU 1999a; Internet Software Consortium 2000*

The lowest host presence occurs for 47 countries with fewer than 10 hosts, of which 15 countries did not have any hosts, including Zaire, Libya, Laos, Sudan, and Surinam. A number of countries also have much higher levels of domain presence than expected, such as Christmas Island, Nuie, Tonga, American Samoa, Turkmenistan, and Moldova, primarily due to the commercial attraction of the domain suffixes. Wilson (2000) notes the attraction of Nuie's .nu, meaning 'now' in Scandinavia, or Moldova's .md in demand by physicians in the USA, and the legal suggestion of trademarks with .tm for Turkmenistan.

INFORMATION TECHNOLOGY AND DEVELOPMENT

The relationship between IT and development has long been observed, with the most advanced countries having, and developing, the most advanced telecommunications infrastructure. The positive relationship between teledensities and GDP is discussed by Kellerman (1993) whose analysis suggests that developed countries tend to encourage telecommunications development, while less developed countries place less emphasis on this infrastructure given other development priorities and lack of access to capital. The relationship between telecommunications densities and economic development is evident when electronic infrastructure measures are plotted against GDP per capita. The data presented in Figures 15.1–15.3 are also presented in terms of GDP in Figures 15.4–15.6. Figure 15.4 presents telephone lines, Figure 15.5 shows cellular subscribers, and Figure 15.6 shows hosts per million in terms of GDP per capita.

In each of Figures 15.4–15.6 a clear and positive relationship emerges, with electronic infrastructure increasing with GDP per capita. The relationship is strongest for telephones, weakens slightly for cellular services, and is even weaker for Internet hosts. Correlation coefficients for telephone lines and GDP is .86, for cellular subscribers and GDP is .84, and for Internet hosts and GDP is .68. In noting this relationship care must be taken as to cause and effect. Wealthier nations may place a higher priority on electronic infrastructure and encourage its growth, or does the existence of the technology create a richer country? Kellerman (1993) notes the causality between telephones and increased income, but also states that the returns are far greater for less developed than developed nations. The contributions of enhanced infrastructure historically show a stronger return for poorer than richer countries due to the far greater marginal benefits present for less developed countries.

The contribution of electronic infrastructure to development has led most countries to introduce public policies designed to encourage the growth of their telecommunications infrastructure. IT development programs occur across the range of development. For example, during the 1980s Ireland completely renovated its telephone system with a digital network, as did Barbados, which introduced a digitalized communications system. In Asia, Singapore became a world leader in IT development, followed by Malaysia and Thailand, with most Southeast Asian countries now having national IT plans in place. Corey (1997, 1998) identifies the strategies used by Singapore and Malaysia to develop their IT infrastructure, while Rimmer (2000) explores telecommunications policy in Indonesia, and Wang (1999) notes how Taiwan has benefited from an aggressive policy to develop its information infrastructure which in turn has

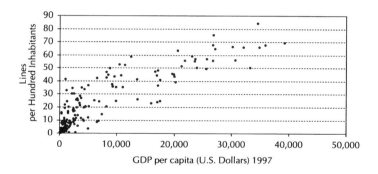

Figure 15.4   *Telephone infrastructure and development. Source: ITU 1999a*

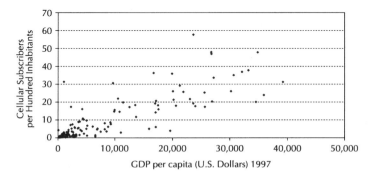

Figure 15.5   *Cellular infrastructure and development. Source: ITU 1999b*

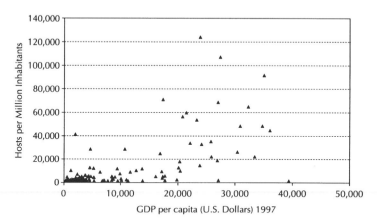

Figure 15.6   *Internet hosts and development. Source: ITU 1999a; Internet Software Consortium 2000*

opened up its knowledge industries. Jussawalla (1999, p. 232) concludes that with '. . . their policies of open economies and export-oriented investment in technology, the Southeast Asian Dragons have proven that such an approach generates increasing returns, trade surplus, and – in spite of the region's recent financial turbulence – can provide the basis for long term economic growth'.

In Africa, South Africa has an established policy for IT development (Hodge and Miller, 1997), and Mgombelo (1997) writes about Tanzania's plans for telecommunication deregulation and development. In North Africa, Kavanaugh (1998) examines trends in Tunisia, Morocco, and Algeria, finding the start of an information infrastructure, although recognizing its very high cost and limited accessibility by only a few scientists, educators, and government officials. The BBC (1999) reports that in late 1999 Somalia opened its first Internet Service Provider (ISP), which had 30 customers and expected to serve 100 accounts in the two largest cities in the country. The cost is high, however: 'The initial installation fee is $120 – the monthly income of some Somali families – while it costs $30 a month to rent a line, but even more exorbitant is the 75 cents a minute it costs to surf the Net'.

Latin America is seen as a major emerging IT market, in part developed by Spanish language e-commerce initiatives in the United States, and the long standing presence of US media and television outlets in South America. As in Africa, many are not able to access information technology. Reuters (1999) reports that the average Internet access cost in Argentina was US$54 a month, far more than in most developed countries, and that the average user was university educated and able to speak English. One successful approach to the high cost of Internet access is the trend in Brazil for free Internet access, led by firms, such as banks and automobile dealers, offering free access with sales of their products. To meet this competition, Brazilian ISPs have moved to a free service model, with one estimate being that 70 percent of users will have free access by the end of 2000 (*San Jose Mercury News* 2000). Costa Rica is using a public approach, with government launching a free e-mail service for all residents, using the public telephone company and post office as the foundation. Residents have Internet and e-mail connectivity in free five-minute blocks through PCs in post offices (Smith 2000).

The development of an electronic infrastructure is not a simple task, and many barriers remain for developing, as well as developed, countries. The same barriers to telecommunications development also apply to the Internet and e-commerce, and it is valuable to remind ourselves of the difficulties developing countries encountered as they initiated telecommunications systems. For example, in the 1950s and 1960s, Citibank in Brazil '. . . created a new job category known as "dialers" – squads of Brazilian youths who did nothing but dial phones all day long. Once a connection was made from Brazil to the United States, Citibank staffers would stay on the line reading newspapers or books, filibustering to keep the line open until someone actually needed it' (Webber 1993).

The Internet equivalent for the developing world is lack of access to ISPs in general, or the need to access distant service providers at very slow modem speeds. In some cases it is necessary to use modems to connect to ISPs in other countries in order to access e-mail and the WWW. Among the challenges confronted by developing countries seeking to advance their information infrastructure are:

1. Access to capital for the development of physical infrastructure, and the cost in terms of worsening terms of trade for developing countries as they seek to import new and costly technology.
2. Deregulating domestic and international electronic interaction, and confronting the monopoly power often held by PTTs in developing countries.

3. Confronting the political and economic implications of restructuring an industry in which governments often have a financial stake and also derive revenue and foreign currency (Melody 1999).

ELECTRONIC COMMERCE AND DEVELOPMENT

Electronic commerce is only a recent phenomenon, but one that merges a great deal of hype and promise. The power and scale of e-commerce is easily apparent to residents of affluent countries in North America, Europe, Asia, and Australia. The promise and scope of e-commerce as a development tool are only just emerging and lagging significantly behind the still unprofitable web industries of the developed world. Among the benefits of an electronic infrastructure, Mansell (1999) points to public sector applications, distance learning, health care, electronic contract tendering, and business information processing as major advantages. Negroponte (1999) also points out that e-commerce may provide ways for developing countries to bypass the traditional economic channels of commerce that have been closed to them.

Online commerce can be divided into two broad groups. One form of e-commerce is the use of the Internet and corporate intranets to manage information within and between firms. This firm-to-firm or business-to-business (B2B) interaction is important in many industries, and a significant source of savings as sourcing, accounting, and information is quickly and efficiently traded and utilized. In addition to B2B applications is B2C, or business to consumer online transactions. B2C takes the form of direct sales, in some cases by existing retailers using a new technology (Barnes and Noble selling books online), and in other cases by new firms established as online retailers (Amazon.com selling books online). A study by Computer Economics (2000) finds that e-commerce will be dominated by firms in North America, Europe, and Asia/Pacific, with these regions controlling 94 percent of e-commerce in 2000. Despite the challenges for developing countries, there is a range of motivations and reasons for exploiting an Internet presence.

First, the cost savings of B2B transactions online may allow production gains in developing countries as occurs in the developed world. Online B2B may allow much faster resolution of financial transactions and information flows than currently possible. Vonk (1997) emphasizes the value of international telecommunications and Internet networks for Shell Oil, while Rees (1997) finds similarly for the international aviation industry. For a major market, such as China, the benefits of B2B can be considerable, but the infrastructure is not yet in place. Only 10 percent of China's firms are online, which limits B2B applications, although the use of pagers and mobile phones is far greater and these technologies may offer an alternative approach (Romeo 2000).

Second, to protect and trade on a known corporate identity or brand name that captures the trust, goodwill, and name recognition firms have spent considerable time and money developing. In this case, an Internet presence may be simply an information source about a firm and its products, or serve as a sales outlet. Establishing a web presence may be competitive. As the web allows only one .com name globally, firms with similar names across several countries will be forced to compete for the best

WWW location. Previously, firms with operations in one country did not have to be concerned with similarly named firms operating elsewhere. On the web, similar names must be differentiated, most easily by country specific top-level domain names, which may also limit online expansion into other countries. A common complaint made about access to domain names is that the early development of the USA meant that American users and speculators have consumed the most popular domain names and also preempted firms from other countries with similar names.

Third, to establish a new corporate identity specializing in online services, such as online banking or travel services. The advantages of lower barriers to entry and transaction costs that attract online operations in wealthy countries may find parallels in developing countries, with the Internet offering new opportunities to serve existing needs or new markets. New entrants to South Korea, such as E*Trade Korea or Yahoo Korea, aim to develop their identities as portals for new markets. Softbank has also established new B2B firms, such as Alibaba.com in China to initiate new brands of online commerce. The International Finance Corporation of the World Bank and Softbank (www.soft-bank.com/sbem) have developed an emerging markets strategy to incubate Internet businesses in developing countries. Softbank Emerging Markets (SBEM) will provide seed money and expertise to entrepreneurs in developing countries with the goal of creating local versions of leading Internet companies.

Fourth, to provide information or propaganda about a product, firm, individual or country. The Internet provides an efficient and low-cost information system and allows locations and organizations to market themselves locally and internationally, and to be found through search engines. Romero (2000) offers the example of weavers in Guyana selling handwoven hammocks to an international market through the web (www.gol.net.gy/rweavers), which shows how the Internet can be used to export products. Information for tourism or events can be available online for much lower cost than the traditional printed matter mailed to those seeking information. The Internet offers opportunities for providing information and marketing abroad at much lower cost than was previously possible. The web also serves to inform or misinform and to be used as a commercial or political weapon against competitors. For example, Taiwan.com was registered by China.com, which is a web site owned in part by China's Xinhua, the state-operated news agency.

In addition to commercial and government initiatives, nonprofit organizations are actively seeking grassroots and low-cost alternatives to enhance access to telecommunications services in the poorest countries. For example, Bangladesh's Grameen Bank, renowned for its microlending program, has established both cellular telephone and Internet projects to provide income to entrepreneurs, who may own only one cellular telephone and sell calls to the public, and at the same time establish telecommunications services where none previously existed (www.Grameen-info.org). Grameen Telecom provides mobile phone service and aims to deliver telecom access to rural villages, either by offering loans to families to purchase mobile phones and sell calls, or by serving area institutions, such as schools and community centers. In 1996, the Grameen Bank started GrameenCyberNet to provide ISP services in Bangladesh.

Another nonprofit initiative is the Sustainable Development Networking Program (SDNP) (www.sdnpk.org) in Pakistan, which is supported locally and through the United Nations, providing Internet access and information online about sustainability issues. For SDNP, developing Internet linkages was a means to their goal of providing information on sustainable development, yet in order to reach their goal they had to become active in the establishment of electronic infrastructure in Pakistan, and train nonprofit organizations how to use the medium.

The Association for Progressive Communications (APC) (www.apc.org) is actively engaged with nonprofit organizations, many in Africa, seeking to develop their access to and use of IT. For example, South African APC member, SANGONeT, 'has been commissioned to build a web site which will connect 14 electoral commissions in the Southern African Development Community (SADC). This project aims to foster cooperation between its members in order to promote a culture of democracy and free and fair elections in SADC countries' (APC 2000a).

In Senegal, Cyberpop (www.enda.sn/cyberpop) shows how grassroots organizations established community development initiatives around information technology:

> The eight community groups chose two young people from the community to be trained by ENDA for five months to be the technical operators of the telecenters. The people chosen tend be university students, who act as an interface between the technology and illiterate community members. ENDA also trained the operators in information searches, adult education, community animation, group dynamics, techniques for social survey and impact assessment, and management of community centers.
>
> The Community Resources Centers provide access to e-mail and the Internet as well as support and training in word processing and database management and accounting. During the first year, the centers were equipped with phone and fax so that they could begin to earn some revenue and get experience of managing a community telecenter (APC2000b).

Challenges for Electronic Development

Electronic commerce also presents many challenges for development. There is the challenge of developing an infrastructure that reaches a critical mass of population who can then access online services. In most developing countries, online access is costly, and only available in the largest cities. The concentration of access points in major cities means that most people in a developing economy do not have easy access to telephone or Internet services. Where services are available, the cost is very high. For example, Kavanaugh (1998) calculates that a year of Internet access in Morocco would incur fixed costs of US$1150 plus a monthly charge that averages US$116. Even among OECD countries, access costs remain high, with the monthly cost of 20 off-peak hours per week being over US$70 in Hungary, Poland, and around US$55 in Portugal and the Czech Republic. This compares with the lowest rates of a little over US$20 in Italy and Finland and US$30 in the USA.

A study of the state of web sites in Africa by Yavo (1999) finds strong growth but still very few sites designed for African markets:

> Despite a very strong growth in the number of web sites and with the exception of South Africa, the number of web sites is still low. This is primarily due to: (1) the lack of appropriate (and expensive) Internet/computers/telecom infrastructures, (2) the lack of national regulations in the areas of copyrights/use of security and authentication mechanisms, (3) the lack of expertise in the area of web design, content production and management, and (4) the low awareness of the benefits that the Internet can bring and the risk management of the Internet activities of an organization.

Given differences in technology and use, it is highly likely that e-commerce will grow differently in developing countries, so that the models seen today in North America and Europe may not apply elsewhere. In their study of Latin American e-commerce, Jupiter Communications (2000) notes that: 'Low PC penetration, low credit card ownership and inefficient fulfillment mechanisms mean that businesses need to focus on alternative solutions. Access devices such as set-top boxes, banks facilitating e-commerce and the "piggybacking" of e-commerce onto existing retail outlets will mark the regional market'.

A byproduct of developing infrastructure for domestic firms to sell internationally also provides an entry point for international firms seeking new markets. Large firms with well-developed business models and capacities may easily be able to out-compete domestic firms in developing countries. It is possible that a large international retailer, such as Amazon.com, could make a significant impact on domestic sales if the cost differential is great between protected domestic sales compared to discounted international sales. As many developing countries lack the inventory and range of products found in affluent countries, online sales could challenge the existing distribution system for goods and services. In many countries, domestic firms need to prepare to compete with the large online retailers that are primarily based in the USA.

Another set of issues relates to the security and efficiency of online transactions, which is a challenge in all economies. Among the security issues is access to encryption technologies that currently are reserved solely for use in the USA and by US residents. Firms and governments outside the USA argue that not being able to access the most secure systems possible places them at a commercial and security disadvantage. A further factor is the existence of an established and workable legal environment that supports electronic commerce and quickly resolves disputes and contractual arrangements. Advanced economies have yet to establish a comprehensive legal framework for e-commerce, placing developing countries at a further advantage as they seek to develop their legal institutions. The currency of the Internet, the credit card, is not widespread in many countries, presenting a barrier to online e-commerce. A related issue can be the availability of hard currencies, with residents of countries with limited foreign exchange not able to access e-commerce.

Establishing a global e-commerce legal environment is a further challenge, with the structure designed by advanced economies with little or no input from the developed world. Johnson and Post (1997) note the problem of applying a legal system based on territory and jurisdiction to the Internet, and questions about the standing of copyright, intellectual property, and contract law. Burk (1997) examines digital piracy, and the ease of copying and distributing software without compensating the owners of the intellectual property. This issue is particularly relevant for developing countries, where there are few controls on intellectual property and the cost of official sources of software far exceeds the resources available.

The social context can often be the most challenging to the development of IT. For many developing countries, the impact of e-commerce may not be the direct financial benefits and costs, but the related implications of access to information. Opening up channels of e-commerce also opens up channels for news and information, which some governments and residents may see as a challenge to the established political or moral order. Finally, developing an information infrastructure has an opportunity cost that may be as basic as a well, a year of elementary education, new roads, or a vaccination program. The expansion of telecommunications in developing countries has long had a similar experience, of high-cost imported technology drawing on domestic development resources. The private sector can be encouraged and supported to provide the infrastructure, but that may also produce a monopoly or uncompetitive market. As governments in developing countries often own part or all of their PTT, they are often wary of increasing competition and compromising the stream of profits and hard currency.

CONCLUSION

New ITs offer many opportunities to developing countries as they make choices about their development. At the same time, the emerging electronic and commercial arena is new and emerging in even the most advanced countries. Developing countries are naturally wary of the power of IT, with fresh memories of past technologies that were used to reinforce divisions between rich and poor despite any accompanying rhetoric to the contrary. IT is presented all over the world as offering new ways of making progress and advancing our economies, but this comes at a high cost.

Many challenges lie ahead, not only for developing, but for all countries. Information economies and e-commerce demand: a global electronic infrastructure; the institutionalization of political, legal, trade, and financial relationships that smooth transactions; access to the technology, both in terms of physical access as well as the skills needed to navigate electronically; awareness of the 'digital divide' that occurs on many spatial levels, from community to globally; and the social acceptance of new technologies and economic activity.

One of the primary attributes of a well-developed electronic infrastructure is that it affords easy access, which brings closer the economic advantages possessed by places, in particular, new markets, low-cost labor or services inputs, and production cost advantages. IT is important, especially the connection of telecommunications and computers, precisely because it can open up new markets or allow new production possibilities. Harvey (1988, p. 124) reminds us, however, that: 'The problem of space is not eliminated but intensified by the crumbling of spatial barriers'.

Handwritten notes:

1) Global DD documented
2) Challenges faced by LDCs
   - Financing infrastructure
   - reluctant to deregulate PTTs
   - opp. costs (what else is foregone
   - enhanced competition from outside.
   - creating a matching financial/legal environ
3) Motivations
   · Firms benefit from an Internet presence

16

Corporate Nations: the Emergence of New Sovereignties

THOMAS M. EDWARDS

Microsoft Corporation, Redmond, WA, USA

INTRODUCTION

Some of us may recall a movie from the 1970s, one in which the rousing strains of Bach's Toccata and Fugue in D Minor played out among the setting of an indoor stadium built for the aggressive and violent sport known as Rollerball. What is interesting about this particular movie is not the sport, but the milieu in which the action occurs, a 21st century world controlled entirely by huge corporations, where athletes compete on behalf of corporations not countries, where corporate battles are symbolically fought in an arena instead of on a military battlefield, and where access to information is controlled wholly by the corporations who create and maintain the infrastructure. It plays like a piece of alarmist science fiction, but regardless of its place in time and artistic value, the movie tried posing some interesting questions to its audience: What is a corporation? How much power can/should it wield? Is the world heading toward a corporate-run power structure? Are nation-states going to become historical artifacts of a society based primarily on consumption of goods and information?

This discussion, while not about Rollerball or its world, is an exploration into the question of the tenuous and changing relationship between government, corporations, people, economy, and politics in light of a world being overrun by technological change and the new economic paradigm: e-commerce. The geopolitical landscape of the past several decades has seen an upheaval and redirection of the Westphalian model of nationality that is unprecedented in relation to the decades that came before. This includes with it the cultures, economies, and controlling philosophies that contribute to geographic differentiation. However, there is an emerging trend that reveals a strong movement of the power base away from the focus on simple territorial sovereignty and more towards one centered on economic control based upon virtual interconnectivity. Stated simply, this trend represents 'the receding power of the state relative to the global economy in mastering space' (Tuathail 1996, p. 251). Much attention in this area has already been assigned to the transnational corporations that have been growing exponentially in response to robust international markets demanding their goods and services. While this situation has worked well for the transnationals, it leaves open many questions as to how such corporate entities are affecting, altering, and shaping the territorial entities in which they thrive. By operating on such a global scale to generate a palpable e-commerce network, within and between geopolitical entities, the transnationals have in turn begun to operate with a degree of sovereignty that is analogous to sovereign nations when it comes to protecting their interests abroad.

This chapter is about the convergence of TNCs (transnational corporations) and nation-states in the context of new information spaces of interaction. First I briefly address the redefinition of geopolitics in order to provide a conceptual background for the components of 'sovereignty' and its meaning. The discussion then turns to Microsoft as an example of an evolving TNC and the role of cartographic representation in that transition. The notion of the 'corporate nation' is introduced as the evolution of both the nation-state and TNC, arriving with new spaces of interactions made possible through e-commerce and widespread IT. The discussion concludes with a brief exploration into other forms of sovereignty that could arise in the info-economic system and how they may affect our current perception of geopolitics and identity.

DEFINING INFORMATION GEOPOLITICS

Geopolitics has been a guiding discipline for helping to define various kinds of global political interactions, yet we need to be clear about the definition of the term as it is used in the context of this discussion. The term itself is often associated today with concepts or perceptions that do not always agree with Rudolf Kjellen's original intentions in 1899, but they do not necessarily have to conform – new times require new definitions. The classical definitions of geopolitics deal primarily with the notion of political spheres of influence, e.g. the Eastern Bloc, the West, and other supranational aggregations. However, with the dynamic political and economic changes of recent times, the definition of geopolitics has evolved from the classic Mackinder example. Critical geopolitical discourse seeks to use geopolitics as a filter for discerning the nature of the global power structure and its various influences on political, economic, and social systems. In this way, it helps to draw out the deus ex machina behind real world events. Geopolitics should not be viewed as a static study of political, economic, and social environments; we are no longer in the era where 'geopolitics rested on the realist theory of international relations, and on the geography of states' (Black 1997, p. 110).

When simplified, geopolitics recognizes a geographic effect from interactions in a political domain, as well as a political effect from interactions in a geographic domain. There are two 'spaces' of interaction defined here, one defined through physical and cultural geography, another defined through political regimes and the diplomatic craft. However, these spaces do not adequately support the much broader and complex range of interactions emerging from the political–economic system that is quickly developing, that is, the information-based economy. This lacuna is where yet another refinement of the definition of geopolitics is required, and that refinement is labeled **information geopolitics** (Edwards 2001). As with traditional geopolitics, information geopolitics addresses two 'spaces' of interaction, the geographic and the virtual (i.e. an information space as described by Johnson (1997, p. 12) and others), but they are two dynamics superimposed upon the existing geopolitical process. One dynamic describes the geopolitical effect (that is, the effect upon politics and geographic space) from interactions in the virtual information space, while the other dynamic describes the information space effect from interactions in the geopolitical space. Interactions in the information space are chiefly the conflicts between a global information context and local information contexts. Information geopolitics is an attempt to describe an emerging motivation behind a changing geopolitical landscape, the influence of information and representation on the realm of statecraft, sovereignty, and national identity.

Information geopolitics discerns the motivational relationship between state action and the persistence or even illusion of geopolitical representation and finding the 'boundary' in between (no pun intended). In one way, it represents something of what Foucault (1997, p. 50) talked about by saying there is 'a process of discerning those things which give light to our thoughts and practices that have not yet been revealed'. It operates within the context of a response of the local to the global; how does a local sovereign entity protect its sovereignty and the perception of its sovereignty in both the geopolitical and information spaces? After all, 'how a state views itself and the world becomes increasingly important as images, symbols, and actions are observed by others' (Brunn *et al.* 1994, p. 298). Conversely, it asks how transnational entities of global extent can gain access to the local without incurring cultural rejection. In either case, the resultant effect on geographic space may be the same as that in traditional statecraft: sanctions, diplomatic rebuke, expulsion or detainment of citizens, and potentially armed conflict.

Information-based causation of real, geographic action is tied to a definition of globalization proposed by Tuathail (1998, p. 76), in which globalization is a pervasive and inevitable ideology of transnational corporations and entities. As such, globalization and the emerging e-commerce form of economy becomes a key factor in information geopolitics. From the information geopolitics perspective, e-commerce is simply about bridging contextual differences between cultural and political realities, to invent a consumer-oriented culture where one did not exist or inadequately existed before. Globalization involves the creation of content and connectivity to a broad market while e-commerce is the transaction. Despite the hype about a completely borderless world, often illustrated by science fiction authors, well-funded think tanks, futurists, and popular media, authors such as Castells (1996, p. 98) caution us that 'there is not, and there will not be in the foreseeable future, a fully integrated, open world market for labor, technology, good, and services, as long as nation states . . . exist'. For all the technopunk glamour placed on the borderless, fully networked world hypothesis, geographic boundaries are still a viable concept. Try convincing occupants of the West Bank that boundaries are virtual and that their reality is information-based. Similarly, we must remember that information space is not necessarily a new concept, as Johnson (1997, pp. 11–15) and Rosecrance (1999) indicate. However, what is unique about the information space of our age is the degree of reality ascribed to it by individuals and cultures and their increasing 'belief' in the validity of this space. We have seen hints of this trend with the pervasiveness of radio and television in the past (the infamous Orson Welles radio broadcast of 'War of the Worlds' in 1938 can easily be compared in believability to the numerous 'urban legends' circulating daily via networks today). This change in mind set yields a motivational dynamic that can affect the real world, that is, actions taken in the information space (transactions of capital, goods, services, identity, propaganda, etc.) will have observable effects on geographic space – whether or not intended. The proposition that actions in geographic space are initiated on the basis of perceptions formed in the information space is one cornerstone of information geopolitics.

THE NOTIONS OF 'NATION' AND 'SOVEREIGNTY'

'What forces define the aggregation of people into a homogeneous political body that then declares itself "sovereign"? The concept of the nation-state needs to be revisited briefly in light of evidence telling us "the clarity of the state frontier is now fading because the exercise of sovereign authority in certain domains is becoming either very difficult or impossible"' (Anderson, 1996, p. 178). As Brunn *et al.* (1994, p. 292) also points out, 'the very definitions of state and nation are challenged by worlds made possible through advances in information and communication technologies'. How will the notion of the nation-state survive under the dynamic e-commerce mechanisms implanted locally by TNCs? This is a fundamental question because, up to this point in time, the Westphalian sovereign state model frames the concepts of trade and regulation – but will this always be the case?

There is no single, universally accepted definition for what defines a 'nation'. In fact, the terms 'nation-state', 'nation', 'state', and 'country' are often used interchangeably in many discussions (Table 16.1).

If one were to examine the many interpretations of the 'nation' idea, we are left open to accepting the presence of many possible nations in today's geopolitical landscape. In fact, in the so-called 'fourth world', 'estimates of the number of stateless nations in the world run as high as 9000' (Minahan 1996, p. xvi). The notion becomes clear that 'the nation is the basis of political legitimacy . . . all assume that the nation is bounded, that it has frontiers' (Anderson 1996, p. 42). To be more accurate, a 'nation-state' is a nation that wholly controls its geographic space and by so doing has obtained its sovereign status. So the generic 'nation' definition can be refined to reflect the 'nation-state' as follows:

1. People: a homogeneous group that demonstrates a national consciousness.
2. Space: a geographically defined area exclusively controlled by the governing body.
3. Authority: an organizing, governmental body that solely represents the national interests beyond its borders.

The nation-state serves as the fundamental geopolitical entity through which international political and economic systems interact, evolve, and conflict and as such their

Table 16.1   *Common definitions of a 'nation'*

Term	Encarta World English Dictionary definition
Nation-state:	an independent state recognized by and able to interact with other states, especially one composed of people who are of one, as opposed to several, nationalities
Nation:	a community of people or peoples who live in a defined territory and are organized under a single government
State:	a country or nation with its own sovereign independent government
Country:	a nation or state that is politically independent, or a land that was formerly independent and remains separate in some respects

Source: *Encarta® World English Dictionary* © & (P) 1999 Microsoft Corporation. All rights reserved. Developed for Microsoft by Bloomsbury Publishing Plc.

overarching power hammer called 'sovereignty' needs to be critically examined. This is very important to consider since 'in the broad sweep of history, nation-states have been a transnational form of organization for managing economic affairs' (Ohmae 1995, p. 141). Do the conditions of human nature that allow geographic sovereignty – the people, space, and authority – hold any significant meaning in an information-based economy. In the face of rapidly changing technology and the increased presence of global information among local societies through mere exposure to e-commerce outlets, it is not human nature that is changing but rather the outcome. Cultural identities continue to remain strong in many regions, yet without a doubt, 'the processes of economic modernization and social change throughout the world are separating people from longstanding local identities. They also weaken the nation state as a source of identity' (Huntington, 1998, p. 161).

Kenichi Ohmae's commentaries on the conditions of nation-states and the emerging information commerce reveal this change in the human behavior. As he points out:

> It is a new kind of social process, something we have never seen before, and it is leading to a new kind of social reality: a genuinely cross-border civilization, nurtured by exposure to common technologies and sources of information, in which horizontal linkages within the same generation in different parts of the world are stronger than traditional, vertical linkages between generations in particular parts of it' (Ohmae 1995, p. 38).

This could be a temporary trend, a transitional step as technology is further introduced into many aspects of life on the small and large scale beyond Western culture. Marketing and merchandising experts have realized for decades that the key to revenue – anywhere in the world – is creating identity-building relationships between consumers and products. The more the local individuals identify with global information and products, the less strength the local forces of identity creation will possess. Ohmae concludes his point by mentioning 'as more and more individuals pass through the brutal filter separating old-fashioned geographies from the global economy, power over economic activity will inevitably migrate from the central governments of nation states to the borderless network of countless individual, market-based decisions' (Ohmae 1995, p. 39). What we begin to see in an e-commerce world is a social phenomenon where the individual and small interests become potential 'players' in the broader system. Brunn (1998, p. 114) concurs that 'the growing importance of information and communications producers is positioning a new group of actors who will have a great influence on state and non-state decisions'. Commonality – through physical or virtual interaction – is a strong identity-building experience for individuals. Undoubtedly, nation-states will desperately attempt to regulate the degree of the globalization of its people by restricting information flow or technological implementation. But as some local markets have already proven, the forces of information piracy and transborder information flow far exceed any government's ability to enforce identity.

Consider this pertinent and recent example from Microsoft's presence in Iceland. The Windows$^©$ operating system can be found in practically every country in the world, in fact it is a cornerstone of much of the global e-commerce activity. For its primary markets (those with the highest revenues), Microsoft produces language-specific versions such as British English, French, German, Japanese, and so forth. Iceland is a fully developed, mature country that values its information infrastructure as much as anyone else, perhaps more so being geographically remote. But when Microsoft initially decided not to produce an Icelandic language version of Windows 98 because of the relatively small market size compared to the production cost, the local government was concerned. Iceland maintained a strict language-preservation program for decades, trying hard to not allow foreign terminology to be introduced without undergoing a thorough conversion to Icelandic, no matter how prevalent those terms may be outside of Iceland. But because Windows was an essential technological dependency in this computer-literate society and its release in Iceland was to be only as an English version, Icelanders feared the impending flood of non-Icelandic computing terminology polluting their language barriers. In summary, they stated that this 'has everything to do with the shamanistic powers computers seem to exercise over the minds of the young and with the marketing strategies of far-away Microsoft' (Walsh 1998). Eventually, Microsoft did utilize this prime public relations event and decided to localize Windows 98 into Icelandic even though the revenue margins were slim compared to a larger market (Figure 16.1). The corporate strategy to provide a desired technology to a specific culture for the long-term gain of new consumers is abundantly clear; even citizens of remote Iceland can be good consumers if given the e-commerce tools – in their language.

If individuals are conditioned over time by exposure to more global information to disregard the importance of geographic space and resultant identity, then the perceived need for territorial control will diminish. Knight (1994, p. 215) emphasizes that 'territory is more than just a physical and measurable entity. It is also something of the mind because people impute meaning to and gain meaning from territory'. In light of this, we must not overlook the role that cartography plays in reinforcing identity and geographic control. It is a well-known fact that 'claims to an identity between people and territory can be asserted through maps and extended back through time' (Black 1997, p. 143). Maps have served for centuries as spatial surrogates for the abstract spatial concept that we cannot see in the real world – the nation-state. We can cognitively perceive evidence of the existence of a nation-state – the homogeneity of the people, the flag flying overhead, the different language, the currency – all symptoms and symbols of statehood. But at the level of the individual, what really differentiates the stars and stripes from the Nike swoosh or cans of cola? Thinking on this level we

Figure 16.1 A Windows 98 advertisement in Icelandic. Source: Microsoft Corporation

can see that 'even if a few states can still defend their territory against an invading army . . . none can control the flow of images and ideas that shape human tastes and values. The globalized "presence" of Madonna, McDonald's, and Mickey Mouse make a mockery of sovereignty as exclusive territorial control' (Krieger 1993, p. 853).

When one realizes that 'the political boundaries of nation-states are too narrow and constricted to define the scope and activities of modern business' (Korten 1996, p. 125) we begin to discern the forces working against nation-states and cultures, made worse by widespread government inability to comprehend the new spaces of transaction made possible by technology. Even though 'sovereign states have only reluctantly surrendered parts of their sovereignty to supranational groups since the 1950s' (Cole 1983, p. 233) the trend of governments yielding a degree of their spatial sovereignty to a supranational group for the purpose of solidarity in economic and military control is ever-increasing, with the advent of the European Union, and other economic alliances such as GATT, NAFTA, ASEAN, OECD, ECO, and so forth. As sovereign governments work toward an unprecedented level of cooperation, they are quickly discovering that TNCs are already operating at a level of technological sophistication and market penetration that is far beyond the vision of most nation-states. National governments thus scramble to respond with attempts at greater transborder regulation, e-commerce laws, anti-virus task forces, and the possibility of taxation of nongeographic-based business transactions.

There is no question that TNCs have become much more politically active to protect their proprietary interests within nation-states, but is it true that 'all over the world, national, provincial, and local governments have become pawns of global corporations and the Corporate Agenda?' (Brecher and Costello 1998, p. 301). What we must understand is that the basis for international exchange of information, goods, and services is fundamentally shifting from geographic space to virtual information and economic spaces. Nation-states were designed to control geographic space, while TNCs design and control global economic space. Some may argue, as an example, that the Microsoft and US Department of Justice confrontation is not about monopolistic practices at its core, but rather about the USA trying to assert sovereignty over an economic space that it never really had any real control over. TNCs enjoy an almost untouchable status when observed from the geographic space perspective; they appear to have a degree of freedom beyond the law, but the reality is that the unwritten survival laws of the virtual e-commerce space are of Darwinian proportions. Does this mean that the role of a national government is diminishing to the point where it only serves as an unwitting tool for TNCs? When governments begin to legislate or take other formal actions against TNCs at an increasing rate, the perception is that the nation-states are beginning to understand the nature of the global e-commerce and are taking action to secure their role within it, if not as technological innovators alongside TNCs then as technological regulators.

What is becoming clear is that 'the greater the political power of corporations and those aligned with them, the less the political power of the people, and the less meaningful democracy becomes' (Korten 1996, p. 140). This is an issue about stakeholders in the old and new models of spatial control. The old model stakeholders would cringe at Hugill's (1999, p. 2) revision of Mackinder's premise: 'if information is power, whoever rules the world's telecommunications system commands the world'. Meanwhile, the new model stakeholders revel in concepts like 'personal empowerment', 'digital freedom', and 'wireless worlds'. Due to increasingly advanced information technology (IT), the primary unit of spatial interaction is becoming the region, the small group, and even the single individual acting by his/her own accord, within a 'personal sovereignty' that is essentially granted to them as consumers in the e-commerce system. When national societies reach this most intrinsic, personal level, people will connect, interact, aggregate, and socialize according to common factors that transcend nationalism, at which point the significance of the nation-state as a source of personal identity will diminish. This does not infer the disappearance of geographic boundaries, but rather the shift in focus from geographic space to virtual spaces of new interactions.

TRANSNATIONAL INFORMATION

At the global scale, TNCs are fiercely positioning themselves as not only the primary builders of the e-commerce model, but as gateways to information and creators of

content – regardless of nation-state agendas. The notion that 'multinational corporations and nation-states are key actors in shaping the direction of the information
economy' (Carnoy 1993, p. 8) is true; the information economy is not the result of any
one player and certainly not the conception of any single politician or businessperson.
How one views TNCs depends chiefly upon where one stands as a stakeholder in the
perception of future gain from a new economic model. TNCs create the global
information infrastructure while nation-states act as the top-level regulatory systems
with which TNCs must negotiate – but this is typically viewed by TNCs as a 'speed
bump', a local trade filter through which they will pass. Most TNCs realize that 'the
success of an industry or region is not the function of a nation per se, but of the
particular combination of individuals, institutions, and culture in this industry or that
region' (Ohmae 1995, p. 64).

E-commerce is built upon a fundamental suite of IT that is the domain of TNCs,
which realize the three main advantages that can be gained from implementing IT: '(1)
to compress time, (2) to overcome geography, and (3) to alter the structure of relationships, such as bypassing intermediaries' (Malecki 1997, p. 208). The idea of overcoming
geography by the use of high-speed telecommunications and networks goes beyond
the obvious high-speed transmission of information between locations. Stated even
more clearly, information is 'the raw material of the economic process, itself quite
indifferent to space, because the technologies of information transmission are now
supposedly approaching the point where the friction of distance is nil' (Storper 1997,
p. 237). The elimination of distance and the diminution of geographic space are key
factors that characterize the global information economy, for as Brunn (2000, p. 58)
states, 'places that are widely separated in absolute space may not be in the same
communication and time space'. It is in virtual information space, an economic space,
and other nongeographic spaces that TNCs can be found, along with a growing host of
individuals and emergent nations that are finding a home on the global networks for
the purpose of economic gain or (re)assertion of identity.

The process of globalization allows TNCs 'to look for ways to sell their product in as
many different places as possible' (*The Economist* April, 1998, p. 69). If they happen to
disrupt local customs and practices, it is not by conscious intention but by the virtue of
their hegemonic global presence interacting on a local level. TNCs should realize that
a disruption of culture, language, mores, and even sovereignty will occur because
TNCs operate from the global information context. Minimizing the effects as much as
possible should be a primary goal if they value market share, but the information 'war'
between the global and local is being waged now and eventually the conflict between
the global and local will be stabilized. Some fundamental issues to be resolved will be:
Who builds the information economy locally, and globally? Who regulates it? Who
controls access to the system? By what conditions? Will digital information access
become an expected, universal personal freedom?

THE GEOPOLITICS OF KNOWLEDGE MANAGEMENT

How do these issues relate to what is happening on the front lines of e-commerce-
building and globalization? Technology-related TNCs are working very hard to build

their proprietary visions for global e-commerce and consumer access to information. First, realize that we are no longer talking about *if* the information-based economy and society will flourish – it is here. The question is how and by whom. One burgeoning field is that of systems and knowledge management, viewing the total 'solution' of providing infrastructure and content and then delivering on the promise. Microsoft, to the appreciation of some and consternation of others, has been a leader in the development of e-commerce infrastructure built upon a broad knowledge management strategy. From the Microsoft perspective, knowledge management is 'about embracing a diversity of knowledge sources, from databases, web sites, employees, partners, and cultivating that knowledge where it resides, while capturing its context and giving it greater meaning through its relation to other information' (Microsoft Corporation 1999).

Knowledge management is a solutions-based model for how the vast, global interconnectivity of the information space can be leveraged for individual and organizational benefit and it serves as one major aspect of Microsoft's .NET$^©$ strategy where software is not just a product to be packaged and sold, rather it is a service. This is clearly a business-oriented model, but it is not far removed from the practice of the nation-states, especially when we consider that 'the state itself is in the "business" of producing, consuming, disseminating, and even manipulating information about a multitude of products, including those about the natural and knowledge R and D worlds' (Brunn 1998, p. 108). There are many existing barriers to the adoption of knowledge management strategies, but it is not what most people would guess – it is neither the lack of technology nor the lack of need. The primary roadblock to implementation is cultural resistance (Figure 16.2). This is a non-trivial barrier to overcome, but as the economy based on e-commerce further develops with both TNCs and nation-states adopting these strategies to compete on equal ground, we will see the cultural factor resolved, the perceived benefit will eventually outweigh the perceived cultural cost as the value of such technology will be incorporated into local cultural values.

A key part of Microsoft knowledge management is the notion of the digital nervous system$^©$ (DNS). A digital nervous system, put simply, is the way in which information is managed within a homogeneous organization on the small and large scale, whether in one's home, in a corporation, or even within a country (Gates 1997). It is important to be aware that the DNS, like any other by product of a particular organization or national entity, is the DNS for a particular cultural and political information context. If one imagines the eventual existence of many DNSs distributed globally then the interaction of information between context-dependent DNSs can produce a geopolitical crisis, at first in the virtual information space and then, if escalated, to the geographic space.

So if we now view information geopolitics in a world interacting more frequently via information commerce between different contexts we yield a slightly different definition: the political ramifications of a global information context interacting with a local information context. The terms 'global' and 'local' are used here to define the context of scale – information used and/or accepted transnationally as compared to information that remains locally significant – to a country, to an organization, or to any particular group of people. The global information context is the information considered gen-

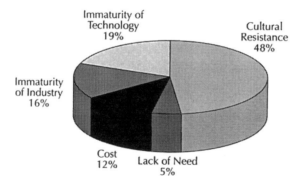

Figure 16.2 Barriers to knowledge management implementation. Source: Microsoft Corporation 1999

erally acceptable on a global basis, it is the 'international' viewpoint or the shared opinion among nation-states and citizens. Mathematics and science are good examples of this, but so is a bottle of Coca-Cola or the image of Mickey Mouse. The local information context contains strong references to local 'reality' that may conflict with the global viewpoint, which could include: geographic facts, historical facts, the naming of people or features, the appearance of a map, etc. For example, declaring Canada as the country that contains the hydrologic feature Hudson Bay is an accepted, international fact that could pass from geographic context to geographic context without challenge. However, declaring a single country as the sole sovereign power over the Senkaku Islands will undoubtedly face opposition from the local information contexts involved with the dispute. [The Senkaku Islands are a group of very small islets northeast of Taiwan that are claimed by China, Taiwan, and Japan. They are the site of frequent student 'occupations' and subsequent removals by Japanese government forces.]

The Microsoft Example

Microsoft realizes, as most TNCs do, that in order to please the customer you must deliver according to their expectations, and this applies to packaged products as well as online web content. Microsoft uses the terms **globalization** and **localization** to refer to the processes through which products and services are tailored for local markets. Globalization is a methodology by which products are cleansed of local information and the product is prepared for international consumption, from the user interface, to the icons, to the menus; that is, to put the product into a global information context. Localization is the process wherein a globalized product is then prepared for local consumption, usually through translation from US English to whatever target local language (e.g. Icelandic). The true aim of localization embodies 'achieving a balance between being global, with the scale advantages associated with size and global scope, and being local within each regional or national market and network of resources' (Malecki 1997, p. 202). But localization is more than just language translation as content is localized as necessary to fit the local information expectations of that market and to fit in within the local context. Microsoft takes great care to study its market geography and analyze the best market penetration strategy, but problems inevitably arise that relate to the breakdown of the appropriate 'interface' between the global information context contained in the Microsoft products and the local information expected in the market. This breakdown can be caused by a number of factors, not the least of which is the lack of geographic understanding. The information producer is in the wrong geographic context to be effectively communicating to another geographic context. While this concept is a well-known diplomatic reality for nation-states, it is new to TNCs and their world; local culture is an often overlooked consideration.

The history of geopolitical errors at Microsoft is a gallery of localization events where the crucial global–local information interface was not diligently established in order for e-commerce to flow freely. Some of the mistakes can be traced to an ignorance of simple world geography on some individuals' parts (which in itself is a commentary on the state of geography education in the USA, but this will not be touched upon here). Other mistakes were a pure lack of local knowledge that probably could not have been foreseen. The majority of the bigger problems Microsoft has encountered involved cartography in its various products, from Windows$^{©}$ to Office$^{©}$ to Encarta World Atlas$^{©}$. This makes a lot of sense, because 'maps can serve as tools of debate, highlighting these spatial implications and thus apparently providing graphic evidence of the nature of the practice of power and of what can be seen as a need to challenge it' (Black 1997, p. 120). Microsoft is aware that in some countries, one of the first things customs agents will examine are the maps in the products – they load the program onto their computer, open it up, and take a look to see if Microsoft's global information is acceptable to the local information market. In other countries, it is true that 'unofficial maps, such as those made by or for one of the parties to a legal dispute, are sometimes admitted in court' (McEwen 1998, p. 19). In Latin American countries, this legal complication can include any cartography sold in the country, regardless of the source, which then makes Microsoft a contributor of evidence in a potential, real-world boundary arbitration, for or against their target market! Microsoft is then forced to make a market decision: comply with the local information needs and change the product, or, bypass the local information market completely and proceed to sell in those nation-states who will accept the globalized information.

Consider a few key examples of geopolitical problems that Microsoft has faced:

Product: Windows 95$^{©}$ – 1995
Location: India
Background: The original specification for Windows 95$^{©}$ included a time zone map, in which users could select their specific country's time zone and the country would be highlighted and outlined on a small bitmap image. The outline for India was lacking the highly sensitive Jammu and Kashmir region, by only a few pixels. This was enough to cause the government of India to ban Windows 95$^{©}$ until the country outline was fixed. The solution involved removing all country outlines from the map completely and showing a borderless world map in the time zone feature. This was hyped up in the media and was generally embarrassing for Microsoft.

Product: Encarta World Atlas$^{©}$ and Encarta Encyclopedia$^{©}$ – 1996
Location: Republic of Korea
Background: This was a case where the revelation of one error in Encarta World Atlas$^{©}$ (EWA) unleashed a public backlash and the uncovering of more errors in Encarta Encyclopedia$^{©}$ (EE). It started initially with a border error on the China/North Korean border, at a location that has high spiritual significance for Koreans. The Encarta World Atlas$^{©}$ map showed the sacred features to be completely within China, which was offensive to the Koreans. After research, it was learned that a border agreement had been reached some time ago between China and North Korea that established a border running through the features, giving half to North Korea and half to China. This fact was not reflected on Microsoft maps, which were using older data from the US government. After more accurate maps defining the new border were received, the data in EWA was fixed – despite the Korean public's claims that Microsoft was conspiring with Japan to undermine Korean culture! Other map issues were the sensitive Liancourt Rocks (aka Tok-do, Take-shima), as well as the lack of the 'East Sea' label for the Sea of Japan.

Product: Several Products, including Windows$^{©}$, Office$^{©}$, Encarta$^{©}$, etc.
Location: China and Taiwan
Problem: The contentious issue between China and Taiwan is a difficult roadblock to companies trying to sell products in both locations, and Microsoft has been no exception. Any hint of Taiwanese sovereignty and independence in a version distributed in China will reap restrictions from the Chinese government. Microsoft has been questioned by the PRC over the unintentional use of the phrase 'Republic of China' for Taiwan. The company, along with other TNCs, has been threatened by China with major sanctions if the government finds any more depictions or descriptions of Taiwan as being a 'country' or in any way independent.

These cartographic examples are very terse glimpses of what a TNC like Microsoft faces when attempting to establish a global e-commerce consumer base. If the potential risks of market penetration outweigh the benefits, then Microsoft may forsake the market in favor of another one of less risk. Some nation-states are more adamant about enforcing their sovereignty, and they do so by reinforcing their local information standard. The reasons for choosing not to enter a market are complex, but in the end it is a decision based on information-based geopolitics. Microsoft, as a producer of knowledge management strategy and globalized content, is unwilling to become embroiled in a dispute over competing local information contexts.

Microsoft strives to avoid the situations where its products and services are being employed as tools for local geopolitical agendas, and it attempts at all turns to reach a fair compromise between differing local information contexts. Microsoft is always taking steps company-wide to be more attentive to these issues, such as through the Geopolitical Product Strategy (GPS) group. The GPS mission is to help protect Microsoft's global markets against closure and in turn preserve local market trust in Microsoft's product integrity. The real challenge, as dictated by information geopolitics, is to proactively discern the proper interfaces between the global and local information contexts long before the products are produced and shipped. This task is the challenge Microsoft and many other TNCs face during the process of globalization and localization (or glocalization as some have come to call it).

In many of the geopolitical issues at Microsoft, the nation-state struggles to reassert its sovereignty over geographic space in the information space. Indeed, they exemplify the truth that 'our very concept of "world", an ideological construct that is usually more philosophical than geographical in content, can be framed and articulated by cartography' (Henrikson 1999, p. 95). Governments are fully aware of the power of cartography, and more so, the power of the global information venue provided by TNCs. Savvy national governments will strive to use TNCs as a means to escalate their local information context into the global information context. Why? If a country is successful in convincing a TNC to incorporate its local context into the global information stream, then that country's local context is globally legitimized, and possibly at the expense of neighboring local contexts that might disagree. When uninformed, the TNC can be played as an ignorant participant in spatial misinformation on the global scale through the use of its own e-commerce mechanism. However, here another interesting dimension comes into play. In order to establish itself and gain access to a local market, a TNC may consciously favor one local information context on the basis of market revenues. The TNC gets what it is really after – the larger revenues from a favored market, and appeases at least one local information market in the process. In fact, clearly biasing itself toward one local context may improve the TNCs ability to thrive in that single market, more than if it had compromised between two or more local contexts. So there are times when a TNC may decide to opt for the conscious inclusion of a particular local information context into its global scheme.

The nation-state, with its unique local information context, is then in the position of having to compete with other nation-states to assert themselves into the global information context via TNCs. Because TNCs are not only the creators of this global information venue but primarily the administrators of it, nation-states struggle to reaffirm their sovereignty in a world where real boundaries, territorial control, and the notion of sovereignty are challenged by e-commerce, globalized information, and technologically empowered individuals.

NEW SOVEREIGNTIES IN INFORMATION GEOPOLITICS

Consider the major trends outlined so far and how they relate to the role of nation-states and TNCs in information geopolitics:

1. *Information access.* The profusion of IT on a global scale and a subsequent, unprecedented level of individual access to knowledge, particularly with the recent advent of 'wearable' computers and portable technology.
2. *Redirection of identity.* People becoming more connected with individuals in other countries than with their own nationalistic tendencies.
3. *Power of image.* Geographic territory becoming less important as compared to information access and the control of the image of territory (e.g. maps).
4. *Nations as corporations.* National governments yielding control to intranational

bodies to form economic alliances to control information flows, protect local information contexts, and drive economic development.

5. *Corporations as nations.* Transnational corporations acting as conveyors of global information, providers of identity, diplomats of the 'global', choosing to accept/reject local contexts as part of the global information system based on market viability.

6. *Global v. local.* Nation-states jockeying for access to the global information stream, each trying to assert its own local context as being globally significant, or else forfeiting the local context in favor of the global one.

These trends solidify the supposition that 'the past two decades have seen the most rapid and sweeping institutional transformation in human history. It is a conscious and intentional transformation in search of a new world economic order in which business has no nationality and knows no borders' (Korten 1996, p. 121). It is evident that both nation-states and TNCs are performing similar roles in the evolving information economy. Up to the present time, nation-states have been pursuing their individual 'manifest destinies' and exercising their right to self-determination as gained through their sovereign status in geographic space. Likewise, TNCs have been fulfilling their own destinies, mastering and controlling the information space and e-commerce. When nation-states realize the advantages of the borderless TNC, they come to realize that 'technological capacity gives many states the possibility of operating beyond boundaries, including space' (Krieger 1993, p. 853). Nation-states, like individuals, are beginning to experience a form of technological empowerment that is applicable beyond the ability to wage war.

Both nation-states and TNCs maneuver for strategic economic positions, and both adopt similar business tactics and both rely heavily on IT as a means to this end. The key difference is that nation-states work in a geographic and political space, while TNCs operate in an economic and information space. But these spaces are converging – political with economic, geographic with information, and so forth. As a result, we may witness a convergence of the nation-state and TNC in both form and function. On one side the nation-states attempt to maintain their sovereign perspective, while on the other side the TNCs attempt to globalize information and homogenize national citizens to create a good pool of transnational consumers. The goal of the two players is essentially the same: maintain the transnational citizens as consumers of your state's/corporation's information. What is also emerging is the role of the individual and communities in dictating how the large, global players can interact in the shared information space. The status of 'global consumer' is an empowerment; nation-states and TNCs are creating customers and thus must respond to them as such. And to these global customers, the expectations on the nation-state and TNC will be the same as in any business; provide what is needed or they will shop elsewhere; it does not matter if it is 'shopping' for the latest DVD or for a solid nationalistic identity.

Corporate Nations

So what becomes of the nation-state and the TNC when citizens are better informed, less ignorant, and are self-aware of their role in the global info-economy? And what becomes of the citizen, the homogeneous groups, and stateless nations of people? In the immediate future, one can foresee a possible evolution of the nation-state and TNC into what is called here a **corporate nation**. The corporate nation synthesizes the powers of the nation-state and the TNC, creating a new geopolitical entity within the context of information geopolitics. A corporate nation is an entity less concerned with geographic space and more concerned about connecting with individuals as consumers of information. A corporate nation is a transnational entity, spreading a global information context that overrides local contexts whenever possible for the purpose of generating e-commerce. Of course, certainly not every TNC shares the same vision of a global information system and, as stated before, all information is ultimately context dependent. Therefore, corporate nations may have slightly differing approaches to the global information context.

People

Individuals are empowered by technology, able to make free consumer choices regardless of local geographic contexts and related limitations. An individual becomes a de facto citizen by using the corporate nation's goods and services. An individual has the right to switch allegiances if the corporate nation fails to provide goods and services as expected. Local cultural rules are viewed as a temporary marketing barrier that will be overcome, or a local 'interface' to the culture that can be exploited.

Space

Geographic space is where consumers physically exist and where resources (skills, raw materials, etc.) for product manufacture are available. Information space, economic space, and other virtual transaction spaces are where the corporate nation thrives and truly exists.

Authority

In corporate nations, a form of government is necessary as an interface to other domains of information goods and services. The status of being the government of a nation-state yields no more clout than being the CEO of a TNC – it is simply a condition of management, it does not matter if it is based on geography, information, people or products.

A corporate nation's sovereignty is based on factors fundamentally different from nation-states (Table 16.2). It guards its sovereignty over information and economic space through a vigorous assertion of its right to self-determination – the right to innovate, to expand, to brand, and to continue to provide services and information on a global basis without impedance from local nation-states. Self-determination is chiefly driven by the desire for financial gain, but it may also include a genuine desire to improve quality of life for the local market and/or a vision to better the world as a whole. For a nation-state, becoming a corporate nation means relinquishing sovereignty over their unique local information context and embracing a global context in order to be competitive. This will be a 'brutal filter' for nation-states, particularly ones that build national identity on 'folk' culture (i.e. historical imagery). For the TNC, becoming a corporate nation involves the adoption of state-like accountability and responsibility for the actions they take. A corporate nation represents itself on the international scene and cannot hide behind the protective laws of its host nation-state (with which it will probably compete).

While a corporate nation might have some geographic territory in its possession, the entity primarily acts in the information space, i.e. it exists through the information products it generates and disseminates. In this way, the real citizens of the corporate nation are not necessarily the end-users of the products; it is the products themselves. Much criticism has been leveled at TNCs for disregarding the welfare of local national citizens; the Seattle riot in December 1999 over the World Trade Organization meeting is a strong indication of public backlash over this issue. If true, this would only reinforce the concept that is carried over to a corporate nation: the products are the citizens and it is the duty of the corporate nation to protect its citizens abroad. Over time, as more and more localities build their digital nervous systems, the precedent of accepting these 'virtual citizens' (i.e. products) will be well established. Undoubtedly, just as with TNCs and nation-states today, the corporate nation will take all necessary action to protect its citizens and keep them viable in and between their targeted markets. It is extremely doubtful one will ever see a corporate nation positioning company warships off the coast of a nation-state, but it is very likely that a corporate nation may cut off access to global networks or withdraw some vital information infrastructure services from a nation-state in order to reinforce its position. A corporate nation can turn the table and let the 'sovereignty' of its information prevail in a globalized market existing in the information space. What if the corporate entity refuses to sell needed information infrastructure to a nation-state? What if a TNCs information product continues to reinforce the virtual existence of ideas in opposition to the nation-state's – in every nation outside of the target state, in schools, in homes, in news sources? In the end, who will be the real victor in this 'battle' without a single bullet ever being fired?

The corporate nation is not too dissimilar from an existing TNC, but it is a form of convergence for both the TNC and the nation-state. The implication is that the current nation-state will have to evolve more than the current TNC in order to become a corporate nation. TNCs already have an advantage in the global markets because, as stated before, they are chiefly responsible for creating the infrastructure upon which the markets are built. But more than the technology itself, what is really at stake for the nation-states is their sovereignty based on their control of territory (geographic space). This notion will change over time, and in the final analysis, the nation-states which make the transition into the global information economy and become more of a corporate nation will simply be corporate nations with control over some geographic space – a distinction from nonterritorial corporate nations that may not be very substantial from the info-economic perspective. This notion is similar to what Rosecrance (1986) mentions about the existence of two types of nation-states: trading states focused more on economic expansion and trade, and territorial states based more on acquiring and exploiting territory and requiring a military presence. In this proposed model, a new schema would perhaps arise with geographic nations, information nations, economic nations, and so forth, emphasizing once again that sovereignty no longer requires geographic territory to be valid.

A Spectrum of New Geopolitical Entities

As the global information economy develops further into the future, we will see unique roles evolve for the primary players of the former geopolitical model, and more than just the corporate nation. The corporate nation is proposed as a next plausible development for nation-states and TNCs. The convergence of the geographic and information spaces, and the subsequent empowerment of previously nonplayer groups in the global economy will allow for many new types of geopolitical interaction.

New players will enter the information geopolitics scene and new roles in the system will be possible. We may see many roles being performed by many diverse geopolitical entities, widely ranging in scale and power, and also varying in the amount of technological adaptation that has taken place. While the primary fuels of the system – information and technology – will be more clearly defined as commodities, the acting players and their interactions will become very complex. The spectrum proposed here is based on a notion of scale, starting with the single individual citizen and propagating the concept to the highest aggregation possible, the global state. In a way, this is a significant elaboration of the 'virtualization continuum' suggested by Rosecrance (1999, pp. 43–55), but with an emphasis on aggregations of people and communities, not the change in status of a static entity. Table 16.2 provides a brief summary.

The implications of such a system are prodigious, but this is only one possible model. This is not a strict hierarchy with a simple transition from one state of existence to the next. Many of these new entities will exist unto themselves with no need to evolve, while others may aggregate and expand. When viewing this possible system, 'we need to ask again about the ways in which electronic information and mapping technologies are reconfiguring the contemporary world . . . the techniques of data exchange and representation legitimize new social practices and institutions in ways we have only begun to recognize and regulate' (Pickles 1995, p. 231). At this point in time, we can only begin to surmise what kinds of geopolitical entities may arise in response to the e-commerce shift that is underway. The key point is that a system that may allow such geopolitical entities is emerging. Whether or not any new forms of sovereignty and identity evolve will depend on the outcome of current, dynamic battles, such as:

- The contest for economic control between nation-states and TNCs.
- The competition for cultural control between the global and local information contexts.
- The emergence of sovereignty on new social and political levels, seen through a struggle between individual freedoms and national oppression in the name of state security.

In the course of this discussion, not a great deal of emphasis has been directly placed on the concepts of geographic boundaries and territoriality. Being byproducts of a geographic space of interaction however, the implications are clear. If a fully globalized

Table 16.2 *New geopolitical entities arising out of an InfoEconomy*

	People	Territory	Government
Individual	A citizen empowered by information technology; an information user with a distinct identity.	The virtual networks; a virtual 'home', local geography	Adheres to the local information context as a convenience while accessing the global.
Community	A group of citizens united with a common identity; information users and distributors.	Shared virtual spaces, neighbourhoods, and small regions.	Builds its own local context while accessing the global.
Nation	A homogeneous aggregation of individuals and clans, united by a common identity or purpose, connected via information technology; creates, distributes, and uses information.	Large, distributed virtual spaces, possible geographic space.	Self-determining with its own local context, with its own global access
Info-nation or Virtual nation	A virtual nation-state, comprised of a people, virtual territory, and a governing system; maintains a unique information domain.	A nation without geographic territory; possesses a well-established, influential virtual presence. Sovereignty is based on control of information.	Self-governed nation, answering to itself on a virtual basis. New local context is created, or, a new interface to the global context within a local one.
TNC	A transnational business operation established for the purpose of creating, disseminating and controlling information technology.	Exists both real and virtually, distributed across many geographic contexts. May be based in one nation-state.	Follows nation-state regulations as much as necessary to penetrate local markets. Thinks globally, acts locally.
Nation-state	Classic definition: a defined people, geographic territory, and government body.	Exists geographically – sovereignty is based on control of territory.	Governments exist to regulate and legislate, to protect national citizenry (i.e., reinforce the local context).
Corporate nation	A unified corporate body of individuals, together for the purpose of succeeding in the global economy	Exists virtually or geographically or both; geographic territory is secondary to control of information assets	Self-governing, tolerates nation-state governments (local contexts) as a hindrance, interfaces better with other corporate nations (other global contexts).
Supranation	An aggregation of nations, info-nations, nation-states, and/or corporate nations, based on common goals and regional information contexts.	Virtual or geographic, the space is an aggregation of individual national entities.	Control is relinquished to a higher body for decision making, local contexts are aggregated into regional contexts for better interface to the global context.
Global state	A fully aggregated political–economic system wherein the global information context has absorbed all local information contexts.	Exists virtually and geographically, de facto control over most territory – despite possible rogue nations.	Disaggregated sovereignty is gone; self-determination exists only at the highest level by a governing body.

info-economy is realized, and individuals, regardless of geographic location, social capacity, and mobility are connected to it, we are likely to see a decrease in the overall emphasis placed on territory and borders. That is not to say that boundaries will cease to exist under the new economic and political model – not at all; this discourse is not advocating a borderless world. In fact, borders will continue to be necessary delineations in geographic space for the purpose of control, for social control, political, economic, and otherwise. The geopolitical entities that arise out of the information-based model, corporate nation or not, will still require a basis for control in order to conduct and maintain business. Under the Westphalian nation-state model, that basis was geographic territory. Under the information geopolitics model, that basis may include geographic territory, but it is more likely to be based in other 'spaces' as well, chiefly the information and economic.

CONCLUSIONS

The road to corporate nation is ready to be traveled, even though the current geopolitical paradigm is in the process of adapting to the info-economy. Are TNCs and nation-states the only viable candidates for this kind of transition? In reality, it is a possibility ripe for many varied forms of organization. Within the TNCs label, we could include the many global financial institutions, telecommunications companies, computer hardware and software manufacturers, and a plethora of others. But what of academic institutions, centers of learning and knowledge (e.g. libraries), biological and technological think tanks, and nongovernment organizations (NGOs)? All of these are key centers of information development that will likewise find empowerment through e-commerce. By developing their own spatial destiny or through partnering with TNCs, corporate nations, and others, they may fully realize the economic potential of their depositories, research, and proven data mining methods.

As for citizen-consumers, their position in the information economy is conditionally secure. They are a necessary and fundamental piece of the system, upon which the success and failure of both TNCs and nation-states are based. Yet how much independence and freedom of choice will individuals truly maintain in a well-packaged information world where TNCs, nation-states, and other powers seek to create information consumers in their image? It may be true that the TNC 'strategy for creating global markets depends on a systematic rejection of any genuine consumer autonomy or any costly program variety – deftly coupled, however, with the appearance of infinite variety' (Barber 1996, p. 116). If so, individuals will need to find an exit from the prefabricated information spaces and develop their own spaces of interaction. The advent of portable devices and wireless networking can make this more of a possibility as it removes confinement to regulatory boundaries imposed by various authorities. Individuals will always find ways to adapt and modify e-commerce tools and methods to their advantage, and in the end most will prevail as independent information consumers. If perceived as necessary, some may even resort to cyber-terrorism as a negative assertion of personal sovereignty in information space; the May, 2000 global attack of the 'Love Bug' virus is one such example.

There are many remaining barriers that can prevent global e-commerce from reaching the point at which corporate nations and other entities can emerge and thrive. Some of these barriers are sadly blatant, such as the fact that 'more than 1.3 billion people live on less than a dollar a day, about 60 percent of them in South Asia and Sub-Saharan Africa. Infant mortality rates remove over 90 per thousand live births in Sub-Saharan Africa and 70 in South Asia, compared with 40 in East Asia' (World Bank 1997, p. 4). Or equally troubling is that 'in far too many countries the private sector continues to struggle under severe trade restrictions and high taxes. Poor public infrastructure acts as a drag on market efficiency by increasing costs, reducing competitiveness, and restricting access to domestic and international markets' (World Bank 1997, p. 38). While one may find Coca-Cola in a poor country, this is by no means an indication that the country is benefiting from the presence of a TNC, or that this nation-state is poised to transition into a corporate nation. In addition, there exist many contentious and unresolved territorial issues in some areas of the world that will exist due to long-standing cultural and political differences. The adoption of an information-based economy and society will not likely bring any of these geopolitical flash points to a peaceful conclusion in the near future, although the affect of generating commonality between the two sides will be powerful.

There are several directions from which to proceed from this discussion. A more in-depth analysis of the reality of information geopolitics, for example, is necessary for a theoretical framework upon which the exploration of info-economic sovereignties can proceed (the forthcoming Edwards (2001) text will attempt this). Just as important, however, is a critical examination of alternative cultural perspectives on e-commerce: an exploration into the local information contexts and how they perceive information technology, TNCs, and the role of nation-states. Much research and development is undoubtedly pursued from Westernized notions of globalization and IT, but there is great value in analyzing the cross-cultural aspects of e-commerce. Are East Asian consumers really the same as Europeans? How do Sub-Saharan African cultures view these issues, as a potential economic promise or continued Western economic colonialism? These are issues that Microsoft and others in the software development field, for example, are only now beginning to address.

We are living in a time of transition and as such, there will be both positive and negative results. Regardless of one's perspective on the outcome, it is prudent for individuals, nation-states, and TNCs to realize that 'the production of information is shaping politics and, by default, establishing new rules for postindustrial society' (Barnet and Cavanagh 1994, p. 334). The author does not adhere to the illusion that the current global system is a only small step away from the world of corporate nations as outlined here; it is quite unlikely we will be seeing Rollerball competitions between Microsoft and Sony! However, the potential exists for a larger and more significant role of corporations in the political–geographic spaces and for nation-states in the information–economy spaces. As we focus our attention on the state of geopolitics and the future viability of nation-states and transnational entities in an information-based economy, let us carefully consider what new geopolitical rules are being written, and who will be writing them.

NOTE

The ideas and opinions expressed by the author in this text do not represent any official ideas and opinions of the Microsoft Corporation.

References

Aaronson, D. and Housinger, K. (1999) The impact of technology on displacement and re-employment. *Economic Perspectives* (Federal Reserve of Chicago), **23**, second quarter, 14–30. (Chapter 1)

ABN–AMRO (1999) *Wire or Shop? E-Commerce and Retail in the Netherlands* (in Dutch). Amsterdam: ABN–AMRO. (Chapter 10)

ABN–AMRO, *Annual Reports* (various years). Amsterdam: ABN–AMRO. (Chapter 10)

Adams, P. (1998) Network topologies and virtual place. *Annals of the Association of American Geographers*, **88**, 88–106. (Chapter 5)

Adams, P.C. (1997) Cyberspace and virtual places. *Geographical Review*, **87**, 155–71. (Chapter 5)

Agnew, J. (1998) *Geopolitics: Re-visioning World Politics*. New York: Routledge. (Chapter 16)

Agnew, J. and Corbridge, S. (1995) *Mastering Space: Hegemony, Territory, and International Political Economy*. London and New York: Routledge. (Chapter 12)

Akers, M.A. (1998) Congress may make gambling on the Internet a federal crime, [http://www.sunherald.com/casinos/docs/intgam012898.htm]. (Chapter 14)

Alessandrini, P. and Zazzaro, A. (1999) A 'possibilist' approach to local financial systems and regional development: the Italian experience. In Martin, R. (ed.), *Money and the Space Economy*. Chichester: John Wiley, pp. 71–92. (Chapter 10)

Almond, G.A. and Verba, S. (eds) (1963) *Civic Culture: Political Attitudes and Democracy in Five Nations*. Princeton: Princeton University Press. (Chapter 14)

Amaha, E. (1999) Japan's mobile-phone users link to the Internet. *Far Eastern Economic Review*, **12**, August. (Chapter 6)

Amazon.com. (1998) Amazon.com acquires three leading Internet companies, 13 August [http://www.amazon.com]. (Chapter 3)

American Electronics Association (1999a) *California Cybercities: California's Hottest High-Tech Metropolitan Areas*. Washington, DC. (Chapter 1)

American Electronics Association (1999b) *CyberEducation: U.S. Education and the High Technology Workforce, A National and State-by-State Perspective*. Washington, DC, April. (Chapter 1)

American Electronics Association (1999c) *Cybernation: The Importance of High Technology Industry to the American Economy*. Washington, DC. (Chapter 1)

American Electronics Association (1999d) *Cyberstates 3.0*. Washington, DC. (Chapter 1)

Americans for Responsible Alcohol Access (2000) [http://www.araa.org]. (Chapter 14)

Amin, A. (1999) An institutionalist perspective on regional economic development. *International Journal of Urban and Regional Research*, **23** (2), 365–78. (Chapter 8)

Amin, A. and Graham, S. (1997) The ordinary city. *Transactions of the Institute of British Geographers*, New Series, **22** (4), 411–29. (Chapter 8)

Amin, A. and Thrift, N. (1992) Neo-Marshallian nodes in global networks. *International Journal of Urban and Regional Research*, **16** (4), 571–87. (Chapters 8, 13)

Andersen, A. (1999) Geographic differences in Internet access among corporate executives narrows, [http://www.ac.com/news/5.99/news_051199.html]. *Andersen Consulting News*, **11**, May. (Chapter 6)

Anderson, M. (1996) *Frontiers: Territory and State Formation in the Modern World.* Oxford, UK: Polity Press. (Chapter 16)

Andressen, M. (1997) Future of the Internet. Address at the National Press Club, Washington, DC, 20 June. (Chapter 1)

Angel, D. (1989). The labor market for engineers in the U.S. semiconductor industry. *Economic Geography,* **65,** 99–112. (Chapter 7)

Angelides, M.C. (1997) Implementing the Internet for business: a global marketing opportunity. *International Journal of Information Management,* **17** (6), 405–19. (Chapter 8)

Antonelli, C. (ed.) (1992) *The Economics of Information Networks.* Amsterdam: Elsevier Science Publishers. (Chapter 7)

APC (2000a) Building free and fair electoral processes in South Africa, [http://www.apc.org/english/news/archive/sn_003.htm]. (Chapter 15)

APC (2000b) Collective access to technology for poor Senegalese neighborhoods, [http://www.apc.org/english/news/archive/enda_001.htm]. (Chapter 15)

Arai, Y. and Yamada, H. (1994) Development of convenience store system in Japan, 1970s–1980s. In Terasaka, A. and Takahashi, S. (eds), *Comparative Study on Retail Trade: Tradition and Innovation.* Conference Proceedings of the IGU Commission on the Geography of Commercial Activities, Tokyo and Kobe, 9–13 September 1993. Ibaraki: Ryutsu Keizai University. (Chapter 6)

Arnum, E. and Conti, S. (1998) Internet deployment worldwide: the new superhighway follows the old wires, rails, and roads. *INET '98 Proceedings.* Reston, VA: Internet Society, [www.isoc.org/inet98/proceedings/5c/5c_5.htm]. (Chapter 5)

Arrowsmith, C.A. and Wilson, M.I. (1998) Telecom tectonics using geographic information systems. *Cartography,* June, **27,** 1–8. (Chapter 15)

Arthur, B. (1989) Competing technologies, increasing returns, and lock-in by historical events. *Economic Journal,* **99** (394), March, pp. 116–31. (Chapter 6)

Arthur, B. (1994) *Increasing Returns and Path Dependency in the Economy.* Ann Arbor: University of Michigan Press. (Chapter 10)

Arthur, B. (1996) Increasing returns and the new world of business. *Harvard Business Review,* July–August, 100–109. (Chapter 10)

Arthur, W.B. (1994) *Increasing Returns and Path Dependence in the Economy.* Ann Arbor: University of Michigan Press. (Chapter 3)

Asia Computer Weekly (1999) Thailand starts on the E-commerce track, 5–11 July, p. 6. (Chapter 8)

Åslund, A. (1998) Russia's financial crisis: causes and possible remedies. *Post-Soviet Geography and Economics,* **39,** 309–28. (Chapter 12)

Atkinson, R. (1998) Technological change and cities. *Cityscape: A Journal of Policy Development and Research,* **3** (3), 129–71, [www.huduser.org:80/periodicals/cityscpe/vol3num3/current.html]. (Chapter 5)

Audretsch, D.B. (1998) Agglomeration and the location of innovative activity. *Oxford Review of Economic Policy:* 18–29. (Chapter 10)

Bagley, M.N. and Mokhtarian, P.L. (1999) *The Role of Lifestyle and Attitudinal Characteristics in Residential Neighborhood Choice.* Department of Civil Engineering, Davis: University of California. (Chapter 2)

Bailey, J.P. (1997) The economics of Internet interconnection agreements. In McKnight, L.W. and Bailey, J.P. (eds), *Internet Economics.* Cambridge, MA: MIT Press, pp. 155–68. (Chapter 5)

Baker, A.M. (1997) The Global Socio-Economic Controversy of United States Public Policy for Internet Gambling, (January), [http://www.siue.edu/~albaker/Inetgaming.htm]. (Chapter 14)

Bank for International Settlements (1999a) *Central Bank Survey of Foreign Exchange and Derivatives Market Activity, 1998.* Basel. (Chapter 11)

Bank for International Settlements (1999b) *Statistics on Payment Systems in the Group of Ten Countries.* Basel. (Chapter 10)

Banker, The (1997) Facing up to the public, September. (Chapter 10)

Banker, The (1999a) The dawn of a new e-economy. July. (Chapter 10)

Banker, The (1999b) Top 1000, July. (Chapter 10)

Bar, F. and Murase, E. (1998) Charting cyberspace: a U.S.–European–Japanese blueprint for electronic commerce. *Transatlantic Trade Cooperation in Asia: Sectors, Issues, and Modalities.* Washington, DC: Council on Foreign Relations. (Chapter 3)

Barber, B.R. (1996) *Jihad vs McWorld: How Globalism and Tribalism are Reshaping the World.* New York: Ballentine Books. (Chapter 16)

Barnet, R.J. and Cavanagh, J. (1994) *Global Dreams: Imperial Corporations and the New World Order.* New York: Simon and Schuster. (Chapter 16)

Barrett, R. (1997) ISPs deny pornography liability. *Inter@ctive Week* (13 May), [http://www5.zdnet.com/zdnn/content/inwk/0415/inwk0048.html]. (Chapter 14)

Barro, R.J. and Sala-i-Martin, X. (1992) Convergence. *Journal of Political Economy*, **100**, 223–51. (Chapter 2)

Barua, A., Pinnell, J., Shutter, J. and Whinston, A.B. (1999) Measuring the Internet economy: an exploratory study. Presented at Brookings Institution Workshop on E-Commerce, September 1999, [http://www.brookings.org/es/research/projects/productivity/workshops/19990924]. (Chapter 5)

Batty, M. (1993) The geography of cyberspace. *Environment and Planning B: Planning and Design*, **20**, 615–16. (Chapter 7)

Batty, M. (1997) Virtual geography. *Futures*, **29**, 337–52. (Chapters 3, 5)

Batty, M. and Barr, B. (1994) The electronic frontier: exploring and mapping cyberspace. *Futures*, **26**, 699–712. (Chapter 7)

Bayers, C. (1999) The inner Bezos. *Wired*, March 1999, 115ff. (Chapter 9)

BBC (1999) Somalia to go online, BBC News, [http://news.bbc.co.uk/hi/english/world/africa/newsid_459000/459319.stm]. (Chapter 15)

Beaverstock, J.V., Smith, R.G. and Taylor, P.J. (2000) *World-City Network: A New Meta-geography? Annals of the Association of American Geographers*, **90** (1), 123–34. (Chapter 11)

Bell, D. (1973) *Coming of the Post-Industrial Society: A Venture in Social Forecasting.* New York: Basic Books. (Chapter 6)

Bell, T.W. (1999) Internet gambling: popular, inexorable, and (eventually) legal. *Policy Analysis*, No. 336 (8 March), [http://www.cato.org]. (Chapter 14)

Berkman, H. and Hayes, L. (2000) The role of floor brokers in the supply of liquidity: an empirical analysis. *Journal of Futures Markets*, **20**, 205–18. (Chapter 13)

Berkman, H., Bradbury, M. and Magan, S. (1997) An international comparison of derivatives use. *Financial Management*, **26**, 69–79. (Chapter 13)

Bernstein, J.R. (1997) 7-Eleven in America and Japan. In McCraw, T.K. (ed.), *Creating Modern Capitalism: How Entrepreneurs, Companies, and Countries Triumphed in Three Industrial Revolutions.* Harvard University Press, pp. 493–530. (Chapter 6)

Berry, B.J.L. and Parr, J.B. (1988) *Market Centers and Retail Location: Theory and Applications.* Englewood Cliffs: Prentice-Hall. (Chapter 4)

Beyers, W.B. and Lindahl, D.P. (1997) Strategic behavior and development sequences in producer services businesses. *Environment and Planning*, A, **29**, 887–912. (Chapter 7)

Bianco, A. (1997) Virtual bookstores start to get real. *Business Week Online*, 27 October, [http://www.businessweek.com]. (Chapter 3)

Bicknell, C. (1998) Here comes AltaVista. *Wired News*, 13 October, [http://www.wired.com/news/news/business/story/15589.html]. (Chapter 9)

Biederman, D. (1998) Who benefits from Bolero? *Traffic World*. 16–18 November. (Chapter 11)

Bikker, J.A. and Groeneveld, J.M. (1998) Competition and concentration in the EU banking industry. *DNB Staff Reports 26.* Amsterdam: De Nederlandsche Bank. (Chapter 10)

Binder, L., Pye, L.W., Coleman, J.S., Verba, S., LaPalmobara, J. and Weiner, M. (1971) *Crises and Sequences in Political Development.* Princeton: Princeton University Press. (Chapter 14)

Black, J. (1997) *Maps and Politics.* Chicago, IL: University of Chicago Press. (Chapter 16)

Blasi, J., Kroumova, M. and Kruse, D. (1997) *Kremlin Capitalism: The Privatization of the Russian Economy.* Ithaca: Cornell University Press. (Chapter 12)

Blejer, M. (1998) Financial crisis in Russia: a comment. *Post-Soviet Geography and Economics*,

39, 329–31. (Chapter 12)

Boardwatch (1999) *Boardwatch Magazine's Directory of Internet Service Providers*, 11th edn. Golden, CO: Penton, [boardwatch.Internet.com/isp/index.html]. (Chapter 5)

Bodnar, G., Hayt, G. and Marston, R. (1998) Wharton survey of financial risk management by U.S. non-financial firms. *Financial Management*, **27** (4). (Chapter 13)

Boltanski, L. (1975) Les usages sociaux de l'automobile. *Actes de la Recherche en Sciences Sociales*, **1**, 25–49. (Chapter 2)

Boone, P., Breach, A. and Johnson, S. (1998) Institutions and prospects for a currency board in Russia: perspectives on a deepening crisis. *Post-Soviet Geography and Economics*, **39** (7), 371–8. (Chapter 12)

Booz Allen and Hamilton and Ministry of Economic Affairs (2000) *The Competitiveness of Europe's ICT Markets. The Crisis Amid the Growth. Ministerial Conference*, 9–10 March 2000, Noordwijk, the Netherlands. (Chapter 10)

Bransten, L. (1998) There's more to E-commerce than just the lowest prices. *Wall Street Journal Interactive Edition*, [http://interactive.wsj.com]. (Chapter 3)

Brecher, J. and Costello, T. (1998) Reversing the race to the bottom. In Tuathail, G., Dalby, S. and Routledge, P. (eds), *The Geopolitics Reader*. London: Routledge, pp. 299–304. (Chapter 16)

Brenner, N. (1997) Global, fragmented, hierarchical: Henri Lefebvre's geographies of globalization. *Public Culture*, **10** (1), 135–67. (Chapter 8)

Brenner, N. (1998) Global cities, glocal states: global city formation and state territorial restructuring in contemporary Europe. *Review of International Political Economy*, **5** (1), 1–37. (Chapter 8)

Brohman, J. (1996) Postwar development in the Asian NICs: does the neoliberal model fit reality? *Economic Geography*, **72**, 107–30. (Chapter 12)

Bromley, R.F. (1980) Trader mobility in systems of periodic and daily markets. In Herbert, D.T. and Johnston, R.J. (eds), *Geography and the Urban Environment: Progress in Research and Applications*, vol. 3. New York: John Wiley, pp. 133–74. (Chapter 4)

Brown, J. (2000) MP3 free-for-all, [http://www.salon.com/tech/feature/2000/02/03/napster/index.html]. (Chapter 3)

Brugge, R. (1991) Logistical developments in urban distribution and their impact on energy use and the environment. In Kroon, M., Smit, R. and van Ham, J. (eds), *Freight Transport and the Environment*. Elsevier: Amsterdam. (Chapter 2)

Brunn, S.D. and Leinbach, T.R. (eds) (1991) *Collapsing Space and Time: Geographic Aspects of Communication and Information*. New York and London: HarperCollins Academic. (Chapters 4, 5)

Brunn, S. (1998) A treaty of silicon for the Treaty of Westphalia? New territorial dimensions of modern statehood. *Geopolitics*, **3** (1), 106–31. (Chapter 16)

Brunn, S. (2000) Human rights and welfare in the electronic state. In Wilson, M. and Corey, K. (eds), *Information Tectonics*. Chichester: John Wiley, pp. 41–64. (Chapter 16)

Brunn, S.D. and Cottle, C.D. (1997) Small states and cyberboosterism. *The Geographical Review*, **87** (2), 240–58. (Chapter 1)

Brunn, S., Jones, J. and O'Lear, S. (1994) Geopolitical information and communications in the twenty-first century. In Demko, G. and Wood, W.B. (eds), *Reordering the World*. Boulder, CO: Westview Press, pp. 292–318. (Chapter 16)

Brynjolfsson, E. and Smith, M.D. (1999) Frictionless commerce? A comparison of Internet and conventional retailers. Paper presented at Understanding the Digital Economy: Data Tools and Research Conference, 25–26 May 1999, Washington DC. [http://www.digitaleconomy.gov/]. (Chapter 9)

Bryson, J., Henry N., Keeble D. and Martin R. (eds) (1999) *The Economic Geography Reader*. Chichester: John Wiley. (Chapter 10)

Budd, L. (1995) Globalisation, territory and strategic alliances in different financial centres. *Urban Studies*, **32**, 345–60. (Chapter 13)

Budd, L. (1998) Territorial competition and globalisation: Scylla and Charybdis of European cities. *Urban Studies*, **35**, 663–85. (Chapter 13)

Burk, D.L. (1997) The market for digital piracy. In Kahin, B. and Nesson, C. (eds), *Borders in Cyberspace*. Cambridge, MA: MIT Press, pp. 205–34. (Chapter 15)

Bush, J. (2000) Russia's new dawn? *Business Central Europe*, March 2000. Website edition. [http://www.bcemag.com/y2000/mar00/cover/0003cover.htm] March 20, 2000. (Chapter 12)

Business Times, The (1999) Singapore consumers nearly quadruple net-spending, 8 November, p. 14. (Chapter 8)

Business Week (1998a) Amazon's wild world, 21 December, 70–4. (Chapter 9)

Business Week (1998b) The 21st century economy, 24 August, pp. 58–71. (Chapter 7)

Business Week (1998c) Saying adios to the office: telecommuting, 12 October, pp. 152–3. (Chapter 7)

Business Week (1999a) Going, going, gone, 12 April, pp. 30–1. (Chapter 7)

Business Week (1999b) The Internet economy, 22 February, pp. 40–2. (Chapter 9)

Business Week (1999c) In the ring: eBay vs Amazon.com, 31 May, pp. 48–55. (Chapter 9)

Button, K.J. (1991) Transport and communications. In Rickard, J.H. and Larkinson, J. (eds), *Long Term Issues in Transport*. Avebury, Aldershot. (Chapter 2)

Button, K.J. and Nijkamp, P. (1998) Economic stability in network industries. *Transportation Research E*, **34**, 13–24. (Chapter 2)

Buyske, G. (1998) Foreign investment and political economy in Russia. In Kahler, M. (ed.) *Capital Flows and Financial Crises*. Ithaca: Cornell University Press, pp. 229–46. (Chapter 12)

Cabot, A.N. (1998) Testimony before the National Gambling Impact Study Commission (21 May), [http://casino.aw.com/links/cabot_testimony.html]. (Chapter 14)

Cairncross, F. (1997) *The Death of Distance: How the Communications Revolution Will Change Our Lives*. Cambridge, MA: Harvard Business School. (Chapters 5, 10, 11, 12)

Capello, R. (1994) *Spatial Economic Analysis of Telecommunications Network Externalities*. Aldershot: Avebury. (Chapter 10)

Carl, J. (1999) The imprecise art of tracerouting. In Boardwatch (1999a), *Boardwatch Magazine's Directory of Internet Service Providers*, 11th edn. Golden, CO: Penton, pp. 22–5, [boardwatch.Internet.com/isp/summer99/tracerouting.html]. (Chapter 5)

Carnoy, M. (1993) Multinationals in a changing world economy – whither the nation-state? *The New Global Economy in the Information Age*. University Park, PA: Pennsylvania State University Press. (Chapter 16)

Carter, D. and Sinkey, J. (1998) The use of interest rate derivatives by end-users: the case of large community banks. *Journal of Financial Services Research*, **14**, 17–34. (Chapter 13)

Castells, M. (1989), *The Informational City: Information Technology, Economic Restructuring and the Urban–Regional Process*. Oxford: Basil Blackwell. (Chapters 5, 8)

Castells, M. (1993), The informational economy and the new international division of labor. In Carnoy, M., Castells, M., Cohen, S.S. and Cardoso, F.H. (eds), *The New Global Economy in the Information Age: Reflections on Our Changing World*. University Park, PA: Pennsylvania State University Press, pp. 15–43. (Chapter 8)

Castells, M. (1996) The Rise of the Network Society. *The Information Age*, vol. 1. Oxford: Blackwell. (Chapters 5, 6, 7, 8, 11, 12, 16)

Castells, M. (1997) *The Information Age*, vol. II: *The Power of Identity*. Cambridge: Blackwell. (Chapter 12)

Castells, M. (1998) *End of Millennium. The Information Age: Economy, Society and Culture*, vol. 3. Oxford: Blackwell. (Chapter 11)

Castells, M. (1999) Grassrooting the space of flows, *Urban Geography*, **20** (4), May, 294–302. (Chapter 6)

Castells, M. and Aoyama, Y. (1993) *Paths Towards the Informational Society: A Comparative Analysis of the Transformation of Employment Structure in the G-7 Countries, 1920–2005*. Working Paper No. 61, Berkeley Roundtable on the International Economy, University of California, Berkeley, March. (Chapter 6)

Castells, M. and Aoyama, Y. (1994) Paths towards the informational society: employment structure in G-7 countries, 1920–1990. *International Labour Review*, **133** (1), 5–33. (Chapter 6)

Cavanagh, J.P. (1998) *Frame Relay Applications: Business and Technology Case Studies.* New York: Morgan Kaufman. (Chapter 5)

Cen, R. and Rubleske, B. (1998) Software jobs go begging, threatening technology boom: computer services employment in US metropolitan areas, 1982 and 1983. *Professional Geographer*, **50**, 358–71. (Chapter 7)

Center for Democracy and Technology (CDT) (1997) *Internet Family Empowerment White Paper: How Filtering Tools Enable Parents to Protect Their Children Online* (16 July), [http://www.cdt.org/speech/empower.html]. (Chapter 14)

Chance, D. (1999) Research trends in Derivatives and risk management since Black–Scholes. *Journal of Portfolio Management, Special Issue*, May

Chancellor, E. (1999) *Devil Take the Hindmost: A History of Financial Speculation.* New York: Farrar Straus and Giroux.

Chandler, C. (1999) Phone costs hamper growth of E-commerce in Japan. *San Jose Mercury News*, 18 August. (Chapter 6)

Chaplin, H. (1999) E-commerce: don't believe the hype. *Salon Magazine*, 22 January, [http://www.salon.com/money/col/chap/1999/01/22chap.html]. (Chapter 9)

Chase-Dunn, C. (1998) *Global Formation: Structures in the World-Economy* 2nd edn. Oxford: Basil Blackwell. (Chapter 12)

Chia, S.Y. (1997) Singapore: advanced production base and smart hub of the electronics industry. In: Dobson, W. and Chia, S.Y. (eds), *Multinationals and East Asian Integration.* Canada: IDRC, pp. 31–61. (Chapter 8)

Chilcoat, Y. and DeWine, S. (1985) Teleconferencing and interpersonal communication perception. *Journal of Applied Communication Research*, **13**, 14–32. (Chapter 2)

Chiu, S.W.K., Ho, K.C. and Lui, T-L. (1997) *City-States in the Global Economy: Industrial Restructuring in Hong Kong and Singapore.* Boulder, CO: Westview. (Chapter 8)

Choi, S-Y., Stahl, D. and Whinston, A. (1997) *The Economics of Electronic Commerce.* Indianapolis: Macmillan Technical Publishing. (Chapter 7)

Choo, C.W. (1997), IT2000: Singapore's vision of an intelligent island. In Droege, P. (ed.), *Intelligent Environments: Spatial Aspects of the Information Revolution.* Amsterdam: Elsevier, pp. 49–65. (Chapter 8)

Christaller, W. (1966) *Central Places in Southern Germany.* Translated by Baskin, C.W. Englewood Cliffs: Prentice-Hall. (Chapter 4)

Christopherson, S. (1989) Flexibility in the U.S. service economy and the emerging spatial division of labor. *Transactions of the Institute of British Geographers*, **14**, 31–43. (Chapter 7)

Clark, G. (1981) The employment relation and spatial division of labor: a hypothesis. *Annals of the Association of American Geographers*, **71**, 412–24. (Chapter 7)

Clark, G. (1993) Global interdependence and regional development: business linkages and corporate governance in a world of financial risk. *Transactions of the Institute of British Geographers*, **18**, 309–25. (Chapter 12)

Clark, G.L. (1997) Rogues and regulation in global finance. *Regional Studies*, **31**, 221–36. (Chapter 13)

Clarke, R., Dempsey, G., Nee, O.C. and O'Connor, R.F. (1998) The technical feasibility of regulating gambling on the Internet. Available at: http://www.anu.edu.au?people/Roger.Clarke/II/IgambReg.html. (Chapter 14)

Clausing, J. (1998) Senators again take up Internet restrictions. *New York Times* on the Web (11 February), [http://www.nytimes.com/library/cyber/week/021198porn.html]. (Chapter 14)

Cline, R.J. and Neubig, T.S. (1999) Masters of complexity and bearers of great burden: the sales tax system and compliance costs for multistate retailers. *Ernst and Young Economics Consulting and Quantitative Analysis.* 8 September, [http://www.ey.com/ecommerce]. (Chapter 14)

Cobb, S. (1998) Internet recruiting industry: state of the industry, research manuscript, unpublished. (Chapter 7)

Coe, N. (1998) Exploring uneven development in producer services sectors: detailed evidence from the computer service industry in Britain. *Environment and Planning A*, **30**, 2041–68. (Chapter 7)

Coe, N. and Yeung, H.W-C. (2000) Grounding global flows: constructing an E-commerce hub in

Singapore, in this volume. (Chapter 8)

Cohen, A. (1998) The IMF and the Russian economic bailout. Testimony before the Subcommittee on General Oversight and Investigation, the House Banking Committee on Banking and Financial Services. US House of Representatives. Washington, DC, September, **10**, 140–8. (Chapter 12)

Cohen, B. (1998) *The Geography of Money*. Ithaca: Cornell University Press. (Chapter 12)

Cohn, L. and Brady, D. (2000) B2B: The hottest net bet yet? *Business Week*, 17 January, pp. 36–7. (Chapter 2)

Cole, J.P. (1983) *Geography of World Affairs*. London, UK: Butterworths, 6th edn. (Chapter 16)

Commission of the European Communities (1992a) *Green Paper on the Impact of Transport on the Environment*: *A Community Strategy for Sustainable Development*, COM(92)46/FIN, Brussels. (Chapter 2)

Computer Economics (1999) *Computer Economics*, 5841 Edison Place, Carlsbad, CA 92008, [www.compecon.com]. (Chapter 7)

Computer Economics (2000) Business on the web is not worldwide, [http://www.computereconomics.com/new4/pr/2000/pr000222.html]. (Chapter 15)

Cooke, P. and Morgan, K. (1998) *The Associational Economy*: *Firms, Regions, and Innovation*. Oxford: Oxford University Press. (Chapter 8)

Corbridge, S., Martin, R. and Thrift, N. (1994) *Money, Power and Space*. Oxford: Blackwell. (Chapter 12)

Corey, K.E. (1991) The role of information technology in the planning and development of Singapore. In Brunn, S. and Leinbach, T. (eds), *Collapsing Space and Time*. London: Harper-Collins, pp. 217–31. (Chapter 12)

Corey, K.E. (1993) Using telecommunications and information technology in planning an information-age city: Singapore. In Bakis, H. Abler, R. and Roche, E.M. (eds), *Corporate Networks, International Telecommunications and Interdependence*: *Perspectives From Geography and Information Systems*. London: Belhaven Press, pp. 49–76. (Chapter 8)

Corey, K.E. (1997) Digital dragons and cyber communities: the application of information technology and telecommunications public policies and private partnerships to the planning of urban areas. *International Journal of Urban Sciences*, **1** (2), 184–96. (Chapters 8, 15)

Corey, K.E. (1998) Information technology and telecommunications policies in Southeast Asian development: cases in vision and leadership. In Savage, V.R., Kong, L. and Neville, W. (eds), *The Naga Awakens*: *Growth and Change in Southeast Asia, Singapore*. Times Academic Press, pp. 145–200. (Chapters 8, 15)

Cornish, S. (1996) Marketing software products: the importance of 'being there' and the implications for business services exports. *Environment and Planning A*, **28**, 1661–82. (Chapter 7)

Corporation of London and London Business School (1993) *The Use of Technology for Competitive Advantage*: *A Study of Screen v. Floor Trading*. London: Corporation of London. (Chapter 13)

Cortada, J. (ed.) (1998) *Rise of the Knowledge Worker*. Boston: Butterworth-Heinemann. (Chapter 6)

Coyle, D. (1998) *The Weightless World*. Cambridge, MA: MIT Press. (Chapter 5)

Craddock, A. (1997) ACLU takes on Virginia net decency law. *Wired News*, 8 May, [http://www.wired.com/news/news/politics/story/3732.html]. (Chapter 14)

Cringely, R.X. (1996) *Accidental Empires: How the Boys of Silicon Valley Make Their Millions, Battle Foreign Competition, and Still Can't Get a Date*. Harperbusiness. (Chapter 9)

Crockett, B. (1997) Web merchants duck sales-tax crackdown – for now, MSNBC (21 November), [http://www.zdnet.com/zdnn/content/msnb/1113/237624.html]. (Chapter 14)

Cronin, M.J. (1996) *Global Advantage on the Internet*. New York: Van Nostrand Reinhold. (Chapter 1)

Cukier, K.N. (1998) The global Internet: a primer. In Staple, G.C. (ed.), *Telegeography 1999*. Washington: Telegeography, pp. 112–45. (Chapter 5)

Cukier, K.N. (1999) Bandwidth colonialism? The implications of Internet infrastructure on international E-commerce. Paper presented at INET'99 Conference, June 1999, San Jose,

USA, [http://www.isoc.org/inet99/proceedings/1e/1e_2.htm]. (Chapters 5, 9)

Cumings, B. (1984) The origins and development of the northeast Asian political economy: industrial sectors, product cycles, and political consequences. *International Organization*, **38**, 1–40. (Chapter 12)

Curry, J. and Kenney, M. (1999) Beating the clock: corporate responses to rapid change in the PC industry. *California Management Review*. (Chapter 3)

Cusumano, M.A. and Yoffie, D.B. (1998) *Competing on Internet Time*. New York: Free Press. (Chapter 5)

Dalton, G. (2000) The suppliers' demands. *Industry Standard*, 13 March, p. 59. (Chapter 3)

Daniels, P.W. (1993) *Service Industries in the World Economy*. Oxford: Blackwell. (Chapters 7, 10)

Datamonitor (1998), [http://www.nua.ie/survey/graphs].

David, P. (1986) Understanding the Economics of QWERTY: the necessity of history. In Parker, W. (ed.), *Economic History and the Modern Economist*. New York: Blackwell. (Chapter 3)

David, P.A. (1985) Clio and the economics of QWERTY. *American Economic Review*, **75**, 332–7. (Chapter 6)

Davis, S. and Meyer, C. (1998) *Blur: The Speed of Change in the Connected Economy*. Reading, MA: Addison-Wesley. (Chapter 3)

De Jonge, P. (1999) Riding the wild, perilous waters of Amazon.com. *The New York Times*, 14 March 1999, section 6, pp. 36ff. (Chapter 9)

De Landa, M. (1991) *War in the Age of Intelligent Machines*. New York: Zone Books. (Chapter 3)

DejaNews (1998) Deja.com, Inc., 9430 Research Boulevard, Echelon II, Suite 300, Austin, TX, 78759, [www.dejanews.com]. (Chapter 7)

DeMeyer, A. (1993) Management of an international network of industrial R&D laboratories. *R&D Management*, **23**, 109–20.

Dempster, J. (1999) Have you done your homework on Japan? *Target Marketing*, **22** (10), (October), 172–80. (Chapter 6)

Department of Commerce (1998) *The Emerging Digital Economy*, Washington, DC: US Department of Commerce. (Chapter 3)

DiBona, C., Ockman, S. and Stone, M. (1999) *Open Sources: Voices from the Open Source Revolution*. Sebastopol, CA: O'Reilly. (Chapter 3)

Dicken, P. (1994) Global-local tensions: firms and states in the global space-economy. *Economic Geography*, **70**, 101–28. (Chapter 11)

Dicken, P. (1998) *Global Shift: Transforming the World Economy*, 3rd edn. London: Paul Chapman. (Chapters 8, 11)

Diederen, P., Kemp, R., Muysken, J. and De Wit, R. (1991) Diffusion of process technology in Dutch banking. *Technological Forecasting and Social Change*, **39**, 201–19. (Chapter 10)

Dizard, W. (1997) *Meganet: How the Global Communications Network will Connect Everyone on Earth*. New York: Westview Press. (Chapter 7)

Dodge, M. (1998) The geographies of cyberspace: a research note. *NETCOM – Networks and Communications Studies*, December, **12** (4), 383–96. (Chapter 9)

Domowitz, I. (1993) A taxonomy of automated trade execution systems. *Journal of International Finance*, **12**, 607–31. (Chapter 13)

Domowitz, I. (1995) Electronic derivatives exchanges: implicit mergers, network externalities and standardization. *Quarterly Review of Economics and Finance*, **35**, 163–75. (Chapter 13)

Donovan, J. (1997) *The Second Industrial Revolution: Reinventing Your Business on the Web*. New Jersey: Prentice-Hall. (Chapter 7)

Downes, T. and Greenstein, S. (1998) Universal access and local commercial Internet markets, [skew2.nwu.edu/~greenste/research/papers/]. (Chapter 5)

Drennan, M. (1989) Information intensive industries in metropolitan areas of the United States of America. *Environment and Planning A*, **21**, 1603–18. (Chapter 7)

Drummond, R. (1996) Safe and secure electronic commerce. *Network Computing*, **7** (19), (December), 116–21. (Chapter 1)

DSA Analytics (1999) The Internet user and online commerce in Japan, [http://www.dsasiagroup.com/]. (Chapter 6)

Duffee, G. (1996) On measuring credit risks of derivative instruments. *Journal of Banking and Finance*, **20**, 805–33. (Chapter 13)

Dunford, M. (1998) Differential development, institutions, modes of regulation and comparative transitions to capitalism: Russia, the Commonwealth of Independent States and the former German Democratic Republic. In Pickles, J. and Smith, A. (eds), *Theorising Transition: The Political Economy of Post-Communist Transformations*. London: Routledge, pp. 76–111. (Chapter 12)

Dupuy, G. (1999) From the 'magic circle' to 'automobile dependence': measurements and political implications. *Transport Policy*, **6**, 1–17. (Chapter 2)

Duranton, G. (1999) Distance, land, and proximity: economic analysis and the evolution of cities. *Environment and Planning A*, **31**, 2169–88. (Chapter 5)

Dykes, J., Moore, K. and Wood, J. (1999) Virtual environments for student fieldwork using networked components. *International Journal of Geographical Information Science*, **13** (4), 397–416. (Chapter 4)

E-Commerce Promotion Council of Japan. (1999a) EC ga nihon keizai ni motarasu impakuto bunseki. February. (Chapter 6)

E-Commerce Promotion Council of Japan. (1999b) EC ni kansuru ishiki chousa kekka: Osaka hen. October. (Chapter 6)

Economides, N. (1996) Network externalities, complementaries and innovations. *European Journal of Political Economy*, **12**, 211–33. (Chapter 10)

Economist, The (1997) In search of the perfect market, November, [http://www.economist.com/editorial/freeforall/14-09-97/ec1.html]. (Chapter 3)

Economist, The (1997) A connected world: a survey of telecommunications. *The Economist*, 13 September. (Chapter 7)

Economist, The (1998) Robots per 10,000 persons employed in the manufacturing industry, 1997. 17 October. (Chapter 6)

Economist, The (1998a) Can pay, won't pay, 14 February, p. 13. (Chapter 7)

Economist, The (1998b) Working with the web, 28 February, p. 67. (Chapter 7)

Economist, The (1998c) Headhunters: search and destroy. *The Economist*, 27 June, p. 63. (Chapter 7)

Economist, The (1998) The science of alliance. Author unknown, 4 April, pp. 69–70. (Chapter 16)

Economist, The (1999) How real is the new economy? 24 July, pp. 17–19.

Economist, The (1999) The net imperative: business and the Internet. *The Economist*, 26 June. (Chapters 6, 9)

Economist, The (2000) Banking at your convenience: how the Internet is helping Japan's corner shops become banks, 22 January. (Chapter 6)

Edwards, J.G. (1998) Gambling experts see future for net betting. *Las Vegas Review Journal* (28 September), [http://www.lvrj.com/lvrj_home/1998/Sep-28-Mon-1998?business/8287844.html]. (Chapter 14)

Edwards, T. (2001) Information geopolitics. PhD dissertation in geography. Seattle: University of Washington, (to be published). (Chapter 16)

Egenhofer, M.J., Glasgow, J., Günther, O., Herring, J.R. and Peuquet, D.J. (1999) Progress in computational methods for representing geographical concepts, *International Journal of Geographical Information Science*, **13** (8), 775–96. (Chapter 4)

Electronic Privacy Information Center (EPIC) (1997) Faulty filters: how content filters block access to kid-friendly material on the Internet, [http://www2.epic.org/reports/filter-report.html]. (Chapter 14)

Elliot, E.X. (1997) No net taxes in New York. [http://www.zdnet.com/cshopper/content/9704/cshp0176.html]. (Chapter 14)

EU Council Directive (1990) *Council Directive on the Establishment of the Internal Market for Telecommunications Services through the Implementation of Open network Provision*, Directive 90/387/EEC, Brussels, 28 June. (Chapter 10)

Exodus Communications Inc. (1999) Peering, [www.exodus.com/network/peering.html]. (Chapter 5)

Falk, T. and Abler, R. (1980) Intercommunications, distance, and geographical theory. *Geografiska Annaler*, Series B, **62**, 35–56. (Chapter 5)

Family PC (1997) Family PC detail findings of 'Net parent' survey, (1 December), [http://www.zdnet.com/zdnn/content/zdnn/1201/249834.html]. (Chapter 14)

Farrell, J. and Katz, M.L. (1998) Public policy and private investment in advanced telecommunications infrastructure. *IEEE Communications Magazine*, **36** (7), 87–92. (Chapter 5)

Farrell, J. and Saloner G. (1986) Installed base and compatibility. *American Economic Review* **76**, 940–55. (Chapter 10)

Federal Express (1998) 6 June, [http://www.fedex.com/us/].

Feldstein, M. (1998) Refocusing the IMF. *Foreign Affairs*, **77** (2), 20–33. (Chapter 12)

Findlay, M. (1999) *The Globalisation of Crime: Understanding Transitional Relationships in Context*. Cambridge: Cambridge University Press. (Chapter 11)

Fischer, M. and Nijkamp, P. (eds) (1999) *Spatial Dynamics in European Integration*. Berlin: Springer-Verlag. (Chapter 10)

Fleming, S. (1999) Web sites liable under law of country where accessed. *The Register* (28 July), [http://www.theregister.co.uk/990728-000008.html]. (Chapter 14)

Forer, P. (1974) Space through time. In Cripps, E.L. (ed.), *Space–Time Concepts in Urban and Regional Models*. London: Pion, pp. 22–45. (Chapter 4)

Fossato, F. (1998) 1998 in review: Russia's economic collapse. *Radio Free Europe/Radio Liberty Newsline*. 18 December, [http://www.rferl.org/nca/features/1998/12/F.RU.981218145814.html]. (Chapter 12)

Foucault, M. (1997) *The Politics of Truth*. New York: Semiotext(e). (Chapter 16)

Francis, S. (1998) Asia gropes for Japan's bootstraps. *Christian Science Monitor*, 17 August, p. 1. (Chapter 12)

Frauenfelder, M. (1999) Remote possibilities. *Business* 2.0, 1 June 1999, [www.business2.com/content/magazine/indepth/1999/06//01/17030].

Free the Grapes (2000) [http:///www.freethegrapes.org/html/print.html]. (Chapter 14)

Frieden, R. (1998) Without public peer: the potential regulatory and universal service consequences of Internet balkanization. *Virginia Journal of Law and Technology*, **3** (Fall), [vjolt.student.virginia.edu/graphics/vol3/vol3_art8.html]. (Chapter 5)

Friedman, T. (1999) *The Lexus and the Olive Tree*. New York: Farrar Straus Giroux.

Friedmann, J. (1986) The world city hypothesis. *Development and Change*, **17**, 69–83. (Chapter 8)

Friedmann, J. and Wolff, G. (1982) World city formation: an agenda for research and action. *International Journal of Urban and Regional Research*, **6**, 309–44. (Chapter 8)

Fukuyama, F. (1996) *Trust – The Social Virtues and the Creation of Prosperity*. New York: Free Press Paperbacks. (Chapter 2)

Garcia, D.L. (1997) Networked commerce: public policy issues in a deregulated communication environment. *The Information Society* **13** (1), (January–March), 17–31. (Chapter 1)

Garcia-Mila, T. and McGuire, T. (1998) A note on the shift to a service-based economy and the consequences for regional growth. *Journal of Regional Science*, **38**, 353–63. (Chapter 7)

Gardiner, G. (2000) Dot com logistics. *Logistics and Materials Handling*, **9**, 11–16. (Chapter 2)

Gaspar, J. and Glaeser, E.L. (1996) *Information Technology and the Future of Cities*, National Bureau of Economic Research, Working Paper 5562, Cambridge. (Chapter 2)

Gaspar, J. and Glaeser, E.L. (1998) Information technology and the future of cities. *Journal of Urban Economics*, **43**, 136–56. (Chapter 5)

Gates, B. (1997). Speech to the national Governor's Association. Microsoft Corporate Information (Microsoft intranet source), 30 July. (Chapter 16)

Gattuso, G. (1993) Big book is gone, but not forgotten. *Direct Marketing*, **55** (11) (March): 6–8. (Chapter 6)

Geczy, C., Minton, B. and Schrand, C. (1997) Why firms use currency derivatives. *Journal of Finance*, **52**, 1323–54. (Chapter 13)

Geenhuizen, M. van (1999) Shifts in urban hierarchy: the case of financial services in the Netherlands. *Geographica Polonica*, **72** (1), 107–24. (Chapter 10)

Geenhuizen, M. van (2000) Information and communication technologies and regional development: experiences in the Netherlands. In Heitor, M. (ed.), *Innovation and Regional Develop-*

ment. Cheltenham: Edward Elgar, (forthcoming). (Chapter 10)

Geenhuizen, M. van and Knaap, G.A. van der (1998) *Financial Services and the Urban System in the Netherlands. TPM Studies in Urban and Regional Development*, vol. 2. Delft: University of Technology, Faculty of Technology, Policy and Management. (Chapter 10)

Geenhuizen, M. van, and Nijkamp, P. (1999) Regional policy beyond 2000. *European Spatial Research and Policy*, **6** (2), 5–20. (Chapter 10)

Geenhuizen, M.S. van (1993) A longitudinal analysis of the growth of firms. PhD Thesis, Erasmus University Rotterdam. (Chapter 10)

Gertler, M. (1997) Globality and locality: the future of 'geography' and the nation-state. In Rimmer, P.J. (ed.), *Pacific Rim Development: Integration and Globalisation in the Asia–Pacific Economy*. Sydney: Allen and Unwin, pp. 12–33. (Chapter 11)

Gibson, C. (1999) Subversive sites: rave culture, spatial politics and the Internet in Sydney, Australia. *Area*, **31**, 19–33. (Chapter 7)

Gibson, W. (1984) *Neuromancer*. London: Gollancz. (Chapter 7)

Gilder, G. (1997) Inventing the Internet again. *Forbes ASAP*, 2 June, also at [http://www.seas.upenn.edu/~gaj1/inventgg.html]. (Chapter 7)

Gillespie A. (1998) Tele-activities and the city: emerging technologies, emerging mythologies. Paper presented at the Telecommunications and the City Conference, March, Athens, GA, USA. (Chapter 9)

Gillespie, A. and Robins, K. (1989) Geographical inequalities: the spatial bias of the new communications technologies. *Journal of Communications*, **39** (3), 7–18. (Chapter 5)

Gillespie, A. and Williams, H. (1988) Telecommunications and the reconstruction of regional comparative advantage. *Environment and Planning A*, **20**, 1311–21. (Chapter 10)

Gimein, M. (2000) The information laundromat, 26 October, [http://www.salon.com/tech/feature/1999/10/26/whisper_numbers/index.html].

Global Internet Liberty Campaign (1997) GILC submission on PICS, December, [http://www.gilc.org/speech/ratings/gilc-pics-submission.html]. (Chapter 14)

Goddard, J.B. (1991) New technology and the geography of the UK information economy. In Brotchie, J., Batty, M., Hall, P. and Newton, P. (eds), *Cities of the 21st Century: New Technologies and Spatial Systems*. Melbourne: Longman Cheshire, pp. 191–213. (Chapter 5)

Goddard, J.B. and Richardson, R. (1996) Why geography will still matter: what jobs go where? In Dutton, W.H. (ed.), *Information and Communication Technologies: Visions and Realities*. Oxford: Oxford University Press, pp. 197–214. (Chapter 5)

Goldman, D. and Armstrong, C. (1999) E-commerce is a likely windfall for wine industry volumes. *Wine Business Monthly*, November, [http://smartwine.com/wbm/1999/1199/bmk9934a.htm]. (Chapter 14)

Goodchild, M.F. (1972) The trade area of a displaced hexagonal lattice point. *Geographical Analysis*, **4**, 105–7. (Chapter 4)

Goodchild, M.F. (1997) Towards a geography of geographic information in a digital world. *Computers, Environment and Urban Systems*, **21** (6), 377–91. (Chapter 4)

Gordon, R. (1999) Has the 'New Economy' rendered the productivity slowdown obsolete? Department of Economics, Northwestern University, 14 June, unpublished paper.

Gorman, S.P. and Malecki, E.J. (2000) The networks of the Internet: an analysis of provider networks. *Telecommunications Policy*, **24**, 113–34. (Chapter 5)

Gould-Davies, N. and Woods, N. (1999) Russia and the IMF. *International Affairs*, **75**, 1–22. (Chapter 12)

Government of Japan (1998a) Basic guidelines on the promotion of an advanced information and telecommunications society, 9 November, [http://www.kantei.go.jp/jp/it/981110kihon.html]. (Chapter 6)

Government of Japan (1998b) A Japanese initiative in promoting E-commerce, June, [http://www.kantei.go.jp/jp/it/980622honbun.html]. (Chapter 6)

Graham, S. (1997) Telecommunications and the future of cities: debunking the myths. *Cities*, **14** (1), 21–9. (Chapters 5, 9)

Graham, S. (1998) The end of geography or the explosion of place? Conceptualizing space, place and information technology. *Progress in Human Geography*, **22** (2), 165–85. (Chapter 8)

Graham, S. (1999) Global grids of glass: on global cities, telecommunications and planetary urban networks. *Urban Studies*, **36** (5–6), 929–49. (Chapters 5, 8, 10, 12, 13)

Graham, S. and Marvin, S. (1996) *Telecommunications and the City: Electronic Spaces*. London: Routledge. (Chapters 1, 5, 10)

Grant, L. (1997) Why FedEx is flying high. *Fortune*, 10 November. (Chapter 3)

Grant, S., Kajii, A. and Polak, B. (1998) Intrinsic preference for information. *Journal of Economic Theory*, **83**, 233–59. (Chapter 13)

Greenfeld, K.T. (1999) Clicks and bricks. *Time Magazine*, 27 December, **154** (26), 78ff. (Chapter 9)

Greenstein, S. (1998) Universal service in the digital age: the commercialization and geography of U.S. Internet access, [skew2.nwu.edu/~greenste/research/papers/]. (Chapter 5)

Gregerman, I.B. (1981) *Knowledge Worker Productivity*. New York: AMACOM. (Chapter 6)

Group of Thirty (1997) *Global Institutions National Supervision and Systemic Risk* (Group of Thirty, 1990, Washington). (Chapter 13)

Guay, W. (1999) The impact of derivatives on firm risk: an empirical examination of new derivatives users. *Journal of Accounting and Economics*, **26**, 319–51. (Chapter 13)

Gurbaxani, V. (1996) The new world of information technology outsourcing. *Communications of the ACM*, **39** (7), July, 45–7. (Chapter 1)

Hagel, J. and Armstrong, A. (1997) *Net Gain: Expanding Markets through Virtual Communities*. Boston: Harvard Business School Press. (Chapter 3)

Haggett, P. and Chorley, R. (1969) *Network Analysis in Geography*. New York: St Martins Press. (Chapter 5)

Haltiwanger, J. and Jarmin, R.S. (2000) Measuring the digital economy. In Brynjolfsson, E. and Kahin, B. (eds), *Understanding the Digital Economy*. Cambridge, MA: MIT Press, pp. 13–33. (Chapters 5, 9)

Hamilton, J. (1999) Take off your coat and stay a while. *Business Week*, 19 April, 30B-D. (Chapter 7)

Hamnett, C. (1995) Controlling space: global cities, in a shrinking world? In Allen, J. and Hamnett, C. (eds), *Global Uneveness and Inequality*. Oxford: Oxford University Press, pp. 104–27. (Chapter 11)

Handley, P. (1998) Hong Kong's counter challenge. *Institutional Investor*, **32** (9) September, 142–3. (Chapter 11)

Hanson, S. (1998) Off the road? Reflections on transportation geography in the information age. *Journal of Transport Geography*, **6**, 241–9. (Chapter 5)

Harary, F., Norman, R.Z. and Cartwright, D. (1965) *Structural Models: An Introduction to the Theory of Directed Graphs*. New York: John Wiley. (Chapter 5)

Hargittai, E. (1999) Weaving the Western web: explaining differences in Internet connectivity among OECD countries. *Telecommunications Policy*, **23**, 701–18. (Chapter 10)

Harpold, T. (1999) Dark continents: a critique of Internet metageographies. *Postmodern Culture*, **9** (2), [muse.jhu.edu/journals/postmodern_culture/v009/9.2harpold.html]. (Chapter 5)

Harrington, J.W. (1995) Empirical research on producer service growth and regional development: international comparisons. *Professional Geographer*, **47**, 66–9. (Chapter 7)

Harris, R. (1998) The Internet as a GPT: factor market implications. In Helpman, E. (ed.), *General Purpose Technologies and Economic Growth*. Cambridge, MA: MIT Press, pp. 140–65. (Chapter 5)

Hart, H.W.T and Piersma, J. (1990) Direct representation in international financial markets: the case of foreign banks in Amsterdam. *Journal of Social and Economic Geography*, **81** (2), 82–92. (Chapter 10)

Harutoshi, Y. (1994). *Demand Forecast and Financial Feasibility of New Freight Transport Systems*. OECD Seminar TT3 on Advanced Road Transport Technologies. Paris: OECD. (Chapter 2)

Harvey, D. (1982) *The Limits to Capital*. Chicago: University of Chicago Press. (Chapter 13)

Harvey, D. (1989) *The Condition of Postmodernity: An Enquiry into the Origins of Cultural Change*. New York: Blackwell. (Chapters 5, 12, 15)

Hashimoto, K. (1998) Shutoken ni okeru kobiniensu sutoa no tenpo ruikeika to sono kuukanteki tenkai: POS deta ni yoru uriage bunseki wo tsujite. *Chirigaku Hyoron (Geographical Review)*, **71A** (4), 239–53. (Chapter 6)

Hashimoto, K. (1999) Personal interview, 4 December, Osaka, Japan. (Chapter 6)

Held, D., McGrew, A., Goldblatt, D. and Perraton, J. (1999) *Global Transformations: Politics, Economics and Culture*. Cambridge: Polity. (Chapter 8)

Henderson, C. (1998) *Asia Falling*. NY: McGraw-Hill. (Chapter 12)

Henrikson, A.K. (1999) The power and politics of maps. In Demko, G. and Wood, W.B. (eds), *Reordering the World*. Boulder, CO: Westview Press, 2nd edn. (Chapter 16)

Henry, D., Cooke, S., Buckley, P., Dumagan, J., Gill, G., Pastore, D. and LaPorte, S. (1999) *The Emerging Digital Economy II*. Washington, DC: US Department of Commerce, Secretariat on Electronic Commerce, [www.ecommerce.gov]. (Chapter 5)

Hepworth, M. (1990) *Geography of the Information Economy*. London: Guilford. (Chapters 5, 7, 8, 15)

Hepworth, M. (1991) Information technology and the global restructuring of capital markets. In Brunn, S. and Leinbach, T. (eds), *Collapsing Space and Time: Geographic Aspects of Communications and Information*. London: HarperCollins, pp. 132–48. (Chapter 12)

Herod, A. and Tuathail, G. (eds) (1998) *An Unruly World? Globalization, Governance and Geography*. London: Routledge. (Chapter 16)

Hewson D. (1999) Start talking and get to work. *Business Life*, November, 72–6. British Airways, London. (Chapter 2)

Hill, R. (1997) Electronic Commerce, the World Wide Web, Minitel, and EDI. *The Information Society*. 13: 1 (January–March), 33–41. (Chapter 1)

Hillis, K. (1998) On the margins: the invisibility of communications in geography. *Progress in Human Geography*, **22**, 543–66. (Chapter 5)

Hippel, E. von (1994) Sticky information and the locus of problem solving: implications for innovation. *Management Science*, 429–39. (Chapter 10)

Hodge, J. and Miller, J. (1997) IT policy for South Africa. In Mgombelo, H.R. and Werner, M.C.M (eds), *Telecommunications for Business in Africa*. Amsterdam: IOS Press, pp. 81–116. (Chapter 15)

Hof, R. (1999) Now it's your web. *Business Week*, 5 October, pp. 164–76. (Chapter 7)

Hoffman, D.L. and Novak, T.P. (1998) *Bridging the Racial Divide on the Internet, Science*, April, **17**, 280, 390–91. (Chapter 9)

Holland, T. (1998) Singapore currency trading rises 32%, *Asian Wall Street Journal*, 1 October, p. 5. (Chapter 11)

Hove, L. van (1999) Electronic money and the network externalities theory. *Netnomics*, **1**, 137–71. (Chapter 10)

Howton, S. and Perfect, S. (1998) Currency and interest-rate derivative use in US firms. *Financial Management*, **27**, 4. (Chapter 13)

Huff, W.G. (1994) *The Economic Growth of Singapore: Trade and Development in the Twentieth Century*. Cambridge: Cambridge University Press. (Chapter 8)

Hugill, P.J. (1999) *Global Communications since 1844: Geopolitics and Technology*. Baltimore, MD: Johns Hopkins University Press. (Chapter 16)

Huitema, C. (1995) *Routing in the Internet*. Englewood Cliffs: Prentice-Hall PTR. (Chapter 5)

Huitema, C. (1997) *IPv6: The New Internet Protocol*. Englewood Cliffs: Prentice-Hall PTR. (Chapter 5)

Huntington, S.P. (1968) *Political Order in Changing Societies*. New Haven: Yale University Press. (Chapter 14)

Huntington, S.P. (1998) The clash of civilizations? In Tuathail, G. and Dalby, S. (eds), *The Geopolitics Reader*. London: Routledge, pp. 159–69. (Chapter 16)

Huston, G. (1999a) *ISP Survival Guide*. New York: John Wiley. (Chapter 5)

Huston, G. (1999b) Interconnection, peering, and settlements. *INET99 Proceedings*. Reston, VA: Internet Society, [www.isoc.org/inet99/proceedings/1e/1e_1.htm]. (Chapter 5)

IBN (1998) *1999 Electronic Recruiting Index: The Industry Matures*, 1. IBN: [interbiznet.com]. (Chapter 7)

Iconocast (1999) Iconocast, Inc., 470 Third St. #102, San Francisco, CA 94107, [www.iconocast.com]. (Chapter 7)

IGY (1998) Personal comments from Internet recruiting facilitator. (Chapter 7)

Illeris, S. (1994) Proximity between service producers and service users. *Journal of Social and Economic Geography*, **85**, 294–302. (Chapter 10)

Illeris, S. (1996) *The Service Economy: A Geographical Approach*. Chichester: John Wiley. (Chapter 7)

IMF (International Monetary Fund) (1999) *World Economic Outlook: Part II. Boxes. Annexes and Statistical Appendix*. Washington, DC. (Chapter 11)

Industry Standard (2000a) Behind the numbers: the mystery of B-to-B forecasts revealed. *Industry Standard*, February, **28**, 158–61. (Chapter 3)

Industry Standard (2000b) Financial spotlight: inside the dot-com VC billions. *Industry Standard*, February, **28**, 163–6410. (Chapter 3)

InfoCom Research (2000) Decline in the number of telephone subscribers Domestic Trend [http://www.icr.co.jp/topics/topics01.html]. (Chapter 6)

ING Bank (previously NMB), *Annual Report* (various years), Amsterdam. (Chapter 10)

Inktomi Corporation (2000) Web surpasses one billion documents, [www.inktomi.com/new/press/billion.html]. (Chapter 5)

Inoue, Y. (1999) Sony to build its own E-bank. *ZDNet News: Technology News Now*, 13 December, [http://www.zdnet.com/]. (Chapter 6)

Interactive Gaming Council (2000) [http://igcouncil.org/info_main.html] (Chapter 14)

International Monetary Fund (1999) *Annual Report of the Executive Board for the Financial Year Ended April 30, 1999*. [http://www.imf.org/external/pubs/ft/ar/1999/pdf/file3.pdf]. (Chapter 12)

International Organization of Securities Commissions (1996) *International Regulation of Derivative Markets, Products and Financial Intermediaries: A Report of the General Secretariat*. IOSCO: Montreal. (Chapter 13)

International Telecommunication Union (1999a) Basic indicators [http://www.itu.org] (Chapter 15)

International Telecommunication Union (1999b) Cellular subscribers [http://www.itu.org]. (Chapter 15)

Internet Gaming Commission (2000) [http://www.Internetcommission.com]. (Chapter 14)

Internet Software Consortium (2000) *Internet Domain Survey* 2000. [http://www.isc.org/ds/new-survey.html]. (Chapter 15)

Janelle, D.G. (1968) Central place development in a time–space framework. *Professional Geographer*, **20**, 5–10. (Chapter 4)

Jenkins, R. (1991) The political economy of industrialization: a comparison of Latin American and East Asian newly industrializing countries. *Development and Change*, **22**, 197–231. (Chapter 12)

Jimeniz, E. and Greenstein, S. (1998) The emerging Internet retail market as a nested diffusion process, [http://skew2.kellogg.nwu.edu/~greenste/research.html]. (Chapter 6)

Johnson, D.R. and Post, D.G. (1997) The rise of law on the global network. In Kahin, B. and Nesson, C. (eds), *Borders in Cyberspace*. Cambridge: MIT Press, pp. 3–47. (Chapter 15)

Johnson, S. (1997) *Interface Culture: How New Technology Transforms the Way We Create and Communicate*. New York: HarperCollins. (Chapters 9, 16)

Johnson, S. (1999) The sim salesman, *FEED Magazine*, 26 January, [http://www.feedmag.com/column/interface/ci164_master.html]. (Chapter 9)

Jones, M.R. and MacLeod, G. (1999) Towards a regional renaissance? Reconfiguring and rescaling England's economic governance. *Transactions of the Institute of British Geographers*, **24** (3), 295–314. (Chapter 8)

Jupiter Communications (2000) Low PC penetration, low credit card usage and infrastructure hinder Latin American Internet markets, [http://www.jup.com/company/pressrelease.jsp?doc=pr000215]. (Chapter 15)

Jussawala, M. (1995) Telecommunications privatization and capital formation in the ASEAN. In Mody, B., Bauer, J. and Straubhaar, J. (eds), *Telecommunications Politics*. Mahwah, NJ: Lawrence Erlbaum Associates. (Chapter 12)

Jussawalla, M. (1999) The impact of ICT convergence on development in the Asian region. *Telecommunications Policy*, **23**, 217–34. (Chapter 15)

Jutaku Shimpo (1999) Tenanto katsuyo kara rodo saido bizinesu made, 26 November. (Chapter 6)

Kagarlitsky, B. (1998) [www.house.gov/banking/91098kag.htm]. Accessed 28 August 2000.

Kahler, M. (ed.) (1998) *Capital Flows and Financial Crises*. Ithaca, NY: Council on Foreign Relations. (Chapter 12)

Kalakota, R. and Whinston, B. (1996) *Frontiers of Electronic Commerce*. New York: Addison-Wesley. (Chapter 7)

Kansky, K. (1963) *Structure of Transportation Networks: Relationships Between Network Geometry and Regional Characteristics*. Chicago: University of Chicago, Department of Geography, Research Papers. (Chapter 5)

Katz., M.L. and Shapiro J. (1985) Network externalities, competition, and compatibility. *American Economic Review*, **75**, 424–40. (Chapter 10)

Kavanaugh, A.L. (1998) *The Social Control of Technology in North Africa*. Westport, CT and London: Praeger. (Chapter 15)

Kellerman A. (1993) *Telecommunications and Geography*. Chichester: John Wiley, Belhaven. (Chapter 15) (Chapter 5)

Kelly, K. (1998) *New Rules for the New Economy*. New York: Viking. (Chapter 5)

Kelly, P.F. (1999) *The Geographies and Politics of Globalization, Progress in Human Geography*, **23** (3), 379–400. (Chapter 8)

Kempf, A. and Korn, O. (1998) Trading system and market integration. *Journal of Financial Intermediation*, **7**, 220–39. (Chapter 13)

Kennard, W.E. (1999) Remarks before the Federal Communications Bar, northern California Chapter, San Francisco, 20 July, [www.fcc.gov]. (Chapter 5)

Kennedy, J. and Morrow, T. (1995) *Electronic Job Search Revolution*, 2nd edn. New York: John Wiley. (Chapter 7)

Kenney, M. and Curry, J. (1999) E-commerce: implications for firm strategy and industry configuration. *Industry and Innovation*, **6** (2), 131–51. (Chapter 3)

Kerwin, K. and Stepanek, M. (2000) At Ford E-commerce is job 1. *Business Week*, February, **28**, 74–8. (Chapter 2)

Khosla, V. (2000) The Terabit tsunami, 7 March, [http://www.kpcb.com/team/vinod.html]. (Chapter 3)

Kim, E-K. (1997) States are cracking down on shipments of wine and beer. Last call for spirits by mail? *The Philadelphia Inquirer* (22 August). [http://www.phillynews.com/inquirer/97/Aug/22/business/BOOZ22.htm]. (Chapter 14)

Kitchin, R. (1998a) *Cyberspace: the World in the Wires*. Chichester: John Wiley. (Chapters 5, 7, 8)

Kitchin, R. (1998b) Towards geographies of cyberspace. *Progress in Human Geography*, **22**, 385–406. (Chapters 5, 7, 8)

Klopfenstein, B. (1998) Internet economics: an annotated bibliography. *The Journal of Media Economics*, **11**, 33–48. (Chapter 7)

Knight, D.B. (1994) People together, yet apart: rethinking territory, sovereignty, and identities. In Demko, G. and Wood, W.B. (eds), *Reordering the World*. Boulder, CO: Westview Press, pp. 71–86. (Chapter 16)

Knight, R.W. (1995) Knowledge-based development: policy and planning implications for cities. *Urban Studies*, **32**, 225–60. (Chapter 10)

Knox, P. and Taylor, P.J. (eds) (1995) *World Cities in a World-System*. Cambridge: Cambridge University Press. (Chapters 5, 8)

Kobrin, S. (1997) Electronic cash and the end of national markets. *Foreign Policy*, summer, pp. 65–77. (Chapter 12)

Korten, D.C. (1996) *When Corporations Rule the World*. San Francisco: Berrett-Koehler. (Chapter 16)

Koski, J. and Pontiff, J. (1999) How are derivatives used? Evidence from the mutual fund industry. *Journal of Finance*, **54**, 791–816. (Chapter 13)

Kotabe, M. (1995) The return of 7-11 from Japan: the Vanguard program. *Columbia Journal of*

World Business, **30** (4), Winter, 70–81. (Chapter 6)

Kotha, S. (1998) Competing on the Internet: the case of Amazon.com, [http://www.netes-teem.com/Studies/studies_amazon.htm]. (Chapter 3)

Kotha, S. and Rindova, V. (1999) *Building Corporate Reputation on the Internet: The Case of Amazon.com*. University of Washington Business School Working Paper, January. [http://us.badm.washington.edu/kotha/Internet/handouts/Reputation.pdf]. (Chapter 9)

Krawiec, K. (1998) Derivatives, corporate hedging, and shareholder wealth. *University of Illinois Law Review*, **4**, 1039–104. (Chapter 13)

Krieger, J. (1993) Sovereignty. In Krieger, J. (editor-in-chief), *Oxford Companion to Politics of the World*. Oxford: Oxford University Press, pp. 851–3. (Chapter 16)

Kristof, N. (1998) Experts question roving flow of global capital. *New York Times*, 20 September, p. 6. (Chapter 12)

Krugman, P. (1994) The myth of the Asian miracle. *Foreign Affairs*, **73**, 62–78. (Chapter 12)

Krugman, P. (1996) *The Self-Organizing Economy*. Oxford: Blackwell. (Chapter 2)

Kurozumi, T. (1993) *Nihon tsushin hanbai hattatsushi*. Tokyo: Doyukan. (Chapter 6)

Kurtzman, J. (1993) *The Death of Money*. Boston: Little, Brown (Chapter 12)

Lamberton, D. (1992) Information economics: introductory remarks. In Antonelli, C. (ed.), *The Economics of Information Networks*. Amsterdam: Elsevier, pp. 29–34. (Chapter 7)

Lambooy, J.G. (1998) Polynucleation and economic development: the Randstad. *European Planning Studies*, **6** (4), 457–66.

Lambooy, J.G. and Moulaert, F. (1996) The economic organization of cities: an institutional perspective. *International Journal of Urban and Regional Research*, **20** (2), 217–37. (Chapter 1)

Landers, P. (1999) In Japan, the hub of E-commerce is a 7-Eleven: without credit cards, shoppers order online and pick up at a local convenience store. *Wall Street Journal*, 1 November. (Chapter 6)

Landers, P. (2000) Seven-Eleven Japan, Sony set E-commerce plan: venture to offer products at convenience stores or on firm's web site. *Wall Street Journal*, 7 January. (Chapter 6)

Langdale, J.V. (1983) Competition in the United States long distance telecommunications industry. *Regional Studies*, **17**, 393–409. (Chapter 5)

Langdale, J.V. (1985) Electronic funds transfer and the internationalisation of the banking and finance industry. *Geoforum*, **16**, 1–13. (Chapter 12)

Langdale, J.V. (1989) The geography of international business telecommunications: the role of leased networks. *Annals of the Association of American Geographers*, **79**, 501–22. (Chapter 5)

Langdale, J.V. (1990) Telecommunications and international banking and finance: Asia–Pacific perspectives. In Wedemeyer, D.J. and Lofstrom, M. (eds), *Proceedings of the 12th Annual Conference of the Pacific Telecommunications Council*. Pacific Telecommunications: Weaving the Technological and Social Fabric, Honolulu, pp. 759–62. (Chapter 11)

Langdale, J.V. (1997) International competitiveness in East Asia: broadband telecommunications and interactive multimedia. *Telecommunications Policy*, **21** (3), 235–49. (Chapter 11)

Langdale, J.V. (1999) Singapore and Hong Kong as world cities in the Asia–Pacific region. *Geography Bulletin*, **31** (1), 28–33. (Chapter 11)

Langdale, J.V. (2000) Telecommunications and twenty-four hour trading in the international securities industry. In Corey, K.E. and Wilson, M.I. (eds), *Information Tectonics: Space, Place, and Technology in an Information Age*. Chichester: John Wiley, pp. 89–99. (Chapter 11)

Lanvin B. (1995) Why the global village cannot afford information slums. In Drake, W.J. (ed.), *The New Information Infrastructure*. New York: The Twentieth Century Fund Press, pp. 205–22. (Chapter 15)

Lappin, T. (1996) The airline of the Internet. *Wired*, December, 234–41. (Chapter 3)

Laulajainen, R. (1998) *Financial Geography*. Gothenburg: Gothenburg School of Economics. (Chapter 12)

Lawrence, S. and Giles, C. (1998) Searching the World Wide Web. *Science*, **280**, April, 98–100. (Chapters 5, 7)

Lawrence, S. and Giles, C.L. (1999) Accessibility of information on the Web. *Nature 400*, 8 July, 107–9. (Chapter 5)

Lawson Software (1999) Kaisha Gaiyo, [http://www.lawson.com/]. (Chapter 6)

Lee, E. (1997) *The Labour Movement and the Internet*. London: Pluto. (Chapter 7)

Lee, E. (1998) *The Asian Financial Crisis*. Geneva: International Labour Office. (Chapter 12)

Lefebvre, H. (1991) *The Production of Space*. Translated by Nicholson-Smith, D. Oxford: Basil Blackwell. (Chapter 8)

Leinbach, T.R. (1991). Asian venture capital: financing risk opportunities in the Pacific rim. In Green, M. (ed.), *Venture Capital: International Comparisons*. New York: Routledge, pp. 248–61. (Chapter 1)

Leinbach, T.R. and Amrhein, C. (1987) A geography of the venture capital industry in the United States. *Professional Geographer*, **39** (2), 146–58. (Chapter 1)

Leo, E. and Huber, P. (1997) The incidental, accidental deregulation of data . . . and everything else. *Industrial and Corporate Change*, **6**, 807–28. (Chapter 5)

Lessani, A.M. (1998) How much do you want to bet that the Internet gambling Prohibition Act of 1997 is not the most effective way to tackle the problems of online gambling? The UCLA Online Institute for Cyberspace Law and Policy (May), [http://www.gseis.ucla.edu/iclp/alessani.html]. (Chapter 14)

Lessig, L. (1999) *Code, and Other Laws of Cyberspace*. New York: Basic Books. (Chapter 3)

Leyshon, A. (1992) The transformation of regulatory order: regulating the global economy and environment. *Geoforum*, **23**, 249–67. (Chapter 12)

Leyshon, A. (1994) Under pressure: finance, geo-economic competition and the rise and fall of Japan's postwar growth economy. In Corbridge, S., Martin, R. and Thrift, N. (eds), *Money, Power and Space*. Oxford: Blackwell, pp. 116–46. (Chapter 12)

Leyshon, A. (1997) True stories? global dreams, global nightmares, and writing globalization. In Lee, R. and Wills, J. (eds), *Geographies of Economies*. London: Arnold, pp. 133–46. (Chapter 8)

Leyshon, A. and Thrift, N. (1992) Liberalisation and consolidation: the single European market and the remaking of European financial capital. *Environment and Planning A*, **24**, 49–81. (Chapter 12)

Leyshon, A. and Thrift, N. (1997) *Money/Space: Geographies of Monetary Transformation*. London and New York: Routledge. (Chapters 10, 12)

Lindstrom, P. (1997) The Internet: Nielsen's longitudinal research on behavioral changes in use of this counterintuitive medium. *The Journal of Media Economics*, **10**, 35–40. (Chapter 7)

Lipton, B. (1998) New territory for Net travel, CNET NEWS.COM, 3 April. (Chapter 3)

Litan, R. and Niskanen, W. (1998) *Going Digital! A Guide to Policy in the Digital Age*. Washington, DC: Brookings Institution Press and Cato Institute. (Chapter 7)

Lohr, S. (1996) Sizing up the Internet as an engine of regional development. *The New York Times*, 16 September. (Chapter 1)

Lohse, G. and Spiller, P. (1999) Internet retail store design: how the user interface influences traffic and sales. *Journal of Computer-Mediated Communication*, **5** (2), December, [http://www.ascusc.org/jcmc/vol5/issue2/lohse.htm]. (Chapter 9)

London First Centre and British Telecom (1998) *London Business Briefing: Telecommunications*. London: London First Centre. (Chapter 13)

Loomis, J.M., Golledge, R.G. and Klatsky, R.L. (1998) Navigation system for the blind: auditory display modes and guidance. *Presence–Teleoperators and Virtual Environments*, **7** (2), 193–203. (Chapter 4)

Lorentzon, S. (1995) The use of ICT in TNCs: a Swedish perspective on the location of corporate functions. *Regional Studies*, **29**, 673–85. (Chapter 5)

Lösch, A. (1954) *The Economics of Location*. Translated by Woglom, W.H. New Haven, CT: Yale University Press. (Chapter 4)

Love, R.F., Morris, J.G. and Wesolowsky, G.O. (1988) *Facilities Location Models and Methods*. New York: North-Holland. (Chapter 4)

Low, L. (1998) *The Political Economy of a City-State: Government-made Singapore*. Singapore: Oxford University Press. (Chapter 8)

Lucas, R.E. (1990) Why doesn't capital flow from the rich to poor countries? *American Economic Review*, **80**, 92–6. (Chapter 2)

Lundvall, B-Å. (ed.) (1992) *National Systems of Innovation: Towards a Theory of Innovation and*

Interactive Learning. London: Pinter. (Chapter 13)

Lyle, R. (1998) 1998 in review: the global economy. *Radio Free Europe/Radio Liberty Newsline*, 18 December, [http://www.rferl.org/nca/features/1998/12/F.RU.981218145937.html]. (Chapter 12)

MacDonald, S. and Williams, C. (1992) The informal information network in an age of advances telecommunications. *Human Systems Management*, **11**, 77–87.

Mackintosh, J. (2000) Old timers start to play catch-up. *Financial Times, Supplement on Stock and Derivatives Exchanges*, 31 March, V. (Chapter 11)

Malecki, E. (1999) Regional policy in the Internet age. Unpublished paper, Uddevalla Workshop, Sweden. (Chapter 10)

Malecki, E.J. (1997) *Technology and Economic Development: The Dynamics of Local, Regional and National Change.* Addison-Wesley Longman. (Chapters 7, 16)

Malone, T., Yates, J. and Benjamin, R. (1987) Electronic markets and electronic hierarchies. *Communications of the Association of Computing Machinery*, **6**, 485–97. (Chapter 1)

Malone, T., Yates, J. and Benjamin, R. (1989) The logic of electronic markets. *Harvard Business Review*, **3**, 166–72. (Chapter 1)

Mandel, M.J. (1998) The 21st century economy. *Business Week*, 24–31 August, pp. 58–63. (Chapter 1)

Mandel, M.J. (1999) The Internet economy. *Business Week*, 22 February, pp. 30–2. (Chapter 5)

Mansell, R. (1999) Information and communication technologies for development: assessing the potential and the risks. *Telecommunications Policy*, **23**, 35–50. (Chapter 15)

Marcial, G.G. (1997) A new chapter for Barnes & Noble? *Business Week Online*, 13 October, [http://www.businessweek.com].

Marshall, J.N. and Bachtler, J.F. (1984) Spatial perspectives on technological changes in the banking sector of the United Kingdom. *Environment and Planning A*, **16**, 437–50. (Chapter 10)

Marshall, J.N. and Richardson, R. (1996) The impact of 'telemediated' services on corporate structures: the example of 'branchless' retail banking in Britain. *Environment and Planning A*, **28**, 1843–58. (Chapter 10)

Marshall, J.N. and Wood, P.A. (1995) *Services and Space: Key Aspects of Urban and Regional Development.* London: Longman.

Martie, C.W. (1999) Issues in use tax administration: increasing the compliance rate. In Childress, M. (ed.), *Collecting Taxes in the Cyberage: How Online Purchases Could Affect Revenue Collections.* (Frankfort, KY: The Kentucky Long-Term Policy Research Center). [http://www.ltprc@lrc.state.ky.us] (Chapter 14)

Martin, C. (1997) *The Digital Estate: Strategies for Competing, Surviving, and Thriving in an Internetworked World.* New York: McGraw-Hill. (Chapter 7)

Martin, R. (1994) Stateless monies, global financial integration and national economic autonomy: the end of geography? In Corbridge, S., Martin, R. and Thrift, N. (eds), *Money, Power and Space.* Oxford: Blackwell, pp. 253–78. (Chapter 12)

Martin, R. (ed.) (1999) *Money and the Space Economy.* Chichester: John Wiley. (Chapters 10, 12)

Maslow, A. (1954) *Motivation and Personality.* New York: Harper. (Chapter 2)

Massey, D. (1994) *Space, Place and Gender.* Cambridge: Polity. (Chapter 8)

Massey, D. (1995) *Spatial Divisions of Labour: Social Structures and the Geography of Production*, 2nd edn. London: Macmillan. (Chapter 7)

McConnaughey, J.W. and Lader, W. (1999) Falling through the Net: defining the digital divide. *National Telecommunications and Information Administration*, July 1999, [http://www.ntia.doc.gov/ntiahome/fttn99/contents.html]. (Chapter 9)

McEwen, A. (1998) Temple of dispute – the fine line of border negotiation. *Mercator's World*, **3** (4), July/August, pp. 16–19. (Chapter 16)

McGrew, A.G. and Lewis, P.G. (eds) (1992) *Global Politics: Globalization and the nation-state.* Cambridge: Polity Press. (Chapter 11)

McIntyre, J. (1994) Competition in Japan's information technology sector. *Competitiveness Review*, **4**, 1–12. (Chapter 12)

McKenzie, J. (1998) Rescue of Russia's battered ruble may be a job for IMF. *Christian Science*

Monitor, 29 May, p. 1. (Chapter 12)

McKnight, L. and Bailey, J. (1998) *Internet Economics*. Cambridge, MA: MIT Press. (Chapter 7)

Melody, W.H. (1999) Telecommunications reform: progress and prospects. *Telecommunications Policy*, **23**, 7–34. (Chapter 15)

Mgombelo H.R. (1997) Regulation for premium and value added services – Tanzania. In Mgombelo, H.R. and Werner, M.C.M. (eds), *Telecommunications for Business in Africa*. Amsterdam: IOS Press, pp. 117–24. (Chapter 15)

Microsoft Corporation (1999) *Practicing Knowledge Management: Turning Experience and Information into Results*. Microsoft White Paper, [http://www.microsoft.com/], 1999. (Chapter 16)

Miller, M. (1999) The derivatives revolution after thirty years. *Journal of Portfolio Management*, *Special Issue*, May, pp. 10–16. (Chapter 13)

Minahan, J. (1996) *Nations Without States*. Westport, CT: Greenwood Press. (Chapter 16)

Ministry of International Trade and Industry (MITI) (1999a) Size of market study for E-commerce, [http://www.jipdec.or.jp/chosa/andersen/index.htm], March. (Chapter 6)

Ministry of International Trade and Industry (MITI) (1999b) Changes in the employment structure brought about by the IT revolution, [http://www.jipdec.or.jp/chosa/IT_kakumei/ITkakumeimain.htm]. Machinery and Information Industries Bureau, Electronics Policy Division, September. (Chapter 6)

Ministry of International Trade and Industry (MITI) (1999c) Johoka Hakusho. (Chapter 6)

Ministry of International Trade and Industry (MITI) (1999d) 1997 Retail Census, [http://www.miti.go.jp/stat-j/syougyou/1997-kak/gyoutai/page_01.htm]. (Chapter 6)

Ministry of Trade and Industry (1998) *Committee on Singapore's Competitiveness*. Singapore: MTI. (Chapter 8)

Mirchandani, P.B. and Francis, R.L. (1990) *Discrete Location Theory*. New York: Wiley. (Chapter 4)

Mitchell, D. (1997) The annihilation of space by law: the implications of anti-homeless laws in the United States. *Antipode*, **29**, 303–35. (Chapter 13)

Mitchell, W.J. (1995) *City of Bits: Space, Place and the Infobahn*. Cambridge, MA: MIT Press. (Chapters 5, 10)

Mokhtarian, P. and Salomon, I. (1994) Modelling the choice of telecommuting: setting the context. *Environment and Planning A*, **26**, 749–66. (Chapter 2)

Moore, G.A. (1999) *Crossing the Chasm: Marketing and Selling High-Tech Products to Mainstream Customers*. New York: Harper Business. (Chapter 6)

Morris, J., Richardson, A.J. and McPherson, A. (1996) The emerging needs of the majority – women, young and old. *Conference. Proceedings of the Australasian Transport Research Forum*. (Chapter 2)

Moss, M. (1998) Technologies and cities. *Cityscape*, **3** (3), 107–27, [www.huduser.org:80/periodicals/cityscpe/vol3num3/current.html]. (Chapter 5)

Moss, M.L. (1991) The information city in the global economy. In Brotchie, J., Batty, M., Hall, P. and Newton, P. (eds), *Cities of the 21st Century: New Technologies and Spatial Systems*. Melbourne: Longman Cheshire, pp. 181–9. (Chapter 5)

Moss, M.L. and Townsend, A.M. (1998) Spatial analysis of the Internet in US cities and states. Paper given at Urban Future – Technological Futures Conference at Newcastle upon Tyne, England, 23–5 April 1998, [urban.nyu.edu/]. (Chapters 2, 5)

Moss, M.L. and Townsend, A.M. (1999) The Internet backbone and the American metropolis, [www.informationcity.org/research/Internet_backbone_american_metropolis/index.htm]. (Chapter 5)

Mougayar, W. (1998) *Opening Digital Markets: Battle Plans and Business Strategies for Internet Commerce*, 2nd edn. New York: McGraw-Hill. (Chapter 7)

Moulaert, F. and Gallouj, C. (1993) The locational geography of advanced producer service firms: the limits of economies of agglomeration. In Daniels, P., Illeris, S., Bonamy, J. and Philippe, J. (eds), *The Geography of Services*. London: Frank Cass, pp. 91–106. (Chapter 10)

Murnion, S. and Healey, R.G. (1998) Modeling distance decay effects in web server information flows. *Geographical Analysis*, **30** (4), 285–303. (Chapter 4)

Murphy, A. (1999) The realities of electronic commerce. Paper presented at the Association of American Geographers 95th Annual Meeting, 23–7 March, Honolulu, Hawaii. (Chapter 9)

Nairn, G. (1998) IT is still changing the face of trading. *Financial Times*, 24 March, p. viii. (Chapter 12)

Nanoka I. and Takeuchi, H. (1996) *The Knowledge-creating Company*. Oxford University Press. (Chapter 10)

National Conference of State Legislatures (2000) Executive Committee Task Force on State and Local Taxation of Telecommunications and Electronic Commerce. Voluntary Zero Burden Sales Tax Administration System. Summary of key findings. (January 10) [http://www.ncsl.org/programs/fiscal/tc0bsum.htm]. (Chapter 14)

National Research Council (1999a) *A Question of Balance: Private Rights and the Public Interest in Scientific and Technical Databases*. Washington, DC: National Academy Press. (Chapter 4)

National Research Council (1999b) *Distributed Geolibraries: Spatial Information Resources*. Washington, DC: National Academy Press, also [http://www.nap.edu]. (Chapter 4)

NCB (1986) *National IT Plan*. Singapore: NCB. (Chapter 8)

NCB (1992) *A Vision of an Intelligent Island: The IT2000 Report*. Singapore: NCB. (Chapter 8)

NCB (1998) Press release, 13 April [http://www.ncb.gov.sg/]. (Chapter 8)

NCB (1999) Press release, 15 August. (Chapter 8)

Needle, D. (1998) Traveling the information highway. *Upside*, May, 88–92, 154–60. (Chapter 3)

Negroponte, N. (1999) quoted in M. Seminerio, E-commerce in the Third World. *ZD Net News*, [http://www.zdnet.com/zdnn/stories/news/0,4586,2231190,00.html].

Neilsen, J. (1995) *Multimedia and Hypertext: The Internet and Beyond*. Boston: AP Professional.

Neilsen, J. (1999) *Designing Web Usability: The Practice of Simplicity*. Indianapolis: New Riders Publishing.

Nippon Keizai Shimbun (2000b) 99nen no pasoken shukka 36% zou. 16 February. Available: Mail Service: [mailservice@nikkeimailgoo.ne.jp].

Nua Internet Surveys (1995, 1999) Nua Ltd, Merrion House, Merrion Road, Dublin 4, Ireland. [http://www.nua.ie/surveys].

Nunn, S., Warren, R. and Rubleske, B. (1998) Software jobs go begging: threatening technology boom: computer services in the US metropolitan areas. 1982 and 1983. *Professional Geographer*, 50, 358–71.

Nystuen, J.D. and Dacey, M.F. (1961) A graph theory of nodal regions. *Papers and Proceedings of the Regional Science Associations*, 7, 29–42.

O hUallachain, B. and Reid, N. (1991) The location and growth of business and professional services in American metropolitan areas, 1976–86. *Annals of the Association of American Geographers*, **81**, 254–70. (Chapter 7)

O'Brien, R. (1992) *Global Financial Integration: The End of Geography*. Washington: Council on Foreign Relations. (Chapters 5, 8, 12, 13)

O'Brien, R. (1995) Who rules the world's financial markets? *Harvard Business Review*, **73**, 144–50. (Chapter 13)

O'Connell, V. (1995) Brokerage firms are moving into cyberspace. *Wall Street Journal*, July 6, p. C1. (Chapter 12)

Odlyzko, A. (1998) The Internet and other networks: utilization rates and their implications. [www.research.att.com/~amo/doc/Internet.rates.pdf]. (Chapter 5)

OECD (1999) OECD Internet access price comparison [http://www.oecd.org/dsti/sti/it/cm/stats/isp-price99.htm]. (Chapter 15)

OECD (1999a) *Communications Outlook*. Paris: OECD (Chapter 10)

OECD (1999b) *The Economic and Social Impacts of Electronic Commerce: Preliminary Findings and Research Agenda*. Paris: OECD. (Chapters 6, 9)

OECD (1999c) OECD *Communications Outlook* 1999. Paris: OECD. (Chapter 9)

OECD (1999d) *Electronic Commerce Web Site*. Paris: OECD. [http://www.oecd.org/subject/e_commerce/]. (Chapter 9)

OECD (2000) OECD Indicators on Internet and electronic commerce [www.oecd.org/dsti/sti/it/cm/stats/newindicators.htm)]. (Chapter 10)

Ohmae, K. (1990) *The Borderless World: Power and Strategy in the Interlinked Economy*.

London: Collins; Fontana. (Chapters 8, 13)

Ohmae, K. (1995) *The End of the Nation State: The Rise of Regional Economies*. New York, NY: Simon and Schuster, and London, UK: HarperCollins. (Chapters 8, 16)

OTA (Office of Technology Assessment) (1995) *The Technological Reshaping of Metropolitan America*. Washington, DC: US Government Printing Office. (Chapter 5)

OTA (US Congress, Office of Technology Assessment) (1990) *Trading Around the Clock: Global Securities Markets and Information Technology – Background Paper*. Washington, DC: US Government Printing Office. (Chapter 11)

Paddock, R. (1998) Russia lied to get loans, says aide to Yeltsin. *Los Angeles Times*, Wednesday, 9 September, p. 1. (Chapter 12)

Palmer, J.W. (1997) Electronic commerce in retailing: differences across retail formats. *The Information Society*, **13** (1), 75–92. (Chapter 1)

Paltridge, S. (1998a) *Internet Traffic Exchange: Developments and Policy*. Paris: OECD, [www.oecd.org/dsti/sti/it/cm/prod/ traffic.htm]. (Chapter 5)

Paltridge, S. (1998b) *Internet Infrastructure Indicators*. Paris: OECD, [www.oecd.org/dsti/sti/it/cm/prod/tisp98_7e.htm]. (Chapter 5)

Paxson, V. (1997) End-to-end routing behavior in the Internet. *IEEE Transactions on Networking*, **5**, 601–15. (Chapter 5)

Peck, J.A. (1995) Moving and shaking: business elites, state localism and urban privatism. *Progress in Human Geography*, **19** (1), 16–46. (Chapter 8)

Peck, J. and Tickell, A. (1994) Searching for a new institutional fix: the after-Fordist crisis and the global-local disorder. In Amin, A. (ed.), *Post-Fordism: A Reader*. Oxford: Blackwell.

Peet, J. (2000) Shopping and the Web, *Economist Survey*, 26 February. (Chapter 2)

Peitchinis, S.G. (1992) Computer technology and the location of economic activity. *Futures*, **24**, 813–20. (Chapter 5)

Pelletiere, D. and Rodrigo, G.C. (1999) Does the Internet complement or substitute for regional external economies: a proposed framework for analysis and preliminary results, presented to the Association for Public Analysis and Management Annual Conference, Washington. (Chapter 2)

Perry, M. (1992) Promoting corporate control in Singapore. *Regional Studies*, **26** (3), 289–94. (Chapter 8)

Perry, M. (1995) New corporate structures, regional offices and Singapore's new economic directions. *Singapore Journal of Tropical Geography*, **16** (2), 181–96. (Chapter 8)

Perry, M., Kong, L. and Yeoh, B. (1997) *Singapore: A Developmental City State*. Chichester: John Wiley. (Chapter 8)

Perry, M., Poon, J. and Yeung, H. (1998a) Regional offices in Singapore: spatial and strategic influences in the location of corporate control. *Review of Urban and Regional Development Studies*, **10** (1), 42–59. (Chapter 8)

Perry, M., Yeung, H., and Poon, J. (1998b), Regional office mobility: the case of corporate control in Singapore and Hong Kong. *Geoforum*, **29** (3), 237–55. (Chapter 8)

Petrazzini, B. and Kibati, M. (1999) The Internet in developing countries. *Communications of the ACM*, June, **42** (6), 31–6. (Chapter 9)

Pickles, J. (ed.) (1995) *Ground Truth – The Social Implications of Geographic Information Systems*. New York: Guilford Press. (Chapter 16)

Pirie, G.H. (1979) Measuring accessibility: A review and proposal. *Environment and Planning A*, **11**, 299–312. (Chapter 4)

Plaut, P.O. (1997) Telecommunication vs transportation. *Access*, No. 10. Davis: University of California Transportation Center. (Chapter 2)

Pollard, J. and Storper, M. (1996) A tale of twelve cities: metropolitan employment change in dynamic industries in the 1980s. *Economic Geography*, **72**, 1–22. (Chapter 7)

Poon, J. and Perry, M. (1999) The Asian economic 'flu': a geography of crisis. *Professional Geographer*, **51**, 184–96. (Chapter 12)

Poon, S. and Swatman, P.M.C. (1999) An exploratory study of small business Internet commerce issues. *Information and Management*, **35** (1), 9–18. (Chapter 8)

Porat, M.U. (1977) *The Information Economy: Definition and Measurement*. US Department of

Commerce. (Chapter 6)

Porteous, D. (1999) The development of financial centres: location, information, externalities and path dependence. In Martin, R. (ed.), *Money and the Space Economy*. Chichester: John Wiley, pp. 95–114. (Chapter 10)

Porter, M. (1990) *The Competitive Advantage of Nations*. New York: The Free Press. (Chapter 1)

Porter, M. (1996) Competitive advantage, agglomeration economies, and regional policy. *International Regional Science Review*, **19** (1 and 2), 85–94. (Chapter 1)

Power, D. (2000) Exchanges, markets, cities and futures: London, ICT and the integration of European stock exchanges, unpublished manuscript. (Chapter 13)

Pratt, D.J. (1998) Replacing money: the evolution of branch banking in Britain. *Environment and Planning A*, **30**, 2211–26. (Chapter 10)

Pritchard, W. (1999) Local and global in cyberspace: the geographical narratives of US food companies on the Internet. *Area*, **31**, 9–17. (Chapter 7)

Pro Active International (2000) *National Internet Monitor*. Amsterdam: Pro Active International. (Chapter 10)

Pryke, M. and Lee, R. (1995) Place your bets: towards an understanding of globalisation, socio-financial engineering and competition within a financial centre. *Urban Studies*, **32**, 329–44. (Chapter 13)

Quittner, S. (1999) The laughing billionaire. *Time Magazine*, 27 December, **154** (26), pp. 46ff. (Chapter 9)

RABO Bank, *Annual Reports* (various years). Utrecht. (Chapter 10)

Rabobank Press Release (1999, 2000) 8 December 1999, 9 February 2000. (Chapter 10)

Radecki, J., Wenniger, J. and Orlow, D. (1997) Industry structure: electronic delivery's potential effects on retail banking. *Journal of Retail Banking Services*, **XIX** (4), 57–63. (Chapter 10)

Radio Free Europe/Radio Liberty Newsline (1997) Luzhkov says dependence on the IMF is a 'national disgrace', 30 December, p. 1. (Chapter 12)

Raper, J., McCarthy, T., and Williams, N. (1999) Georeferenced four-dimensional virtual environments: principles and applications. *Computers, Environment and Urban Systems*, **22** (6), 529–39. (Chapter 4)

Rees, J. (1997) International wide area networking for business applications. In Mgombelo, H.R. and Werner, M.C.M. (eds), *Telecommunications for Business in Africa*. Amsterdam: IOS Press, pp. 27–40. (Chapter 15)

Regan, P.M. (1995) *Legislating Privacy: Technology, Social Values, and Public Policy*. Chapel Hill: University of North Carolina. (Chapter 14)

Reidenberg, J. (1997) Governing networks and rule-making in cyberspace. In Kahin, B. and Nesson, C. (eds), *Borders in Cyberspace: Information Policy and the Global Information Infrastructure*. Cambridge: MIT Press. (Chapter 14)

Reimer, S. (1999) Contract services firms in local authorities: evolving geographies of activities. *Regional Studies*, **33**, 121–30. (Chapter 7)

Reuters (1999) Net remains privilege of Argentinean elite, [http://www.nua.ie/surveys/?f= VS&art_id=905355182&rel=true]. (Chapter 15)

Richardson, A.J., Morris, J. and Loeis, M. (1996) Changing employment and income profiles – new environment for travel demand. *Conference. Proceedings of the Australasian Transport Research Forum*. (Chapter 2)

Rickard, J. (1996) Mapping the Internet with traceroute. *Boardwatch Magazine*, December, [boardwatch.Internet.com/mag/96/dec/bwm38.html]. (Chapter 5)

Rickard, J. (1998) The Internet – what is it? *Boardwatch Directory of Internet Service Providers*. Boulder, CO: Penton, pp. 11–16, [www.boardwatch.com/isp/summer99/Internetarch.html]. (Chapter 5)

Ridding, J. (1998) Rival markets battle for the top spot. *Financial Times*, 27 April, p. 30. (Chapter 11)

Rimmer, P (2000) Near neighbors: Australian and Indonesian telecommunications connections. In Wilson, M. and Corey, K. (eds), *Information Tectonics: Spatial Organization in the Electronic Age*. Chichester: John Wiley, pp. 165–98. (Chapter 15)

Rindova, V. and Kotha, S. (2000) The dynamics of form and function: how Yahoo! and excite pursue competitive advantage, [http://www.netesteem.com/downloads/Research%20Papers/yahoo_pap.pdf]. (Chapter 3)

Robison, R. and Rosser, R. (1998) Contesting reform: Indonesia's new order and the IMF. *World Development*, **26**, 1593–609. (Chapter 12)

Rodan, G. (1989) The political economy of Singapore's industralization: nation state and international capital, Kuala Lumpur, Forum. (Chapter 8)

Rogers, E.M. (1964) *Diffusion of Innovations*. New York: Free Press of Glencoe. (Chapter 6)

Rogers, E.M. (1995) *Diffusion of Innovations*, 4th edn. New York: The Free Press. (Chapter 10)

Rogers, J. (1998) Safety Nyet. *Testimony before the Subcommittee on General Oversight and Investigation, The House Banking Committee on Banking and Financial Services*, US House of Representatives. Washington, DC, September, **10**, 162–9. (Chapter 12)

Romeo, J. (2000) Wireless B2B E-commerce developing in China. *Ecommerce Times*, 21 January. [http://www.ecommercetimes.com/news/articles2000/000121-4.shtml]. (Chapter 15)

Romer, P.M. (1990) Endogenous technical change. *Journal of Political Economy*, **98**, S71–S102. (Chapter 2)

Romero, S. (2000) Weavers go dot.com, and elders move in. *New York Times*, 28 March, 1. (Chapters 1, 15)

Root, A., Schintler, L. and Button, K.J. (2000) Women, travel and the idea of sustainable transport. *Transport Reviews*, **20** (3), pp. 369–83. (Chapter 2)

Rosecrance, R. (1986) *The Rise of the Trading State*: *Commerce and Conquest in the Modern World*. New York: Basic Books. (Chapter 16)

Rosecrance, R. (1999) *The Rise of the Virtual State*: *Wealth and Power in the Coming Century*. New York: Basic Books. (Chapter 16)

Rosenberg, S. (1999) Amazon vs. the ants. *Salon Magazine*, 10 March 1999, [http://www.salon.com/21st/rose/1999/03/10straight.html]. (Chapter 9)

Rosenberg, S. (2000) The Napster files. *Salon*, 4 February, [http://www.salon.com/tech/col/rose/2000/02/04/napster_swap/index.html]. (Chapter 3)

Rycroft, R.W. and Kash, D.E. (1999) *The Complexity Challenge*: *Technological Innovation for the 21st Century*. London: Pinter. (Chapter 2)

Saburov, E. (1998) The IMF and the Russian banking industry. *Testimony before the Subcommittee on General Oversight and Investigation, The House Banking Committee on Banking and Financial Services, US House of Representatives*. Washington, DC, September, **10**, 177–83. (Chapter 12)

Salant, J.D. (1999) Lawmakers try to stop legislation restricting wine sales, DetroitNews.Com (27 May), [http://www.detroitnews.com/1999/technology/9905/29/05270248.htm]. (Chapter 14)

Salomon, I. (1985) Telecommunications and travel – substitution or modified mobility? *Journal of Transportation Economics and Policy*, **19**, 219–35. (Chapter 2)

Salomon, I. (1986) Telecommunications and travel relationships: a review. *Transportation Research*, **20A**, 223–38. (Chapter 2)

Salomon, I. (1996) Telecommunications, cities and technological opportunism. *Annals of Regional Science*, **30**, 75–90. (Chapter 5)

Salomon, I. (2000) Can telecommunications help solve transportation problems? In Button, K.J. and Hensher, D. (eds), *Handbook of Transport Modelling*, Oxford: Elsevier. (Chapter 2)

Salomon, I. and Mokhtarian, P. (1997) Why don't you telecommute? *Access*, No. 10. Spring. Davis: University of California Transportation Center. (Chapter 2)

Salomon, I. and Mokhtarian, P. (1998) What happens when mobility-inclined market segments face accessibility-enhancing policies? *Transportation Research D*, **3**, 129–40. (Chapter 2)

San Jose Mercury News (2000) Brazil's unusual ISPs causing net boom, 9 February, [http://www.nua.ie/surveys/?f=VS&art_id=905355582&rel=true]. (Chapter 15)

Sarkar, A. and Tozzi, M. (1998) *Electronic Trading on Futures Exchanges*. New York: Federal Reserve Bank of New York. (Chapter 11)

Sarkar, M., Butler, B. and Steinfield, C. (1998) Cybermediaries in Electronic Marketspace: Toward Theory Building. *Journal of Business Research*, **41** (3), 215–21. (Chapter 8)

Sassen, S. (1991) *The Global City*: *New York, London, Tokyo*. Princeton NJ: Princeton University Press. (Chapters 8, 13)

Sassen, S. (1994) *Cities in a World Economy*. London: Sage; Thousand Oaks, CA: Pine Forge Press. (Chapters 5, 11)

Sassen, S. (1995) The state and the global city: notes towards a conception of place-centered governance. *Competition and Change*, **1** (1), 31–50. (Chapter 8)

Sassen, S. (1996) Cities in the global economy. *Proceedings of the Seoul Metropolitan Fora 96*, Seoul. (Chapter 10)

Sassen, S. (1999) Global financial centers. *Foreign Affairs*, **78** (1), 75–87. (Chapter 11)

Saunders, R., Warford, J. and Welleniuis, B. (1994) *Telecommunications and Economic Development*. Baltimore: Johns Hopkins University Press. (Chapter 7)

Saw, T.C. (1999) Wired Singapore? The impact of electronic networks on the geography of business linkages in Singapore, Honours Thesis, Department of Geography, National University of Singapore. (Chapter 8)

Saxenian, A. (1994) *Regional Advantage: Culture and Competition in Silicon Valley and Route 128*. Cambridge, MA: Harvard University Press. (Chapters 7, 8)

Schiller, D. (1999) *Digital Capitalism: Networking and the Global Market System*. Cambridge, MA: MIT Press. (Chapters 1, 5, 7, 12)

Scholes, M. (1996) Global financial markets, derivatives securities and systematic risks. *Journal of Risk and Uncertainty*, **12**, 271–86. (Chapter 13)

Schumpeter, Joseph (1969) *Business Cycles*. New York: McGraw-Hill (abridged by Reindig Fels). (Chapter 3)

Scott, A. (1995) The geographic foundations of industrial performance. *Competition and Change: Journal of Global Business and Political Economy*. **1**, 51–66. (Chapter 13)

Scott, A.J. (1988) *Metropolis: From the Division of Labor to Urban Form*. Los Angeles: University of California Press. (Chapter 8)

Scott, A.J. (1996) Regional motors of the global economy, *Futures*, **28** (5), 391–411. (Chapter 8)

Scott, A.J. (1998) *Regions and the World Economy: The Coming Shape of Global Production, Competition and Political Order*. Oxford: Oxford University Press. (Chapter 8)

Scripps Howard News Service (1997) Rolling the dice on the Internet, [http://abcnews.aol.com/sections/scitech/Internetgambling1119/index.html]. (Chapter 14)

Sears, Roebuck and Co. (1999) *Sears History*, [http://www.sears.com/]. (Chapter 6)

Segal, L. and Sullivan, D. (1997) The growth of temporary services work. *Journal of Economic Perspectives*, **11**, 117–36. (Chapter 7)

Seven-Eleven Japan (1999a) Shutten Jokyo, [http://info.sej.co.jp/]. (Chapter 6)

Seven-Eleven Japan (1999b) *Corporate Outline 1999*, [http://info.sej.co.jp/]. (Chapter 6)

Shapiro, C. and Varian, H.R. (1998) *Information Rules: A Strategic Guide to the Network Economy*. Boston: Harvard Business School Press. (Chapters 2, 7)

Shapiro, C. and Varian, H.R. (1999) *Information Rules: A Strategic Guide to the Network Economy*. Boston: Harvard Business School Press. (Chapters 3, 9, 10)

Shaw, R. (1997) Internet domain names: whose domain is this? In Kahin, B. and Keller, J. (eds), *Coordinating the Internet*. Cambridge, MA: MIT Press. (Chapter 9)

Shephard, S. (1997) The new economy: what it really means. *Business Week*, 17–23 November, 38–40. (Chapter 1)

Simons, K. (1997) Model error. *New England Economic Review*, November–December, pp. 17–25. (Chapter 13)

Singapore (1998) Bank for International Settlements (BIS) *Survey of Foreign Exchange and Derivatives Markets Activities*, 29 September. Singapore: Monetary Authority of Singapore. (Chapter 11)

Singh, A. (1994) Global economic changes, skills, and international competitiveness. *International Labour Review*, pp. 133, 2, 167–183 (Chapter 1)

Singh, S. (1999) Electronic money: understanding its use to increase the effectiveness of policy. *Telecommunications Policy*, **23**, 753–73. (Chapter 10)

Smith, E.B. (2000) Costa Rica online with free e-mail for all. *USA Today*, 1 June, p. 20A. (Chapter 15)

Solomon, E. (1997) *Virtual Money*. Oxford: Oxford University Press. (Chapter 12)

Solomon, R. (1999) *Money on the Move: The Revolution in International Finance since 1980.* Princeton, NJ: Princeton University Press. (Chapter 12)

Solow, R.A. (1956) A contribution to the theory of economic growth. *Quarterly Journal of Economics*, **70**, 65–94. (Chapter 1)

Sonnemans, M.A.A. (1996) *Banking Firms Start a Payment Experiment on Internet* (in Dutch). Bank-en Effectenbedrijf, July/August, 7–10. (Chapter 10)

Southwick, K. (1996) Interview with Jeff Bezos, Amazon.com. *Upside*, October, pp. 29–34. (Chapter 3)

Spohrer, J.C. (1999) Information in places. *IBM Systems Journal*, **38** (4), 602–28. [http://www.research.ibm.com/journal/sj/384/spohrer.html]. (Chapter 4)

Steinfield, C. and Klein, S. (1999) Local vs. global issues in electronic commerce. *Electronic Markets*, **9** (1/2), 1–6. (Chapter 9)

Steinfield, C. and Whitten, P. (1999) Community level socio-economic impacts of electronic commerce. *Journal of Computer-Mediated Communications*, December, **5** (2). (Chapter 9)

Sternberg, R. (1996) Regional growth theories and high tech regions. *International Journal of Urban and Regional Research*, **20**, 3, 518–38. (Chapter 1)

Stiroh, K. (1999) Is there a new economy? *Challenge*, July–August **42** (4), 82–84. (Chapter 1)

Storper, M. (1995) The resurgence of regional economies, ten years later: the region as a nexus of untraded interdependencies. *European Urban and Regional Studies*, **2** (3), 191–221. (Chapter 8)

Storper, M. (1997) *The Regional World: Territorial Development in a Global Economy.* New York: Guilford Press. (Chapters 8, 16)

Storper, M. and Walker, R. (1989) *The Capitalist Imperative: Territory, Technology, and Industrial Growth.* Oxford: Blackwell. (Chapter 13)

Straits Times, The (1998) Masterplan to make Singapore e-commerce hub, 24 September, 1. (Chapter 8)

Straits Times, The (1999a) Mustafa let down by e-commerce, 13 December, p. 64. (Chapter 8)

Straits Times, The (1999b) E-commerce takes hold: business to close in on $1.5 bn mark, 24 August, p. 42. (Chapter 8)

Straits Times, The (2000) First e-commerce tax incentives, 14 January, p. 1. (Chapter 8)

Strange, S. (1994) From Bretton Woods to the casino economy. In Corbridge, S., Martin, R. and Thrift, N. (eds), *Money, Power and Space.* Oxford: Blackwell, pp. 49–62. (Chapter 12)

Strange, S. (1998) *Mad Money: When Markets Outgrow Governments.* Ann Arbor, MI: University of Michigan Press. (Chapter 12)

Struye de Swielande, H. (2000) Internet as a challenge for financial service providers (in Dutch). *Bank- en Effectenbedrijf*, January/February, pp. 34–8. (Chapter 10)

Stuck, B. (1996) Internet transactions still yield small change. *Business Communications Review*, **26** (10), 51–4. (Chapter 1)

Stutz, F. and de Souza, A. (1998) *The World Economy: Resources, Location, Trade, and Development.* NJ: Prentice-Hall. (Chapter 7)

Sullivan, J. (1998a) Using bots to buy books. *Wired News*, 14 May, [http://www.wired.com/news/news/business/story/12280.html] (Chapter 9)

Sullivan, J. (1998b) Wal-Mart sues web upstarts. *Wired News*, 16 October, [http://www.wired.com/news/news/business/story/15672.html]. (Chapter 9)

Sumser, J. (1998) Regional excellence. *Electronic Recruiting News*, 27 March, p. 1. (Chapter 7)

Sutton, J. (1997) Sell no wine online in the south. Nando.net. Available at [www.nando.net/newsroom/ntn/info/093097/info6_29429_noframes.html].

Swann, D. (1996) *European Economic Integration.* Cheltenham: Edward Elgar. (Chapter 10)

Swyngedouw, E. (1996) Producing futures: international finance as a geographical project. In Daniels, P. and Lever, B. (eds), *The Global Economy in Transition.* Harlow: Longman, pp. 135–63. (Chapter 13)

Tapscott, D. (1996) *The Digital Economy.* New York: McGraw-Hill. (Chapter 12)

Taylor, P. (1994) The state as container: territoriality in the modern world-system. *Progress in Human Geography*, **18**, 151–62. (Chapter 12)

Taylor, S.Y. (1999) *Review of Freight Transport Chain Case Studies.* Austroads Project

NRSM.9804. ARRB Transport Research, South Vermont. (Chapter 2)

Taylor, S.Y., Button, K.J., and Stough, R. (2000) *Telecommunications and Transport Effects: A Review of Interaction Tendencies and Travel,* Mason Enterprise Center Working Paper 2000/1, George Mason University. (Chapter 2)

TCA (2000) Number of Subscribers by Carriers. Telecommunication Carriers Association. Online. Available: [http://skew2.kellogg.nwu.edu/greenste/.research.html].

Teitelman, R. and Davis, S. (1996) How the cash flows. *Institutional Investor,* August, pp. 58–73.

Telecommunications Carriers Association (2000) Keitai denwa, PHS to musen yobidashi no ruikei kanyusha su. End-January. [http://www.tca.or.jp/index.html]. (Chapter 6)

Telegeography (1998) *Global Telecommunications Traffic Statistics and Commentary.* Washington, DC: Telegeography, Inc. (Chapter 12)

Telegeography, Inc. (1999) *Telegeography 2000.* Washington, DC: Telegeography, Inc. (Chapter 5)

Terkowitz, R.S. (1999) Tulip frenzy revisited: are Internet stocks another bubble? *Information Impacts Magazine,* April. [http://www.cisp.org/imp/]. (Chapter 9)

Tessler, J. (1999) Web surfing is fast way to go job hopping. *The Wall Street Journal,* 27 May, B12. (Chapter 7)

Thomas, G. and Wyatt, S. (1999) Shaping cyberspace – interpreting and transforming the Internet. *Research Policy,* **28,** 681–98. (Chapter 5)

Thord, R. (ed.) (1993) *The Future of Transportation and Communication.* Berlin: Springer-Verlag. (Chapter 10)

Thrift, N. (1994) On the social and cultural determinants of international financial centres: the case of the City of London. In Corbridge, S., Martin, R. and Thrift, N. (eds), *Money, Power and Space.* Oxford: Blackwell, pp. 327–55. (Chapter 7)

Thrift, N. (1996) New urban eras and old technological fears: reconfiguring the goodwill of electronic things. *Urban Studies,* **33** (8), 1463–93. (Chapter 8)

Thrift, N. (2000) Less mystery, more imagination: the future of the City of London. *Environment and Planning A,* **32,** 381–4. (Chapter 13)

Thrift, N. and Leyshon, A. (1994) A phantom state? The de-traditionalization of money, the international financial system and international financial centres. *Political Geography,* **13,** 299–327. (Chapters 12, 13)

Tickell, A. (1996) Making a melodrama out of a crisis: reinterpreting the collapse of Barings Bank. *Environment and Planning D: Society and Space,* **14,** 5–33. (Chapter 13)

Tickell, A. (1999a) European financial integration and uneven development. In Hudson, R. and Williams, A. (eds), *Divided Europe: Society and Territory.* London: Sage, pp. 63–78. (Chapter 13)

Tickell, A. (1999b) Unstable futures. In Leys, C. and Panitch, L. (eds), *Socialist Register 1999.* London: Merlin Press, pp. 248–77. (Chapter 13)

Tickell, A. (2000) Dangerous derivatives: controlling and creating risks in international money. *Geoforum,* **31,** 87–99. (Chapter 13)

Toffler, A. (1980) *The Third Wave.* New York: Morrow. (Chapters 6, 8)

Toffler, A. and Toffler, H. (1995) *Creating a New Civilization: The Politics of the Third Wave.* Atlanta: Turner Publishing. (Chapter 8)

Touraine, A. (1971) *The Post Industrial Society; Tomorrow's Social History.* New York: Random House. (Chapter 6)

Tuathail, G.Ó (1996) *Critical Geopolitics.* Minneapolis, MN: University of Minnesota Press. (Chapter 16)

Tyner, J. (1998) Asian labor recruitment and the World Wide Web. *Professional Geographer,* **50,** 331–44. (Chapter 7)

UK Royal Commission on Environmental Pollution (1994) *Eighteenth Report: Transport and the Environment.* Cm. 2674. HMSO, London. (Chapter 2)

United States Federal Communications Commission (1999) *Trends in the US International Telecommunications Industry.* [http://www.fcc.gov/Bureaus/Common_Carrier/Reports/FCC-State_Link/Intl/itltrd99.pdf]. (Chapter 15)

US Census Bureau (1999a) *1997 Economic Census – Retail Trade, Geographic Area Series,*

25 October, [http://www.census.gov/prod/ec97/97r44-dc.pdf]. (Chapter 6)

US Census Bureau (1999b) *State Population Estimates and Demographic Components of Population Change: July 1, 1998 to July 1, 1999*, [http://www.census.gov/population/estimates/state/st–99–1.txt]. ST–99–1. 29 December. Population Estimates Program, Population Division. (Chapter 6)

US Census Bureau (2000) *Land Area, Density and Population for Metropolitan Areas*, [http://www.census.gov/]. US Census Bureau, Population Division, Population and Housing Programs Branch. (Chapter 6)

US Department of Commerce (1998) *The Emerging Digital Economy I*. Washington, DC: US Department of Commerce, [http://www.ecommerce.gov]. (Chapters 1, 7)

US Department of Commerce (1999) *The Emerging Digital Economy II*, June 1999. GPO, Washington, DC, [http://www.ecommerce.gov/]. (Chapters 1, 6, 9)

US Department of Transportation (1992) *Transportation Implications of Telecommuting*, US-DOT, Washington (Chapter 2)

Varian, H.R. (1999) Market structure in the network age, presented to the Understanding the Digital Economy Conference, Washington. (Chapter 2)

Vernon, R. (1966) International investment and international trade in the product cycle. *Quarterly Journal of Economics*, **80**, 190–207. (Chapter 2)

Vernon, R. (1971) *Sovereignty at Bay*. New York: Basic Books. (Chapter 12)

Vervest, P. and Dunn A. (2000) *How to Win Customers in the Digital World?* Berlin: Springer-Verlag. (Chapter 10)

Vesely, R. (1999) Pounding the virtual pavement. *Business* 2.0, 4, 24–6. (Chapter 7)

Virtual Vineyards Responds to Sting Allegations, [http://www.pathfinder.com/money/latest/press/PW/1997Dec16/539.html]. (Chapter 14)

Vonk, E. (1997) International telecommunications requirements within a multinational company. In Mgombelo, H.R. and Werner, M.C.M. (eds), *Telecommunications for Business in Africa*. Amsterdam: IOS Press, pp. 19–26. (Chapter 15)

Waddell, C.D. (1999) The growing digital divide in access for people with disabilities: overcoming barriers to participation. Paper presented at Understanding the Digital Economy: Data Tools and Research Conference, 25–6 May, Washington, DC, [http://www.digitaleconomy.gov/]. (Chapter 9)

Walsh, M.W. (1998) Icelanders, Microsoft in war of words. *Los Angeles Times*, 29 June. (Chapter 16)

Walther, J.B. (1996) Computer-mediated communication: impersonal, interpersonal and hyperpersonal interaction. *Communication Research*, **23**, 3–43. (Chapter 2)

Wang, E.H. (1999) ICT and economic development in Taiwan; analysis of the evidence. *Telecommunications Policy*, **23**, 235–43. (Chapter 15)

Warf, B. (1989) Telecommunication and the globalization of financial services. *Professional Geographer*, **41**, 257–71. (Chapter 10)

Warf, B. (1995) Telecommunications and the changing geographies of knowledge transmission in the late 20th century. *Urban Studies*, **32**, 361–78. (Chapter 12)

Warf, B. (1998) Reach out and touch someone: AT&T's global operations in the 1990s. *Professional Geographer*, **50**, 255–67. (Chapter 12)

Warf, B. (1999) The hypermobility of capital and the collapse of the Keynesian state. In Martin, R. (ed.), *Money and the Space Economy*. Chichester: John Wiley, pp. 227–40. (Chapters 10, 12)

Warf, B. (2000) Japanese information services in the late twentieth century. In Wilson, M. and Corey, K. (eds), *Information Tectonics: Spatial Organization in the Electronic Age*. Chichester: John Wiley, pp. 101–14. (Chapter 12)

Warf, B. and Grimes, J. (1997) Counterhegemonic discourses and the Internet. *The Geographical Review*, **87**, 259–74. (Chapter 7)

Warntz, W. (1967) Global science and the tyranny of space. *Papers and Proceedings of the Regional Science Association*, **19**, 7–19. (Chapter 4)

Watson, R., Akelsen, S. and Pitt, L. (1998) Attractors: building mountains in the flat landscape of the World Wide Web. *California Management Review*, **40** (2), 36–56. (Chapters 3, 7)

Wawine Home (1997) What do people in the following states have in common? [http://

www.wawine.com/move.htm]. (Chapter 14)

Webber, A.M. (1993) What's so new about the new economy? *Harvard Business Review*, January–February, 24–42. (Chapter 15)

Weber, A. (1929) *Alfred Weber's Theory of the Location of Industries*. Translated by Friedrich, C.J.. Chicago: University of Chicago Press. (Chapter 4)

Weber, M. (1947) *The Theory of Social and Economic Organization*. New York: The Free Press. (Chapter 14)

Weiner, S.E. (1999) Electronic payments in the US economy: an overview. *Bulletin of the Federal Reserve Bank of Kansas City*, 4th quarter, pp. 53–64. (Chapter 1)

Weisbrot, M. (1998) Testimony of Mark Weisbrot. *Testimony before the Subcommittee on General Oversight and Investigation, House Banking Committee on Banking and Financial Services, US House of Representatives*. Washington, DC, September, 10, 157–61. (Chapter 12)

Weiss, L. (1998) *The Myth of the Powerless State*: Governing the Economy in a Global Era. Cambridge: Polity Press. (Chapter 8)

Wenninger, J. (2000) The emerging role of banks in E-commerce. *Current Issues in Economics and Finance*, 6 (3), 1–6. (Chapter 11)

Westland, J.C. and Clark, T.H.K. (1999) *Global Electronic Commerce. Theory and Case Studies*. Cambridge, MA: MIT Press. (Chapters 1, 10, 11)

Wheeler, D. and O'Kelly, M.E. (1998) *A Method for Generating Cyber Trade Areas: A Case Study of the Ohio State University*. Presentation at the 1998 Annual Meeting, East Lakes Division, Association of American Geographers (31 October). (Chapter 4)

Wheeler, D. and O'Kelly, M.E. (1999) Network topology and city accessibility of the commercial Internet, *Professional Geographer*, 51 (3), 327–39. (Chapters 4, 5)

Wheeler, J.O., Aoyama, Y., and Warf, B. (eds) (2000) *Cities in the Telecommunications Age*: The Fracturing of Geographies. New York: Routledge. (Chapter 6)

Whinston, A.B., Stahl, D. and Choi, S-Y. (1997) *The Economics of Electronic Commerce*. Indianapolis: Macmillan Technical Publishing. (Chapter 1)

Wigand, R. (1997) Electronic commerce: definition, theory, and context. *The Information Society*, 13 (1), March, 1–16. (Chapter 1)

Williamson, J. (1983) *The Exchange Rate System*. Washington, DC: Institute for International Economics. (Chapter 12)

Willis, C. (1998) Does Amazon.com really matter? *Forbes ASAP*, 6 April. (Chapter 3)

Wilson, J.P. (1999) Local, national, and global applications of GIS in agriculture. In Longley, P.A., Goodchild, M.F., Maguire, D.J. and Rhind, D.W. (eds), *Geographical Information Systems: Principles, Techniques, Management and Applications*, vol. 2. New York: John Wiley, pp. 981–98. (Chapter 4)

Wilson, M. (1999) Fall of the mall? The urban impact of electronic retailing. Paper presented at the Association of American Geographers 95th Annual Meeting, 23–7 March 1999, Honolulu, Hawaii. (Chapter 9)

Wilson, M. (2001) Location, location, location: the geography of the dot com problem. *Environment and Planning B*, 27, forthcoming. (Chapter 15)

Wine Institute (1997) What's happened so far this year on the direct shipping front. *Wine Business Monthly*, (August), [http://smartwine.com/wbm/1997/9708/bmh9709.htm]. (Chapter 14)

Winter, M. (1999) Scarborough Bill impacts Internet wine sales. Or does it? *Wine Business Monthly*, (November), [http://smartwine.com/wbm/1999/1199/bmk9923.htm]. (Chapter 14)

Wired (1999) Mall browser, June, p. 201. (Chapter 9)

Wong, P-K. (1998) Leveraging the global information revolution for economic development: Singapore's evolving information industry strategy. *Information Systems Research*, 9 (4), 323–41. (Chapter 11)

Woody, T. (1999) Online wine sales Turn to grapes of wrath, CNN.com (13 April). [http://www.conn.com/TECH/computing/9904/13/grapes.html]. (Chapter 14)

World Bank, The (1997) *World Bank Atlas*. (Chapter 16)

WorldCom (1999) MAE services, [www.mfsdatanet.com/MAE/doc/maedesc/maedesc1.html]. (Chapter 5)

Wurman, R.S. (1997) *Information Architects*. Graphis Press Corp. (Chapter 9)

Yankee Group (1999) Business-to-business e-commerce, 9 March. (Chapter 3)

Yavo, N. (1999) Top 50 African web sites: in search for quality web content, [http://www.woyaa.com/topweb/top50report.html]. (Chapter 15)

Yeung, H.W.C. (1998a), Capital, state and space: contesting the borderless world. *Transactions of the Institute of British Geographers*, **23** (3), 291–309. (Chapter 8)

Yeung, H.W.C. (1998b), Competing for transnational corporations? The regional operations of foreign firms in Hong Kong and Singapore. In Cook, I.G., Doel, M.A., Li, R.Y.F. and Wang, Y. (eds), *Dynamic Asia: Business, Trade and Economic Development in Pacific Asia*. Aldershot: Ashgate, pp. 78–119. (Chapter 8)

Yeung, H.W.C. (1998c) The political economy of transnational corporations: a study of the regionalisation of Singaporean firms. *Political Geography*, **17** (4), 389–416. (Chapter 8)

Yeung, H.W.C. (1999) Regulating investment abroad? The political economy of the regionalisation of Singaporean firms. *Antipode*, **31** (3), 245–73. (Chapter 8)

Yeung, H.W.C. (2000a) Organising 'the firm' in industrial geography I: networks, institutions and regional development. *Progress in Human Geography*, **24**. (Chapter 8)

Yeung, H.W.C. (2000b) State intervention and neoliberalism in the globalising world economy: lessons from Singapore's regionalisation programme. *The Pacific Review*, **13** (1), 133–62. (Chapter 8)

Yeung, H.W.C. and Olds, K. (1998) Singapore's global reach: situating the city-state in the global economy. *International Journal of Urban Sciences*, **2** (1), 24–47. (Chapter 8)

York City Council (1999) Personal Communication. York City Council, York. (Chapter 2)

Zimine, D. and Bradshaw, M. (1999) Regional adaptation to economic crisis in Russia: the case of Novgorod Oblast. *Post-Soviet Geography and Economics*, **40**, 335–53. (Chapter 12)

Zook, M. (2000) Growth of domains in US and the World, [http://socrates.berkeley.edu/~zook/domain_names/us_and_world.html]. (Chapter 15)

Zook, M. (2001) Old hierarchies or new networks of centrality?: The global geography of the Internet content market. *American Behavioral Scientist*, forthcoming. (Chapter 6)

Zook, M.A. (2000) The web of consumption: the spatial organization of the Internet industry in the United States. *Environment and Planning A*, **32**, 411–26. (Chapter 5)

Zwass, V. (1999) Structure and macro-level impacts of electronic commerce: from technological infrastructure to electronic marketplaces. In Kendall, K.E. (ed.), *Emerging Information Technologies*. Thousand Oaks, CA: Sage, pp. 289–315. (Chapter 5)

Zysman, J. (1999) The digital economy in international perspective: common construction or regional rivalry, [http://e-conomy.berkeley.edu/events/deip/summary.html]. Presented at a Conference of the University of California E-conomy(tm) Project, 27 May, Washington, DC. (Chapter 6).

Index

Note: Page reference in *italics* refer to figures; those in **bold** refer to Tables

Index compiled by Annette Musker

what's new (46)

is e-commerce ≡ e-economy? (Is prod ≡ exchange)

(E-commerce ideal : more [flexible, quicker, closer, "collapsing class + geog divisions" (13)
                                    more informed (?)
↘ Intranets ?

isolating the e-commerce effect   (techn. determinism)
separating
            ⇒ theorize dependence on other processes
                            (Leah back a bit)

space : geog of infrastructure
: spat econ dynamics
: loc^n (firms, customers)
: phys tsptn.
: geog of cyberspace: what is distance?
: geog of regulation?
~~task~~
: F2F